Multilingualism, Second Language Learning, and Gender

Language, Power and Social Process 6

Editors

Monica Heller
Richard J. Watts

Mouton de Gruyter
Berlin · New York

Multilingualism, Second Language Learning, and Gender

Edited by

Aneta Pavlenko
Adrian Blackledge
Ingrid Piller
Marya Teutsch-Dwyer

Mouton de Gruyter
Berlin · New York 2001

Mouton de Gruyter (formerly Mouton, The Hague)
is a Division of Walter de Gruyter GmbH & Co. KG, Berlin.

♾ Printed on acid-free paper which falls within the guidelines
of the ANSI to ensure permanence and durability.

Library of Congress Cataloging-in-Publication-Data

Multilingualism, second language learning, and gender / edited by
Aneta Pavlenko ... [et al.].
   p. cm. − (Language, power, and social process ; 6)
Includes bibliographical references and index.
ISBN 3110170264 (alk. paper) − ISBN 3110170272 (pbk. : alk. paper)
   1. Multilingualism.   2. Language and sex.   3. Second language
acquisition.   4. Language and languages − Study and teaching.
I. Pavlenko, Aneta, 1963−   II. Series.
P115.M83   2001
404'.2−dc21

                        2001044540

Die Deutsche Bibliothek − Cataloging-in-Publication Data

Multilingualism, second language learning, and gender / ed. by Aneta
Pavlenko .... − Berlin ; New York : Mouton de Gruyter, 2001
   (Language, power and social process ; 6)
   ISBN 3-11-017027-2
   ISBN 3-11-017026-4

Printing: WB-Druck, Rieden/Allgäu.
Binding: Lüderitz & Bauer GmbH, Berlin.
Cover design: Christopher Schneider.
Printed in Germany.

Preface

The story of this book illustrates, in itself, the multilingual, international, and cross-cultural communication characteristic of late modernity of which it speaks. We worked on it from locations in three different continents, and the four of us have only met face-to-face twice, but we have developed intense virtual relationships over the past three years. In 1997 each of us found individually that our interest in language and gender was not widely shared in the community of Second Language Acquisition researchers, our "primary academic home". Luck had it that three of us (Aneta, Adrian, and Marya) presented papers at the First International Symposium on Bilingualism in Newcastle-upon-Tyne, UK, in early 1997, and that Aneta, Ingrid, and Adrian presented papers on multilingualism and gender at the similarly named First International Symposium on Bilingualism in Vigo, Spain, in late 1997. It was Aneta who realized how related all our papers were and who suggested and organized a panel on Multilingualism, Second Language Learning, and Gender at the Fourth Berkeley Women and Language Conference in April 1998, where the four of us met for the first time and conceived the idea of this volume. One year later, we had organized another panel on Multilingualism, Second Language Learning and Gender at the Annual Meeting of the American Association of Applied Linguistics in Stamford, CT, in March 1999. By the time we met there, we had commitments from all of our contributors and some first draft chapters. To ensure some continuity in the middle of change – as well as some buzz – both in Berkeley and in Stamford we conducted our meetings at Starbucks Coffee, which provided us with enough caffeine to keep Ingrid and Adrian productive despite their jetlags. Our main debt is, however, to the wonders of modern technology, as most of our brainstorming, editing, proofreading, and related communication took place in the jetlag-free world of virtual space.

No book is possible without the collaboration of many, many people and we appreciate the help of all who have supported our work in diverse ways. First and foremost, we would like to thank each other for being extremely efficient, patient, and pleasant co-workers and supportive friends.

Material support for our travel – and, in some cases, also for research – was provided by our home institutions: University of Birmingham (Adrian), St. Cloud State University (Marya), Temple University (Aneta), and Hamburg University, the University of Sydney, and the German Research Council (DFG) (Ingrid).

Intellectual support has come from our colleagues all over the world and from our editorial team at Mouton de Gruyter, and we are particularly indebted to all those who read (parts of) the manuscript and/or helped us in the editorial process: Anke Beck, Monica Heller, Richard Watts, Rebecca Walter, and the two anonymous reviewers for Mouton de Gruyter.

Our families and friends, many of whom are multilinguals and second language learners in many diverse ways, have cheerfully or stoically suffered through our days and nights filled with writing, back and forth e-mailing, and musings about multilingualism, second language learning, and gender.

Our largest debt is, of course, to our contributors who believed in this book and whose work made possible our original vision: to provide a varied and comprehensive portrayal of the relationship between multilingualism, second language learning, and gender, firmly grounded in diverse communities of practice and informed by contemporary social theory.

March 2001

Aneta Pavlenko   Philadelphia, PA, USA
Adrian Blackledge   Birmingham, UK
Ingrid Piller   Sydney, Australia
Marya Teutsch-Dwyer   St. Cloud, MN, USA

Table of contents

3. Gender in multilingual educational settings

Contributors

Adrian Blackledge (Ph.D. Birmingham University, 1998) is Senior Lecturer in English and Director of Research at the University of Birmingham, Westhill. His publications include *Teaching Bilingual Children* (Trentham Books, 1994) and *Literacy, Power, and Social Justice* (Trentham Books, 2000). He is co-editor (with Aneta Pavlenko) of a Special Issue of *The International Journal of Bilingualism*, 'Negotiation of Identities in Multilingual Contexts' (2001). His main area of research is multilingualism and social justice in linguistic minority settings. He is also interested in discursive construction of identities, and relations of power and ideology in multilingual contexts. His e-mail address is A.J.Blackledge@bham.ac.uk.

Susan Ehrlich is Professor in the Department of Languages, Literatures, and Linguistics and Women's Studies at York University, Toronto. Her areas of research include discourse analysis, linguistic approaches to literature, language and gender, and second language acquisition. She has published in journals such as *Journal of Pragmatics, Language in Society, Discourse and Society, Text*, and *Studies in Second Language Acquisition*. Her books include: *Point of View: A Linguistic Analysis of Literary Style* (Routledge, 1990), *Teaching American English Pronunciation* (with Peter Avery, Oxford University Press, 1992) and the recent *Representing Rape: Language and Sexual Consent* (Routledge, 2001). Her e-mail address is sehrlich@yorku.ca.

Tara Goldstein is Associate Professor at the Ontario Institute for Studies in Education of the University of Toronto (OISE/UT) where she teaches in both the pre-service teacher education and graduate education programs. She is also the Academic Director of Student Services which offers a range of co-curricular teacher development programs for students at OISE/UT. Tara's research and teaching interests include the education of immigrant students, multilingualism, equity in education, critical ethnography, and applied theater research. These interests have come together in the writing and performances of *Hong Kong, Canada*, her first play. Her e-mail address is tgoldstein@oise.utoronto.ca.

Monica Heller is Professor in the Department of Sociology and Equity Studies and the Centre de recherches en éducation franco-ontarienne at the Ontario Institute for Studies in Education of the University of Toronto (OISE/UT). Her main area of interest is the role of language in the construction of social difference and social inequality. Recent publications include *Linguistic Minorities and Modernity: A Sociolinguistic Ethnography* (Longman, 1999), *Voices of Authority: Education and Linguistic Difference* (co-edited with Marilyn Martin-Jones; Ablex, 2001); and *Éléments d' une sociolinguistique critique* (Hatier, forthcoming).

Claire Kramsch is Professor of German and Foreign Language Acquisition at the University of California, Berkeley, and Director of the Berkeley Language Center. She has published widely on the relation of language and culture in language learning, and on the application of second language research, discourse analysis, and stylistics to the teaching and learning of foreign languages in institutional settings. Her latest books are *Context and Culture in Language Teaching* (Oxford University Press, 1993) and *Language and Culture* (Oxford University Press, 1998). She is a past president of the American Association of Applied Linguistics and current co-editor of *Applied Linguistics*. Her e-mail address is ckramsch@socrates.berkeley.edu.

Cheiron McMahill is Associate Professor of English communication at Gunma Prefectural Women's University. She studied Japanese and TESL at Georgetown and the University of Washington. She is a long-time social activist and a founder of two professional organizations, Women Educators and Language Learners (WELL) and Gender Awareness in Language Education (GALE). McMahill's research interests center on women's social identities, personal narratives, and linguistic resistance to oppression. Her work has appeared in *TESOL Quarterly*, she also co-authored the textbook *Springboard to Success* (Prentice Hall, 1996), and co-edited a book on the life stories of gays in Japan *Queer Japan* (New Victoria, 1998). She is currently researching the oral narratives of women in a rural community in Gunma for her Ph.D. at Lancaster University. She can be reached at cheiron@gpwu.ac.jp.

Yumiko Ohara recently received her Ph.D. from the University of Hawai'i and is currently working as a visiting foreign researcher at the National Language Research Institute in Japan. In addition to employing phonetic analyses to examine the social meanings of voice pitch in Japanese, she has also been using the perspective of critical discourse analysis to examine how gender is portrayed and expressed in the Japanese media. She can be reached at yumikoo@hawaii.edu.

Aneta Pavlenko (Ph.D. Cornell University, 1997) is Assistant Professor of TESOL and Director of the International Teaching Assistant program at Temple University, Philadelphia. Her research interests include the relationship between language and identity, language and cognition, language and gender, bilingualism, and second language acquisition. Her work has appeared in *Applied Linguistics, Annual Review of Applied Linguistics, Issues in Applied Linguistics, Bilingualism: Language and Cognition, The International Journal of Bilingualism, Multilingua*, and *Pragmatics and Cognition*. Together with Adrian Blackledge, she co-edited a Special Issue of *The International Journal of Bilingualism*, 'Negotiation of Identities in Multilingual Contexts' (2001). Currently, she is working on a book *Crosslinguistic Influence in Language and Cognition* (co-authored with Scott Jarvis; Lawrence Erlbaum, forthcoming). Her e-mail address is apavlenk@astro.temple.edu.

Ingrid Piller (Ph.D. Dresden, 1995) is Lecturer in Linguistics at the University of Sydney, and Coordinator of the MA program in Applied Linguistics. Her teaching and research interests are in discourse analysis, sociolinguistics, and applied linguistics. She is the author of *American Automobile Names* (Essen, 1996). Her current research is on the linguistic practices of bilingual couples, and includes issues of language choice, the linguistic construction of identity, and linguistic ideologies. For further information visit her website at http://www.arts.usyd.edu.au/~ingpille

Marya Teutsch-Dwyer (Ph.D. Stanford University, 1995) is Associate Professor in the English Department and Director of the Intensive English Center at St. Cloud State University, Minnesota. Her teaching and research interests include second language acquisition, language learning in tutored and untutored settings, language learning and identity, and issues in teacher development. Her e-mail address is mteutsch@stcloudstate.edu.

Linda von Hoene is Director of the Graduate Student Instructor Teaching and Resource Center at the University of California, Berkeley. She has published several articles on the intersection of feminist theory, psychoanalysis, and second language learning. Her research in German literature and cultural studies focuses on psychoanalysis, fascism, and gender. Her e-mail address is vonhoene@socrates.berkeley.edu

Introduction: Multilingualism, second language learning, and gender

Ingrid Piller and Aneta Pavlenko

Multilingualism, second language learning (SLL), and gender? Don't we already know that women are 'better at languages' and more willing to interact in their second language (L2)? Or that immigrant women don't learn the language of their new country because their husbands don't let them out of the house? Or that women are more prestige-conscious, which leads them to spearhead language shift? And that they are a subordinate group with no option but to maintain minority languages? Even this short list of widely held assumptions about multilingualism, SLL, and gender reveals how contradictory these assumptions are. So, no, as a matter of fact, we don't know any of these things. The main goal of the present volume is not only to problematize these and other commonly held assumptions about 'women', 'men', 'second language acquisition', and 'bilingualism', but to deconstruct the very categories and to argue for alternative approaches to the study of multilingualism, SLL, and gender. In order to do so, in what follows, we will use the accepted terms 'bilingualism' and 'SLA' to refer to already existing fields of study, and favor the more comprehensive and inclusive terms 'multilingualism' and 'SLL' in the discussion of our own theoretical approach.

1. Monolingual bias in the study of language and gender

In recent years, many researchers in the field of language and gender have abandoned the assumption that the meaning of gender is shared across cultures and that it is fixed, unproblematic, and can be easily isolated from other aspects of social identity such as class, race, ethnicity, culture, sexuality, age, nationality, (dis)ability, as well as from power relations, social setting, context, and discourse functions. They have steered away from variationist sociolinguistic approaches where language was taken to be the phenomenon to be explained and gender constituted the explanation (Cameron 1996). Instead, many feminist researchers started talking about 'doing' and 'performing' gender (Butler 1990; West and Zimmerman 1987), and came to view language and gender as rooted and jointly constructed in particular communities of practice (Eckert and

McConnell-Ginet 1992; Holmes and Meyerhoff 1999). Significant differences in ideologies and meanings of gender and gendered linguistic practices were established for several speech communities around the world (Burton, Dyson, and Ardener 1994; Freed 1994; Günthner 1996; Philips, Steele, and Tanz 1987). Due to these and other developments, the field of language and gender has become one of the most lively, sophisticated, and interdisciplinary areas of linguistic inquiry. Only in the last five years, scholars in the field produced several highly influential monographs (Cameron 1996; Coates 1996; Holmes 1995; Pauwels 1998), edited volumes (Bergvall, Bing, and Freed 1996; Bucholtz, Liang, and Sutton 1999; Hall and Bucholtz 1995; Harvey and Shalom 1997; Johnson and Meinhof 1997; Kotthof and Wodak 1997; Livia and Hall 1997; Mills 1995; Wodak 1997), readers (Cameron 1998; Coates 1998), and textbooks (Crawford 1995; Goddard and Patterson 2000; Romaine 1999; Talbot 1998), and there is no doubt that many more are on the way.

One shortcoming that many of these monographs, collections, and textbooks have in common is their monolingual bias in the treatment of language and gender: a few include a chapter or two dealing with second language learners and bilinguals (Coates 1998; Hall and Bucholtz 1995; Johnson and Meinhof 1997; Kotthof and Wodak 1997; Romaine 1999); most, however, reduce multilingualism and SLL to a passing mention and/or an obligatory reference to Gal's (1978) study. Some do not mention these topics at all. As a result, theoretical debates on the nature of the relationship between language and gender – which include a variety of languages and contexts and are eloquent about many previously marginalized groups such as gays and lesbians (e.g., Livia and Hall 1997) – continue to ignore the fact that more than half of the world's population is bi- and multilingual (Romaine 1995). This oversight is largely due to the fact that the field has burgeoned in the US, which – despite its linguistic diversity – is characterized by a strong monolingual bias (Lippi-Green 1997). However, multilingualism has important implications for the relationship between language and gender. Therefore, the first goal of the present volume is to transcend the monolingual bias that has characterized much of the field of language and gender studies by establishing a new interdisciplinary field – multilingualism, SLL, and gender – which investigates the relationship between gender, ideology, and linguistic practices in bi- and multilingual communities. Theoretical implications of widespread multilingualism for the study of language and gender will be explored in the first chapter by Pavlenko and Piller, while empirical implications will be demonstrated in the remaining chapters.

2. Gender-blindness of Second Language Acquisition (SLA) research

While language and gender studies have been characterized by a widespread monolingual bias, research in mainstream bilingualism and SLA has suffered from just as widespread gender-blindness (for a more detailed discussion see chapters by Pavlenko and Piller, and by Ehrlich). SLA, in particular, has been characterized by an almost ubiquitous gender-blindness due to the prevalence of psycholinguistic and Universal Grammar approaches in the field, which assume a generic language user and disregard inter-individual variation as 'noise', i.e., a distraction that cannot be avoided but which cannot in any way contribute to our understanding of the universal facts of SLA. As McKay and Wong put it:

> Conceptualizing a second-language learner as a complex social being is a relatively recent trend in second-language-acquisition (SLA) research. For many years, error analysis and interlanguage analysis dominated this research..., encouraging a focus on the second language as formal code, referenced to native-speaker proficiency as the norm. Little recognition was given to learning processes, individual variables, or the social context in which the second language was learned and used. (1996: 577–578)

In recent years, sociolinguistic and sociocultural perspectives have started to gain some currency in the field, but gender continues to be under-theorized and under-researched. When considered at all, gender has often been treated from a binary and essentialist (be it biological or social) standpoint and reduced to the status of a variable designating undifferentiated groups of boys and girls, or women and men (see, for example, studies reviewed in Edwards 1994; Ellis 1994). Furthermore, it is not only human beings who are considered outside of the social context – the same holds true for languages. Neither speaker status nor language status have been adequately attended to in mainstream SLA research, in particular, in conjunction with gender. The enumerated shortcomings call unequivocally for the introduction of a more context-sensitive approach which treats gender as a system of social relations and discursive practices whose meaning varies across speech communities. As will be demonstrated in the present volume, such a context-sensitive approach is of crucial importance in explaining the variable outcomes of language learning and language contact, and in illuminating ways in which ideologies of language and gender institutionalize social inequalities and serve to 'naturalize' not only white male dominance but also the dominance of speakers of a majority language. The second goal of the present volume is, therefore, to bring a more nuanced understanding of gender as a system of social relations and discursive practices into research on second language learning and use, and on language contact.

We situate the new field in two ways. In the first chapter we will provide a comprehensive theoretical framework for the study of multilingualism, SLL, and gender, which is informed by feminist and poststructuralist approaches currently adopted in the field of language and gender. The other chapters in the volume, while not necessarily embracing this framework fully, will enrich the understanding of the relationship between multilingual practices and gender with a wealth of empirical data, collected in a variety of contexts in North America, Europe, and Asia. The volume is divided into three sections which reflect three central areas of the interaction between multilingualism, SLL, and gender: institutional (or, more generally, public), private, and educational settings. Below we will provide a short overview of the papers in each section.

3.   Gender, society, and ideology in multilingual settings

The chapters brought together in Section 1 are concerned with the interaction of multilingualism, SLL, and gender in institutional settings. They are characterized by a common focus on gatekeeping and discrimination which take place in various communities of practice. As indicated at the beginning of this introduction, the results of findings in research on SLA, bilingualism, and gender may appear controversial. Some studies present women as 'cultural brokers', sensitive to the demands of the linguistic marketplace, and, thus, as faster L2 learners and users of more prestigious language varieties (e.g., Gal 1978; Nichols 1983). In contrast, other work depicts women as guardians of the home language and culture and as slower L2 learners for a variety of reasons, including restricted access or symbolic resistance to mainstream culture (e.g., Dabène and Moore 1995; Hill 1987). These results are explained alternatively in Section 1 as gender-mediated outcomes whereby gendered social practices in which particular language learners and users participate are critical for a better understanding of their language learning trajectories. The focus of Section 1 is, therefore, on experiences, linguistic choices, and performances of women and men in minority language groups. Among the issues of particular concern in this section are the interaction between majority schools and minority families in literacy education (Blackledge's chapter), language choice in the workplace (Goldstein's chapter), and ways in which sexual harassment practices impinge on L2 learning and use in target language contexts (Ehrlich's chapter). Despite the diversity of the issues discussed, these three chapters share a common focus: the role of gendered social and discursive practices in the production and reproduction of identities and social inequalities in multilingual communities.

Another central issue of the utmost importance in Section 1 is how speakers respond symbolically to relations of power between their group and the dominant group in society. Accordingly, the papers in this section locate L2 users' language and literacy performance and choice in the context of these relations of gender and power. For instance, it is often incumbent on minority and immigrant women to approach the dominant language market (e.g., of the school), where they are disadvantaged by coercive relations of power which insist on the use of the majority language. As a result, their linguistic capital (Bourdieu 1991) may often go unnoticed by societal institutions such as schools. In response to this discrimination, minority group women either learn to play by the rules of the dominant group game, or put at risk their children's educational success and their own access to services in the community. Playing the game means accepting the rules; but – as pointed out in Blackledge's chapter – the rules are normally skewed in favor of the dominant group which created them. In his chapter, Blackledge describes how working-class mothers, immigrants to Britain from Bangladesh, who are literate in Bengali, and sometimes in Arabic, are constructed as illiterate, incompetent caregivers in their interactions with their children's teachers. Whatever accomplishments they may have, their lack of competence in English and in the rules of 'middle-class white culture' condemn them in the eyes of British educators. Thus, these women find themselves in a double bind: their efforts at supporting the children's learning of Bengali and Arabic literacy go unacknowledged; at the same time, the lack of support from schools renders them unable to support the learning of English literacy. The Portuguese immigrant women in Canada whose linguistic practices are examined by Goldstein find themselves in a similar double bind: the rules of their workplace are built upon the solidarity among Portuguese workers. Not only is speaking English unnecessary but it is also seen as an exclusionary practice which could break up the solidarity code among the workers. While Portuguese is thus crucial to the women's well-being at this particular workplace, it also keeps them from looking for and finding more skilled, rewarding, and better-paid work. Keeping such opportunities from them is easily rationalized through their 'lack of English' – an assumption that leads many researchers, educators, language policy makers, and employers to ignore the fact that for these women an investment in English amounts to trading off the visible benefits of solidarity, support, and companionship for intangible future benefits of career advancement. Finally, Ehrlich discusses ways in which sexual harassment genders the study-abroad experience for female second language learners. She demonstrates that sexual harassment or the fear of such harassment may curtail the women's interactions in their host society and target language. While they learn to 'say no' in their target language, a speech act which involves considerable pragmatic skills, this knowledge is not tested on their L2 proficiency tests. Thus, the assumption that L2 learning is ungendered hurts these women twice. First, their classroom language learning experiences poorly prepare them to deal with sexual harassment in the host society; as a result, they get less out of their stay than their male peers. Second, the skills they gain through negotiating this interactional challenge are not validated by the proficiency tests upon their return home.

Each of these three chapters highlights the bind in which bi- and multilingual women may find themselves. Of course, the existence of a double bind – 'damned if you do, damned if you don't' – has also been described for white, middle-class, English monolingual women with regard to the use of more direct language, typically associated with men (Lakoff 1975; Tannen 1994). The work collected in this volume suggests that in multilingual settings, the 'double bind' may become a 'multiple' one.

4.   Negotiation and performance of gender in multilingual contexts

The chapters in Section 2 shift the focus to negotiation and performance of gender in private settings, as well as to assimilation and resistance to particular ideologies of language and gender in the processes of L2 learning and use. Drawing on Cameron's (1996) work, we emphasize the constitutive role of language in gender performance and posit that it is speech communities that produce gendered styles, while individuals make accommodations to these styles in the process of producing themselves as gendered subjects. Recent research has persuasively demonstrated that individuals continuously construct or produce themselves as particular kinds of women or men by engaging in discursive practices that are associated with culturally- and community-defined norms of gender performance (see, for example, Bucholtz, Liang, and Sutton 1999; Hall and Bucholtz 1995). The papers in Section 2 of our volume show equally persuasively that in the process of geographic, cultural, and linguistic transitions individuals may undergo drastic transformations in their understanding and discursive performance of gender.

The chapter by Pavlenko draws on autobiographies by successful L2 learners to show ways in which gender performance is being transformed in the process of L2 learning and use: gender ideologies which were perceived as 'natural' before the transition from one language and culture to another are being questioned by these L2 users, and new gendered discursive practices are being resisted or assimilated to. The areas in which transformations of gender performance occur most often include private relationships – such as intimate, family, and friendship relationships – as well as public ones such as the workplace. Pavlenko argues that successful L2 learning may entail a modification of one's gender performance in order to ensure validation and legitimacy in the target language and culture. While Pavlenko focuses on femininities in transition, Teutsch-Dwyer is concerned with masculinities. Her chapter describes a linguistic trajectory of a Polish immigrant, Karol, whose gendered experiences in the US (interactions with his American girlfriend, excelling as handyman, telling jokes to appreciative female audiences) resulted in an early fossilization of certain aspects of his English. As long as his girlfriend is ready to write his checks for him and as long as his female co-workers are amused by his jokes and comical stories, there is no need for Karol to improve his English any further. He can lead a satisfactory social life in an English-speaking environment despite his limited English because he is primarily perceived as a 'nice guy' rather than a poor speaker of English – his gender identity overrides his linguistic identity in the perception of his circle of women friends. Teutsch-Dwyer challenges widely held assumptions that naturalistic learning is best and that simplified input aids the acquisition process. In the case of Karol these are gendered practices that bring his progress to a premature halt. Piller is likewise concerned with the relationship between performance and perception of gendered and linguistic identities. She investigates linguistic practices of couples who come together from two linguistic backgrounds, English and German. Piller shows that for female L2 users perception may not work quite as advantageously as for male ones: not only are the women in her study often denied linguistic and gender competence in their L2 but they are also denied their status as competent L1 users in their communities of origin. As a result, they lose either way, becoming marginal members in both their linguistic and national communities of origin and of choice and learning to inhabit the borderlands and forge new multicultural, postnational identities for themselves. A slightly different approach to gender performance is taken by Ohara. Her study is based on the fact that women employ different voice pitch levels in English and Japanese, and that for English speakers the high pitch of Japanese women's language often has negative associations. Ohara's study demonstrates that bilingual women are keenly aware of the different gender performances expected of them in different linguistic environments. As a result, some American women who are proficient in Japanese raise their pitch levels when speaking Japanese, and others refuse to conform to this gendered performance which they perceive as 'overly humble' and 'silly'.

A further concern of Section 2 is with bringing new and diverse methods to the study of the negotiation and performance of gender in multilingual contexts. Teutsch-Dwyer ingeniously combines ethnographic interviews with detailed linguistic analysis in her longitudinal case study. Ohara relies on experimental tasks which allow her to compare mean fundamental frequencies of English-Japanese and Japanese-English bilinguals. Pavlenko introduces language memoirs as a relatively recent source of data in SLL studies. She reflects upon the value and reliability of such data and also on their constructed nature: autobiographies as an overwhelmingly feminized genre are shown to be gendered performances in themselves. Finally, Piller examines a number of methods used in the study of private communication, and describes how each method presents a certain trade-off between naturalness, reliability, and ethical procedures. After an overview of the various methods available, multi-methodological approaches to data collection are advocated.

5.   Gender in multilingual educational contexts

Section 3 is concerned with gender in multilingual educational settings. Possible ways in which inequalities can be uncovered and dealt with in the classroom are addressed and implications for the field of second and foreign language teaching and learning are mapped out. While recent research in the teaching and learning of second and foreign languages has acknowledged the complexities and challenges that learners face when they participate in a new linguistic community, little attention has been given to gendered speech communities and/or the (re)construction of gendered identities in the language classroom. The chapters in the present section remedy this oversight and present a number of approaches to the study of gender in multilingual educational contexts. Heller examines ways in which public discourses in a Francophone school in Toronto, Canada, shape the students' orientation towards bilingualism in French and English. She demonstrates that both visions, of bilingualism and of 'international French', are shaped by and for boys, and argues that languages are never neutral but come with a baggage of gender ideologies. For instance, female Nerds, one of the few groups in the school who attempt to carve alternative non-hegemonic gender identities for themselves, often prefer to do so in English. The authors in this section critique a reductionist view of the social context of language which informs many contemporary communicative approaches to second and foreign language teaching and results in a seemingly genderless and therefore often male-centered language in the classroom. Kramsch and von Hoene illuminate ways in which the teaching and learning of foreign languages in the US has often supported colonialist and masculinist discourses of traveling to other cultures. Drawing on feminist and postmodern theory and data from widely-used German textbooks they suggest an alternative discourse of cross-cultural travel, one that explores and re-signifies notions of difference, hybridity, and living between cultures and languages – a theme that connects their chapter with the contributions in Section 2. While Kramsch and von Hoene attempt to link feminist discourses with foreign language classroom materials in the US, McMahill describes a similar link between English as a Foreign Language (EFL) and feminism in a Japanese EFL class. For students in this feminist class, the use of English facilitates the disclosure of personal experiences, the acceptance of emotions as a source of knowledge, self-interpretation as 'survivor' instead of as 'victim', and a continuous challenging of oppressive ideologies of gender and race. Thus, the EFL classroom becomes a collective endeavor to construct new linguistic, racial, and gender identities.

Together with the chapters in Section 1, the chapters in Section 3 map out a number of new directions in reconceptualizing language and education policies, language and literacy curricula, classroom materials, and everyday interactions in a variety of multilingual educational contexts.

6. Aims and scope

The central aim of this volume is to place the new field of multilingualism, SLL, and gender firmly on the map of linguistic and educational inquiry. Within this overall aim our hopes for the volume are twofold. It has recently been remarked that "much of what we 'know' about gender and discourse is really about white, middle-class, heterosexual women and men using English in Western societies" (West, Lazar, and Kramarae 1997: 137). By challenging this Anglocentric, monolingual view, this volume intends to contribute to the body of knowledge in the field of language and gender, both by demonstrating the benefits of the multilingual perspective on gender and by portraying a variety of women and men who perform and negotiate gender in more than one language. At the same time, we are hoping to contribute to the body of knowledge in the fields of SLA and bilingualism, by presenting a theoretical framework for the conceptualization of gender, based on recent developments in poststructuralist and feminist theory, and by demonstrating how this framework allows for a deeper understanding of language contact phenomena and of the processes involved in L2 learning and use. In short, this volume aims at raising awareness about the complex interactions between ideologies of language, gender, and power in multilingual contexts.

References

Bergvall, Victoria, Janet Bing, and Alice Freed (eds.)
1996   *Rethinking Language and Gender Research: Theory and Practice.* London: Longman.

Bourdieu, Pierre
1991   *Language and Symbolic Power.* Cambridge: Polity Press.

Bucholtz, Mary, A.C. Liang, and Laurel Sutton (eds.)
1999   *Reinventing Identities: The Gendered Self in Discourse.* Oxford/New York: Oxford University Press.

Burton, Pauline, Ketaki Kushari Dyson, and Shirley Ardener (eds.)
1994   *Bilingual Women: Anthropological Approaches to Second-Language Use.* Oxford: Berg.

Butler, Judith
1990   *Gender Trouble: Feminism and the Subversion of Identity.* London/New York: Routledge.

Cameron, Deborah
1996   *Feminism and Linguistic Theory.* London: Macmillan.
(ed.) 1998 *The Feminist Critique of Language: A Reader.* Second edition. London/New York: Routledge.

Coates, Jennifer
1996   *Women Talk: Conversation between Women Friends.* Oxford: Blackwell.
1998   *Language and Gender: A Reader.* Oxford: Blackwell.

Crawford, Mary
1995   *Talking Difference: On Gender and Language.* London: Sage.

Dabène, Louise and Danièle Moore
1995   Bilingual speech of migrant people. In Milroy, Lesley and Pieter Muysken (eds.), *One Speaker, Two Languages: Cross-Disciplinary Perspectives on Code-Switching.* Cambridge: Cambridge University Press, 17–44.

Eckert, Penelope and Sally McConnell-Ginet
1992   Think practically and look locally: Language and gender as community-based practice. *Annual Review of Anthropology* 21, 461–490.

Edwards, John
1994   *Multilingualism.* London: Penguin.

Ellis, Rod
1994   *The Study of Second Language Acquisition.* Oxford: Oxford University Press.

Freed, Alice
1994   A cross-cultural analysis of language and gender. In Bucholtz, Mary, A.C. Liang, Laurel Sutton, and Caitlin Hines (eds.), *Cultural Performances: Proceedings of the Third Berkeley Women and Language Conference.* Berkeley: University of California, 197–204.

Gal, Susan
1978   Peasant men can't get wives: Language and sex roles in a bilingual community. *Language in Society* 7, 1, 1–17.

Goddard, Angela and Lindsey Patterson
2000   *Language and Gender.* London/New York: Routledge.

Günthner, Susanne
1996   Male-female speaking practices across cultures. In Hellinger, Marlies and Ulrich Ammon (eds.), *Contrastive Sociolinguistics.* Berlin/New York: Mouton de Gruyter, 447–473.

Hall, Kira and Mary Bucholtz (eds.)
1995   *Gender Articulated: Language and the Socially Constructed Self.* London/New York: Routledge.

Harvey, Keith and Celia Shalom (eds.)
1997   *Language and Desire: Encoding Sex, Romance and Intimacy.* London/New York: Routledge.

Hill, Jane
1987   Women's speech in modern Mexicano. In Philips, Susan, Susan Steele, and Christine Tanz (eds.), *Language, Gender, and Sex in Comparative Perspective.* Cambridge: Cambridge University Press, 121–160.

Holmes, Janet
1995   *Women, Men and Politeness.* London: Longman.

Holmes, Janet and Miriam Meyerhoff (eds.)
1999   Communities of Practice in Language and Gender Research. Special Issue of *Language in Society* 28, 2.

Johnson, Sally and Ulrike Meinhof (eds.)
1997   *Language and Masculinity.* Oxford: Blackwell.

Kotthof, Helga and Ruth Wodak (eds.)
    1997   *Communicating Gender in Context*. Amsterdam/Philadelphia: John Benja-
            mins.

Lakoff, Robin
    1975   *Language and Woman's Place*. New York: Harper and Collins.

Lippi-Green, Rosina
    1997   *English with an Accent: Language, Ideology, and Discrimination in the
            United States*. London/New York: Routledge.

Livia, Anna and Kira Hall (eds.)
    1997   *Queerly Phrased: Language, Gender, and Sexuality*. Oxford/New York:
            Oxford University Press.

McKay, Sandra Lee and Sau-Ling Cynthia Wong
    1996   Multiple discourses, multiple identities: Investment and agency in second-
            language learning among Chinese adolescent immigrant students. *Harvard
            Educational Review* 66, 3, 577–608.

Mills, Sara (ed.)
    1995   *Language and Gender: Interdisciplinary Perspectives*. London: Longman.

Nichols, Patricia
    1983   Linguistic options and choices for Black women in the rural South. In
            Thorne, Barrie, Cheris Kramarae, and Nancy Henley (eds.), *Language,
            Gender, and Society*. Boston: Newbury House, 54–68.

Pauwels, Anne
    1998   *Women Changing Language*. London: Longman.

Philips, Susan, Susan Steele, and Christine Tanz (eds.)
    1987   *Language, Gender, and Sex in Comparative Perspective*. Cambridge: Cam-
            bridge University Press.

Romaine, Suzanne
    1995   *Bilingualism*. Oxford: Blackwell.
    1999   *Communicating Gender*. Mahwah, NJ: Lawrence Erlbaum.

Talbot, Mary
    1998   *Language and Gender: An Introduction*. Oxford: Polity Press.

Tannen, Deborah
1994   *Talking from 9 to 5. Women and Men in the Workplace: Language, Sex and Power*. New York: William Morrow.

West, Candace and Don Zimmerman
1987   Doing gender. *Gender and Society* 1, 2, 125–151.

West, Candace, Michelle Lazar and Cheris Kramarae
1997   Gender in discourse. In Van Dijk, Teun (ed.), *Discourse as Social Interaction*. London: Sage, 119–143.

Wodak, Ruth (ed.)
1997   *Gender and Discourse*. London: Sage.

1. Gender, society, and ideology in multilingual settings

New directions in the study of multilingualism, second language learning, and gender

Aneta Pavlenko and Ingrid Piller[1]

1. Introduction

Recently, several researchers have pointed to the ever-growing gap between the study of second language acquisition (SLA) and bilingualism and the study of language and gender (Burton, Dyson, and Ardener 1994; Ehrlich 1997; Pavlenko 2001; Woolard 1997). The goal of the present chapter is to write second language learning (SLL) and multilingualism into the theory of language and gender and to adopt recent developments in the field of language and gender for the study of multilingualism and SLL.

In order to argue for a reconceptualization of any area of research, it is necessary to pinpoint the problems with the existing framework. Thus, we will first challenge essentialist assumptions underlying many earlier treatments of bilingualism, SLA, and gender, which present 'men' and 'women' as undifferentiated groups. Subsequently, we will outline a poststructuralist theoretical framework for the study of multilingualism, SLL, and gender, and discuss four promising research directions which can significantly contribute to our understanding of the field. In doing so, we will focus on ways in which gender as a system of social relations and discursive practices mediates the learning and use of additional languages, and on ways in which gender relations and performances may be transformed in the process of second language socialization.

2. Essentialist approaches to the study of multilingualism, second language learning, and gender

The relationship between language and gender emerged as a separate field of inquiry in the 1970s, prompted by feminist concerns about the connections between sex, power, and language. The controversy sparked off by Lakoff's (1975) *Language and Woman's Place*, and by Thorne and Henley's (1975) anthology *Language and Sex: Difference and Dominance* stimulated unparalleled interest on the part of sociolinguists and linguistic anthropologists in relationships between gender and linguistic practices. Almost immediately researchers looked at the relationship between multilingualism, SLL, and gender, suggesting that this, too, may be a promising area of inquiry (Gal 1978; Schlieben-Lange 1977; Solé 1978). Lakoff (1975: 47) underscored how important it is for language teachers "to realize that social context is relevant in learning to speak a second language fluently", and warned them to pay close attention to ways in which language practices and performances may be gendered. Gal (1978) demonstrated that not only language practices but also motivation and agency in learning the second language may be gendered and that in some cases this learning may be more advantageous for one group – young Hungarian women in her study – than for others. Unfortunately, for more than fifteen years Gal's (1978) work was rarely followed up, if at all. It was not until Burton, Dyson, and Ardener (1994) published a volume entitled *Bilingual Women: Anthropological Approaches to Second-Language Use* that conversation on multilingualism, SLL, and gender resumed. In what follows, we will discuss three paradigms in which research on multilingualism, SLL, and gender was conducted between 1975 and the early 1990s. All three originated in the field of language and gender and focused on differences between women's and men's language, attempting to explain them through a generalized feature of gender identities or relations: deficit, difference, or dominance.

In the *deficit* framework, theorized in Ardener (1975) and exemplified in Lakoff (1975), women are presented as inferior language users and oftentimes as 'the muted group'. Lakoff (1975) suggested that women speak a 'powerless language' – uncertain, weak, excessively polite – and rely on hedges, tag questions, emphatic stress, and hypercorrect grammar. She also claimed that this language is forced on them as the price of social approval for being appropriately 'feminine'. In the study of multilingualism, this approach translated into the *linguistic lag* hypothesis, the view of minority women as less bilingual than men, and, thus, lagging linguistically behind them (see, for example, Stevens 1986). The deficit framework has been severely criticized in the field of language and gender for assuming a male-as-norm language standard and thus problematizing women, for treating women as an undifferentiated group, and for postulating a one-to-one mapping between linguistic phenomena and their meaning (Cameron, McAlinden, and O'Leary 1988; Holmes 1990; O'Barr and Atkins 1980). With regard to bilingual women, Borker (1980), Gal (1991), and Spedding (1994) argued that at times it is the ethnographic practice that renders women mute and monolingual and that the findings of the earlier studies may not adequately represent reality: some women may prefer to hide the extent of their bilingualism in the 'unequal encounters' with white middle-class male anthropologists, linguists, and ethnographers.

Another way to view Lakoff's (1975) work is in terms of the *dominance* paradigm which sees male dominance and female oppression as the key factors in linguistic interaction, suggesting that speech differences uncovered by researchers stem from institutionalized patriarchy. Theorized in Lakoff (1975), Thorne and Henley (1975), and Spender (1980), this approach found support in studies which demonstrated that in cross-sex conversations men dominate and/ or interrupt women (West and Zimmerman 1983; Zimmerman and West 1975) or simply don't listen, leaving women to do the conversational 'shitwork' (Fishman 1983). In the study of multilingualism, the dominance approach offered an alternative interpretation of women's greater monolingualism, portraying them as linguistically oppressed by men (Burton 1994). In their theoretical critiques of the dominance model, feminist linguists pointed out that while this approach does acknowledge the importance of power relations, it fails to recognize the social, historical, and political situatedness of power, the effects of which are mediated not only by gender, but also by class, race, ethnicity, and sexuality (Cameron 1992; Eckert and McConnell-Ginet 1992). As a result, the model oversimplifies patriarchy and gender relations, portraying 'women-as-a-group' as dominated by 'men-as-a-group' and obfuscating the fact that hegemonic masculinities often oppress both women and other men (who do not or cannot conform) and that hegemonic femininities also participate in oppressive practices. In language contact situations, the interaction is further complicated by historical and social complexities of the relationship between majority and minority language groups. In addition, it was also shown that the proponents of the model ignored the ambiguity of linguistic strategies and failed to systematically investigate the links between linguistic practices and production of and resistance to hegemony (James and Clarke 1993; Tannen 1993). In the study of multilingualism, several researchers challenged the portrayal of women as less bilingual than men, pointing out that at times women are not only more bilingual but also the initiators of language shift (Constantinidou 1994; Gal 1978; Holmes 1993; McDonald 1994; Schlieben-Lange 1977; Solé 1978)

A closer look at linguistic practices was taken in the *sex differences* approach, assumed in variationist sociolinguistics. This approach focused on correlating particular linguistic variables with the sex of the speaker, whereby sex was seen as one of several attributes, such as class, age, or race, determining an individual's relation to linguistic variation, in particular, phonological patterns and orientation towards standard grammar. The best-known claim in this paradigm is that women tend to use more standard and/or prestigious linguistic forms and registers (Labov 1966, 1972; Trudgill 1972, 1974). In the study of multilingualism, this approach strove to explain instances of language shift spearheaded by women as caused by women's preference for more prestigious languages and/or varieties. In the field of SLA, it led researchers to posit that female learners generally do better than males (Ellis 1994) and to explain their achievement through more positive attitudes and better use of learning strategies (Oxford 1993, 1994). Feminist critics take issue with variationist sociolinguistics research both from theoretical and empirical standpoints. With regard to theory, they enumerate the inherent problems in measuring women's linguistic behavior against that of men, and argue against the speculative nature of 'female superiority' claims. They point out that no independent evidence supports these claims and suggest that the social meanings of linguistic variables cannot be defined on the basis of identities of those who use them most frequently (Cameron and Coates 1988; Eckert and McConnell-Ginet 1992; Holmes 1992). Other scholars provide evidence that the claims are not borne out in cross-linguistic studies, in particular in Arabic-speaking countries (Haeri 1996; James 1996). In the study of bilingualism and SLA, the 'female superiority' claim finds no support either: in some contexts male learners outperform female ones (Polanyi 1995), and in others men are found to be more bilingual than women (Harvey 1994; Hill 1987; Holmes 1993; Spedding 1994; Stevens 1986).

The *gender differences* or 'two-cultures' approach, introduced by Maltz and Borker (1982) and developed and popularized by Tannen (1990), shifted the focus from linguistic features to male and female styles in cross-gender communication. The merit of this approach is in discussing male styles on a par with female ones, as opposed to considering male behavior as a norm: no explicit judgments are passed about the comparative value of either style. Stemming from work on cross-cultural miscommunication, the two-cultures view suggests that men and women constitute different cultures (learned mainly in single-sex preadolescent peer groups), and as a result, cannot always communicate successfully. Women are said to focus on rapport and affective functions of conversation, while men focus on report and informational aspects, often seeing conversations as status contests. This approach was transferred to the study of SLA by Gass and Varonis (1986), who suggested that men interact to produce more output, while women interact to obtain more input. Pica et al. (1991) found that the gender of the learner played no role in native/non-native speaker (NS/NNS) interaction but the gender of the interlocutor did: female NSs were shown to ask more helpful questions and to negotiate meaning more consistently than male NSs. Therefore, it was hypothesized that the interaction with a female NS may lead to better results in SLL than interaction with a male NS (see Teutsch-Dwyer's chapter for a critical evaluation of this thesis).

While Tannen's (1990) book was extremely popular with the general public, quickly becoming an international bestseller, in academia her arguments were heavily criticized. Feminist linguists identified several problems with the 'two-cultures' approach, the first of which was the oversimplification of the assumption of separate cultures. "Girls and boys, women and men ... live together in shared linguistic worlds, be it in the family, in schoolrooms, in the streets, in colleges, in jobs; they are probably spending more time in mixed-sex contexts than in single-sex contexts, and, above all, they are not victims of constant misunderstandings," stated Trömel-Plötz (1991: 490) in her scathing review of Tannen's (1990) book. Eckert and McConnell-Ginet (1992) pointed out that to assume lack of knowledge of the interactional norms of the 'other culture' is to ignore individuals' agency in making interactional choices and to presuppose that in any given context individuals choose only possibilities judged typical for their gendered subculture. Later research convincingly demonstrated that both men and women can be involved in both rapport and report talk, depending on the activity they are engaged in and the community of practice they are associated with (see Cameron 1997a). In the field of SLA, Günthner (1992) demonstrated that NS/NNS status may override any possible gender effects in cross-cultural communication.

In sum, critical analyses of the deficit, dominance, and difference paradigms, conducted in the early 1990s, demonstrated that all three undertheorized gender and language and, as a result, were grounded in problematic universalizing assumptions, speaking of 'women' and 'men' in ways that obscure heterogeneity across and within cultures (Cameron 1992; Eckert and McConnell-Ginet 1992; Gal 1991; Trömel-Plötz 1991). These analyses demonstrated that the studies in all three paradigms focused on and problematized women, thus normalizing the status of men's language as unmarked and ungendered. Several researchers also pointed out that the designs of the studies from which these models were derived have not systematically identified or sought out participants representing the diversity of men's and women's experience. Most importantly, feminist linguists argued for the reevaluation of the categories of 'language' and 'gender', and for the need to move beyond static oppositions such as 'difference and dominance', to the study of how gender and hegemony are produced in discourse in a variety of contexts (Cameron 1992, 1996, 1997b, 1998; Eckert and McConnell-Ginet 1992; Gal 1991; West and Zimmerman 1987).

3.   Feminist poststructuralist approaches to the study of multilingualism, second language learning, and gender

In the last decade, many researchers have embraced feminist poststructuralist approaches to the study of language and gender (Cameron 1992, 1996, 1997b, 1998) and to the study of second language learning and multilingualism (Peirce 1995; Norton 2000). In this section, we will attempt to demonstrate how these fields can be brought together in the poststructuralist paradigm and provide definitions of the key terms that will be used throughout the chapter.

While the terms 'poststructuralism' and 'critical inquiry' serve as an umbrella for a variety of theoretical approaches, in the present chapter we will use the terms interchangeably, emphasizing similarities which they share. Similarly, we see various feminist movements as having a common aim of challenging the dominant patriarchy and improving life conditions of oppressed groups. Thus, for us, *feminist poststructuralism*, outlined by Cameron (1992, 1997b) and Weedon (1987), is an approach which strives to theorize and to investigate the role of language in the production of gender relations, and the role of gender dynamics in language learning and use. Of particular importance to us is the poststructuralist focus on *language* as the locus of social organization, power, and individual consciousness, and as a form of symbolic capital (Bourdieu 1991). *Learning*, in turn, is seen here as socialization, or a situated process of participation in particular communities of practice, which may entail the negotiation of ways of being a person in that context (Wenger 1998).

Our view of gender will also differ significantly from that espoused in earlier research. Contemporary theorists of gender present a convincing argument for why gender cannot be fully understood as an individual attribute: femininities relate to masculinities and all are connected to other social categories (Cameron 1992; Crawford 1995; Eckert and McConnell-Ginet 1992; Nicholson 1994; West and Fenstermaker 1995). Conceiving of gender as composed of separate masculinities and femininities also prevents us from addressing issues of power and inequality. Consequently, we will approach *gender* not as a set of traits, a variable or a role, but as a product of social doings, "a system of culturally constructed relations of power, produced and reproduced in interaction between and among men and women" (Gal 1991: 176). If gender is viewed as a social, historical, and cultural construct, then it comes as no surprise that normative masculinities and femininities, as well as beliefs and ideas about relations between the sexes, may vary across cultures as well as over time within a culture (for a comprehensive discussion of diverse meanings of gender see Bonvillain 1995). Moreover, anthropological evidence indicates that not all so-

cieties limit the view of gender to the binary opposition. While in Western societies intersexed infants have to undergo surgery so that the male/female dichotomy can be medically enforced (Bing and Bergvall 1996), other cultures
allow for a 'third' or 'fourth' gender, such as neither man/nor woman *hijra* in
India (Nanda 1990) or half man/half woman *berdache* or 'two-spirit' in Native
American tribes (Lang 1997).

This view of gender as a system of social relations and discursive practices
has important implications for both the 'gender' and the 'language' parts of
language and gender research. With language seen as a collection of heterogen-
eous discourses, individual linguistic strategies can no longer be directly linked
to gender and cease to be the main focus of research. Instead, the locus of study
shifts to ideologies of language and gender, which embody speakers' normative conceptions of gender identities, gender relations, and gender-appropri-
ate uses of language, and are produced, reproduced, challenged, and negotiated
in talk, and other forms of discourse (Bergvall 1999; Gal 1991; Kulick 1998;
Ochs 1992; Talbot 1998; West and Zimmerman 1987). Therefore, with gender
seen as a system of social relations and discursive practices, the goal of the
study of language and gender becomes twofold: on the one hand, to study ways
in which gender is constructed and negotiated in multiple discourses, and, on
the other, to investigate the effects of gender on individuals' access to linguistic
resources and possibilities of expression.

Finally, it is not only the locus of study that has shifted with time, but also
the primary unit where research is conducted. Early research on language and
gender focused on interpersonal encounters and on speech communities, defined by Gumperz (1972) as a group of speakers who share rules and norms for
the use of language. Lately, the latter notion had been found wanting as it did
not directly address the mediating role of activity and practice in the relationship between language and society. A pioneering article by Eckert and McConnell-Ginet (1992) "Think practically and look locally: Language and gender as
community-based practice" shifted the locus of research to a more concrete site
of communities of practice (Lave and Wenger 1991; Wenger 1998). *Communities of practice* are defined in this work as groups "whose joint engagement in
some activity or enterprise is sufficiently intensive to give rise over time to a
repertoire of shared practices" (Eckert and McConnell-Ginet 1999: 185). They
can be small or large, formal or informal, and embrace a variety of settings,
such as a factory floor (Goldstein's chapter), an English-as-a-foreign-language
(EFL) classroom (McMahill's chapter), or even a married couple (Piller's
chapter). Communities of practice present a very useful framework for future
research on multilingualism, second language learning, and gender, as they
allow us to focus on the learning process, to examine ways in which gender me-

diates access to various practices, and to theorize the gender-based marginalization of particular community members.

In short, we believe that the feminist poststructuralist view of the relationship between language and gender allows us to view the processes of learning and use of additional languages in a new light. In the present chapter we outline four areas which we see as most promising in terms of the current and future study of the relationship between gender and additional language learning and use: (1) the study of gendered access to linguistic resources, (2) the study of gendered agency, motivation, and investment in second language learning and language shift, (3) the study of gender performance in multilingual contexts, and (4) the study of ways in which critical and feminist pedagogy may transform contemporary educational practices. Clearly, these areas are not entirely new, as can be seen in the amount of research conducted in each, as well as in the fact that we can trace some research strands back to the 1960s (Ervin-Tripp 1967) and 1970s (Gal 1978; Schlieben-Lange 1977; Solé 1978). At the same time, these diverse attempts to investigate the links between multilingualism, SLL, and gender have not yet been brought together and theorized in a way offered in the present chapter (see also Pavlenko 2001). Consequently, we see the main contribution of our chapter as attracting attention to this new field of research, explicating the theoretical framework in which the research has been conducted, demonstrating what has been established to date, and outlining ways in which the field can move forward.

4. New directions in the study of multilingualism, second language learning, and gender

4.1. Gendered access to linguistic resources in multilingual contexts

One of the key findings in the field is that gender as a system of social relations and discursive practices structures differential opportunities for access to linguistic resources. Numerous studies demonstrate that in some minority and immigrant communities, where second language skills are highly valued and associated with social and economic benefits, men have privileged access to this symbolic capital, while women are prevented from learning and using the language by a number of gatekeeping practices which restrict women's mobility, access to majority language education, and the workplace (Goldstein 1995; Harvey 1994; Hill 1987; Holmes 1993; Kouritzin 2000; Loftin 1996; Losey

1995; Spedding 1994; Stevens 1986; Swigart 1992; see also chapters by Black-ledge, Ehrlich, Goldstein, Heller, and Teutsch-Dwyer).

Recent studies show that immigrant and minority women's access to edu-cation in majority languages may be significantly constrained by language and gender ideologies and practices of both majority and minority communities. To begin with, women's status as housekeepers and mothers, in conjunction with the lack of governmentally funded daycare, may result in complete immobility. In some contexts, their status as financially dependent on the breadwinner males may also bar them from government-funded English-as-a-second-lan-guage (ESL) classes (Kouritzin 2000). However, as Kouritzin (2000) insight-fully points out, it is overly simplistic to equate access with availability: lives of immigrant and minority women may be complicated not only by gendered and systemic inequalities but also by cultural conflicts. Even in contexts where classes, professional training, and other linguistic resources are available, ac-cess problems may arise. The availability of daycare solutions did not appear to help an Indian woman in Kouritzin's (2000) study, as her husband was adamant that only family should care for the children. Similarly, lack of family respon-sibilities did not help young Portuguese women in Goldstein's (1995) study: they couldn't take ESL classes because being in the same classroom with male strangers was considered inappropriate in their community. Thus, even the best of solutions, such as evening and weekend classes and externally funded day-care, do not help women who are culturally required to be home with their children and to prioritize their roles as housekeepers, mothers, wives, care-takers, and 'guardians of the home language'. Blackledge's chapter convin-cingly shows that the majority society also constrains women's access to lin-guistic resources: positioning Bengali mothers as illiterate, the school in Bir-mingham does not provide them with bilingual books which would have sim-ultaneously helped them to improve their own English and to assist the English literacy learning of their children.

Moreover, as demonstrated by Heller (1999) and Losey (1995), even when immigrant and minority women do access the classroom, they may get signifi-cantly less classroom interaction time than either minority men or majority men and women. Losey's (1995) study of classroom participation patterns of American and Mexican-American students in a community college classroom persuasively demonstrated that Mexican-American women were doubly mar-ginalized in the class, both as ethnic minority members and as women, and thus prevented from taking their turns, expressing themselves, and interacting in the target language. Similarly, Heller (1999) shows that older immigrant girls are the ones who are alienated most in a French-language high school in Toronto, Ontario, and have least access to its linguistic resources, in particular, English.

In contrast, middle-class white boys have the best chance to become bilingual in the way envisaged by the school (see also Heller's chapter).

Another discursive space where access to linguistic resources may be gendered is the workplace. While many researchers attribute minority and immigrant men's greater bilingualism to their role as breadwinners (see, for example, Stevens 1986), Holmes (1993) and Goldstein (1995, and this volume) argue that participation in the workforce alone does not guarantee access to the majority language: in many cases, gatekeeping practices may prevent women from learning and using the second language even when they are working. Holmes (1993) shows that while immigrant men in Australia and New Zealand are more often employed where English is required, immigrant women often-times work in places where they use their native language. Goldstein's (1995, and this volume) investigation of linguistic practices in a Canadian factory demonstrates that the unspoken rules of this workplace prevent immigrant Portuguese women from using English by positing Portuguese as a solidarity code. Since all the co-workers are either native speakers of Portuguese or at least proficient L2 users (in the case of the speakers of Spanish and Italian), there is no need for English, and many women on the line do not speak or understand it well. Thus, tradition prohibits the use of English, positioning it as a secret language that some may not understand. The researcher points out that while this practice ensures solidarity and cooperation on the factory floor, it may also keep the women from social and economic advancement, enjoyed by Portuguese men, more fluent in English. A similar link between education and the workforce is made in Hill's (1987) study of the use of Spanish and Mexicano (Nahuatl), an indigenous language of Mexico, in rural communities in the region of the Malinche Volcano. The researcher shows that women in this community have less access to education than men and speak less Spanish; as a result, they cannot join the industrial labor force, for which the use of Spanish is crucial, and have limited opportunities to practice whatever Spanish they know.

Studies conducted in indigenous communities in South America paint a very complex picture of ways in which ideologies of language and gender conspire in restricting indigenous women's access to Spanish (Harvey 1994; Hill 1987; Loftin 1996; Spedding 1994). The researchers suggest that the images of ideal masculinity, constructed by local ideologies, attach high value to bilingualism and thus present men as skillful "mediators between the inside world of kinship and community and the outside world of finance and knowledge" (Harvey 1994: 60). In contrast, the images of ideal femininity place women firmly inside the community, making them the transmitters of the home language, and of cultural, ethnic, and religious traditions. In doing so, these ideologies obfuscate the fact that the 'guardian' role is predicated upon lesser bilingualism and is not highly valued. Moreover, it is argued that local ideologies construct indigenous women as more Indian than the men, both in their looks and in their speech. This Indianness, in turn, positions women simultaneously as 'guardians of the home language' and as backward members of the community. In an attempt to explain the origins of women's linguistic oppression, Cameron (1992) suggests that in some communities men may be threatened by women becoming bilingual. She points to the paradoxical situation in which many immigrant and minority men find themselves with regard to assimilation: while beneficial socially and economically, it may also undermine one's way of life, values, beliefs, and ultimately ethnic and cultural identity. Positioning women in charge of language maintenance may become a way out: "In a male-dominated society, men can resolve this problem [of assimilation] by taking the rewards of cultural change for themselves while requiring the community's women to be living symbols of tradition" (Cameron 1992: 202). Harvey (1994) shows that women in Ocongate, Peru, clearly recognize that their inability to use Spanish has negative implications for their social position. However, their attempts to use Spanish are met with negative attitudes from the men in the community and their performance is subject to ridicule and insults, in which they are portrayed as trying to pass themselves off as better and more educated than they are in reality. Similar situations are depicted in studies which look at minority language communities in Africa, India, and South America, and at immigrant communities in Australia, New Zealand, and the US (Harvey 1994; Hill 1987; Holmes 1993; Stevens 1986; Swigart 1992; Zentella 1987).

Interestingly, it is not only disadvantaged immigrant and minority women who may be denied access to linguistic resources or allowed limited access only, but also middle- and upper-middle class Western females, who temporarily live abroad as students or expatriates and temporary workers. Several studies conducted with Americans studying abroad suggest that some contexts in Russia, Japan, or Spain also provide unequal opportunities for male and female learners to participate in informal interactions (Polanyi 1995; Siegal 1996; Talburt and Stewart 1999). Pichette (2000) interviewed a number of male and female Westerners living in Japan comparing contexts in which they use the language and their linguistic achievements. She concluded that white Western men have many more chances to participate in informal interactions – and, as a result, acquire the language in a wider range of contexts – than Western women. The men spend a lot of time in the local *izakaya* (Japanese pub) where they can 'pick up' the language from the regular customers; they also practice the language with their Japanese girlfriends. In contrast, Western women do not as often form relationships with Japanese men, and are discouraged from going to pubs and bars alone as their attempts to strike up a conversation may be misinterpreted by the locals. Gender, in conjunction with race, also appears to have limited the interactional opportunities of Misheila, an African-American student on a study abroad trip to Spain (Talburt and Stewart 1999). During the trip, Misheila had found herself consistently singled out and sexually harassed by Spanish males. This sexual harassment, whether real or perceived, provoked a negative reaction in her toward Spanish and its speakers, and curtailed any future investment in learning Spanish. In contrast, the men in Polanyi's (1995) study conducted in Russia and in Pichette's (2000) study conducted in Japan explicitly stated that they had enjoyed their opportunity to be different and visible as it brought them a lot of attention, in particular from local women.

At the same time, we would like to emphasize that women are not always positioned at a double disadvantage as L2 learners. In certain contexts, ideologies of language and gender may conspire against men in achievement of success in second language learning. Thus, Günthner (1992) demonstrated that while Chinese women in her study kept asking native speakers of German for help and assistance in their learning of German, Chinese men were resigned to solving their problems by themselves, as revealing their communicative deficits would have been face-threatening to them. Similarly, Moon (2000) found that Asian women coming to the US as immigrants or international students have a greater chance of forming relationships with American men and, as a result, have more opportunities to be engaged in meaningful interactions in the target language; consequently, they may achieve higher proficiency than their male peers. At the same time, a high amount of interaction does not necessarily lead to higher proficiency: Teutsch-Dwyer's chapter clearly shows that linguistic accommodations made by the American girlfriend and the English-speaking co-workers of an immigrant Polish man slowed down his acquisition of English.

In sum, we can see that unequal gender relations may mediate access to linguistic resources and structure differential interactional opportunities for male and female L2 users of different ages, class, and ethnic backgrounds. Sexual harassment in particular emerges as an important gatekeeping practice which may complicate women's access to the target language community and inhibit their language learning (Ehrlich 1997, this volume; Goldstein 1995, this volume; Polanyi 1995; Siegal 1996; Talburt and Stewart 1999). We see this feminist understanding of ways in which ideologies and identities, in particular gender identities, mediate access to linguistic resources as critical both for theoretical treatments of language contact and language learning outcomes in the fields of bilingualism and SLA, and for practical attempts to devise new pedagogical approaches to language teaching, and new language and education policies and curricula.

4.2. Gendered agency in second language learning and use

Another important finding in the study of multilingualism, SLL, and gender is the intrinsic relationship between gender and agency – i.e., individual decisions and actions – in the process of L2 learning and use. While many SLA theories view L2 learners as passive vessels for input and output, poststructuralist approaches portray them as agents in charge of their own learning (Pavlenko, 2001). This view implies that in some cases L2 users may decide to learn the second, or any additional, language only to a certain extent, which allows them to be proficient, but without the consequences of losing the old and adopting the new ways of being in the world. In other contexts, their L2 learning may be accompanied by a full transition to the new linguistic community and L1 loss. And yet in others they may resist the language that positions them unfavorably. Moreover, an individual's choice is only part of the story in the poststructuralist framework which sees agencies as co-constructed and learning options as predicated on language ideologies and power structures within a particular society.

Gender as a system of social relations and discursive practices emerges as one of the key factors that in certain contexts may influence the decision-making process, and, as a result, the outcomes of second language learning and language shift (see chapters by McMahill, Pavlenko, and Teutsch-Dwyer). To begin with, differences in gender relations between particular speech communities may motivate individuals – oftentimes women – to learn a second language which will ensure them a higher, more respectable social and economic status (Gal 1978; McDonald 1994). Gal's (1978) pioneering study of the bilingual Austrian-Hungarian peasant community of Oberwart demonstrated that women in this community spearheaded language shift from Hungarian to German escaping the peasant life hierarchy in which they were kept in subservient positions. Motivated by a symbolic link between German and a newly available worker status, the young women chose both jobs and prospective mates in industrial urban centers where German was spoken, and not in their native Hungarian villages. Similar findings are reported by Swigart (1992), who shows that while a large majority of women in Dakar, Senegal, works on preserving and transmitting Wolof, there is a small but visible group of younger women who identify with Western culture, wear Western clothes, and refuse to speak Wolof, using exclusively French. Close attention paid to multiple aspects of identity in both studies suggests that linguistic innovation may be restricted to a particular group of women who are best able to take advantage of social change in progress – often, these may be younger and better educated women (Gal 1978; Holmes 1993; Kobayashi 2000; Swigart 1992).

Another way in which women were found to initiate language shift is by deciding not to transmit the primary language of the community to their children (Constantinidou 1994; Mascarenhas-Keyes 1994; McDonald 1994; Schlieben-Lange 1977). Schlieben-Lange (1977) and McDonald (1994) describe, respectively, Provençal and Breton mothers who in the 1960s and the 1970s started speaking French to their children. French for them was associated with modernity, urbanity, refinement, and higher social status, while Provençal and Breton "smelled of cow-shit" (McDonald 1994: 103). The dominant society encouraged the shift, forbidding and punishing the use of local languages in school settings. Similarly, Constantinidou (1994) documents the death of East Sutherland Gaelic, prompted by the fact that in the 1930s women stopped transmitting the language to their children. Constantinidou (1994) suggests that, motivated by the death of the fishing industry and opening employment opportunities in other domains, these women were in the process of redefining themselves: Gaelic symbolized the bond with their fishing past from which they wanted to break loose.

Several studies indicate that nowadays learning English in particular is seen by many women around the globe as a way of liberating themselves from the confines of patriarchy (Kobayashi 2000; Matsui 1995; Solé 1978; McMahill's and Pavlenko's chapters). Solé (1978) documents a greater tendency to use English – at times exclusively – among Mexican-American college women, striving to escape the confines of traditional Mexican culture. Kobayashi's (2000) survey of 555 high school students in Japan provides evidence that female Japanese students are significantly more positive toward – and more interested in – learning English, training for English-language related professions, and traveling to English-speaking countries, than their male peers. It is not surprising then, that in 1998, according to the Japanese Ministry of Education, 67% of foreign language majors among the university students were female, with English being the most popular and socially expected choice for women as a major and as an occupational choice (Kobayashi 2000). The researcher explains these trends by pointing to the marginalized status of young women in mainstream Japanese society and to ways in which the media discourses of language and gender legitimize female career choices linked to English. One cannot help but notice that this steering of women toward career choices in the language professions – which tend to be lower-paid and more marginal than most other professional careers – is very much in line with the traditional patriarchal distribution of career options. McMahill's chapter in the present volume takes a different approach to the same phenomenon, suggesting that the links perceived between feminism and English allow female Japanese learners in a feminist EFL class to use English as a language of empowerment. Similarly, an analysis of personal narratives of second language learners in Pavlenko's chapter shows that some immigrant and minority women learn English in order to escape gender relations and gendered linguistic practices of their cultures, perceived by them as hierarchical and demeaning.

It is important to point out here that women are not always the ones prompted to shift allegiances by unequal gender relations. Fortune (1998) tells about a young man who grew up in Brazil speaking Karaja, an indigenous language where the use of certain morphological and lexical forms is sex-exclusive. The young man's parents did not correct his use of women's forms in speech when he was growing up; as a result, his linguistic behavior was considered inappropriate by the wider Karaja community and he was ridiculed as a 'misfit'. Becoming bilingual was a liberating experience for this man, as Portuguese provided a new and much more respectable linguistic and gender identity for him. Herbert (1992, cited in James 1996: 104) shows that among the Thonga people in South Africa, where women have higher prestige and more power than in the dominant Zulu culture, men lead the shift to Zulu, since assimilation to Zulu language and culture would improve their economic and social status. The changing nature of gender relations and the meaning of bilingualism is underscored by Aikio (1992), who discusses the Sámi community in Finland, where women historically enjoyed a comparatively high social and economic status and freedom to travel, while Finnish women were perceived by them as economically disadvantaged, dependent on their husbands, and forced to stay in one spot. As a consequence, up until World War II Sámi women attempted to protect themselves from the dominant culture by refusing to learn Finnish. Once the traditional social and economic status began to change during – and as a result of – World War II, Sámi women followed Sámi men in their shift to Finnish.

It is equally important to indicate that gender as a system of social relations and discursive practices may not only prompt second language learning and language shift but may also elicit resistance to learning a language which invalidates individuals' gender subjectivities and replaces them with other ones, seen as problematic. A particularly poignant case is an outcome of a widespread shift from Native American languages to English for those previously categorized as 'berdache' or 'two-spirit'. Since these subjectivities, which treat gender and sexuality in terms of spirituality rather than biology, were not easily understood by members of the majority community, many 'berdache' Native

Americans had no choice but to identify themselves as gays and lesbians. In doing so, they acquired identities which could be read in Western terms, but, at the same time, moved from highly respectable identities to highly problematized ones (Lang 1997; Medicine 1997). While these Native Americans had no choice but to learn English, Pavlenko's chapter presents a number of cases in which learners choose to abandon – or at least limit – their attempts to learn and use the second language which positions them unacceptably in terms of gender.

In sum, we can see that paying attention to gender enhances our understanding of agency that may lead to investment in L2 learning or resistance to it. The studies discussed above convincingly demonstrate that it is not the essential nature of femininity or masculinity that defines the patterns of language shift or linguistic trajectories of particular individuals, but rather the nature of gendered social and economic relations, and ideologies of language and gender that mediate these relations. We also believe that much more work remains to be done in this area, in particular, with regard to gendered choices prompted by legitimization of particular sexual identities. An intriguing glimpse into ways in which sexuality may influence linguistic and cultural transitions is offered in Cant's (1997) collection of testimonies of gays and lesbians who migrated either from a rural area to a metropolitan one or from a country where homosexuality is illegal to a more tolerant one. While second language learning was not a factor in some transitions, switching speech communities was critical for Nacho, who left Franco's Spain for London, and for Anna, who left London's Chinese community for the city's multicultural lesbian scene.

4.3. Gendered discursive interactions in multilingual contexts

Another promising direction for future research is the study of gender and discursive interactions in multilingual contexts. Above we discussed ways in which gender may mediate access to interactional opportunities in the second language. In the present section, we will pay close attention to ways in which the presence of more than one language simultaneously multiplies and constrains possibilities for gendered self-expression. We see five main areas in which investigation of multilingual contexts may enhance the understanding of the relationship between language and gender: (1) investigation of the discursive construction of gendered subjectivities in language contact situations, which illuminates clashes in ideologies of language and gender (see Heller's chapter); (2) examination of the use of multiple languages in indexing and performing gender (see Ohara's chapter); (3) study of transformations of gender performances in linguistic transitions (see Ohara's and Pavlenko's chapters), (4) inquiry into ways in which gender, ethnic, and national identities, NS/NNS status, language proficiency, and the degree of acculturation interact in multilingual contexts (see Piller's chapter), and (5) consideration of ways in which affect and affiliation are implicated in multilingual contexts (see Piller's and Teutsch-Dwyer's chapters).

With regard to the first area of research, multilingual and multicultural contexts present a fertile site for investigation of the discursive construction of gendered subjectivities in public and private discourses. While multiple ideologies of language and gender also clash in seemingly homogeneous monolingual environments, the clashes are especially visible and severe when two or more clearly delineated linguistic, ethnic, and cultural communities are involved. For instance, in a study that compared the discursive construction of German and Turkish women in essays of German students, Räthzel (1997) found that both groups of women were portrayed as subordinated to men. At the same time, German women were seen as subordinating themselves actively, while Turkish women were depicted as "victims of men, of their nature (they are often pregnant) and of ideologies (honour)" (Räthzel 1997: 67). Blackledge's chapter further elaborates on discursive constructions of minority women by the majority society demonstrating how the British school system views Bengali women as illiterate because their literacy is in Bengali and not English. At times, minority communities conspire with the majority culture in oppressive practices. A pioneering study by Ledgerwood (1990) identifies storytelling as an important gender policing resource in a Cambodian immigrant community in the US. Transition to a society with less rigid and more equal gender roles resulted in a loss of social order in the Cambodian community, as Khmer women are entering the workforce, becoming mobile, literate, educated, and able to control cash from both public assistance and wages. Understanding that American laws can protect them against abusive marriages, and that job opportunities and financial assistance are available to help them end unsatisfactory marriages, some women have less interest in family and community matters and engage in dating or having affairs instead. While not all Khmer women participate in these changes, the very possibility of the choices – threatening to Khmer patriarchal social order – led to the creation of a new genre of stories about improper women: (1) improper wives who consider themselves equal to men and, thus, are sexually promiscuous; (2) improper daughters, who are involved in premarital sexual behavior and/or run away from home; (3) improper widows and orphans who are considered unguarded and at greater risk of sexual promiscuity. Performed as 'urban legends' by older men and women, these stories are always told as true and serve as a warning to disobedient women, since any kind of deviation in these stories always results in serious consequences such as illness or death.

Like other types of identity, gender identities are not only constructed *by* discourse, but also accomplished *in* discourse. In recent years, the field of language and gender has come to recognize that the relationship between gender and language is neither direct nor unilinear, and that most linguistic behaviors and practices index gender indirectly, mediated through ideologies of language and gender (Gal 1991; Eckert and McConnell-Ginet 1992; Ochs 1992). A useful distinction between two types of gender indexicals is proposed by Silverstein (1985): categorical/ overt and statistical/covert. Overt linguistic practices index the gender of the speaker, listener, or both directly, independent of the context of the conversation. Covert indexicals – such as directness or politeness – do not directly point to but are typically associated with speakers of a particular gender group. Since only "few features of language directly and exclusively index gender" (Ochs 1992: 340), it is the latter group that has long been the focus of attention in the field of language and gender. To date, linguistic indexing of gender has been attested in prosody, phonology, syntax, morphology, lexicon, communicative styles, narrative styles, strategic uses of silence, and access to and use of discursive genres (Bonvillain 1995; Freed 1995; Gal 1991; Ohara, this volume; Philips, Steele and Tanz 1987; Romaine 1999; Yokoyama 1999; for a comprehensive review, see Günthner 1996). The study of multilingualism and SLL indicates that in multilingual contexts gender can additionally be indexed by language use, language choice, language maintenance, language shift, and code-switching.

Most cases of gender indexing in bi- and multilingual communities constitute covert indexing, mediated by ideologies of language, gender, and power, so that particular languages or ways of using them are positioned as predominantly feminine or masculine. Thus, in many language contact communities, the dominant language, perceived as a power code, is associated with masculinity, and the minority language with domestic values and femininity (Harvey 1994; Loftin 1996). In other communities, the minority language is viewed as a solidarity code and is associated with masculinity (Hill 1987; McDonald 1994; Schlieben-Lange 1977) or with femininity (Spedding 1994). In their review of research on code-switching and gender, Cheshire and Gardner-Chloros (1998), who are writing from a gender-differences perspective, indicate that, while there exists no direct relationship between the two, different meanings that code-switching practices acquire in different contexts may mediate their relationship to gender. The framework adopted in the present chapter leads us to suggest that in contexts where the majority language is more valued, through association with power, people with more access to that language, oftentimes men, will exhibit higher degrees of code-switching and loan-word use in the minority language. In contrast, when the local language is more valued, through association with solidarity, code-switching may be restricted and one group of speakers may insist on implementing linguistic purism in the minority language. Thus, in Dakar men are found to speak a code-switched variety, Urban Wolof (Swigart 1992), while in Mexico their speech is considered to be a 'cleaner' version of the local language Mexicano than that spoken by women (Hill 1987).

A related and quite intriguing area of investigation is research that links differences in gender performances between different communities to transformation of these performances in linguistic transitions. To date, however, very little research has been conducted in this area. More than three decades ago, Ervin-Tripp's (1967) study of Japanese women living in the US suggested that some bilingual women may perform drastically different gendered selves depending on the context, interlocutor, and the language of the interaction. Her insights were not built upon until recently, when researchers started looking again at possibilities of self-expression afforded to individuals by different languages. While Ohara's chapter discusses transformations of pitch in the speech of women who are bilingual in English and Japanese, McMahill's and Pavlenko's chapters talk about ways in which some languages may be seen as more advantageous than others for free self-expression. Pavlenko's chapter also discusses transformations in discursive performances of gender experienced by individuals in the process of linguistic transition. A recent study by Pujolar (1997) reminds us that ideologies of language and gender differ also within multilingual communities based on a number of factors, such as class, ethnicity, or sexuality. In his work, Pujolar (1997) found that men in Catalonia, bilingual in Spanish and Catalan, construct masculinity in different ways: while working-class Catalan men perform masculinity through verbal dueling in Catalan (oftentimes involving insults related to alleged homosexuality), more urban sons of Spanish-speaking parents mock their ways, using silly voices in Catalan to present unmasculine individuals.

Poststructuralist inquiry into multilingualism, SLL, and gender, also brings a new dimension into investigations of intercultural communication and miscommunication. To begin with, it is suggested that individual and institutional interactions in multilingual contexts cannot afford to ignore ways in which power can be differentially distributed based on gender, social status, the native/non-native speaker status, the speakers' degree of proficiency in the more prestigious language, or the degree of acculturation to the majority culture (Günthner 1992; Singh and Lele 1990). The interplay between status, gender, and power in conversational interaction is well illustrated in Günthner's (1992) study of conversational conflicts between German counselors and Chinese students in a Chinese university, where German counselors attempt to give Chinese students a more realistic perspective on their future stay in Germany. The researcher found that in four conversations, conducted in German, Chinese women hardly contradicted their German interlocutors and gave up their own positions, while Chinese men were willing to handle disagreement and remained argumentative all the way through. At the same time, the female German counselors employed highly assertive discursive strategies, due to their high status as counselors and as native speakers of German.

Finally, recent studies also follow up on Eckert and McConnell-Ginet's (1992) contention that the emphasis on economic and social power should not obfuscate other aspects of gender relations such as affiliation and affect. This trend finds reflections in the study of language use and language choice in cross-cultural couples (Heller and Lévy 1992; Piller's chapter) and investigations of bilingualism, gender, and friendship (Hruska 2000; Willett 1995; Woolard 1997). Piller's chapter provides a detailed discussion of various factors which contribute to language choice and language use in cross-cultural couples' communication. Other recent studies look at ways in which gendered peer networks may impact both language use and language learning outcomes. Woolard's (1997) ethnographic case study of high school students in the Barcelona area indicates that gendered friendship practices can affect the use of the bilingual repertoire. The researcher shows that being more solidary and cohesive than the boys' groups, girls' friendship circles favor ethnic and linguistic homogeneity and set stronger constraints on linguistic behavior. In contrast, boys' peer groups can be ethnically mixed and linguistically diverse, with Catalan and Castilian boys mixing more freely than Catalan and Castilian girls. As a result, boys and girls profit differently from the patterns of language use imposed on them by their gendered peer networks: girls' friendships and language behavior may have greater consequences for the social identities they are able to project. Similar gendered patterns in affiliation and language practices were documented in Hruska's (2000) and Willett's (1995) studies of young ESL learners. Willett's (1995) study of four 7-year old ESL children in a mainstream classroom showed that the combined effects of differences in gendered peer cultures and the seating arrangements – which were designed to keep the boys apart but allowed the girls to sit together – favored the three female learners. The friendship between three ESL girls allowed them to collaborate and support each other, thus earning a high status in the girls' subculture and the status of 'good learners' in the eyes of the teacher. In contrast, the working-class Mexican-American boy, Xavier, did not get any help from his female seatmates and was not allowed to get out of his seat to get help from his male bilingual friends. As a result, he had to rely on adults for help, thus acquiring the status of a needy child, unable to work independently.

In sum, we can see that multilingual and multicultural contexts offer multiple opportunities for researchers interested in the relationship between language and gender. These settings offer a productive site for investigation of the interaction between diverse constructions of gender, sexuality, and privilege which may co-exist – or clash – with each other. They also provide us with a unique opportunity to examine ways in which gendered performances may be transformed in the process of second language socialization. Finally, these contexts offer unparalleled insights not only into the relationship between language, gender, and power, but also into the links between language, gender, and the dynamics of sexual attraction and affiliation.

4.4. Critical and feminist pedagogy

Given the fact that many of the studies in the field are concerned with the mediated relationship between language and social justice, it is clear that mere critical analyses are not enough and that practical outcomes of research in the new field of multilingualism, SLL, and gender are most desirable. Over the years, numerous researchers have engaged in projects that aimed to investigate how critical and feminist pedagogies can contribute to learners' enrichment and empowerment (Casanave and Yamashiro 1996; McGregor, 1998; Peirce 1995; Norton 2000; Papatzikou Cochran 1996; Schenke 1996; Vandrick 1995, 1999 a; Yamashiro 2000). Four key topics have been explored in this research: (1) gendered access to educational opportunities (see Blackledge's and Heller's chapters); (2) the gendered nature of classroom interaction (see Heller's chapter); (3) gender representation in teaching materials (see Kramsch and von Hoene's chapter); and (4) development of feminist approaches to language pedagogy (see McMahill's chapter).

Considering that readers may be more familiar with this line of research and practice, we will be brief in our review (for a comprehensive review of the issues of language and gender in second and foreign language education, see Sunderland 2000). In particular, we will omit discussion of the first two topics since they have already been dealt with in sections 4.1 and 4.3, which discuss ways in which gender may mediate access to educational opportunities and patterns of classroom interaction, oftentimes doubly discriminating against immigrant and minority women. In section 4.3, we also presented Willett's (1995) study which shows that in some contexts gendered peer networks may work to the advantage of female learners. Similarly, McMahill's chapter discusses a unique type of class which combines the learning of English with a feminist agenda and targets an almost exclusively female audience. Together, studies investigating ways in which gender mediates access to and interaction in educational contexts suggest that more attention needs to be paid to locally constructed relations of power which are predicated not only on gender, but also on age, ethnicity, sexuality, class, and linguistic and cultural background. At the same time, feminist educators warn us that this complex approach should not distract attention from the fact that female learners are still disadvantaged in the majority of contexts (Vandrick 1999 b).

The third topic, gender representation in language teaching materials, has been for a long time a focus of attention in the fields of applied linguistics (AL) and teaching English-as-a-second/foreign-language (TESL/TEFL). In particular, content analyses of ESL textbooks, published in the 1970s and early 1980s, revealed that many texts stereotyped male and female roles and excluded women from the narrative through omission of females in texts and illustrations, firstness of males in any pair of categories, privileging of males in occupational visibility, and the use of masculine generics such as 'he', 'man', or 'mankind' (Hartman and Judd 1978; Porreca 1984; Sunderland 1992). While the situation has been steadily improving in ESL, recent textbook analyses of EFL textbooks published in Japan (McGregor 1998), Japanese textbooks published in Japan and the US (Siegal and Okamoto 1996), and Russian textbooks published in the US (Shardakova 2000) reveal that many second and foreign language textbooks continue to portray stereotypical gender roles with men occupying higher social positions and women more subordinate roles. Siegal and Okamoto (1996) in particular found that textbooks aimed at teaching Japanese to American students present highly stereotypical linguistic 'norms' based on hegemonic ideologies of class, language, and gender. Kramsch and von Hoene's chapter expands on this theme, insightfully analyzing ways in which discourses of gender and travel interlink in contemporary German textbooks. Together, these studies suggest that there is still a lot to accomplish in order for classroom language teaching materials, in particular textbooks, to fairly represent gender relations and practices and to reflect the gendered nature of linguistic exchanges. The inclusion of sexual harassment issues in the curriculum is particularly important in order to enable female learners to use the language skillfully to protect themselves from potential attacks and to avoid misunderstandings. For instance, in a Spanish classroom, some discussions may deal with multiple meanings of *piropos*, Spanish male complements, which are at times perceived as sexual harassment by American women (Talburt and Stewart 1999).

Finally and most importantly, we believe that the appearance of feminist approaches to language pedagogy (Casanave and Yamashiro 1996; McGregor,

1998; Peirce 1995; Norton 2000; Papatzikou Cochran 1996; Schenke 1996; Vandrick, 1995, 1999 a; Yamashiro 2000; see also chapters by Kramsch and von Hoene and McMahill), concerned with empowering the students through discussions of gender, sexuality, and the teaching of non-sexist language, signals the beginnings of a steady movement toward equality and social justice in educational contexts.

5. Conclusions

To conclude, we hope to have demonstrated the importance of forging new links between the fields of multilingualism, SLL, and language and gender. We have argued that the field of language and gender will benefit from considering multilingual contexts, which can provide a unique perspective on the effects of gender as a system of social relations and discursive practices on individuals' access to linguistic resources. Multilingual contexts also offer an unparalleled opportunity to explore construction and negotiation of gender in discourse through examination of gender indexing in multilingual communities, individual gender performances in two or more languages, and the interplay between gender and the NS/NNS status in the construction of authority.

We have also argued that the fields of bilingualism and SLA will similarly benefit from incorporating gender among other social factors that influence multiple language learning and use. We suggested a theoretical framework which foregrounds ideologies of language and gender in the explanation of language contact and SLL processes and outcomes. This framework posits that in certain contexts language contact and language learning outcomes can be explained by the difference in gender relations in majority and minority communities and the meaning assigned by ideologies of language and gender to specific linguistic resources and practices. Thus, in the study of SLA this framework will allow the field to investigate how differences in the meaning and performance of gender could motivate L2 learning.

Two types of questions, macro and micro, need to be explored in future investigations of the interaction between multilingualism, gender, and ideology. With regard to the societal level of linguistic interaction, among the many questions are the following: What – possibly conflicting – gender ideologies and discourses are at work in a particular society? How are they reflected in language ideologies and linguistic practices? What are the power relations and how do they define access to particular linguistic resources? What discourses of resistance are available to the members of particular communities and how do they make use of them? Are gender ideologies currently in the process of change and, if so, how is this change reflected in linguistic practices?

To acknowledge the fact that language, gender, and power interaction is best studied on a local level, researchers may then ask what ideologies of gender and language are at work in a particular community of practice and how do they relate to the ideologies of society at large?

With regard to gender, how do different gender, age, class, and race groups participate in the local economy and how is this participation mediated linguistically? With regard to language, what are the values of languages and language varieties used in the community and how is gender reflected in these beliefs? What are the attitudes toward various language contact phenomena, from language maintenance to code-switching? Who has access and who controls particular discourses? How are gatekeeping practices instituted in the community? What are the possibilities for resistance to the predominant hierarchy and how do different groups of speakers engage in this resistance?

Shifting the focus of attention to individuals, we need to know what are the communities of practice/linguistic markets in which particular bi- and multilinguals participate? How are these communities positioned with regard to society? Which communities are easier accessed and by whom? Who gets silenced in particular encounters, when and why? And, finally, if the individuals in question are engaged in cross-cultural transitions, how were they positioned by the dominant ideologies of language and gender in their first language communities of practice? Only when these and many other related questions are answered for a number of postcolonial, minority, and migrant communities, as well as for individuals in cross-cultural marriages and cross-linguistic transitions, will we be able to paint a sufficiently comprehensive picture of the relationship between multilingualism, SLL, and gender.

Note

1.   Parts of this chapter appear in Pavlenko, A. (2001) Bilingualism, gender, and ideology. *The International Journal of Bilingualism* 5, 2.

References

Aikio, Marjut
  1992   Are women innovators in the shift to a second language?: A case study of Reindeer Sámi women and men. *International Journal of the Sociology of Language* 94, 43–61.

Ardener, Edwin
  1975   The problem of women revisited. In Ardener, Shirley (ed.), *Perceiving Women*. London: Malaby/Dent.

Bergvall, Victoria
  1999   Toward a comprehensive theory of language and gender. *Language in Society* 28, 2, 273–293.

Bing, Janet and Victoria Bergvall
  1996   The question of questions: Beyond binary thinking. In Bergvall, Victoria, Janet Bing, and Alice Freed (eds.), *Rethinking Language and Gender Research: Theory and Practice*. London/New York: Longman, 1–30.

Bonvillain, Nancy
  1995   *Women and Men: Cultural Constructs of Gender*. Englewood Cliffs, NJ: Prentice-Hall.

Borker, Ruth
  1980   Anthropology: Social and cultural perspectives. In McConnell-Ginet, Sally, Ruth Borker, and Nelly Furman (eds.), *Women and Language in Literature and Society*. New York: Praeger, 26–44.

Bourdieu, Pierre
  1991   *Language and Symbolic Power*. Cambridge: Polity Press.

Burton, Pauline
  1994   Women and second-language use: An introduction. In Burton, Pauline, Ketaki Kushari Dyson, and Shirley Ardener (eds.), *Bilingual Women: Anthropological Approaches to Second-Language Use*. Oxford/Providence: Berg, 1–29.

Burton, Pauline, Ketaki Kushari Dyson, and Shirley Ardener (eds.)
  1994   *Bilingual Women: Anthropological Approaches to Second-Language Use*. Oxford/Providence: Berg.

Cameron, Deborah
  1992   *Feminism and Linguistic Theory*. Second ed. London: Macmillan.

1996   The language-gender interface: Challenging co-optation. In Bergvall, Victoria, Janet Bing, and Alice Freed (eds.), *Rethinking Language and Gender Research: Theory and Practice*. London/New York: Longman, 31–53.

1997 a   Performing gender identity: Young men's talk and the construction of heterosexual masculinity. In Johnson, Sally and Ulrike Meinhof (eds.), *Language and Masculinity*. Oxford: Blackwell, 47–64.

1997 b   Theoretical debates in feminist linguistics: Questions of sex and gender. In Wodak, Ruth (ed.), *Gender and Discourse*. London: Sage, 21–36.

1998   Gender, language and discourse: A review essay. *Signs* 23, 4, 945–973.

Cameron, Deborah and Jennifer Coates
1988   Some problems in the sociolinguistic explanation of sex differences. In Coates, Jennifer and Deborah Cameron (eds.), *Women in their Speech Communities: New Perspectives on Language and Sex*. London/New York: Longman, 13–26.

Cameron, Deborah, Fiona McAlinden, and Kathy O'Leary
1988   Lakoff in context: The social and linguistic functions of tag questions. In Coates, Jennifer and Deborah Cameron (eds.), *Women in their Speech Communities: New Perspectives on Language and Sex*. London: Longman, 74–93.

Cant, Robert (ed.)
1997   *Invented Identities? Lesbians and Gays Talk about Migration*. London: Cassell.

Casanave, Christine Pearson and Amy Yamashiro (eds.)
1996   Gender issues in language education (Special issue). *Keio University Shonan Fujisawa Campus Journal*.

Cheshire, Jenny and Penelope Gardner-Chloros
1998   Code-switching and the sociolinguistic gender pattern. *International Journal of the Sociology of Language* 129, 5–34.

Constantinidou, Evi
1994   The 'death' of East Sutherland Gaelic: Death by women? In Burton, Pauline, Ketaki Kushari Dyson, and Shirley Ardener (eds.), *Bilingual Women: Anthropological Approaches to Second-Language Use*. Oxford/Providence: Berg, 111–127.

Crawford, Mary
1995   *Talking Difference: On Gender and Language*. London: Sage.

Eckert, Penelope and Sally McConnell-Ginet
1992   Think practically and look locally: Language and gender as community-based practice. *Annual Review of Anthropology* 21, 461–490.
1999   New generalizations and explanations in language and gender research. *Language in Society* 28, 2, 185–201.

Ehrlich, Susan
1997   Gender as social practice: Implications for second language acquisition. *Studies in Second Language Acquisition* 19, 421–446.

Ellis, Rod
1994   *The Study of Second Language Acquisition*. Oxford: Oxford University Press.

Ervin-Tripp, Susan
1967   An Issei learns English. *The Journal of Social Issues* 23, 78–90.

Fishman, Pamela
1983   Interaction: The work women do. In Thorne, Barrie, Cheris Kramarae, and Nancy Henley (eds.), *Language, Gender, and Society*. Rowley, MA: Newbury House, 89–102.

Freed, Alice
1995   Language and gender. *Annual Review of Applied Linguistics* 15, 3–22.

Fortune, Gretchen
1998   *Sex-exclusive differentiation in the Karaja language of Bananal island, Central Brazil*. Ph.D. dissertation, Lancaster University.

Gal, Susan
1978   Peasant men can't get wives: Language and sex roles in a bilingual community. *Language in Society* 7, 1, 1–17.
1991   Between speech and silence: The problematics of research on language and gender. In Di Leonardo, Micaela (ed.), *Gender at the Crossroads of Knowledge*. Berkeley: University of California Press, 175–203.

Gass, Susan and Evangeline Varonis
1986   Sex differences in NS/NNS interactions. In Day, Richard (ed.), *Talking to Learn: Conversation in Second Language Acquisition*. Rowley, MA: Newbury House, 327–351.

Goldstein, Tara
1995   "Nobody is talking bad": Creating community and claiming power on the production lines. In Hall, Kira and Mary Bucholtz (eds.), *Gender Articu-*

lated: Language and the Socially Constructed Self. New York/London: Routledge, 375–400.

Gumperz, John
1972   Introduction. In Gumperz, John and Dell Hymes (eds.), *Directions in Sociolinguistics.* New York: Holt, Rinehart & Winston, 1–25.

Günthner, Susanne
1992   The construction of gendered discourse in Chinese-German interactions. *Discourse and Society* 3, 167–191.

1996   Male-female speaking practices across cultures. In Hellinger, Marlies and Ulrich Ammon (eds.), *Contrastive Sociolinguistics.* Berlin/New York: Mouton de Gruyter, 447–473.

Haeri, Niloofar
1996   *The Sociolinguistic Market of Cairo: Gender, Class, and Education.* London: Kegan Paul.

Hartman, Pat and Elliott Judd
1978   Sexism and TESOL materials. *TESOL Quarterly* 12, 4, 383–393.

Harvey, Penelope
1994   The presence and absence of speech in the communication of gender. In Burton, Pauline, Ketaki Kushari Dyson, and Shirley Ardener (eds.), *Bilingual Women: Anthropological Approaches to Second-Language Use.* Oxford/Providence: Berg, 44–64.

Heller, Monica
1999   *Linguistic Minorities and Modernity: A Sociolinguistic Ethnography.* London/New York: Longman.

Heller, Monica and Laurette Lévy
1992   Mixed marriages: Life on the linguistic frontier. *Multilingua* 11, 1, 11–43.

Herbert, Robert
1992   Language, gender, and ethnicity: Explaining language shift in Thongaland. Paper presented at the Annual Meeting of the Linguistic Society of America, Los Angeles, CA.

Hill, Jane
1987   Women's speech in modern Mexicano. In Philips, Susan, Susan Steele, and Christine Tanz (eds.), *Language, Gender, and Sex in Comparative Perspective.* Cambridge: Cambridge University Press, 121–160.

Holmes, Janet
1990   Hedges and boosters in women's and men's speech. *Language and Communication* 10, 3, 185–205.

1992   *An Introduction to Sociolinguistics.* London: Longman.

1993   Immigrant women and language maintenance in Australia and New Zealand. *International Journal of Applied Linguistics* 3, 2, 159–179.

Hruska, Barbara
2000   Bilingualism, gender, and friendship: Constructing second language learners in an English dominant kindergarten. Paper presented at the Annual AAAL Conference, March 2000, Vancouver, Canada.

James, Deborah
1996   Women, men and prestige speech forms: a critical review. In Bergvall, Victoria, Janet Bing, and Alice Freed (eds.), *Rethinking Language and Gender Research: Theory and Practice.* London/New York: Longman, 98–125.

James, Deborah and Sandra Clarke
1993   Women, men, and interruptions: A critical review. In Tannen, Deborah (ed.), *Gender in Conversational Interaction.* New York: Oxford University Press, 231–280.

Kobayashi, Yoko
2000   Young Japanese women's perceptions about English study. Paper presented at the Annual TESOL Conference, March 2000, Vancouver, Canada.

Kouritzin, Sandra
2000   Immigrant mothers redefine access to ESL classes: Contradiction and ambivalence. *Journal of Multilingual and Multicultural Development* 21, 1, 14–32.

Kulick, Don
1998   Anger, gender, language shift, and the politics of revelation in a Papua New Guinean village. In Schieffelin, Bambi, Kathryn Woolard, and Paul Kroskrity (eds.), *Language Ideologies: Practice and Theory.* New York/Oxford: Oxford University Press, 87–102.

Labov, William
1966   *The Social Stratification of English in New York City.* Washington, DC: Center of Applied Linguistics.

1972   *Language in the Inner City.* Philadelphia: University of Pennsylvania Press.

Lakoff, Robin
    1975   *Language and Woman's Place*. Harper and Row Publishers.

Lang, Sabine
    1997   Various kinds of two-Spirit people: Gender variance and homosexuality in
            Native American communities. In Jacobs, Sue-Ellen, Wesley Thomas, and
            Sabine Lang (eds.), *Two-Spirit People: Native American Gender Identity,
            Sexuality, and Spirituality*. Urbana/Chicago: University of Illinois Press,
            100–118.

Lave, Jean and Etienne Wenger
    1991   *Situated Learning: Legitimate Peripheral Participation*. Cambridge: Cam-
            bridge University Press.

Ledgerwood, Judy
    1990   *Changing Khmer Conceptions of Gender: Women, Stories, and the Social
            Order*. Ph.D. dissertation, Cornell University.

Loftin, Jonathan
    1996   "Women's knowledge" and language choice at the Fourth Cultural Con-
            gress in Otavalo, Ecuador. In Warner, N., J. Ahlers, L. Bilmes, M. Oliver,
            S. Wertheim and M. Chen (eds.), *Gender and Belief Systems. Proceedings
            of the Fourth Berkeley Women and Language Conference, April 19–21,
            1996*. Berkeley, CA: University of California, BWLG, 447–454.

Losey, Kay
    1995   Gender and ethnicity as factors in the development of verbal skills in bilin-
            gual Mexican American women. *TESOL Quarterly* 4, 635–661.

Maltz, Daniel and Ruth Borker
    1982   A cultural approach to male-female miscommunication. In Gumperz, John
            (ed.), *Language and Social Identity*. Cambridge: Cambridge University
            Press, 196–206.

Mascarenhas-Keyes, Stella
    1994   Language and diaspora: The use of Portuguese, English, and Konkani by
            Catholic Goan women. In Burton, Pauline, Ketaki Kushari Dyson, and
            Shirley Ardener (eds.), *Bilingual Women: Anthropological Approaches to
            Second-Language Use*. Oxford/ Providence: Berg, 149–166.

Matsui, Machiko
    1995   Gender role perceptions of Japanese and Chinese female students in
            American universities. *Comparative Education Review* 39, 3, 356–378.

McDonald, Maryon
   1994   Women and linguistic innovation in Brittany. In Burton, Pauline, Ketaki
           Kushari Dyson, and Shirley Ardener (eds.), *Bilingual Women: Anthropo-
           logical Approaches to Second-Language Use.* Oxford/Providence: Berg,
           85–110.

McGregor, Laura (ed.)
   1998   Special issue: Gender issues in language teaching. *The Language Teacher*
           22, 5.

Medicine, Beatrice
   1997   Changing Native American roles in an urban context *and* changing Native
           American sex roles in an urban context. In Jacobs, Sue-Ellen, Wesley Tho-
           mas, and Sabine Lang (eds.), *Two-Spirit People: Native American Gender
           Identity, Sexuality, and Spirituality.* Urbana/Chicago: University of Illinois
           Press, 145–155.

Moon, Seonjoo
   2000   Ideologies of language and gender among Korean ESL students and South
           American ESL students: Shaping language learning processes. *Gender Is-
           sues in Language Education: Temple University Japan Working Papers in
           Applied Linguistics* 17, 148–163.

Nanda, Serena
   1990   *Neither Man nor Woman: The Hijras of India.* Belmont, CA: Wadsworth.

Nicholson, Linda
   1994   Interpreting gender. *Signs* 20, 1, 79–105.

Norton, Bonny
   2000   *Identity and Language Learning: Gender, Ethnicity, and Educational
           Change.* London: Longman.

O'Barr, William and Bowman Atkins
   1980   "Women's language" or "powerless language"? In McConnell-Ginet,
           Sally, Ruth Borker, and Nelly Furman (eds.), *Women and Language in Lit-
           erature and Society.* New York: Praeger, 93–110.

Ochs, Elinor
   1992   Indexing gender. In Duranti, Alessandro and Charles Goodwin (eds.), *Re-
           thinking Context.* Cambridge: Cambridge University Press, 335–358.

Oxford, Rebecca
    1993   Gender differences in styles and strategies for language learning: What do
            they mean? Should we pay attention? In Alatis, James (ed.), *Strategic In-
            teraction and Language Acquisition: Theory, Practice, and Research.*
            Washington, DC: Georgetown University Press, 541–557.
    1994   La différence continue ... Gender differences in second/foreign language
            learning styles and strategies. In Sunderland, Jane (ed.), *Exploring Gender:
            Questions and Implications for English Language Education.* London:
            Prentice Hall, 140–147.

Papatzikou Cochran, Effie
    1996   Gender and the ESL classroom. *TESOL Quarterly* 30, 159–162.

Pavlenko, Aneta
    2001   Bilingualism, gender, and ideology. *The International Journal of Bilin-
            gualism,* 5, 2.

Peirce, Bonny Norton
    1995   Social identity, investment, and language learning. *TESOL Quarterly* 29, 1,
            9–31.

Philips, Susan, Susan Steele, and Christine Tanz (eds.)
    1987   *Language, Gender, and Sex in Comparative Perspective.* Cambridge: Cam-
            bridge University Press.

Pica, Teresa, Lloyd Holliday, Nora Lewis, Dom Berducci, and Jeanne Newman
    1991   Language learning through interaction: What role does gender play?
            Studies in Second Language Acquisition 13, 343–376.

Pichette, Mary Jo
    2000   *The influence of gender on the acquisition of the Japanese language by
            white Western men and women living and working in Japan.* Unpublished
            manuscript, Temple University Japan.

Polanyi, Livia
    1995   Language learning and living abroad: Stories from the field. In Freed, Bar-
            bara (ed.), *Second Language Acquisition in a Study Abroad Context.* Am-
            sterdam/Philadelphia: John Benjamins, 271–291.

Porreca, Karen
    1984   Sexism in current ESL textbooks. *TESOL Quarterly* 18, 4, 705–724.

Pujolar, Joan
    1997   Masculinities in a multilingual setting. In Johnson, Sally and Ulrike Mein-
            hof (eds.), *Language and Masculinity.* Oxford: Basil Blackwell, 86–106.

Räthzel, Nora
  1997   Gender and racism in discourse. In Wodak, Ruth (ed.), *Gender and Discourse*. London: Sage, 57–80.

Romaine, Suzanne
  1999   *Communicating Gender.* Mahwah, NJ: Lawrence Erlbaum.

Schenke, Arleen
  1996   Not just a "social issue": Teaching feminist in ESL. *TESOL Quarterly* 30, 155–159.

Schlieben-Lange, Brigitte
  1977   The language situation in Southern France. *Linguistics* 19, 101–108.

Shardakova, Marya
  2000   *Identity construction in Russian textbooks.* Unpublished manuscript, Bryn Mawr College.

Siegal, Meryl
  1996   The role of learner subjectivity in second language sociolinguistic competency: Western women learning Japanese. *Applied Linguistics* 17, 356–382.

Siegal, Meryl and Shigeko Okamoto
  1996   Imagined worlds: Language, gender, and socio-cultural "norms" in Japanese language textbooks. In Warner, N., J. Ahlers, L. Bilmes, M. Oliver, S. Wertheim and M. Chen (eds.), *Gender and Belief Systems. Proceedings of the Fourth Berkeley Women and Language Conference, April 19–21, 1996.* Berkeley, CA: University of California, BWLG, 667–678.

Silverstein, Michael
  1985   Language and the culture of gender: At the intersection of structure, usage, and ideology. In Mertz, Elizabeth and Parmentier, Richard (eds.), *Semiotic Mediation: Sociocultural and Psychological Perspectives.* New York: Academic Press, 219–259.

Singh, Rajendra and Jayant Lele
  1990   Language, power, and cross-sex communication strategies in Hindi and Indian English revisited. *Language in Society* 19, 541–546.

Solé, Yolanda
  1978   Sociocultural and sociopsychological factors in differential language retentiveness by sex. *International Journal of the Sociology of Language* 17, 29–44.

Spedding, Alison
  1994   Open Castilian, closed Aymara? Bilingual women in the Yungas of La Paz
            (Bolivia). In Burton, Pauline, Ketaki Kushari Dyson, and Shirley Ardener
            (eds.), *Bilingual Women: Anthropological Approaches to Second-Lan-
            guage Use*. Oxford/ Providence: Berg, 30–43.

Spender, Dale
  1980   *Man Made Language*. London: Routledge and Kegan Paul.

Stevens, Gillian
  1986   Sex differences in language shift in the United States. *Sociology and Social
            Research* 71, 1, 31–34.

Sunderland, Jane
  1992   Teaching materials and teaching/learning processes: Gender in the class-
            room. *Working Papers on Gender, Language, and Sexism* 2, 2, 15–26.
  2000   Issues of language and gender in second and foreign language education.
            Language Teaching 33, 4, 203–223.

Swigart, Leigh
  1992   Women and language choice in Dakar: A case of unconscious innovation.
            Women and Language 15, 1, 11–20.

Talbot, Mary
  1998   *Language and Gender: An Introduction*. Oxford: Polity Press.

Talburt, Susan and Melissa Stewart
  1999   What's the subject of study abroad?: Race, gender, and "living culture".
            The Modern Language Journal 83, 163–177.

Tannen, Deborah
  1990   *You Just Don't Understand: Women and Men in Conversation*. New York:
            Morrow.
  1993   The relativity of linguistic strategies: Rethinking power and solidarity in
            gender and dominance. In Tannen, Deborah (ed.), *Gender and Conversa-
            tional Interaction*. New York: Oxford University Press, 165–188.

Thorne, Barrie and Nancy Henley
  1975   *Language and Sex: Difference and Dominance*. Rowley, MA: Newbury
            House.

Trömel-Plötz, Senta
  1991   Review essay: Selling the apolitical. *Discourse and Society* 2, 4, 489–502.

Trudgill, Peter
1972   Sex, covert prestige and linguistic change in the urban British English of
        Norwich. *Language in Society* 1, 179–195.
1974   *The Social Differentiation of English in Norwich.* Cambridge: Cambridge
        University Press.

Vandrick, Stephanie
1995   Teaching and practicing feminism in the University ESL class. *TESOL
        Journal* Spring, 4–6.
1999 a   Who's afraid of critical feminist pedagogies? *TESOL Matters* 9, 2, 9.
1999 b   The case for more research on female students in ESL/EFL classrooms.
        TESOL Matters 9, 2, 16.

Weedon, Chris
1987   *Feminist Practice and Poststructuralist Theory.* Oxford: Blackwell.

Wenger, Etienne
1998   *Communities of Practice.* Cambridge: Cambridge University Press.

West, Candace and Sarah Fenstermaker
1995   Doing difference. *Gender and Society* 9, 1, 8–37.

West, Candace and Don Zimmerman
1983   Small insults: A study of interruptions in cross-sex conversations between
        unacquainted persons. In Thorne, Barrie, Cheris Kramarae, and Nancy
        Henley (eds.), *Language, Gender, and Society.* Rowley, MA: Newbury
        House, 102–117.
1987   Doing gender. *Gender and Society* 1, 2, 125–151.

Willett, Jerri
1995   Becoming first graders in an L2: An ethnographic study of L2 sociali-
        zation. *TESOL Quarterly* 29, 3, 473–503.

Woolard, Kathryn
1997   Between friends: Gender, peer group structure, and bilingualism in urban
        Catalonia. *Language in Society* 26, 533–560.

Yamashiro, Amy (ed.)
2000   Gender issues in language education. *Temple University Japan Working
        Papers in Applied Linguistics* 17.

Yokoyama, Olga
   1999   Russian genderlects and referential expressions. *Language in Society* 28, 3,
           401–429.

Zentella, Ana Celia
   1987   Language and female identity in the Puerto Rican community. In Pen-
           field, J. (ed.), *Women and Language in Transition*. Albany, NY: SUNY
           Press, 159–166.

Zimmerman, Don and Candace West
   1975   Sex roles, interruptions and silences in conversations. In Thorne, Barrie
           and Nancy Henley (eds.), *Language and Sex: Difference and Dominance*.
           Rowley, MA: Newbury House, 105–129.

Complex positionings: Women negotiating identity and power in a minority urban setting

Adrian Blackledge

1. Introduction

Schools have a crucial role to play in maintaining or challenging structures of power in society. In the education of minority language groups, existing structures of social injustice are reproduced to the extent that the school dictates that only the language of the majority is acceptable as a means of communication in and with the school (Corson 1993, 1998; Shannon 1999). At the same time, language ideologies interact with other elements which affect social and community participation, including gender, cultural identity, class, and race. The sociolinguistic study of schools can make visible the marginalization of minority groups in Western societies who often seem to go unnoticed in their interactions with social institutions, as they make attempts to gain access to structures of institutional power to "take advantage of open doors or to deal with ones that are closed" (Heller 1999: 274).

This chapter presents data in which the mothers and teachers of young Bangladeshi children in a school in Birmingham, UK, articulate their attitudes to the children's schooling, and in particular to the Bangladeshi women's attempts to support their children's literacy learning. The data demonstrate that there were tensions between the Bangladeshi women's views of themselves and the majority-culture teachers' perception of them. These tensions emerged in the teachers' positioning of the women in terms of their literacy, their competence as care providers, their access to cultural resources, and their ability (or willingness) to adopt the values and behaviors of the dominant (white, middle-class) group. The teachers' positioning of the Bangladeshi women as deficient in these areas conflicted with the women's view of themselves. These tensions meant that the women were unable to take advantage of doors which appeared to be open, and were unable to unlock those that were closed.

2. Identity and power in the process of schooling

The analysis presented here draws on the notion that identities are not only socially constructed (Peirce 1995), but also multiple and dynamic (Woolard 1998). In minority language settings, it is often the case that the identity of minority groups and individuals is constructed as being in some way deficient (Norton 2000). If features central to the group's cultural identity are viewed negatively by the dominant society, the group may incorporate a negative view of itself (Blommaert 1999; Bourdieu 1991; Ferdman 1990; Gal 1998). The dominant group's deficit view of features of the minority group can act as a pressure on the minorities to conform to the values and behaviors of majority-culture society. When minority-language parents attempt to interact with majority-language teachers, the most evident feature of the minority group is often that of language. The failure of teachers to communicate effectively with minority-language parents may put pressure on the parents to adopt the language of the majority group. However, for the minority group, a shift to the majority language may put at risk their group identity, as the language of the home country may be invested with symbolic status (Dabène and Moore 1995; Heller 1992, 1995). For the dominant group, in contrast, the minority language may represent no more than a source of inconvenience and frustration, as teachers are unable to communicate with the parents of the children in their class. It is in the terrain of language (Heller, this volume) that features of minority groups' identity are constructed and re-constructed by members of the dominant group. These features of identity include literacy, gender, cultural competence, class, and race.

2.1. The social construction of "illiteracy"

Until recently there has often been an assumption among educators and policy-makers that the homes of poor, minority-culture families are less effective language and literacy learning environments than the homes of middle-class, majority-culture families. Minority groups are massively over-represented among the "functionally illiterate" in Western developed countries (Cummins 1994). But public discourse often absolves schools and society from responsibility for minority-group underachievement, and attributes school failure to minority students' own deficiencies (lack of academic effort), or deficiencies of their families (parental inadequacy). The same person may be regarded as "illiterate" in one culture, while appearing to be quite literate in another culture. When a number of cultures co-exist within the same society it is more likely that a range of versions of what constitutes being literate will be encountered (Ferdman 1990). "Illiteracy" is therefore as much a social construction as "literacy". Street (1993) argues that "school literacy" tends to define what counts as literacy, and that this constructs the lack of school literacy in deficit terms. That is, those who are not literate in the terms determined by the school are seen as illiterate, and therefore lacking essential skills. Adults who lack reading and writing skills are often judged to be intellectually, culturally, and even morally inferior to others, although they see themselves as interdependent, sharing their skills and knowledge with members of their social networks (Lytle and Landau 1987). Lankshear (1987) proposes that the social production of illiteracy is an important political process. In discussing people who are illiterate in Western societies, the literature often talks about incompetence (whether of the individual, family, group, teacher, or school), but not about injustice. As a consequence, the disadvantage of those who are not "literate" in the majority language is not seen as a result of the very structures by which others are advantaged and enabled to maintain and extend their advantage. Those who are "illiterate" are usually situated at the wrong end of the continuum of structural power with respect to their economic, political, and cultural interests. They may find greater difficulties in gaining employment, and if they do find work, it is likely to be poorly paid and low-status. Structured illiteracy seems to explain and legitimate (to those who are dominant and subordinate alike) unequal structures of power in society. Society seems to consider that those who are "illiterate" are economically disadvantaged because they lack literacy skills, rather than vice-versa (Lankshear 1987).

2.2. Identity and power in minority settings

It is not only in the process of literacy teaching and learning itself that relations of power between minority and majority groups may be reproduced, but also in the attitudes and assumptions related to literacy learning. That is, the majority group's attitudes to minority families' ability to contribute to their children's language and literacy learning may maintain structures in society which prevent minority groups' participation in, and access to, institutions of power. Majority-culture teachers may make assumptions about the behaviors and beliefs of members of minority groups, assuming that they are able to explain such behaviors and beliefs from an ethnocentric, monocultural perspective. In fact, behaviors and beliefs related to learning are not only likely to alter within and between cultural groups, but also to interact in complex ways with aspects of social identities such as gender, culture, class, and race (Eckert and McConnell-

Ginet 1992, 1995). When teachers' positioning of minority-language women assumes that they are in some ways inadequate for the task of supporting their children's academic and linguistic development, doors may remain securely closed, denying parents access to involvement in, or information about, their children's schooling.

Teachers may assume that minority-culture families should organize their daily lives in ways which fit with the expectations of the dominant, white middle-class. For women, often the key figures in the organization of the home, this may mean having to make decisions about whether to adopt the cultural and linguistic rules prescribed by the majority-culture institution. To do so may mean putting at risk the maintenance and transmission of cultural traditions and identities; to resist may mean putting at risk their children's academic success. When schools build on the existing language and literacy resources of the home, there is little need for such decisions to be made. However, for minority-culture families there is a high probability that in order for their children to become successful in school literacy, it will be necessary for them to learn and play by the rules of a culture which is skewed in favor of the white middle-class (Heller 1992; Knight 1994; Lareau and Horvat 1999). In fact, schools' attempts to communicate with minority groups about their children's learning may be contrived to inform them precisely of this: that in order for their children to succeed academically (and, consequently, in society), they will have to conform to, and abide by, the rules of the dominant group. The study of interactions between schools and minority-language parents can make visible the ways in which the dominant, majority group constructs the identities of minority groups in terms of their literacy, gender, culture, class, and race, and the effects of these positionings in relations of power between dominant and subordinate groups.

3.   Research design

I investigated questions about language, identity, and power in a primary school with a high minority-language population. This section of the chapter will outline the methodological approaches and techniques used to investigate the relations of power in language and literacy interactions between a group of minority-language women and their children's school, making explicit the selection of participants, the role of the bilingual research assistant, and the use of research tools in the collection of data.

3.1. The research setting

Before beginning the research, I had been a teacher in multilingual primary schools in Birmingham. During this time I had taught many Bangladeshi children, and found that their parents were often the least visible at the school site. At the same time, evidence was emerging that Bangladeshi children were not attaining as highly as other groups in the primary years (Gillborn and Gipps 1996). For these reasons I chose to investigate questions of language, power, and identity in the context of interactions between Bangladeshi families and their children's teachers. The study focused on a single school in an inner-city area of Birmingham. At the time of data collection, in 1996, 21% of children in the school were of Bangladeshi origin, and 73% of Pakistani origin. The remainder were of a variety of groups, including White British, Malay and African-Caribbean. The school provided an extensive number of placements for teacher education students who were attached to local and remote institutions of higher education. The school was well known to me, as I had been a teacher there for three years. I selected this school because I was known to some of the staff, and I already had some knowledge of the local community. This would provide relative ease of access, and assist the school-based interview and observation process, where existing bonds of trust and professional understanding would be invaluable. Several years had put sufficient distance between the data collection period and my time as a teacher in the school, without greatly diminishing the opportunity to capitalize on existing relationships. A further reason for selection of this school was its high standing in the region as a school with an excellent reputation for working positively with its community.

The next decision to take was that of the selection of children and their families. Criterion-based selection referred to the children rather than their families. That is, the criteria for selection were that the children should be Bangladeshi, that they should be six years old, and in Year Two of their primary schooling ("Year Two" refers to the third year of schooling, as Reception Class is the first year). Six-year-old children were selected because they had all been in school for more than two years at the time of data collection. This meant that the school would have had the opportunity to communicate with the children's parents. To select children in their Reception year would have meant that the school and family might have had little opportunity to communicate with each other about the children's literacy learning. The selection of children in their third year of schooling meant that parents and teachers would be able to reflect on the process of the children's literacy learning. At the time of selection there were twenty children in the school who met these criteria. In fact, two of the children's parents refused, or were unable, to become involved in the research, reducing the number of participating families to eighteen.

All of the children were born in Britain to Bangladeshi immigrant parents. Ten of the children were boys, and eight girls. Ten of the children's fathers were unemployed at the time of data collection. The remainder were employed in restaurants, one of them part-time. As the data were collected and analyzed, the children's mothers became important participants in the study. The initial focus of the study was the role of parents in supporting children's reading of school-books. For most of the Bangladeshi families the mother undertook the task of literacy instruction, rather than the father. For this reason the children's mothers were interviewed, rather than their fathers. The only means for "se-lecting" these women for study was that they were the mothers of the Bangla-deshi children selected according to the criteria set out above. All of the women who were interviewed had been born in Bangladesh, and migrated to Britain between seven and seventeen years before the data collection period. Most of them had attended school for five or six years in Bangladesh, although three had never been to school. The spoken language at home for these families was Sylheti. All of the women reported that their children spoke English to each other, and Sylheti when speaking to parents and other adults at home. All of the women were able to read and write Bengali (the standard language of Bangla-desh), except the three who had not attended school. None of the eighteen re-ported that she was a confident reader or writer of English, or a confident speaker of English. The eighteen Bangladeshi women were interviewed about their children's reading and their attempts to support their children's literacy learning. A bilingual/bicultural interpreter, Mrs. Minara Miah, assisted with the interviews, which were conducted in Sylheti. The interviews took place in the women's homes. The children's teachers were also interviewed about the process of teaching literacy, and their attempts to involve Bangladeshi parents in their children's school-related learning. Access to the homes of the eighteen Bangladeshi families was achieved with the support of Mrs. Miah, who lived in the local community, and was a member of the social network of the women re-spondents.

3.2. The role of the bilingual/bicultural research assistant

In describing the role of the bilingual/bicultural research assistant, I will dis-cuss the need for interpretation and translation skills, negotiation of access to participants' homes, and issues of cultural compatibility. The most pressing reason for recruiting a bilingual/bicultural research assistant in the collection of data was that I am unable to speak Sylheti, and the women respondents were unable to speak English. I approached Mrs. Miah, who had been employed by the subject school as a part-time Community Link Worker until shortly before the data collection period. Mrs. Miah agreed to support the research project. She agreed to the use of her name, and to the description of her background, and her role as a research assistant, presented here. A written financial contract was agreed, and signed by all parties. Mrs. Miah was a Bangladeshi woman who spoke Sylheti as a first language, and English as an additional language. Mrs. Miah's father was Sylheti, and her mother was an English woman who spoke Sylheti as an additional language. Sylheti was the main language spoken in her home. Mrs. Miah was married to a Bangladeshi man, and had three young children, two of whom attended the subject school. Neither of the children was involved in the present study. Mrs. Miah's marital status was directly relevant to her role as research assistant. When I first approached Bangladeshi parents to request permission to record their children reading at home, I did so with the support of an unmarried, 17-year-old female interpreter who was employed at the school. The parents were generally unresponsive, and wary of this request. When the request was put later by Mrs. Miah, the same parents were far more inclined to agree to become participants in the study. The difference in the parents' response derived from their perception of Mrs. Miah as someone with a more appropriate social status in the community than the younger interpreter. Mrs. Miah's social network largely consisted of Bangladeshi women whose young children attended the subject school. She was therefore already known to most of the families who became participants in the study.

Part of Mrs. Miah's function as research assistant also involved acting as cultural broker in initiating the participation of the mothers of the eighteen children. Gaining the parents' agreement to become involved in the research involved more than simply interpreting skills. Mrs. Miah usually explained the aims and purposes of the research project to the participants as fully as possible. Having explained the aims of the research, she negotiated access to the home, and asked permission for me to interview the parent a week or so after recording their child reading a school book at home (the literacy interaction data are presented in Blackledge 2000), indicating that she would accompany me to interpret.

3.3. Data collection

3.3.1. Interviews with the Bangladeshi women

The eighteen Bangladeshi children were recorded reading at home, usually with siblings. Results and analysis of these reading interactions are reported elsewhere (Blackledge 2000). The focus of the present chapter is on follow-up interviews with the children's mothers, which were conducted within seven days of recording their children reading. The interviews were conducted in Sylheti with the Bangladeshi women, and interpreted by Mrs. Miah. The interview questions gave the women opportunities to talk about their interactions with the school in their attempts to support their children's literacy learning, and to talk about broader issues of language and literacy use in the home. The presence of the researcher in collecting interview data in the homes of participants can be problematic as Delgado-Gaitan (1990) found in collecting interview data in the homes of Spanish-speaking families in California. In the present study, however, the role of Mrs. Miah as interpreter in the interviews with Bangladeshi women provided an invaluable bridge between outsider researcher and the respondents. The interviews always took place in the living room of the family home. Mrs. Miah would usually position herself somewhere between me and the interviewee, although there were occasions when she placed herself beside the respondent, with both of the women then facing me. Mrs. Miah did this when the interviewee seemed to be apprehensive about the interview. She interpreted my questions, and the women's responses, in manageable sections. As she was accustomed to the role of interpreter at the school site, so this process ran smoothly.

Martin-Jones (1995) notes that in sociolinguistic surveys, respondents' self-reports of language use may be idealizations of actual communicative practices. In the present study no attempt was made to collect the full range of naturalistic speech data in the Bangladeshi households, as language and literacy use per se was not the focus of the research questions. For this reason the women's self-reports of their language use could not be formally checked against recorded data. However, Mrs. Miah, who knew the Bangladeshi women as part of her social network, corroborated the women's statements about their language use. Each interview began with closed questions about language use and demographic data, which enabled the women to give clear, informative answers to unambiguous questions. This structure allowed the women to develop confidence in their role as interview respondent, as they were talking about themselves, and there was no controversy associated with the questions or answers. The subsequent questions were more open, asking the women to talk about their attitudes and concerns in their children's literacy learning. Having gained confidence from answering closed questions, most of the women responded more fully to relatively open questions. When the parents were reticent, prompts such as "Can you say more about that?", or "why is that?" were used to encourage a fuller response. In all cases the women agreed to allow the interviews to be tape-recorded, after confidentiality was guaranteed.

3.3.2. Interviews with the children's teachers

Interviews were conducted with three teachers, who were the class teachers of the eighteen children in the study. The intention of these interviews was to give the teachers the opportunity to talk about their support of parents in their attempts to teach their children to read. The interviews were structured so that the initial questions allowed the teachers to articulate their strategies for teaching reading in the classroom, before moving on to questions about involving parents in the home. This questioning strategy allowed the teachers to talk freely about teaching children to read, and to develop confidence in their role as interview respondent. The protocol allowed a mix of open and closed questions, but with the emphasis more weighted towards open questions than in the parent interviews. The teachers responded fully to individual questions. Their awareness of my background as a primary school teacher, and of my role in teacher education, seemed to lead them to talk comprehensively about teaching reading in the classroom. Prompts were used if answers seemed incomplete. In addition, questions which had not been written in the interview schedule were asked in response to the teachers' answers.

4. Women negotiating identity and power

Transcribed data from the interviews with the eighteen Bangladeshi women, and the three (English women) teachers, were reduced to manageable form by a process of constant comparison. Data were fractured, labeled, categorized, annotated, and summarized to develop analytic categories (Delamont 1992; Goetz and LeCompte 1984). Analytical commentary on the transcripts added clarity and meaning to the data (Ball 1991; Miles and Huberman 1994), which were then re-coded and summarized. The process of analyzing the data led to the emergence of patterns and themes, as aspects of language use and attitudes interacted with features of social identities, including literacy, gender, culture, class, and race.

4.1. "Literacy" and "illiteracy"

The Bangladeshi women were asked about the books their children brought home from school. There was an expectation on the part of the school that parents would support their children's reading of these books, which were in English. Aminur's mother made clear her frustration that she could not read the texts brought home by her son. When asked whether he ever brought home dual language books, in English and Bengali, she responded:

> *Only occasionally, but I would like more of that. I could explain more of the story, as it is I can't understand the English books*
> (Here, and in subsequent quotations from the interviews with the Bangladeshi women, the transcription is of Mrs. Miah's interpretation in English of the women's responses in Sylheti.)

Several of the women made this same point. Sultanas' mother spoke of her attempts to read with her daughter:

> *I can't do it because I can't read English, but if it's a Bengali book I will read the stories to her*

Mohammed Ali's mother spoke of her younger child who was at nursery, where:

> *They give out books which have two languages, the Bengali at the bottom and the English at the top, I read to them now, I think that's a very good idea, I wouldn't have understood them otherwise, I think that's a very good idea that they are in two languages*

There was no indication that these dual-language books were sent home with the six-year-old children. In these data there is a clear picture of parents who understood that their Bengali proficiency was a potentially valuable resource in their children's literacy learning. The teachers' positioning of the Bangladeshi women in terms of their apparent literacy proficiency was also evident in responses to questions which referred to advice received by the women about reading with their children. While most said that they had received no advice about this, two of the women described the advice they had been given:

> *The teacher has told me that if I can't understand a book, I can talk about the pictures. But if the book was in Bengali and English I could read the story myself*

The teacher said make up a story from the pictures. I can't read English, only Bengali

The teachers' advice to the Bangladeshi women assumed that they were "illiterate". The women's responses clearly demonstrated that although they could not read English, they were literate in Bengali, and they could have used this literacy to support their children's reading. A teacher summarized the advice given to the children's mothers:

We have stressed that most of the help they can give their children is talking about books, you don't have to be able to read the book yourself, you can ask questions, or just say "What is your book about? "

The responses of the teachers and the mothers made it clear that the Bangladeshi women were positioned by the teachers as "illiterate", and considered to be unable to contribute substantially to their children's literacy learning.

4.2. Literacy, gender, and identity

Some of the teacher interview data referred to the Bangladeshi women's ability to create and care for home environments which were appropriate for language and literacy learning. These data were located in the context of questions about the women supporting their children's reading. The teachers' view of the women as literacy tutors was expressed as follows:

In many cases mum's at home on her own because dad's either out working or out, you know, out, so there's a mother at home with five, six kids, now it's very hard to have time. Who are you going to choose to be with and you've got often small babies, you know, incredibly busy people ... I think reading is the last thing on their minds really, even though I think they're willing but it's just not possible

Most of the houses I've been to are so incredibly fraught with things going on and children not necessarily behaving as well as they do at school

The teachers seemed to position the women as mothers whose lives were too "fraught" with the difficulties of motherhood to even think about supporting their children's reading.

Other data which referred to the women's competence to organize their homes appropriately included teachers' assumptions and opinions about the type and amount of talk in everyday family interactions. The teachers' view seemed to be that the women did not engage their children in appropriate conversations:

> *Some children don't seem to have been spoken to about where they go, I mean a boy the other day, a year five boy, he hurt his finger and had to go to hospital and I said to him next day which hospital did you go to, he didn't know the name of it, now I would expect a parent to say we are going to Dudley Road Hospital and this is what's happening*

Similarly, a teacher suggested that the women failed to speak to their children when traveling to visit other parts of the country:

> *They haven't known they've gone to Bradford or wherever they've gone to, and they don't know how long it's taken them and they don't know the things they saw on the way, and I think that reaps benefits when it comes to reading*

At the same time, the teacher recognised the "tremendous potential" for talk among the Bangladeshi families, acknowledging that some families had "incredible amounts of conversation", and that the "cultural structure of families" provided opportunities for familial talk which may not have been available to families of different cultural backgrounds. In such families, she said, "you can see there's a high level of interaction, very high level in fact". Nevertheless, the teacher's view was that the importance of talk in the family was "quite a hard thing to get across". These data suggest that the teachers positioned the Bangladeshi women as deficient in the way they talked to their children. There was a clear suggestion (which one of the teachers said "does sound a bit patronizing") that either the amount or quality of talk in the families was insufficient for children's language and literacy learning. The teachers constructed for the women an identity which was based on an inability to create and maintain a stable home, on little interest in their children's learning, and on inadequacy in developing for their children a suitable language environment. This perception was at odds with the women's positioning of themselves and, by implication, based on their perception of gender roles of white, middle-class mothers, as the data in the next section demonstrate.

4.3. Cultural competence and negotiation of identity

The Bangladeshi women answered questions about their attitude to their children's Bengali literacy learning. Bengali was the standard language of community literacy for these families, and different from Sylheti, the spoken language of the home. All eighteen women said that their children were learning to read and write Bengali, or would shortly do so. Typical of their responses were the following:

> *Because we are Bengali, to us it is very important that Muhitur learns to read and write Bengali*

> *It is very important that my daughter knows how to read and write Bengali because otherwise if she goes back home she won't know the language or culture*

These responses made explicit the links between the community language and cultural identity. Most of the women either taught their children to read and write Bengali, or sent them to a local community class to learn. Although they spoke of the importance of Bengali for reading letters from the home country, the language had a significance beyond its function as a means of communication. It represented the group's identification as Bengalis, and their difference from the majority culture, and from other minority cultures:

> *It is very important to me that he learns the language because we are Bengali. It is good that he has English as a second language*

Twelve of the eighteen women took steps to directly support their children's Bengali literacy learning. Common responses were as follows

> *As often as I can I will spend twenty minutes teaching them Bengali*

> *I sit with the children for two hours on Saturdays and Sundays, and I teach them Bengali and Arabic*

Those women who did not offer support at home for the children to read Bengali said that they would send their children to a tutor for this purpose when they were eight years old. The women were able to offer Bengali literacy support to their children without having to acquire a new language, and without having to adopt aspects of the majority culture. Bengali literacy had a symbolic significance beyond its use as a means of communication. For these women, to learn to read and write Bengali was to *be* Bengali. Teaching their children to be literate in Bengali represented a symbol of solidarity with their cultural group. Although economic power was not likely to accrue from their children learning to be literate in Bengali, the women invested considerable resources in Bengali literacy instruction. Literacy in Bengali was a clearly articulated symbol of solidarity with the women's group identity. There was no evidence, however, that the parents' Bengali literacy support was recognized or valued by the school. The teachers' attitude to the children's Bengali literacy learning, and reading of Arabic at the *madressah* (the community school, sometimes held at the mosque, where children read the Qur'an, and may learn to read and write the community language), was characterized in terms of the potentially harmful effect of a pedagogical style which was different from that of the school:

> *At the mosque the emphasis is without doubt on reading without understanding, getting the words right or you'll be smacked. That has a very powerful influence on them*

The teacher did not say in what way this assumed approach to teaching influenced the children. Similarly, one of the teachers assumed the women's attitude to teaching reading to their children to be one which was characterized by brutality:

> *There's still the idea that it's got to be rather a fearsome process, you've got to get it right or there'll be a smack*

There was no evidence of this approach to reading instruction in the home reading data (Blackledge 2000) recorded in the Bangladeshi women's households. The teachers offered a range of reasons for the Bangladeshi women's apparent lack of involvement in their children's learning. They seemed to be aware that the parents perceived their lack of English proficiency as a difficulty in supporting their children's school-focused learning. One perception was that the women "rely very much, certainly, on the school, because of their language". A similar view was articulated by another teacher, who said,

> *They still think that being able to read the English is the most important and would feel that they can't be that helpful because they haven't got the spoken English and the reading of English*

This view seemed to regard negatively the women's perception that English literacy was required to support their children's English learning. However, all the evidence demonstrated that the school presented literacy learning as an activity which was rooted solely in English, using English resources. It cannot be surprising, therefore, that the parents held this view. In fact the source of the view that English proficiency was required to support children's academic learning seemed to be located in the school.

Another teacher considered that the women's apparent lack of involvement in their children's learning was due to two factors:

One there's an attitude it's inappropriate, it's the teacher's job, let the teacher get on with it, and not interfering. That's one attitude, which may come from home countries. The other attitude is, I want to be involved but I do not want to be put in a position whereby I am going to be embarrassed, and a feeling of having poor self-esteem is then compounded by the children adopting that as well

Another teacher agreed with the first point here, saying "there's the old idea of, you know, you learn at school, school is the place for learning". This view is supported by evidence from another study of Bangladeshi parents' school-focused literacy support practices (Tomlinson and Hutchison 1991). However, in the present study the teachers' perception that parents regarded involvement in their children's learning as "inappropriate" was not substantiated by the parent interviews. In fact, the Bangladeshi women would have liked to contribute to their children's literacy learning, but they were disempowered by the cultural and linguistic structures in place in the school, and by the teachers' positioning of them as inadequate language and literacy instructors. Typically, Joyghun's mother argued that "if you get help at home and at school you do well". This view was not consistent with the teachers' assumptions that the women wanted to leave academic teaching entirely to the school. The teacher's second argument, that parents would not become involved in their children's learning because of fear of embarrassment, seems to recognize the parents' lack of empowerment in school-related activities. However, the assumption that parents had "poor self-esteem" may have been a false one. It may be that the parents appeared to the teachers to have little confidence or self-regard in the school setting, because they were disempowered by the linguistic and cultural demands of the dominant-culture institution. In fact, the interview data suggest that the Bangladeshi women were confident of their role in the familiar environment of their local community, where their cultural and linguistic resources were accepted and valued.

The teachers' attitudes to, and perceptions of, the Bangladeshi women's literacy proficiency can be further developed through a literacy framework which incorporates storytelling in the home language, Sylheti. Of the eighteen women, fifteen said that they told stories to their children in the home language. These stories were told regularly and were in a variety of traditions:

I tell the children stories in Sylheti, traditional stories, Islamic stories, and stories I make up myself. I do this two or three times a week

I make up stories for my three boys, like "there were once three princes who became kings", and so on

I tell them Islamic stories which explain what Islam is, the proper stories

These responses make it clear that home-language storytelling was thriving in the homes of these families, and was used to reinforce religious and cultural traditions. That is, storytelling was used by the women to transmit aspects of their culture. However, there was little evidence that their oral literacy skills were incorporated in the school curriculum. Teachers were aware of home-language storytelling as a valuable learning opportunity, but its potential remained unfulfilled in the classroom:

I know there's a strong oral tradition of storytelling; perhaps we don't appreciate that enough, because that's an incredible skill, to be able to tell a traditional story like that

The women's competence in organizing their homes for the transmission of aspects of their culture through regular storytelling, Bengali literacy instruction, and reading of the Qur'an was at odds with the teachers' positioning of them as inadequate language and literacy tutors. In fact, the women only lacked these resources when viewed from a perspective which considered English as the sole acceptable language in the process of education. When viewed from a multilingual perspective, the women were competent and organized providers of opportunities for language and literacy learning.

4.4. Class, competence, and the professional teacher

Another aspect of the teachers' assumptions about the women's ability to support their children's learning concerned references to "class". In response to a question which asked whether teachers attempted to inform parents how to support their children's learning, one of the teachers said:

> *It's a class thing, isn't it, really, in many cases, and you're trying to make people have a set of rules which are really middle-class white rules, aren't they? In order for children to achieve in Britain today you've got to have those really*

This response seemed to assume that the Bangladeshi parents did not have the cultural resources to contribute to their children's learning. There was an assumption, or perhaps an acceptance, that the parents would have to learn to play by the rules of the dominant majority if their children were to succeed academically. The teacher went on to say that parents had to learn "middle class rules", because

> *that's how you achieve in this society, that's the way that society works, but you're not going to if you don't do it*

Implicit in this response was the view that parents should change, to become like *middle-class* parents, or risk consigning their children to academic failure. There was no evidence that the school would consider devising a set of rules which was located in the existing cultural or linguistic resources of the parents. The school view was reinforced when the teacher added that the school planned to extend borrowing of schoolbooks to nursery children, not for the children to read, but for the parents to read to the children:

> *You know, story time at the end of the day, because that's a very white, middle-class thing isn't it, reading a story before your child goes to bed? I don't think that happens*

Implicit in these plans was an intention to teach the parents the behaviours of "white, middle-class" families, in order to ensure the children's academic success. At the same time, the teacher was unaware that many parents told stories to their children in the evening. In the teacher's remarks there seemed to be no intention to build on the existing cultural or linguistic resources of the families. Instead, the explicit plan was to teach minority-language parents to abide by the rules of the "white middle-classes". Those parents who were unable to adopt the rules of the majority, or refused to do so, would not "achieve in this society".

Further evidence of the teachers' positioning of the Bangladeshi women as inadequate contributors to their children's literacy learning emerged in responses to questions about new initiatives in teaching reading and writing in school. The teachers were able to talk extensively about modifications to their classroom practice. When asked whether they would involve parents in the new initiative, however, they were less forthcoming:

Whether you could involve parents in doing that I don't know because it's taken me a lot of training, I've had to re-learn how to teach reading

in a way you've got to get consistency amongst the teachers before you start thinking that deeply about parents doing it because there's inconsistencies among teachers

The teachers' responses seemed to indicate that they viewed the teaching of reading as a task for professionals, which could not be attempted by parents. The clear implication, once again, is that the teachers did not consider that the women possessed the cultural resources to contribute to their children's literacy learning. As before, there were tensions between the teachers' positioning of the women, and the women's own positioning of themselves as competent teachers of community literacies.

4.5. Race, ethnicity, and power

The Bangladeshi women's responses to questions about their communications with the school, more fully reported elsewhere (Blackledge 2000), revealed that they felt disempowered at the school site, as they did not share the language or culture of their children's teachers. Their young children interpreted for them at parents' evenings, and they were frustrated in their attempts to find out information about their children's academic progress. Recognizing a need for more effective communication with the children's parents, the teachers had adopted a strategy which focused on those Bangladeshi women who had been educated in Britain, and who, therefore, were able to speak and understand English:

There are a lot of parents, particularly younger parents that have been educated in this country, and they're, say, in their early twenties, they have some understanding of the system and they do ask a lot of questions

We think that might be quite a captive audience and perhaps do a more formalised meeting with the parents

None of the women in the present study had been educated in Britain. The teachers seemed to position the younger women, who had attended British schools, as an "audience" who could be reached, and who could therefore be taught the cultural and linguistic rules of the school. A corollary of this is that the teachers positioned the women who had been born and educated in Bangladesh as being beyond the reach of the school. That is, those women who presented themselves (linguistically and culturally) as being "more Bangladeshi", and "less British", paid the price of receiving less support and information in the process of their children's schooling. In targeting support at those women who already had some understanding of "the system", the school would potentially increase inequality (Toomey 1989), as those most in need of support remained out of reach.

For the teachers, strategies for teaching Bangladeshi children, and for involving their families in that process, seemed to be based on the reconstruction of the families' ethnic identities on racial grounds:

> *It's to do with – not really thinking about second language learners, but thinking about white people, white families*

It was as if the reconstruction of the Bangladeshi families' identities as "white families" would resolve the difficulties of communication and attainment which were causing frustration on all sides. The Bangladeshi women were positioned by the teachers as inadequate in terms of their ability to support their children's learning, to create an appropriate home environment, and to activate cultural resources. The best thing to do was to become as much like the dominant group as possible. Rather than finding out information about the cultural and linguistic resources of the Bangladeshi families, and incorporating these into curricular and extra-curricular activities, the school would wait until the Bangladeshi women and their families had (at least partly) transformed themselves into "white families".

5.   Conclusions

The data presented here demonstrate that the Bangladeshi women considered themselves to be competent providers of community literacy instruction for their children. Even those women who were not themselves literate were confident that their children would learn to read and write Bengali. Bengali was a strongly-stated symbol of cultural solidarity and identity for the women. Yet the women were positioned by their children's teachers as illiterate individuals who were unable to contribute to their children's literacy learning. The teachers did not consider the children's out-of-school literacy learning to be beneficial or pedagogically sound. They positioned the women as "incredibly busy" mothers, too busy running "fraught" homes to be interested in their children's education.

The data also show that the women reported their use of stories to transmit cultural and religious values to their children, in a structured yet informal environment. The teachers' view of the women's ability to provide rich language and literacy learning environments for their children was quite different, as they assumed that either too little, or poor quality, talk was characteristic of Bangladeshi family life. The teachers thus positioned the women as providers of inadequate language and literacy learning environments. Their view of the teaching of reading was that it was a complex, technical process which would be beyond the skills of the parents. Also, the data make visible the teachers' assumptions that the Bangladeshi women would have to learn and abide by "middle-class, white rules" if their children were to succeed academically. The teachers did not indicate that the school would change its "rules" to build on the women's existing literacy skills and resources.

Interactions between schools and minority groups can be viewed as thresholds between dominant and minority groups, at which reproduction or renegotiation of power occurs. In the data presented here the teachers' positioning of the women as inadequate language and literacy providers was starkly different from the women's positioning of themselves. This difference seemed to derive at least partly from the teachers' view that what "counts" as literacy is school literacy – that is, literacy in English. The teachers' view was that either the women must learn the rules and values of the dominant group, or they would put at risk their children's academic success. These teachers were doing more than most to involve linguistic-minority parents in their children's schooling, and the school was highly-regarded as one which worked successfully with its community. However, the teachers' positioning of the Bangladeshi women reflected the positioning of linguistic-minority women in public discourse in Britain. As such, the teachers' positioning of the women became the site of reproduction of existing relations of power, as the Bangladeshi women's language and literacy resources were ignored by the school, and they were unable to gain access to the rules and values of the dominant group.

References

Ball, Stephen
    1991   Power, conflict, micropolitics and all that! In Walford, Geoffrey (ed.), *Doing Educational Research.* London: Routledge, 166–192.

Blackledge, Adrian
    2000   *Literacy, Power and Social Justice.* Stoke-on-Trent: Trentham Books.

Blommaert, Jan
    1999   The debate is open. In Blommaert, Jan (ed.), *Language Ideological Debates.* Berlin: Mouton de Gruyter, 1–38.

Bourdieu, Pierre
    1991   *Language and Symbolic Power.* Cambridge: Polity Press.

Corson, David
    1993   *Language, Minority Education and Gender: Linking Social Justice and Power.* Clevedon: Multilingual Matters.
    1998   *Changing Education for Diversity.* Buckingham: Open University Press.

Cummins, Jim
    1994   From coercive to collaborative relations of power in the teaching of literacy. In Ferdman, Bernardo, Rose-Marie Weber, and Arnulfo Ramirez (eds.), *Literacy Across Languages and Cultures.* New York: SUNY Press, 295–330.

Dabène, Louise and Danièle Moore
    1995   Bilingual speech of migrant people. In Milroy, Lesley and Pieter Muysken (eds.), *One Speaker, Two Languages: Cross-Disciplinary Perspectives on Code-Switching.* Cambridge: Cambridge University Press, 17–44.

Delamont, Sarah
    1992   *Fieldwork in Educational Settings.* London: Falmer Press.

Delgado-Gaitan, Concha
    1990   *Literacy for Empowerment.* London: Falmer Press.

Eckert, Penelope and Sally McConnell-Ginet
    1992   Communities of practice: Where language, gender and power all live. In Hall, Kira, Mary Bucholtz, and Birch Moonwomon (eds.), *Locating Power: Proceedings of the Second Berkeley Women and Language Conference.* Berkeley: University of California Press, 89–99.

1995   Constructing meaning, constructing selves. Snapshots of language, gender, and class from Belten High. In Hall, Kira and Mary Bucholtz (eds.), *Gender Articulated: Language and the Socially Constructed Self.* New York: Routledge, 469–508.

Ferdman, Bernardo
1990   Literacy and cultural identity. *Harvard Educational Review* 60, 181–204.

Gal, Susan
1998   Multiplicity and contention among language ideologies: A commentary. In Schieffelin, Bambi, Kathryn Woolard, and Paul Kroskrity (eds.), *Language Ideologies: Practice and Theory.* Oxford/New York: Oxford University Press, 317–331.

Gillborn, David and Caroline Gipps
1996   *Recent Research on the Achievements of Ethnic Minority Pupils.* London: HMSO.

Goetz, Judith and Margaret LeCompte
1984   *Ethnography and Qualitative Design in Educational Research.* Orlando: Academic Press.

Heller, Monica
1992   The politics of codeswitching and language choice. *Journal of Multilingual and Multicultural Development* 13, 1, 123–142.

1995   Language choice, social institutions and symbolic domination. *Language in Society* 24, 373–405.

1999   *Linguistic Minorities and Modernity: A Sociolinguistic Ethnography.* London: Longman.

Knight, Ann
1994   Pragmatic biculturalism and the primary school teacher. In Blackledge, Adrian (ed.), *Teaching Bilingual Children.* Stoke-on-Trent: Trentham Books, 101–112.

Lareau, Annette and Erin Horvat
1999   Moments of social inclusion and exclusion. Race, class and cultural capital in family-school relationships. *Sociology of Education* 72, 37–53.

Lankshear, Colin with Moira Lawler
1987   *Literacy, Schooling and Revolution* London: Falmer Press.

Lytle, Susan and Jacqueline Landau
  1987   Adult literacy in cultural context. In Wagner, Daniel (ed.), *The Future of Literacy in a Changing World*. Oxford: Pergamon, 209–215.

Martin-Jones, Marilyn
  1995   Sociolinguistic surveys as a source of evidence in the study of bilingualism: A critical assessment of survey work conducted among linguistic minorities in three British cities. *Working Paper Series,* 13. Lancaster: Center for Language and Social Life.

Miles, Matthew and Michael Huberman
  1994   *Qualitative Data Analysis. An Expanded Sourcebook*. London: Sage.

Norton, Bonny
  2000   *Identity and Language Learning: Gender, Ethnicity and Educational Change*. London: Longman.

Peirce, Bonny Norton
  1995   Social identity, investment, and language learning. *TESOL Quarterly*, 29, 1, 9–31.

Shannon, Sheila
  1999   The debate on bilingual education in the U.S.: Language ideology as reflected in the practice of bilingual teachers. In Blommaert, Jan (ed.), *Language Ideological Debates*. Berlin: Mouton de Gruyter, 171–200.

Street, Brian
  1993   Introduction: The new literacy studies. In Street, Brian (ed.), *Cross-Cultural Approaches to Literacy*. Cambridge: Cambridge University Press, 1–21.

Tomlinson, Sally and Sarah Hutchison
  1991   *Bangladeshi Parents and Education in Tower Hamlets*. London: Advisory Center for Education.

Toomey, David
  1989   How home-school relations policies can increase educational inequality. *Australian Journal of Education* 33, 3, 284–298.

Woolard, Kathryn
  1998   Language ideology as a field of inquiry. In Schieffelin, Bambi, Kathryn Woolard, and Paul Kroskrity (eds.), *Language Ideologies: Practice and Theory*. Oxford: Oxford University Press, 3–47.

Researching women's language practices in multilingual workplaces

Tara Goldstein

A statement of purpose for organizing on-site English-as-a-Second-Language (ESL) workplaces in London, Ontario (Canada):

> It was clear to us, and verified by meeting with students that many have never attended ESL classes and that their level of proficiency in English does not meet basic survival needs although they have been in Canada for several years ... Inability to converse in English is often compounded by illiteracy. There are thousands of immigrant workers who are hampered in their work, community participation and personal lives because of this deficiency ... The daily frustration of working with inadequate communication skills must be tremendous. (Richer 1982: 73)

From "Linguistic terrorism" in *Borderlines/La Frontera: The New Mestiza*:

> Until I can take pride in my language, I cannot take pride in myself. Until I can accept as legitimate Chicano Texas Spanish, Tex-Mex and all the other languages I speak, I cannot accept the legitimacy of myself. Until I am free to write bilingually and to switch codes without having to translate, while I still have to speak English or Spanish when I would rather speak Spanglish, and as long as I have to accommodate the English speakers rather than having them accommodate me, my tongue will be illegitimate.
>
> I will no longer be made to feel ashamed of existing. I will have my voice: Indian, Spanish, white. I will have my serpent's tongue – my woman's voice, my sexual voice, my poet's voice. I will overcome the tradition of silence. (Anzaldúa 1987: 59)

1. Introduction

In 1982, Judy Richer, an ESL programmer working in London, Ontario, wrote an article about the workplace English language classes she was administrating. As can be seen in the first of the two quotes that open this chapter, Richer makes several assumptions about the learners enrolled in her program. She assumes that English is the only language the learners use to communicate not only within – but outside of – the workplace. She also assumes that not being able to communicate in English is a deficiency and that immigrant workers who don't speak English are hampered not only in their work lives, but also in their community and personal lives.

Five years later, writer/poet Gloria Anzaldúa wrote about her childhood along the Texas-Mexico border in the United States. In the second quote that opens this chapter, Anzaldúa challenges Richer's understandings of what constitutes linguistic deficiency and inadequate communication. She writes of her desire to communicate in multiple voices, her desire to feel pride in the many languages she speaks, and her need to have her multilingual tongue legitimized.

Rarely do writers like Richer and Anzaldúa speak to each other in the same text. I have used their writings to open this essay so I could mark the starting and ending points of a research project I recently undertook to better understand my own workplace teaching practice. Like Judy Richer, I was taught by my TESL (Teaching English as a Second Language) training to assume that the language skills that multilingual workers needed in everyday work situations were necessarily English language skills. While I did not use words like 'deficiency' to talk about my students' language learning needs, I did believe that learning English for work was key to workers' success at work. Growing up in a monolingual (English) home and having been trained by teacher educators who were similarly rooted in traditions of monolingualism, I did not know or understand much about everyday bilingual life. This was true even though I had experienced several years of bilingual (French immersion/English) schooling. Since I did not use two languages in my everyday life (French was associated with doing course work at school), I was not sensitive to the issues of pride and legitimacy Anzaldúa writes about on a personal level. I gained some of this sensitivity through a two-year research study on bilingual life at the multilingual workplace in which I taught.

This chapter is a reflection on that two-year study which is most fully described in my critical ethnography *Two Languages at Work: Bilingual Life on the Production Floor* (Goldstein 1997).[1] In addition to reflecting back on my own work, I discuss other research studies that are of interest to readers wanting to learn more about women, multilingualism, and second language learning in the workplace. The chapter is divided into three different sections. In the first section, I review research that is concerned with questions of gender and multilingualism at work by providing a detailed discussion of the theoretical and methodological choices I made in conducting my own study. In the second section, I discuss the implications my own and other workplace studies have for workplace English as a Second Language (ESL) curriculum development. Finally, in the last section, I conclude with a discussion of directions for further research.

2. Women's language practices in a multilingual workplace: An ethnographic interactionist approach

There is a body of literature which researchers can consult when they begin designing a study on women's multilingual practices at work. Relevant research has been undertaken in the fields of multilingualism and work (Belfiore and Heller 1992; Clyne 1994; Gumperz 1992; Heller 1988a; Lippi-Green 1997; Pauwels 1994; Roberts, Davies, and Jupp 1992), language learning at work (Belfiore and Burnaby 1984, 1995; Jupp and Hodlin 1975; Peirce, Harper, and Burnaby 1993) and gender and multilingualism (Gal 1979, 1988, 1991; Kouritzin 2000; Peirce 1995; Norton 2000). The following discussion of my own work includes a review of these studies.

In conceptualizing my research study into women's bilingualism (Portuguese/English) at work, I found anthropological interactionist sociolinguistic approaches to identity formation, language choice, code-switching, and the political economy to be very helpful. I also found that I could effectively weave these sociolinguistic approaches with the methodological strategies and ideologies of critical ethnography. I begin a review of my study with the story that opened my workplace ethnography (Goldstein 1997).

2.1. A story from a multilingual workplace ·

The walls of the classroom begin to shake as the tow-motor speeds by on the old wooden floor. The truck is transporting raw materials needed by some of the assembly line workers down to the production floor. The assemblers themselves, however, are not on the lines. It is lunch time and they are sitting in the English classroom waiting for the noise to pass and for the teacher to begin speaking again. The line workers are all women and most of them are first-generation immigrants from Portugal. The noise dies down, and the teacher, my colleague Peter, continues his lesson on polite ways of asking your co-worker for tools while working on the line. The women smile in amusement, look at each other, begin to laugh quietly, and start talking to each other in Portuguese. The teacher is puzzled and waits for someone to tell him what is funny about talking politely on the lines. Fernanda[2] looks at the teacher, smiles and tells him that on the lines, no one has to be polite. They are all "sisters" and sisters don't have to be polite when asking each other to pass over tools. What Fernanda does not tell the teacher, and what he does not know, is that on the lines, not only do workers not have to be polite with one another, they also do not speak English to each other. The majority of the women working on the lines, like the majority of the women in the English class, are Portuguese. The language used to communicate and do production work on the lines is Portuguese. The communicative task of asking a co-worker for tools, which is the topic of Peter's lesson, is not undertaken in English. It is undertaken in Portuguese.

At the time I conducted my ethnographic study (1988–90), on-site workplace English classes for immigrant workers were often centered on the notion of job-specific language training. In the professional development work we undertook as workplace English language instructors, Peter and I were taught that relevant language activities for immigrant workers were those which were related to the tasks they performed at work. We based our curriculum development on research from the field of applied linguistics which instructed us on how to determine our students' work-related English-language needs (e.g., Belfiore and Burnaby 1984; Jupp and Hodlin 1975). Peter and I, however, had a concern about our curriculum choices. Our mostly high-beginner and intermediate-level Portuguese-speaking students were not using the English they already knew or the English they were learning in class on the production floor. Ready to begin my doctoral research, I decided to undertake a study on workplace language practices that would help me understand why my students were choosing not to use English at work.

2.2. Studying language choice

The study of language choice, that is, the investigation of what makes people in a multilingual society choose to use one language or language variety rather than another in a particular instance, has been undertaken by sociolinguists, sociologists, social psychologists, and anthropologists. Some sociologists and sociolinguists have approached the problem of language choice by looking at the relationship between language use and social structure. Such studies look for a social structure, conduct a survey of a sample of the target population that relates to the proposed social structure, and provide a statistical analysis of the results (see Goldstein 1997: 40 for examples of such work). This kind of research, which links social variables to linguistic variables, however, has been criticized for being limited in its power to explain the phenomenon of language choice (see Heller 1995).

Making use of anthropological perspectives and traditions, interactionist sociolinguists have focused on what it is that links macrosociological factors to people's individual language choice decisions. They aim to uncover the relationship between social processes and language choice in different social contexts and their work has shed light on problems of ethnic stratification, ethnic equality, pluralism, assimilation, multilingualism, and second language learning (see Gal 1979; Gumperz 1982 a, b; Heller 1988 a, b, c; Le Page 1968; Woolard 1989).

In my own study, I undertook 39 ethnographic interviews, spent 59 hours observing everyday work activities and language practices, and recorded 24 hours of workers' interactions on the production lines at Stone Specialities. I then used the ethnographic observational and interview data to explain the recorded linguistic data. Before moving to a review of the interactionist sociolinguistic framework I used to examine language choice at work, I will engage in a brief discussion on linguistic and cultural differences between researchers and research participants.

As a non-speaker of Portuguese whose research involved members of Toronto's Portuguese community, I decided that working with a linguistic and cultural interpreter was necessary. While this meant working with two layers of interpretation, it also meant that I had access to some of the sociocultural and sociolinguistic background knowledge necessary for understanding talk by Portuguese workers participating in the study. This knowledge, the importance – and complexity – of which has been discussed by sociolinguists interested in intercultural interview situations (e.g., Belfiore and Heller 1992; Briggs 1986; Gumperz 1992), was not accessible to me without a linguistic and cultural interpreter. It is the knowledge that I believe strengthened my analysis (see Goldstein 1995 a for a fuller discussion of this issue). However, in a recent article on immigrant women's access to ESL classes, Kouritzin (2000), who conducted life-history interviews with mothers of school-age children, makes a compelling argument for not using translators. She believes that translators can distance participants in an interview, reduce the trust and privacy of an interview and may not be as careful with the affective dimensions of speech as the researcher herself. Given that Kouritzin was conducting life-history interviews about how immigration had influenced the women's lives and expectations, her concerns around the use of translators are noteworthy. It is also important to note that several of the women interviewed by Kouritzin thanked her for giving them confidence in their ability to make themselves understood, and for giving them an extended period of time in which they could practice authentic language use. Clearly, there are many different issues to take into consideration when deciding how to best negotiate linguistic and cultural differences between the researcher and the research participants. When designing a new project, researchers must think about the ways they will work with social differences and whether or not the use of a cultural and linguistic interpreter will enhance the goals of their project or constrain them.

In the next four subsections, I move on to a detailed review of the interactionist sociolinguistic framework I used to examine women's language choice practices at work.

2.3. Language choice, social identities, and social relationships

One way people create and maintain a particular social identity and reality in interaction is through the language or language variety they choose to use with others. An interactionist perspective on language choice argues that people associate particular languages or language varieties with membership in particular social groups and with the cultural values and practices associated with being a member of those social groups. Put a little differently, interactionists believe that particular languages or language varieties symbolize particular social identities. Underlying interactionist descriptions of individual language choice is a belief that stresses the fluidity of individual behavior and the range of choice open to people in their use of language as a means of symbolizing various identities. Le Page, for example, has explained that "The individual creates his [sic] system of verbal behavior so as to resemble those common to the group or groups with which he [sic] wishes from time to time to be identified" (1968: 192). Individuals then, may make different selections among the values and identities available to them at different times. These changes in values and identities are symbolized by changes in language choice within interaction.

The expression of social identity through the use of one language over another acknowledges particular rights, obligations, and expectations people attach to different social roles and relationships they assume in everyday interaction. Unexpected language choices send out a metaphorical message about social roles and relationships. They may reflect a change within a social relationship or an attempt to change an existing relationship. For example, in a study about Canadian French- and English-speaking workers from Québec, Monica Heller (1988 a) showed that while most speakers in the wider community chose to speak only French or English in accordance with their identity as francophone Canadians or anglophone Canadians, anglophones working for a company whose language of work is French code-switched among themselves, that is, changed from the expected use of English to the unexpected use of French. Heller explained this behavior in terms of "authority" which has been defined by sociologist Max Weber (1958) as "legitimate domination" or power exercised through means other than the means of force.

Heller argued that since it was the use of French that legitimized one's role of authority in the company, anglophones code-switched because "it allow[ed] them to assert their voice to claim new roles, new rights, and new obligations"

(1988 a: 93), all of which, in turn, were associated with the use of French. Code-switching routines were useful to the anglophones in the company because they symbolized the anglophones' right to assume all the privileges and obligations associated with French roles without making them assume a francophone identity.

Following those interactionist sociolinguists who take individuals in everyday interaction as the basis of their description of language choice and code-switching, it was possible for me to assume that the Portuguese women participating in my study used Portuguese and English as a way of presenting themselves to others and associating themselves with particular cultural values, activities, and identities that were linked to the use of Portuguese and English. In the next section, I will discuss how I used an anthropological interactionist sociolinguistic perspective to understand people's language choices in the workplace.

2.4. Language choice on the production floor

In the Production Department of Stone Specialities, 24 out of 27 Portuguese workers surveyed (88%) had found a job at the company by relying on Portuguese network ties. Many had heard about a job opening from a "friend", that is a friend of a relative or a relative of a friend or relative. Others had found work at the company by responding to an ad placed in a Portuguese church paper or by following up information given to them by someone working in a Portuguese church. The majority of the Portuguese employees working in the Production Department worked on assembly lines. Almost all of these assembly line workers were women, and most of them had been with the company for 16–22 years.

The company's practice of hiring Portuguese family and friends to work on the production floor and the Portuguese community's practice of finding work through community networks led to the creation of a Portuguese "family"/community in the Production Department. While some members of this Portuguese "family" were actual kin related by blood ties, others were not, but thought of each other as family. People called each other "sister", "brother", "daughter," and *"marida"* which is the feminine form of the Portuguese word for husband, *"marido"*.[3] A problem involving a worker who was unhappy about the boss she was working for was referred to as a "family problem". Thus, for most Portuguese workers on the production floor, work relationships and conditions at the factory were lived and represented as family and community relationships and conditions.

The use of Portuguese functioned as a symbol of solidarity and group membership in the "family"/community on the production floor. Portuguese was associated with the rights, obligations, and expectations members of that community had of each other at work. Members of the "family" who worked on assembly lines were expected to help each other "keep the line up". If one person on a line was ahead because her particular task was easier and took less time to complete, she was expected to help someone else whose work was piling up. Similarly, if a person on a line needed to leave the line, someone else was expected to pitch in and help do that person's work while she was gone.

Making friends on the line and ensuring access to assistance in case one's work piled up or one needed to leave was related to knowing how to talk to people on the line. Furthermore, talk that provided access to friendship on the lines and thus to assistance on the lines was talk in Portuguese. Women on the lines – including women whose first language was not Portuguese, but Spanish or Italian – used Portuguese on the lines to gain access to friendship and assistance when they needed it.[4]

Tara: If I am on the line with you and I want to be your friend, what should I do to be your friend on line?

Angela: So all you have to do is talk with us. And if we see you can't do the job properly, then we will help you.

Odile: We will help show you what you have to do. And you need to talk to the others, so we can know about yourself.

Tara: What kind of things are important to know about me? What should I tell you about myself?

Odile: We would like to know where you worked before. If you like to work with us. We will help you to get your hands on the work so you won't feel nervous on the line.

Tara: What kind of things do people talk about on the lines?

Angela: Mostly family problems or they talk about their sons and daughters. Family matters.

Augusta: Sometimes they talk about cook[ing], movies.

John: If you're married. If you're single. If you're dating. They all want to know that kind of stuff. Or why aren't you married?

Lidia: You talk about your recipes or ask about a person who everyone is talking about. People talk about who's sick, events in people's lives.

Raquel: Some talk everyday about the cook[ing]. Some girls they talk about their husbands. Everyday about the kids. Shopping. Everything. Everything.

Tara: This is mostly in Portuguese.

Raquel: Yeah.

The value of friendship and assistance at work is not to be underestimated. When asked what advice she would give me if I were new to the company and wanted to make friends on the lines, one of the line workers replied, "If you have a good job already, don't come here. Because this is a change and you have to make other friends". Friendships at work were valuable – valuable enough not to leave a job and risk not finding them elsewhere. Without friends on the line, without access to assistance, assembly workers ran the risk of losing their jobs for not being able to meet efficiency standards.

As a language that is associated with the performance of a work role on the production lines, Portuguese was not only associated with finding a job through networks in the Portuguese community, it was associated with keeping a job and getting a paycheck as well. For Portuguese women immigrants who had had no access to English-speaking networks and/or ESL classes upon their arrival, the use of Portuguese was the only accessible linguistic means to economic survival and gain in Canada. On the lines, there were social and economic benefits associated with the use of Portuguese that were not associated with the use of English. Moreover, there were risks to using English at work.

The Portuguese women working on the lines understood and spoke English with varying levels of proficiency. Some were advanced users of English while others were only beginning to understand and speak English. Line workers who didn't understand what a Portuguese speaker was saying to them in English reported it was "an insult" when a Portuguese speaker spoke to them in English since the speaker knew how to speak Portuguese. They also reported that they would tell the speaker to "talk in Portuguese". Accommodating this preference for Portuguese on the line was important to members of the Portuguese "family" who were able to speak English with some fluency. Using English with workers on the lines was risky; if people didn't understand exactly what you were saying, they might assume you were "talking bad" about them and feel insulted (see Goldstein 1995b, 1997 for a further discussion of "talking bad"). The following quote describes how one worker felt when a Portuguese speaker addressed her in English before she had acquired enough of the language to understand what was being said to her. It illustrates how angry people could become if they thought others were talking about them in English:

> Before I'm mad because I don't speak English. I don't understand the people who talk English. It make me crazy because maybe they talk about me... Now, I don't care. Before I don't understand... Now, I don't speak very, very good, but I understand.

The use of English on the production lines then, was associated with social and economic risks for many of the Portuguese line workers. Line workers who depended on their "sisters" for assistance in "keeping the line up" and meeting efficiency standards could risk making others "mad" and losing their friendship by using English on the lines.

2.5. Language choice and the political economy

In an important study comparing several different case studies of code-switching in various European communities, Susan Gal (1988) argues that it is not enough to examine language practices in terms of social roles and relationships, but that there is a need to consider language choice patterns within regional contexts of economic and political power relations as well. She asserts that as members of different ethnic groups, people have specifiable structural positions of power or subordination in their regional economy and that this larger context is crucial in shaping their individual language choices – choices they make when speaking among themselves as well as choices they make when speaking with others. In other words, differences in language practices can be linked to the ways in which communities are differently situated within a regional political and economic system (for a recent framework that explores the way that language practices are bound up with relations of power in local speech and larger political economies, see Heller 1995). Building on this work, Gal (1991) has also pointed to the importance of gender in shaping people's language choices.

The idea that language choice may be seen as a symbolic practice of sociopolitical and gender position was key to thinking through why the women participating in my study did not learn and use the language of economic dominance at work. I was particularly influenced by Jane Hill's (1987) research that demonstrated the ways in which language choice could be related to gender position in the political economy. In her study of language use in the Mexican region of the Malinche Volcano, Hill looked at the different ways men and women talked about Mexicano, an indigenous language of Mexico, and Spanish. She found that women expressed more negative attitudes about Mexicano than men did, and linked this finding to the fact that many women felt hampered by their inadequacies in Spanish in the local economic market. As Hill's pioneering work is discussed in Pavlenko and Piller's chapter, in the next section I will briefly examine how language practices in my own study were related to the class and gender positions Portuguese immigrant workers at Stone Specialities held within the Canadian economy.

2.6. Language, gender, and class on the production floor

The language choices made by the women participating in my study – on the basis of the linguistic resources to which they had access upon their arrival to Canada – can be linked to the gendered structure and dynamics of the Portuguese family and the class positions they held within the Canadian political economy. Although at the time there were several different kinds of government-funded English language programs available to immigrant women in Toronto – full-time regular high school classes at adult learning centers, full-time six-month ESL programs at community colleges, part-time ESL classes offered during the day, and part-time ESL classes at night – access to English instruction was problematic (for other important discussions of access to English language learning, see Kouritzin 2000; Norton 2000; Peirce 1995). Only 1 out of 26 Portuguese women on the lines had ever accessed ESL instruction before joining the workplace language classes. One obstacle to accessing formal ESL instruction had to do with not being permitted to attend language classes because of the presence of men in the classroom. Augusta, who came to Toronto with her family when she was 16 years old, started working two or three days after she arrived. She reported that she had wanted to go to night school to learn English, but had only managed to attend for one or two weeks before her father decided that neither Augusta nor her two sisters could continue studying because of the presence of "so many boys" in the class. Other obstacles that prevented women from attending ESL classes are revealed in the conversations below:

Tara: Some people go to school when they come from another country. Did you have a chance to go to school when you first came?

Olga: Yes. When I came [to Canada], my husband come with me to the employment insurance [Canada Employment Centre] and for make a card for a social insurance number. And the girl [asked me if] I am so young why I don't go to the school? I had 19 years old when I came. I say no I came for work. I make a life. I think I make big mistake, but I never go.

Tara: Did you ever think that you would like to go to night school? Or it was too hard working and coming home?

Olga: I think it's hard, because after 4 years here I have my son. And for working the day and then the night go to the school ... I have to pay to the baby sitter, and the night maybe again. It's very hard for my son, and very hard for me.

In this first conversation, Olga explains how the need to financially support family members was at the heart of her decision to not attend government-funded full-time ESL classes upon her arrival to Canada. She considered work to be a "necessity" – "I came for work". Learning English was an "extravagance" (Wong 1993). Needing to work outside the home all day, Olga could not emotionally or physically afford the time away from her family to attend night school even though it did not cost any money to attend.

Tara: Did you think about going to school when you first came here?

Luísa: I was scared to walk on the streets at night. Because I came in August and in September the school starts. And I was scared because I hear so many strange things.

Tara: So you never wanted to go to night school.

Luísa: I want to go, but I was scared.

Tara: And day school?

Luísa: I had to help my friends because we had to start a new life.

Like Olga, Luísa needed to financially support her family of friends when she first arrived in Canada and chose not to go to ESL classes that were offered during the day. While Luísa did not have the mothering responsibilities Olga had, she did not go to night classes because she was frightened by sights and sounds that were unfamiliar to her and did not feel safe on the streets at night. The threat of violence against women, then, is another obstacle to English language classes for immigrant women.

Tara: When there's two Portuguese speakers speaking English and you are there, what do you think?

Angela: I would like to know English to talk to them. I have a Spanish lady telling me that I could go for six months and learn English and get paid by the government. But I didn't want to at the time ... I was not feeling optimistic, so I didn't want to go to school.

In this conversation Angela talks about her desire to know enough English to talk to English speakers and about the opportunity she had to study English full-time for six months. Unlike Olga and Luísa, she does not mention financial obligation as an obstacle to full-time study. In fact, Angela had the opportunity of joining a program that would have paid her (a modest amount) to study. However, having just left family and friends in Portugal to start a new life in a new country, Angela was too overwhelmed by the changes in her life to consider attending ESL classes and did not take advantage of this opportunity.

Tara: You didn't at that time think about going to school?
Fernanda: No at that time I don't think to go school, because I don't have a father. Me and my mother had to work alone. My [younger] brothers went to school.

In this last conversation, Fernanda talks about her responsibility as the eldest daughter in a single-parent home to financially support the family. Her work outside the home made it possible for her younger brothers to go to school. Looking at all four conversations together, we can see that Olga, Luísa, Angela, and Fernanda all wanted to attend ESL classes to learn English.

However, for three of the women starting a new life in Canada meant the necessity of working full-time outside the home. Such work prevented the possibility of day-time study. For the fourth woman, the work of adjusting to a new community and a new society needed to take place before she could enroll in an English program.

While the women interviewed above found that the use of English was not necessary for finding a job and bringing home a paycheck in the city of Toronto, it can certainly be argued that the use of English is necessary for economic mobility. For example, Grillo (1989) asserts that, in multilingual societies, languages and their speakers are usually of unequal status, power, and authority and that there is commonly a hierarchical ordering of languages, dialects, and ways of speaking. Languages that are associated with authority are "dominant" languages. Following Weber (1958), Grillo understands authority as "legitimated domination" or the exercise of power without force. Thus, dominant languages are associated with authority or the legitimate exercise of power. "Subordinate" languages, on the other hand, are languages that are not associated with authority and are restricted to use in domains from which authority is absent. Grillo argues that in a situation where mass labor migration brings together speakers of languages other than the official language(s) of the "receiving" or "host" society, immigrant language speakers occupy subordinate social, cultural, economic, and political statuses in that receiving society.

While many non-English speakers do indeed hold subordinate economic statuses in societies where English is the dominant language, it is necessary to question assumptions that learning and using English unproblematically provides access to economic power. Not all immigrant workers who learn to speak the dominant language are able to change their subordinate economic status. At Stone Specialities, higher-paying jobs off the production lines (jobs such as Quality Control inspector) were jobs that were not only associated with "good" to "excellent" English language skills, but were also associated with the possession of at least a Canadian grade 12 education. Most of the women line workers who chose to use only Portuguese at work were working-class women who had had access to only four years of elementary school education in the Azores, a set of islands located west of Lisbon (the capital of Portugal) in the Atlantic Ocean. Acquiring "good" to "excellent" English and a grade 12 education was beyond the means of possibility for most – if not all – of the women whose access to educational opportunities was limited to two hours of workplace English language instruction a week.

2.7. Language, gender, and ideology on the production floor

Gal's and Hill's work asks us to consider the ways in which language choice patterns are related to regional contexts of economic and political power relations. However, it is also important to analyze language practices in terms of local power relations. At the beginning of this chapter, I mentioned that sociolinguistic research could be effectively combined with the methodological strategies and ideologies of critical ethnography. A further analysis of the Portuguese "family"/community at Stone Specialities provides a good example of the way a critical ethnographic perspective can shed light on language and local unequal relations of power (see Anderson 1989 and Quantz 1992 for a review of the development of critical ethnography). Earlier, I explored how the ideological representation of work relationships as family relationships impacted on the way workers communicated with each other at work. Understanding one's work place as a "second home" also impacted on the way workers related to the Stone family who owned Stone Specialities.

Employees working at Stone talked about a "family feeling" in the company which was explained as the knowledge and expectation that the Stone family would look after its employees – who were members of the company "family" – in times of crisis. In extending financial aid to employees in crisis, CEO Roger Stone fulfilled his "family" obligations to his employees and expected his employees to fulfill similar obligations to him. This expectation allowed the Stone family to end a strike (in 1971) that was initiated by union organizers attempting to pressure the family into unionizing the factory. While union organizers were able to get many of the Portuguese women workers at the company to attend meetings and sign union cards, they were unsuccessful in getting most of them to go out on strike. There are several reasons why most Portuguese workers chose not to go out on strike even though they agreed to sign union cards. There was distrust of the union organizers who did not work for the company and who could not speak Portuguese. The local Portuguese parish priest – who did speak Portuguese – told them that if the union got in, they were going to lose their jobs and their houses. A third reason had to do with the ideological belief that the Stone family took care of its family of workers. Language played an important role here when Cecília, a recognized leader among the Portuguese women on the lines, was asked by management to talk to Portuguese workers who did go out on strike and see if she could convince them to leave the picket lines and come inside. By using her Portuguese network contacts and appealing to the authority of gendered cultural values and practices, Cecília was successful in convincing three women to leave the picket lines. When asked what she said to the three people to get them to come back to work, Cecília explained:

> There was no problem because one was my husband's niece, the other was a friend of mine who is still working in the factory – she lived very close to me – and while the other was only an acquaintance of mine, she was very friendly with the other two. That was the reason there was no problem. I called my husband's niece who is Graciete ... I called her to my house and made her see a lot of things. She had just recently married, she was only married for two or three months, and I made her see that she should understand that she was already [now] married and the company was going to do the best it could and it was very good for her to be inside. She should leave the picket because it was shameful to behave the way, the way strikers were behaving [calling each other bad names and getting into fights with sticks]. She agreed.

Cecília was successful in bringing Graciete and two other women back to work during the strike because she appealed to gendered cultural values and practices held by Graciete and her co-workers. She pointed out her niece's new responsibilities as a married woman (which included bringing home a salary to pay the bills); criticized her niece's social behavior on the picket lines; and then, after conferring with the line supervisor, offered an invitation to all three women to come back.

When asked why she went on strike, Graciete said it was because she felt "pushed" by those who went on strike, but after realizing that she didn't feel "good with that people outside", she came "inside again". Upon being reprimanded for having broken communal rules of conduct, Graciete reported feeling that she had not made the "right decision" and returning to the lines inside. Even though she had once agreed with those workers who felt that they were not making enough money and were being treated like a "horse", after her talk with Cecília, Graciete felt "uncomfortable".

It was Cecília's common sense (Gramsci 1971) understanding that the Stone family took care of its workers that resulted in her telling Graciete that "the company was going to do the best it could and it was very good for her to be inside". However, this ideological understanding was buttressed by a responsibility to assume the wifely duty of contributing to the family income. Language played an important role in supporting and maintaining local unequal relations of power through its articulation of gendered, ideological values, roles, and practices. I came to this analysis of the relationship between language, gender, ideology, and local relations of power by moving outside the field of sociolinguistics and making use of ideas in other fields of social theory.

3.   Women's language practices in a multilingual workplace: Implications for teaching and learning

The purpose underlying my own research project was to find out why the students in our workplace classes did not choose to use English at work. By developing a better understanding of bilingual life in the workplace I was teaching in, I was pushed to think about my teaching practice differently. One of the most important findings of the study was learning that the use of English at work was associated with risks for many of the Portuguese women. I learned that in my attempt to empower workers though English language instruction, it was important for me to acknowledge and respect the language boundaries that constructed and were constructed by different interactions in people's working and personal lives (see Kouritzin 2000 for related work around ambivalence and contradiction in English language learning). An English language curriculum that was shaped around interactions with non-speakers of Portuguese, however, acknowledged and respected the costs involved with crossing a language boundary. I also learned that while English language instruction was not always necessary for performing everyday work tasks at Stone Specialities and did not provide line workers with access to economic mobility, workers had other reasons for learning English. In a society where English was the dominant language, not speaking English sometimes limited the control the women had over everyday living conditions and relationships. For example, Virginia told me a story of asking a bilingual Portuguese dental assistant to translate for her during an operation for gum surgery being performed by an English-speaking dentist. After the assistant explained the surgical procedure to her, Virginia agreed to undergo the operation, but told the assistant that she wanted to go to the bathroom before the dentist started the procedure. When the assistant translated for Virginia, she told the dentist that Virginia was going to the bathroom because she was frightened of the operation and wanted to run away. Virginia, having spent some time in an English high school, understood everything the assistant said. She was so angry at the assistant's attempt to humiliate her that she decided to use English and speak to the dentist herself.

An English language curriculum that centers on increasing the control people have over everyday working and living conditions and relationships can provide people with expanded possibilities for functioning as members of English-speaking societies. Examples of lessons that would have been more useful to the women in our workplace classes are those that practice the language needed to deal with monolingual English-speaking medical professionals and corporate and government bureaucracies (see Belfiore and Heller 1992; Goldstein 1994). These kinds of lessons also respect the language boundaries that were part of the women's working lives. They are lessons that "legitimize" their "multilingual tongues".

Another difficulty with using a language broker to translate messages is having the force of one's message diluted. At Stone Specialities, the people who assumed the role of language brokers were often in supervisory or management positions. As Tony – one of the bilingual Portuguese-English supervisors in the Production Department – explained, supervisors who assumed the role of language broker were expected to support the authority of management when translating messages between Portuguese workers and English-speaking managers and supervisors. As a result, they would sometimes rephrase and dilute the force of a worker's concern when passing it on to management. A set of English lessons that assisted workers in conveying their messages to English-speaking supervisors themselves would have also been relevant and beneficial to our students (see Peirce, Harper, and Burnaby 1993 for similar findings).

Importantly, the women in our workplace classes who did not speak English fluently were vulnerable to unemployment during times of economic hardship. Workers who get jobs in recessionary times are those who have a variety of skills they can draw upon in addition to their ethnic networks. While it was beyond the scope of our own workplace program to provide our students with

English for finding a job, the possession of such language skills could enhance their chances of finding new employment in case of layoff.

My efforts to develop a curriculum for protection and control that would be more useful to our workplace students than the job-specific language curriculum I had been trained to use have been informed by the "problem-posing" approach associated with the work of Brazilian educator Paulo Freire (e.g., 1970, 1971, 1973, 1985). They have also been informed by the work of progressive North American ESL educators who believe that problem-posing is particularly relevant to immigrant and refugee ESL students who often have little control over their lives (see Auerbach and Wallerstein 1987; Bell and Burnaby 1984; Crawford-Lange 1981; Wallerstein 1985). Briefly, a problem-posing ESL curriculum is centered on talk about shared conflicts and problematic interactions. Such talk enables students to envision different working and living conditions and to generate an individual or community response to problems. Also valuable was the considerable amount of Canadian literature which has advocated for ESL instruction that serves to assist people in becoming "active participants" in society (e.g., Elson 1989; Hernandez 1989; Mohamid 1989; Peirce, Harper, and Burnaby 1993; Sauvé 1989). Finally, I learned that there were established workplace ESL programs that had been working with a curriculum for protection and control for a long time. Interestingly and importantly, these programs were developed with the assistance of union education funding in unionized workplaces (e.g., the Centre for Labour Studies Program at Humber College in Toronto described in Belfiore and Burnaby 1984 and the Metro Labour Education Centre program in Toronto). The curriculum of the union-funded programs reflected an understanding and respect of working-class issues and realities that had been absent from the curriculum we had been taught to develop and use.

My own work in moving from job-specific English-language instruction to a curriculum that worked to increase the control people had over everyday working and living conditions and relationships has been paralleled and expanded upon in the work of other workplace researchers and teachers. For example, in their reflection about the work carried out by the British Industrial Language Training Service, in the 1970s and 80s, Roberts, Davies, and Jupp (1992) explain that there was a shift from language instruction to intercultural communication and race relations research and education in British workplaces. The British researchers and teachers realized that if workers were to have effective communicative relationships with people who had power in the workplace, there had to be a willingness on the part of those with power to build an effective communicative relationship. It was felt that English-speaking supervisors in the workplace – who had a vested interest in the status quo – might not wish to communicate in English with workers who spoke other languages since such communication was to the workers' advantage. In choosing not to communicate with their workers, the researchers and teachers felt that English-speaking supervisors were acting as "gatekeepers" to opportunities for promotion and training (see Peirce 1995 and Norton 2000 for a discussion on what Bourdieu 1977 calls "the power to impose reception"). To help workers access such opportunities, they maintained that communication training in the workplace needed to target supervisors as well as workers. As a result, in addition to the English language instruction they already offered to workers, they began to offer intercultural communication education to those individuals in positions of power who worked with people from different ethnic and cultural groups. Underlying the provision of intercultural communication education for supervisors was the assumption that the lack of communication or ineffective communication between supervisors and workers from different cultural and linguistic groups could lead to incidents of misinterpretation. In turn, cumulative misinterpretation could lead to hardened attitudes, stereotypes, and discrimination which biased supervisors against workers trying to access opportunities for promotion and training.

This move from English language instruction to intercultural communication and race relations research and education in the workplace (see Belfiore and Burnaby 1995 for Canadian research on issues of anti-racist education in the workplace and Clyne 1994 for Australian sociolinguistic research on workplace intercultural communication) represents a change in focus from trying to improve individual relationships and communication skills to recognizing and addressing wider systemic issues of power and access. It is within this very important shift that directions for future research lie.

4. Women's language practices in multilingual workplaces: directions for future research

There is a number of different ways to pursue a research program that looks at issues of gender, power, and access in multilingual and multiracial workplaces. Following the work of Roberts, Davies, and Jupp (1992), researchers can ask how women workers get access to job training and promotion opportunities and inquire into the ways these opportunities may be constrained by intersections of linguistic discrimination, sexism, classism, and racism in the workplace (see Lippi-Green 1997 for an excellent example of such research).

While my own research on gender and bilingual language practices in the workplace has not linked itself to the studies that inquire into gender in monolingual work situations, future research into women's bilingualism at work might make use of the interesting work being undertaken in this field (e.g., Kendall and Tannen 1997; McElhinny 1995; Tannen 1994). To illustrate, researchers might ask how the gendered styles described in monolingual workplace settings are similar to or different from the gendered language practices described in bilingual work settings. Or how gendered style shifting is similar to or different from gendered code-switching practices. When contextualized within a research program that is interested in issues of power and access, such questions can shed light on the ways particular gendered styles or practices are valued or devalued in a particular workplace and, thus, promote or constrain opportunities at work.

In thinking about where to inquire into questions of power and access and intercultural, interethnic, and interracial communication at work, Coleman (1989) and Clyne (1994) have reported that much of the research into language at work has been concerned with language use in professional contexts such as medical care, legal context, and education. They both call for work that spans a wide range of occupations, non-professional as well as professional.

In closing, I'd like to say that no matter what area of investigation we select for our future projects, it is good ethnographic practice to find ways of disseminating our questions into the workplaces we wish to study before undertaking our research. Such work allows research participants to think about our questions in terms of their own insights about their working lives. If we choose to undertake particular research projects in order to inform policies and practices which may affect women workers' life chances, it is important that we work with the workers we research to uncover the questions that might truly be beneficial to a group of women in a particular workplace rather than assume the questions we are asking – from outside the workplace – are necessarily the most relevant.

Notes

1.   *Two Languages at Work: Bilingual Life on the Production Floor* is based upon research I undertook for my doctoral thesis study. I would like to acknowledge and thank my thesis supervisor Dr. Monica Heller and the members of my committee Dr. Roger Simon and Dr. Barbara Burnaby for their interest and expert guidance. I also want to acknowledge and thank Dora Matos for her valuable research assistance. York University provided financial support for my thesis study by making research funding available to part-time faculty. I am most grateful for this initiative.

2. The names of the people in this story and the names of the research participants and the company in the rest of the chapter have been changed to protect their anonymity.

3. Several Portuguese-speaking readers of this text have indicated that they have never heard the word "marida" used. They suggest that its use on the production floor at Stone Specialities may be unique.

4. The following is a collage of data obtained from separate interviews with Portuguese line workers.

References

Anderson, Gary
  1989   Critical ethnography in education: Origins, current status and new directions. *Review of Educational Research* 59, 3, 249–270.

Anzaldúa, Gloria
  1987   *Borderlands/La Frontera: The New Mestiza*. San Francisco: Aunt Lute Books.

Auerbach, Elsa and Nina Wallerstein
  1987   *ESL for Action: Problem Posing at Work*. Reading, MA: Addison-Wesley.

Belfiore, Mary Ellen and Barbara Burnaby
  1984   *Teaching English in the Workplace*. Toronto: OISE Press and Hodder and Stoughton.
  1995   *Teaching English in the Workplace*. Revised and expanded edition. Toronto: OISE Press and Hodder and Stoughton.

Belfiore, Mary Ellen and Monica Heller
  1992   Cross-cultural interviews: Participation and decision-making. In Burnaby, Barbara and Alistair Cumming (eds.), *Sociopolitical Aspects of ESL*. Toronto: OISE Press and Stoughton, 233–240.

Bell, Jill and Barbara Burnaby
  1984   *A Handbook for ESL Literacy*. Toronto: OISE Press.

Briggs, Charles
  1986   *Learning How to Ask: A Sociolinguistic Appraisal of the Role of the Interview in Social Science Research*. Cambridge: Cambridge University Press.

Bourdieu, Pierre
  1977   The economics of linguistic exchanges. *Social Science Information* 16, 6, 645–668.

Clyne, Michael
  1994   *Inter-cultural Communication at Work: Cultural Values in Discourse.* Cambridge: Cambridge University Press.

Coleman, Hywel (ed.)
  1989   *Working with Language: A Multidisciplinary Consideration of Language Use in Work Contexts.* Berlin/New York: Mouton de Gruyter.

Crawford-Lange, Linda
  1981   Redirecting second language curricula: Paulo Freire's contribution. *Foreign Language Annals* 14, 4/5, 257–268.

Elson, Nick
  1989   The teacher as a participating citizen. *TESL Talk* 19, 1, 47–55.

Freire, Paulo
  1970   *Pedagogy of the Oppressed.* New York: Seabury Press.
  1971   To the coordinator of a cultural circle. *Convergence* 4, 1, 61–62.
  1973   *Education for Critical Consciousness.* New York: Seabury Press.
  1985   *The Politics of Education.* South Hadley, MA: Bergin-Garvey.

Gal, Susan
  1979   *Language Shift: Social Determinants of Linguistic Change in Bilingual Austria.* New York: Academic Press.
  1988   The political economy of code choice. In Heller, Monica (ed.), *Codeswitching: Anthropological and Sociolinguistic Perspectives.* Berlin/New York: Mouton de Gruyter.
  1991   Between speech and silence: The problematics of research on language and gender. In di Leonardo, Micaela (ed.), *Gender at the Crossroads of Knowledge: Feminist Anthropology in the Post Modern Era.* Berkeley, CA: University of California Press, 175–203.

Goldstein, Tara
  1994   'We are all sisters, so we don't have to be polite': Language choice and English language training in the multilingual workplace. *TESL Canada* 11, 2, 30–45.
  1995 a   Interviewing in a multicultural/multilingual setting. *TESOL Quarterly* 29, 3, 587–593.

1995b 'Nobody is talking bad': Creating community and claiming power on the production lines. In Bucholtz, Mary and Kira Hall (eds.), *Gender Articulated: Language and the Socially Constructed Self.* New York: Routledge, 375–400.

1997 *Two Languages at Work: Bilingual Life on the Production Floor.* Berlin/ New York: Mouton de Gruyter.

Gramsci, Antonio
1971 *Selections from the Prison Notebooks.* Translated by Quintin Hoare and Geoffrey Nowell Smith. New York: International Publishers.

Grillo, Ralph
1989 *Dominant Languages: Language and Hierarchy in Britain and France.* Cambridge: Cambridge University Press.

Gumperz, John
1982a *Discourse Strategies.* Cambridge: Cambridge University Press.
1982b *Language and Social Identity.* Cambridge: Cambridge University Press.
1992 Interviewing in intercultural situations. In Drew, Paul and John Heritage (eds.), *Talk at Work: Interaction in Institutional Settings.* Cambridge: Cambridge University Press, 302–327.

Heller, Monica
1988a Strategic ambiguity: Codeswitching in the management of conflict. In Heller, Monica (ed.), *Codeswitching: Anthropological and Sociolinguistic Perspectives.* Berlin/New York: Mouton de Gruyter, 77–96.

1988b Introduction. In Heller, Monica (ed.), *Codeswitching: Anthropological and Sociolinguistic Perspectives.* Berlin/New York: Mouton de Gruyter, 1–24.

1988c Speech economy and social selection in educational contexts: A Franco-Ontarian case study. *Discourse Processes* 12, 3, 377–390.

1995 Codeswitching and the politics of language. In Milroy, Lesley and Pieter Muysken (eds.), *One Speaker, Two Languages: Cross-disciplinary Perspectives on Code-switching.* New York: Cambridge University Press, 158–174.

Hernandez, Carmencita
1989 Beyond existence, towards participation. *TESL Talk* 19,1, 62–64.

Hill, Jane
1987 Women's speech in modern Mexicano. In Phillips, Susan, Susan Steele, and Christine Tanz (eds.), *Language, Gender and Sex in Comparative Perspective.* Cambridge: Cambridge University Press, 121–160.

Jupp, Tom and Susan Hodlin
 1975   *Industrial English.* London: Heinemann Educational Books.

Kendall, Shari and Deborah Tannen
 1997   Gender and language in the workplace. In Wodak, Ruth (ed.), *Gender and Discourse.* London: Sage, 81–105.

Kouritzin, Sandra
 2000   Immigrant mothers redefine access to ESL classes: Contradiction and ambivalence. *Journal of Multilingual and Multicultural Development* 21,1, 14–32.

Le Page, Robert
 1968   Problems of description in multilingual communities. *Transactions of the Philological Society,* 189–212.

Lippi-Green, Rosina
 1997   *English with an Accent: Language, Ideology and Discrimination in the United States.* London/New York: Routledge.

McElhinny, Bonnie
 1995   Challenging hegemonic masculinities: Female and male police officers handling domestic violence. In Bucholtz, Mary and Kira Hall (eds.), *Gender Articulated: Language and the Socially Constructed Self.* London/ New York: Routledge, 217–243.

Mohamid, Norman
 1989   Students' themes, students' work. *TESL Talk* 19,1, 68–74.

Norton, Bonny
 2000   *Identity and Language Learning: Gender, Ethnicity and Educational Change.* New York: Longman.

Pauwels, Anne (ed.)
 1994   Cross-Cultural Communication in the Professions (Special issue). *Multilingua: Journal of Cross-Cultural and Interlanguage Communication,* 13, 1/2.

Peirce, Bonny Norton
 1995   Social identity, investment, and language learning. *TESOL Quarterly* 29, 1, 9–31.

Peirce, Bronwyn, Helen Harper and Barbara Burnaby
 1993   Workplace ESL at Levi Strauss: 'Dropouts' speak out. *TESL Canada Journal* 10, 2, 9–32.

Quantz, Richard
   1992   On critical ethnography (with some postmodern considerations). In Le-
            Compte, Margaret, Wendy Milroy, and Judith Preissle (eds.), *Handbook of
            Qualitative Research in Education*. San Diego: Academic Press, 447–506.

Richer, Judy
   1982   Workplace language classes: The management factor. *English in the Work-
            place, TESL Talk* 13, 4, 72–82.

Roberts, Celia, Evelyn Davies, and Tom Jupp
   1992   *Language and Discrimination: A Study of Communication in Multi-ethnic
            Workplaces*. London: Longman.

Sauvé, Virginia
   1989   Power and presence: Reconceptualizing the work of the ESL teacher. *TESL
            Talk* 19, 1, 118–132.

Statistics Canada
   1989   *Profile of Ethnic Groups: Dimensions – Census of Canada 1986*. Ottawa:
            Statistics Canada.

Tannen, Deborah
   1994   *Talking From 9 to 5. Women and Men in the Workplace: Language, Sex and
            Power*. New York: William Morrow.

Wallerstein, Nina
   1985   *Language and Culture in Conflict*. Reading, MA: Addison-Wesley.

Weber, Max
   1958   *From Max Weber: Essays in Sociology*. Translated and edited by Gerth,
            Hans and C. Wright Mills. New York: Oxford University Press.

Woolard, Kathryn
   1989   *Double Talk: Bilingualism and the Politics of Ethnicity in Catalonia*. Stan-
            ford, CA: Stanford University Press.

Wong, Cynthia Sau-Ling
   1993   *Reading Asian American Literature: From Necessity to Extravagance*.
            Princeton, NJ: Princeton University Press.

Gendering the 'learner': Sexual harassment and second language acquisition

Susan Ehrlich

1. Introduction

Theories of second language acquisition have often assumed an idealized, abstract learner devoid of social positioning and removed from the social environment in which learning takes place. Indeed, Rampton (1991: 241) points to "the ubiquity of the phrase 'the learner'", arguing that such a phrase implies a 'normal' or 'natural' course of second language development that exists outside of a social context. In a similar way, Kramsch and von Hoene (1995: 336) have critiqued what they call the "reductionist view of the social context of language" that informs most communicative approaches to language teaching. Such a view assumes a "generic taxonomy of predetermined 'learners' needs' and situations with predetermined scripts" (Kramsch and von Hoene 1995: 336) without regard for the particularities of learners' social identities. That the social location of learners can have a profound effect on learning outcomes is not in itself a new insight. For example, in a now classic study of social distance Schumann (1976: 404) investigated the effects of instruction on the pidginized speech of Alberto and concluded "that instruction is evidently not powerful enough to overcome the pidginization engendered by social and psychological distance". What is challenged, however, in the work of Rampton (1991) and Kramsch and von Hoene (1995), among others, is the claim that the effects of social variation are secondary. As Siegal (1994, 1996) has demonstrated, the nature of learners' interlanguage can be determined to a large extent by the social identities taken on by learners in relation to social stratification in the target culture. In an ethnographic study of four white Western women in Japan, Siegal (1994: 648) found that her learners "created their own language system based on their perceptions of Japanese women's language and demeanor and their awareness of their position in Japanese society". That is, the learners' inadequate use of honorifics and sentence-final pragmatic particles associated with Japanese women's language is explained by Siegal in terms of their resistance to adopting what they perceive as an overly humble, overly silly Japanese feminine identity. Siegal's work portrays female second language learners, not as passive learners acquiring sociolinguistically appropriate forms, but rather as active agents who use the second language to resist a social positioning that is unattractive to them. Without the ethnographic and social contextualization provided by Siegal, the social significance of these learners' interlanguage would be lost and, concomitantly, the possible interaction between social identities and linguistic processes, such as simplification and overgeneralization. While linguistic simplification is a universal property of learners' interlanguages, the particular kind of linguistic simplification displayed by these female learners of Japanese resulted from their distaste for Japanese constructions of femininity as manifested in Japanese women's speech styles. That is, viewing social factors as an analytic category that alters a 'normal' trajectory of second language development misses the fact that learners are always situated by age, race, class, and gender and that these social locations permeate the learning process.

In this chapter, I examine the relationship between a gendered social practice, sexual harassment, and second language acquisition as a way of demonstrating that social categories, such as gender, occupy a crucial role in learners' attempts to acquire second languages. (See Ehrlich (1997) for a slightly different version of this argument.) I begin with a historical overview of research that has investigated the relationship between gender and second language acquisition. Such research, I argue, has not acknowledged the complexity of gender as a social construct and thus has simplified and overgeneralized the relationship between gender and language acquisition. I then elaborate a conception of gender that has not generally informed research in the field – a conception of gender that is highly attentive to the specificities of cultural, social, and interactional contexts – and demonstrate its value for future research.

2.   Historical overview

Many early investigations of sex and gender and second language acquisition investigated the possible superiority of female learners. Burstall (1975), for example, reports that girls had significantly higher scores than boys on all tests measuring French achievement in her study of approximately 6,000 children studying French in British primary schools. Ekstrand (1980) reports on two large scale studies in Sweden, one involving Swedish children learning English and the other involving immigrant children learning Swedish. Ekstrand's conclusions support proficiency differences in favor of girls due, according to Ekstrand, to differences in basic cognitive variables, in attention, in brain function, and in cultural differences. Boyle (1987), in his study of approximately 500 Chinese university students studying English in Hong Kong, found that females were superior in general language proficiency. As Ellis (1994) points out, however, support for female superiority in L2 proficiency is not uncontested; Boyle in the 1987 study found men to outperform women on listening vocabulary tests and Bacon (1992) found no differences between the listening comprehension of men and women.

Other studies have indicated that gender plays a role in the way that learners approach the task of second language acquisition, which in turn is hypothesized to relate to female superiority in classroom language learning. In a series of studies (Ehrman and Oxford 1989, 1990; Oxford, Nyikos, and Ehrman 1988; Oxford and Nyikos 1989; summarized in Oxford 1993, 1994) Oxford and her colleagues have investigated possible differences in the use of learning styles and language learning strategies by female and male learners. Oxford (1993: 549–50) summarizes the results of gender-differentiated L2 learning strategy research:

> When L2 research has considered gender, it has usually ... demonstrated gender differences in strategy frequency, with women consciously choosing to use particular sets of strategies more often than men. Women especially tended to use general study strategies, social strategies, affective strategies, and certain conversational or functional practice strategies more frequently than men across a number of studies, thus usually showing a greater range of frequently used strategy categories.

Bacon and Finnemann (1992) report a similar finding in their self-report study of over 900 students of Spanish at two large institutions in the United States to the extent that women reported a higher level of strategy use and social interaction with Spanish. Although most of these studies did not determine the relationship between language learning outcomes and strategy use or reported strategy use, Oxford (1994: 146) connects the qualitative difference in strategy use by women and men to success in classroom performance: "It may be the qualitative differences in their strategy use that favor women and girls, who often show better classroom performance in a second or foreign language than males." Here, Oxford is drawing on research that has shown that appropriate learning strategy use is frequently related to better learning performance (O'Malley and Chamot 1990; Wenden and Rubin 1987; Wenden 1991).

Hypotheses concerning female superiority in second language learning are generally derived from research in L1 acquisition (e.g., Maccoby and Jacklin 1974) that has established girls' superiority over boys. Larsen-Freeman and Long, in their 1991 textbook, report on "the generally accepted fact" in L1 acquisition that females display a rate advantage, at least in the beginning stages of first language acquisition, and then go on to report on two studies that show female superiority in some aspects of second language acquisition (i.e., Eisenstein 1982; Farhady 1982). Likewise, many of the studies described above are driven very explicitly by sex differences research. Boyle (1987: 274), for example, talks about "the weight of evidence in favor of female superiority over males in verbal ability", evidence that is too powerful to be explained by social factors alone. Ekstrand (1980), although much more cautious about the findings of female superiority in first language acquisition studies, still frames his research question in terms of possible sex differences in second language acquisition. And Bacon and Finnemann (1992: 472) begin their literature review with the following comments: "Psychologists, who have long been interested in the relationship of sex to behavior and cognition, have found significant sex-related differences in social behavior, cognitive activity, and general verbal ability". Not only do these remarks display some confusion about the usual distinction made between sex and gender[1] (i.e., that sex refers to biological categories and gender to social categories), more importantly, they are emblematic, I would argue, of the biological and dualistic conceptions of gender that underlie much work in second language acquisition. Such characterizations of gender exaggerate and overgeneralize differences between women and men in addition to ignoring the social, cultural, and situational forces that shape gender categories and gender relations.

Given the widespread influence of sex differences research (particularly research concerning sex differences in verbal ability) on the kinds of research questions asked by those interested in gender and second language acquisition, I would suggest that this research paradigm warrants some discussion. Crawford (1995), in a general critique of psychological research on sex differences, questions the political neutrality and objectivity of scientific inquiry devoted to the 'uncovering' of sex differences, arguing that the epistemological stances driving questions about 'difference' are inevitably embedded in a system of unequal power relations between men and women. (See Bing and Bergvall 1996 for a similar argument.) Her comments about the interpretation of one such difference are instructive:

> Even if we accept the search for sex differences as a valid question, and the differences obtained in research as veridical, the 'truth' about their meaning is elusive, and ideologically influenced. Consider one highly publicized sex difference: mathematics performance on standardized tests. Janet Hyde and her colleagues ... have provided a compelling example of how the meaning of this difference is distorted as a result of treating it as absolute and interpreting it outside its social context. On average, white males do slightly better than white females

on standardized mathematics ability tests. However, among African-Americans and Asian-Americans, the sex difference is smaller. Age is an important variable, too: girls outperform boys until adolescence. When odd samples (such as specially selected mathematically precocious adolescents) are removed from the overall calculations, the difference shifts in the other direction – girls slightly outperform boys. Like other sex differences, the similarity is much greater than the difference, and the difference itself may be an artifact of sampling (1995: 4–5).

With respect to sex differences in verbal ability, it seems to be a generally accepted fact (perhaps like the generally accepted fact described above that males are superior in mathematical ability) in studies of second language acquisition that females enjoy an advantage in L1 acquisition, at least in the early stages. Although Maccoby and Jacklin's *The Psychology of Sex Differences* (1974) is the text most often cited in connection with the claims about female superiority in L1 acquisition, it is interesting to note that other researchers have interpreted this text somewhat differently, that is, as wary of the sex differences literature: "They [Maccoby and Jacklin] ... warned against uncritical biologizing, noting that there are many possible mechanisms through which female-male differences could come into being. Finally they pointed out that beliefs about sex differences far outstripped reality" (Marecek 1995: 105). In addition, other more recent studies of sex differences in verbal ability have contested claims about female superiority. Macaulay (1978: 361) finds that the evidence of sex differences in first language development is too "tenuous and self-contradictory to justify any claims that one sex is superior to the other". Furthermore, Hyde and Linn (1988), in a meta-analysis of 165 studies involving 1,418,899 subjects, conclude that there is strong evidence to support no difference in verbal ability between males and females. To reiterate Crawford's comments above, even if female superiority in verbal ability is a "true" finding of research, like other sex-differences, "the similarity is much greater than the difference, and the difference itself may be an artifact of sampling" (Crawford 1995: 4–5).

My point here is not to deny the possibility of women's (or men's) greater success in second language acquisition within particular contexts within particular speech communities. Rather, my aim is to challenge claims about sex differences in verbal ability that have provided the impetus for certain kinds of research questions in second language acquisition, that is, overly general questions about women and men, girls and boys that ignore the social, cultural, and situational contexts in which second languages are acquired. Indeed, even when second language researchers have discussed aspects of acquisition that are clearly related to the specificities of certain learning environments or particular social and cultural contexts, dualistic and dichotomous conceptions of gender often emerge. For example, in a recent review of gender differences in second and foreign language learning styles and strategies, Oxford (1994: 141) acknowledges a sociocultural basis to the differences she identifies: "These differences may, at least in part, be innate – and thus in fact sex differences – but most are likely to be *socioculturally* developed" (emphasis mine). However, while invoking sociocultural explanations for gender differences, Oxford, at the same time, appears to view gender-differentiated learning styles and strategies as fixed, unchanging, and immutable, for example, in her comments that global learning styles may be characteristic of females and analytic styles characteristic of males. It strikes me that making generalizations about the relationship between gender and learning styles and strategies is particularly problematic in the context of second and foreign language learning, given that learners typically come from a large number of different racial, ethnic, and social and cultural groups for which the interaction between learning styles (said by Oxford to be "socioculturally developed") and gender is likely to vary widely.

Ellis (1994), in his attempt to provide social explanations for why females have been shown in a number of studies either to have more positive attitudes towards learning a second language (Burstall 1975; Gardner and Lambert 1972; Spolsky 1989) or to outperform males (see studies cited above), also resorts to generalizations about gender that remove it from particular social, cultural, and situational contexts. Drawing on North American work by Maltz and Borker (1982) that suggests men and women learn different communicative styles (competitive vs. cooperative, respectively) based on the segregated same-sex peer groups they play in as children, Ellis (1994: 204) speculates that "the female 'culture' seems to lend itself more readily to dealing with the inherent threat imposed to identity by L2 learning". Maltz and Borker's work has been critiqued by Thorne (1990), among others, for overemphasizing the role of same-sex peer groups in the development of gendered identities; Thorne argues that the situations in which boys and girls are together may be as socially significant as those in which they are apart. In addition, Goodwin (1990) has argued, based on her ethnographic study of African-American children, that in certain activities girls adopted hierarchical speech styles similar to those adopted in the all-boy groups. Of particular relevance here is the fact that, in the absence of cultural, social, and situational contextualization, claims about women's cooperative speech styles are overly general and subject to qualification in the same way that claims about women's more positive attitudes to L2 learning and superior ability are. By contrast, Ellis's final comments about gender link L2 learning to the activities in which women and men are engaged in a specific speech community:

> It will not always be the case ... that females outperform males. Asian men in Britain generally attain higher levels of proficiency in L2 English than do Asian women for the simple reason that their jobs bring them into contact with the majority English-speaking group, while women are often 'enclosed' in their home. (Ellis 1994: 204)

It seems to me that Ellis points to a more fruitful direction for investigations of gender and L2 learning – one which acknowledges the complexity of gender as a social construct and the variation that gender categories and gender relations can exhibit across speech communities and social contexts.[2]

3.   Gender as mediated by social practice

Recent work in sociolinguistics, generally, and language and gender research, more specifically, has rejected categorical and fixed notions of gendered identities (and social identities more generally) in favor of more constructivist and dynamic ones. Cameron (1990a: 86), for example, makes the point (paraphrasing Harold Garfinkel) that "social actors are not sociolinguistic 'dopes'", mindlessly and passively producing linguistic forms that are definitively determined by social class membership, ethnicity, gender, etc. Rather, Cameron argues for an understanding of gender that reverses the relationship between linguistic practices and social identities traditionally posited within the quantitative sociolinguistics or variationist paradigm. Work in this tradition has typically focused on establishing correlations between linguistic variables and social factors such as age, race, ethnicity, and sex, implicitly assuming that these aspects of social identity exist prior to and are determinate of linguistic behavior (and other social behavior). By contrast, more recent formulations of the relationship between language and gender, following Butler (1990), emphasize the performative aspect of gender: linguistic practices, among other kinds of practices, continually bring into being individuals' social identities. Under this account, language is one important means by which gender – an ongoing social process – is enacted or constituted; gender is something individuals *do* – in part through linguistic choices – as opposed to something individuals *are* or *have* (West and Zimmerman 1987). Cameron's (1995: 15–16) comments are illustrative:

> Whereas sociolinguistics would say that the way I use language reflects or marks my identity as a particular kind of social subject – I talk like a white middle-class woman because I am (already) a white middle-class woman – the critical account suggests language is one of the things that *constitutes* my identity as a particular

kind of subject. Sociolinguistics says that how you act depends on who you are; critical theory says that who you are (and are taken to be) depends on how you act. (emphasis in original)

The idea that an individual's linguistic behavior does not simply arise from a set of permanent and invariant social attributes is also suggestive of the contextually-variable nature of social identities. If identities are not fixed and static, then their 'performance' can vary across social, situational, and interactional contexts. It is in this regard that Schiffrin (1996) is critical of variationist studies within sociolinguistics, in particular, the practice of coding aspects of social identity as categorical and invariant across contexts. Schiffrin argues for a different view, one in which social identities are locally situated and constructed: "We may act more or less middle-class, more or less female, and so on, depending on what we are doing and with whom. This view forces us to attend to speech activities, and to the interactions in which they are situated" (Schiffrin 1996: 199). Likewise, Goodwin (1990: 9) in an ethnographic study of urban African-American children in Philadelphia argues that stereotypes about women's speech collapse when talk in a whole range of activities is examined:

> In order to construct social personae appropriate to the events of the moment, the same individuals articulate talk and gender differently as they move from one activity to another. The relevant unit for the analysis of cultural phenomena, including gender, is thus not the group as a whole, or the individual, but rather situated activities. [3]

According to Ochs (1992), one of the major advances in language and gender research has been the adoption of perspectives that are functional and strategic rather than formal. Such approaches focus first on the types of social activities and practices that enter into the construction and constitution of gender within a particular community and then isolate the linguistic structures that are used in the accomplishment of these activities and practices. Under this account, language *indirectly* indexes gender, that is, this relationship is mediated by the social activities and practices symbolically and practically associated with women and men in a particular community.[4] One influential attempt to theorize the relationship between gender and language in terms of the social practices that mediate the two is the 'communities of practice' framework developed by Eckert and McConnell-Ginet (1992 a, b, 1999). Advocating a shift away from overarching generalizations about women, men, and 'gendered' speech styles, Eckert and McConnell-Ginet (1992 a: 462) emphasize the need to "think practically and look locally". They recommend that the interaction between language and gender be examined in the everyday social practices of particular local communities – what they term 'communities of practice' – because gender is not always easily separated from other aspects of social identity and relations nor will it always have an invariant meaning – and linguistic manifestation – across communities. In Eckert and McConnell-Ginet's words (1992 b: 95), "gender is produced (and often reproduced) in differential communities of practice". Put another way, it is not gender *per se* that interacts with linguistic practices, but rather the complex set of 'gendered' social practices in which individuals participate: individuals produce themselves as 'gendered' by habitually engaging in the social practices of a community, i.e., in different communities of practice, that are practically or symbolically associated with a community's notion of masculinities or femininities. And just as women's and men's involvements in 'gendered' communities of practice will vary, so women's and men's relation to normative constructions of femininity and masculinity will vary.

In a discussion of an experimental setting (Freed and Greenwood 1996) that produced similar linguistic behavior, i.e., a cooperative speech style, in both female and male subjects – same sex friends in casual conversation – Freed (1996) provides a more concrete description of the way in which gender is produced through involvement in certain social practices or activities. The study Freed comments on here is one in which Freed and Greenwood (1996) found that women *and* men involved in same-sex dyadic conversations with friends, displayed strikingly similar linguistic behavior – behavior typically associated with the so-called cooperative speech style of women:

> First, participating in the same practice produced in the women and men the same kind of talk; second, outside of this experimental setting, it is possible that women and men would be less likely to find themselves in such similar settings, given the sex- and gender-differentiated society in which we live ....Thus language and gender studies conducted in natural settings may often find differences not similarities in women's and men's speech simply because women and men are frequently engaged in different activities (see M. Goodwin 1990) and not because of any differences in women and men themselves. Since it is increasingly clear that speech patterns are products of the activities that people are engaged in and not inherent to the participants, we can conclude that communicative styles are ... customs related to actions, activities and behaviors differentially encouraged for women and men. (Freed 1996: 67)

Freed, like Eckert and McConnell-Ginet and Ochs, posits an indirect relationship between gender and language, a relationship "mediated by the crucial variable of practice" (Cameron 1996: 45). And, while, as Freed suggests, gender undoubtedly influences the kinds of social activities or communities of practice (in Eckert's and McConnell-Ginet's terms) to which individuals have access and/or in which they participate, the mediating variable of practice leaves open the possibility of linguistic behavior being variable within an individual speaker as well as across speakers of the same sex/gender.

4.   Second language acquisition and gender

If the relationship between language and gender is not a direct one (as argued above), but one mediated by the social activities and practices of particular speech communities, then investigations of gender and language use are most fruitfully carried out in relation to the 'gendered' social practices of those communities. With respect to the acquisition of second languages, a number of studies investigating language choice and acquisition in bilingual and multilingual communities have elucidated the kinds of social practices that may be relevant to gender differentiation in second language acquisition outcomes. Hill (1987) and Harvey (1994), for instance, describe communities in Mexico and Peru, respectively, where women are less proficient than men in the dominant, postcolonial language of Spanish because they are less likely to have access to contexts in which Spanish is spoken: wage labor and education. By contrast, Medicine (1987) and Zentella (1987) describe communities (a Lakota Sioux community and an East Harlem Puerto Rican community) where the women are more often than men proficient bilinguals due to the 'cultural broker' roles the women assume in these communities. That is, in some communities, women are expected to not only be the 'guardians' of the traditional language and culture (Burton 1994) but also to mediate between the dominant and minority cultures. Still another kind of situation is described by Gal (1978). In the Hungarian-German community of Oberwart, Austria, Gal found that young women were leading in the shift from Hungarian to German because, Gal argues, the peasant lifestyle associated with Hungarian was one they wished to reject. Rather than assuming a 'cultural broker' role in the community and mediating between the two cultures and languages, then, Gal's young women rejected Hungarian and strategically adopted German in order to escape their social position as peasants. What these studies demonstrate is the difficulty of drawing generalizations about the precise way that gender (more accurately, the social practices involved in the construction of gender in particular communities) will influence second language acquisition; in particular, these studies do not unequivocally support the finding of female superiority. Indeed, Hill and Harvey describe communities in which women are *less* proficient than men in the dominant, postcolonial language of Spanish and Gal describes a situation in which young peasant women are very deliberately *rejecting* Hungarian. Clearly, the various ways that gender gets constructed and constituted across communities will result in varying acquisition outcomes for women and men across communities.

Given the need to examine the relationship between second language acquisition and gender alongside the social practices that constitute gender within particular communities, I now turn to a social practice that is 'gendered' in many communities and cultures – sexual harassment. Indeed, Polanyi (1995) claims that sexual harassment of women is a regular feature of study-abroad programs and thus elucidates yet another way in which women's participation in the second language acquisition process can be shaped by the 'gendered' social practices of a community or culture.

4.1. Sexual harassment as a 'gendered' social practice

Arguably, one of the major successes of second wave feminism has been the naming and politicizing of sexual harassment – aspects of women's everyday experiences previously personalized and gone unnamed. As Steinem (1983: 149) says of terms such as sexism and sexual harassment: "A few years ago, they were just called life". The coining of new terms to express the experiences and perceptions of many women – phenomena previously unexpressed in a language encoding a male worldview – has enabled women to resist and organize against forms of male violence such as sexual harassment (Kitzinger and Thomas 1995: 32). After all, as Cameron (1990b: 13) points out, "feelings and ideas without words to express them may remain fleeting, inchoate, and unrecognized by the culture at large". Now recognized by the culture at large, sexual harassment is deemed unacceptable and/or illegal by many mainstream cultural institutions, including the legal system (at least in the West).

Despite the seriousness with which sexual harassment is treated within national and international institutions and legal systems, the editors of a recent volume on sexual harassment (Thomas and Kitzinger 1997: 8) maintain that it is "still the case that people (both men and women) fail to recognize it when it occurs". To exemplify, Thomas and Kitzinger cite a Canadian Human Rights Commission survey, conducted in the 1980s, in which 49 per cent of the women interviewed reported one or more instances of "unwanted sexual attention" whereas only 30 per cent of those identified the experiences as "sexual harassment". Furthermore, in their own interview research Thomas and Kitzinger found that there was huge variation among women as to what kinds of behavior they believed the term "sexual harassment" legitimately included. While the term is subject to contestation, it is nonetheless the case that sexual harassment is a descriptor used substantially more by women to describe their experiences than by men. Kitzinger and Thomas (1995: 33) remark:

> Women consistently define more experiences as sexual harassment than do men, and the factor which most consistently predicts variation in people's identification of what constitutes sexual harassment is the sex of the rater. ... Overall, men tend to label fewer behaviours as sexual harassment ... and, in particular, are less likely to see behaviours such as sexual teasing, looks or gestures as harassment.

Indeed, the fact that women and men may respond differentially to sexual behavior and label different types of behavior sexual harassment is beginning to influence jurisprudence in North America, specifically, case law surrounding sexual harassment. Since the early twentieth century, courts in Canada and the United States have found it useful to invoke the notion of a 'reasonable person' in considering whether certain kinds of behavior should be deemed as harmful or offensive and thus punishable. The reasonable person is supposed to represent community norms; thus, whatever would offend or harm a reasonable person is said to be more generally offensive or harmful. Feminist legal scholars (e.g., Abrams 1989) have recently challenged the generalizability of a reasonable person's experiences, arguing that men and women may experience sexual advances or sexual harassment differently. For example, because women, as a group, are more likely than heterosexual men to be victims of men's sexual violence, women may be more threatened by sexual banter than men. Indeed, some state courts and lower federal courts in the U.S. have modified the reasonable person standard and introduced a 'reasonable woman' standard for evaluating charges of sexual harassment. One such U.S. court (Ellison v. Brady 1991) justifies introducing the reasonable woman standard in the following way:

> We realize that there is a broad range of viewpoints among women as a group, but we believe that many women share common concerns which men do not necessarily share. For example, because women are disproportionately victims of rape and sexual assault, women have a stronger incentive to be concerned with sexual behavior. ... We adopt the perspective of a reasonable woman primarily because we believe that a sex-blind reasonable person standard tends to be male-biased and tends to systematically ignore the experiences of women. (Ellison v. Brady, 924 F.2d 872, 878–8 1 (9th Cir.1991))

What is demonstrated in these comments (and those of Kitzinger and Thomas (1995) cited above) is the 'gendered' nature of sexual harassment. The fact that "women are disproportionately victims of rape and sexual assault" is part of the background knowledge that informs women's interpretation of men's sexual behavior. As a result, a communicative act such as sexual banter may be perceived as more threatening to women than to heterosexual men because women's stock of cultural beliefs may include the proposition that sexual banter is potentially "a prelude to violent sexual assault". In other words, socially-structured differences among people (heterosexual men vs. women in this case) can determine the harm of particular sexual behaviors.[5]

In fact, Polanyi (1995), in her examination of journals kept by American students in a Russian study-abroad program, found precisely this. The young men in the study-abroad program described sexual or potentially sexual encounters as pleasant, romantic, and fun, whereas the young women consistently narrated distressing and unpleasant incidents in which Russian men expected or demanded sexual 'favors' of them, often as a condition for continued contact. As Cameron (1997: 31) argues, the routine enactment of gender is often, perhaps always, subject to the "coerciveness" of institutional contexts; in other words, dominant gender ideologies and power relations often mold and/or inhibit the kinds of gendered identities that women (and men) can perform.[6] Within the Russian study-abroad program that Polanyi describes, sexual harassment functioned as a gatekeeping practice, restricting the kinds of gender identities that could be enacted by the young women. And as a social practice involved in the construction of gender, sexual harassment, like the other kinds of social practices described above, may lead to gender-differentiated acquisition outcomes.

4.2. Sexual harassment and second language acquisition

Given the 'gendered' nature of sexual harassment and its presence in at least one second language learning situation (i.e., the situation described by Polanyi 1995), what are the possible consequences of sexual harassment for the second language learning process? Harvey's (1994) research is suggestive of one possible consequence. In her study of Quechua/Spanish speakers in the Peruvian Andes, Harvey found that young women who studied Spanish in school and consequently had a good passive understanding of the language rarely used it in conversation for fear of ridicule and ostracism from local men. Whether or not this behavior on the part of local men constitutes *sexual* harassment or harassment more generally, its effects are comparable to those produced in some of Polanyi's journal writers, when faced with unwanted sexual advances. One woman, Hilda, described herself as falling silent when she realized her male companion was not listening to her expressions of resistance:

> What happened was I had a meeting with a friend of mine who I had known three years ago, who I thought was a really big blackmarketeer, and this meeting didn't go very well because he decided I was his woman immediately and he started to be extremely demanding of me and telling me who I could see, when I could see them, what my life was going to be like and everything like that. And I was feeling extremely uncomfortable during this exchange, and very disgusted, because I couldn't make myself clear to him ... After a while, I just stopped talking, because I just couldn't make myself be understood, and I was feeling, you know, maybe it was my language, maybe I just didn't know the right words. (Polanyi 1995: 281)

Another woman describes her sexual harassment experience as degrading and humiliating. In contrast to the silence and/or degradation engendered by young women's encounters with Russian men, Polanyi cites the journal of a young man whose pleasant flirtation with a Russian woman results in an evening of increased linguistic fluency: "My Russian felt good, and her ongoing barrage of smiles certainly helped ... We joked and chatted ... My Russian was smooth and flexible ... The evening went wonderfully. We discussed music, art, economics, and film, along with politics" (Polanyi 1995: 281). Target language interactions in which learners are reduced to silence or made to feel humiliated as opposed to those in which learners are encouraged to speak by, among other things, "an ongoing barrage of smiles" clearly influence the type of output learners will produce in a second language (e.g., silence vs. joking and chatting). Furthermore, the degradation and humiliation associated with sexual harassment may create in women negative attitudes towards the target language and culture, which, in turn, may adversely affect their acquisition of the target language.

An even more extreme example of sexual harassment is documented by Talburt and Stewart (1999) in their description of a Spanish study-abroad program. They describe the *constant* sexual harassment experienced by an African-American student, Misheila. In interviews, Misheila makes the following comments (translated from Spanish by the authors):

> I just don't like it. Every time I go out, I mean I can't even walk to the corner. I'm not comfortable going out ... My observation is very negative. For me while I've been in Spain I notice that the African woman is a symbol of sexuality. When I walk in the streets I always receive comments on my skin and sexual commentaries, especially with old men and adolescents between the age of 15 and 20 ... Every day, ... someone says something negative. Yesterday two men asked me if I wanted to go back to their house. Every day it's something like that, every day someone says something negative, something sexual to me, every time I go out. (Talburt and Stewart 1999: 169)

While Talburt and Stewart say nothing about the effects of this kind of harassment on Misheila's acquisition of Spanish, they do say that in an interview conducted after little more than a week in Spain she declared "I'm not in a hurry to ever get back to Spain" (Talburt and Stewart 1999: 168). Clearly, then, her negative experiences in the target culture produced in her negative perceptions of Spanish culture. Moreover, her discomfort in 'going out' may have dramatically diminished her interactions in the target language, at least relative to other students in the study-abroad program who were not victims of sexual harassment in the same way.

Goldstein's (1995, and this volume) study of the linguistic choices of Portuguese immigrant women in Toronto demonstrates more concretely the extent to which the threat of sexual harassment (or more severe acts of violence against women) can severely restrict exposure to target language input. Within the Portuguese community to which Goldstein's subjects belong, men have had greater access to English, either in Portugal as soldiers or in Canada in all-day English classes. Several of Goldstein's women interviewees reported that fathers and husbands prevented them from attending English classes once in Toronto because of the presence of so many men in the classroom. Others reported feelings of fear at the prospect of attending classes at night. Not surprisingly, the immigrant women's lack of language training, and therefore lack of proficiency in English, has had profound consequences for their work opportunities. The factory in which Goldstein conducted her research hired low-paid immigrant women who spoke little English. Furthermore, Goldstein reports that the use of English on the assembly line was associated with significant economic and social costs, because Portuguese was used to signal friendship and solidarity on a production line in which cooperation among workers was crucial to productivity. Thus, we see that women's 'gendered' roles as potential victims of sexual violence in this community restricted their access to English language classes and, concomitantly, their proficiency in English. With minimal proficiency in English their restricted participation in the labor market further discouraged the use and acquisition of English.

While Goldstein's work (and Talburt and Stewart's) is suggestive of the way that threats of sexual harassment may restrict women's access to target language input, Kline (1993) argues that, in some contexts, it may function to improve the literacy skills of women. In an ethnographic investigation of the social practice of literacy in a French study-abroad program, Kline (1993) found that the women in the program read more and read a greater variety of texts than the men. Kline hypothesizes that women took refuge in books and reading because of the sexist and hostile attitudes they encountered in the broader French community: "Of the 19 women in the group, 9 were attacked by French men during the course of the year. Most were grabbed; one was raped" (1993: 178). That is, the women's restricted movement in the target culture – the result of sexist and hostile attitudes and behavior – may have enhanced their literacy skills in French.

Increased exposure to written language in the target language may not be the only 'positive' linguistic consequence of sexual harassment.[7] Polanyi (1995: 285) makes the point that when "faced with complex interpersonal situations" the young women in the Russian study-abroad program were acquiring the linguistic skills to cope. Some reported on learning useful vocabulary for dealing with sexually-harassing situations from Russian women:

> So I learned a few words like "pressure" and – "pressure" and words like that, having to do with being fed up with something, being tired of something, feeling caged in and feeling you don't know what to do, and those are really useful vocabulary words in this country. ... So, I – it was a productive conversation. Not just in the fact that I learned language-wise, but that it helps me when I can talk to someone about these kinds of problems. (Polanyi 1995: 285)

Others reported that their linguistic ability to deal effectively with harassing situations in Russian became a source of pride. Indeed, a recent article that applies conversational analysis to the linguistic accomplishment of sexual refusals (Kitzinger and Frith 1999) attests to the sophisticated linguistic and sociolinguistic competence required for the transactions. Within the framework of conversational analysis, refusals are 'dispreferred' responses and as such require much more interactional work than, for example, acceptances do. Included among the interactional features that characterize refusals are delays (e.g., pauses and hesitations), hedges (e.g., expressions such as *well*, *uh*), palliatives (e.g., apologies, token agreements) and accounts (e.g., explanations, justifications). Polanyi's comments below suggest that it was precisely this more complex interactional competence that was being acquired by the young women in the Russian study-abroad program she describes:

> The women in the Living Abroad Programs are learning to negotiate treacherous waters based on gender-related behavior which requires coping with severe gender related problems ... Rather than discussing music, politics and debating the relative merits of a totally free market based economy, they are learning how to get out of humiliating social encounters, how to interpret the intentions of even polite-seeming educated young men, how to get themselves home in one piece after an evening spent in fending off unwanted advances. They are learning to be more subtle about handling encounters in Russian than they would hope to ever need to be in English. They become skilled at saying "No. Get your hands off

me" to young men whose friendship and help they need to get to know the country well and to do the job they came over to do. (Polanyi 1995: 289)

In spite of the considerable linguistic and sociolinguistic sophistication acquired by these women, the linguistic skills developed in response to sexually harassing situations were not the focus of language proficiency tests. Thus, not surprisingly, Brecht, Davidson, and Ginsberg (1995: 56), in their long-term study of the predictors of language gain in the same Russian study-abroad programs, found that women made fewer gains than men in listening and speaking skills and that men were more likely than women to "cross the crucial divide between Intermediate+ to Advanced level", "which is defined as genuine, although basic functionality in the language."[8] It is important to note that the young women performed as well as the young men on Russian tests before the study-abroad program. The problem, according to Polanyi, is not that the young women were less gifted language learners than the young men but rather that a woman will be treated as a "gendered" individual in a language learning situation, yet "she will be penalized on proficiency examinations which will test her listening and speaking as an ungendered person (i.e., a male)" (Polanyi 1995: 290). Whether women are rendered silent by sexual harassment, whether they develop negative attitudes towards the target culture, whether their access to target language input is thwarted, whether they take refuge in books and reading as a result of a sexually hostile climate, or whether they develop sophisticated skills for effectively dealing with sexual harassment, instructional and evaluation practices that do not address the specificities of their social locations neglect their needs. For example, instruction that does not address the gendered or racial discrimination experienced by many students "negatively affects their potential to meet their goals for study abroad" (Talburt and Stewart 1999: 164). Likewise, proficiency tests that take as their norm men's linguistic activities and practices disadvantage women by missing their important linguistic gains. Put another way, because gendered (and racial) social practices, such as sexual harassment, will have very concrete consequences for the kinds of second language practices and proficiencies that learners develop in a second language, second language instruction and evaluation must address the specificities of learners' social identities. As Polanyi (1995) argues in the context of young women's experiences of sexual harassment:

Educators and those charged with shaping foreign language policy and practice... must face up to our responsibilities to teach and to nourish not the faceless, disembodied abstract student, but the story teller, a person always situated by race, social class, and physical disabilities as well as by gender. (Polanyi 1995: 291)

5. Conclusions

I began this paper by interrogating the notion of the abstract, 'disembodied' learner – a notion that lies at the core of much second language acquisition theory and pedagogy. Relying on recent insights from the work of feminist linguists (Cameron 1995, 1996; Eckert and McConnell-Ginet 1992 a, b, 1999), I have argued that individuals produce themselves (or are produced) as 'gendered' by habitually engaging in the social practices of a speech community that are symbolically and practically associated with masculinities or femininities or some combination thereof. It is not gender per se, then, that interacts with linguistic practices, but rather the complex set of 'gendered' social practices in which individuals participate. The previous section has been suggestive of gender-differentiated linguistic practices produced by sexual harassment. For example, sexual harassment or its threat may result in women's and men's differential access to target language input, differential opportunities for interaction in the target language, and differential attitudes toward the target language and culture. While the precise relationship of such differences to acquisition outcomes is unclear, it is clear that real speakers, like Polanyi's journal-writers, are continually engaged in gendered social practices, which in turn have consequences for second language learning.

Who, then, is the abstract, idealized learner that Rampton claims is ubiquitous in the second language acquisition literature? According to Polanyi (1995: 290), in second language pedagogy, as we have seen, the 'generic' learner is male: "In vocabulary acquisition, choice of lesson materials and content, role play, and testing, male activities and linguistic practices are considered the norm and privileged over female practices." Polanyi's work, then, suggests that the idealized, disembodied second language learner who pervades the second language acquisition literature and informs second language pedagogy is, in fact, abstracted from a very specific learner – a male learner.

Recent scholarship in feminist epistemology has questioned the possibility of objective and disembodied knowledge-seekers. Code (1995: 15), for example, talks about the "constraints that location within specific bodies and sets of circumstances impose upon *all* knowledge-seeking" (emphasis mine). Standpoint feminists go further, arguing that "the authoritative and standard-setting knowledge in Western societies is derived from and tested against an abstracted interpretation of the social experiences of a limited segment of the population: white, middle-class, educated men" (Code 1995: 41). In reflecting on the implications of feminist epistemology for what she terms "epistemically responsible" research methods, Code warns against the danger of false universalism – androcentric research projects that falsely universalize the experiences of particular groups of men. For example, if the idealized language learner with a 'normal' or 'natural' course of development is actually abstracted from a very specific language learner, then the second language pedagogy that is informed by such notions of 'normalness' and 'naturalness' fails many learners (as we have seen in Polanyi's work). Indeed, Code claims that questions of gender-specificity (and class, race, age, economics, and other specificities) belong within every research project dealing, directly or indirectly, with human subjects. Like Code, I would suggest that the study of second language learners needs to be more attentive to the specificities of their social locations as these specificities do not merely modify a 'normal' course of second language development but rather, as Rampton (1991) says, "impregnate" the entire process. Thus, it is not just investigations of 'social factors' that require greater ethnographic and social contextualization, but rather investigations of second language acquisition more generally.

Notes

1.   The distinction between sex and gender was originally an attempt by feminist researchers in the 1970s and 1980s to separate biological categories (sex) from social ones (gender). In more recent years, some feminist theorists (e.g., Bem 1993, 1996; Butler 1990) have argued that both sex and gender are socially constructed. Bem (1996) cites the work of developmental geneticist, Anne Fausto-Sterling, who argues that sex is a continuum that ought to be divided not into just two sexes, but into at least five. The fact that intersexed individuals are regularly assigned to the categories of male or female provides some evidence for the claim that sex, like gender, is socially constructed. See Bing and Bergvall (1996) for further discussion.

2.   Ellis' comments about Asians in Britain may be subject to the same kinds of overgeneralizations that I am claiming characterize comments about men and women in much of the second language acquisition literature.

3.   Freeman and McElhinny (1996: 245), in a survey of language and gender research written explicity for applied linguists and language teachers, favor research questions that take Goodwin's notion of activity as the basic unit of analysis and then ask "when, whether and how men's and women's speech are similar and different" within such a unit.

4.   Ochs (1992) claims that a more direct indexical relationship between language and gender is exemplified by personal pronouns that index the gender of a speaker.

5.   For a fuller discussion of these concepts within the context of sexual assault adjudication processes, see Ehrlich (2001).

6.   Cameron (1997: 30–31) makes these comments in her discussion of Butler's (1990) notion of gender as 'performative.' For many feminist theorists, Cameron included, Butler's formulation affords subjects unbounded agency, ignoring the "institutional contexts and power relations within which gender is being enacted". Arguably, Butler's (1990) discussion of performativity does acknowledge the "rigid regulatory frame" within which gendered identities are produced, but as Cameron points out, often philosophical treatments of this "frame" remain very abstract.

7.   I am somewhat reluctant to label any of the effects of sexual harassment 'positive'; however, it does seem clear that even the most unpleasant of experiences can provide second language learners with opportunities for producing target language output.

8.   Brecht, Davidson, and Ginsberg (1995: 56), in explaining their gender effect, assert that "there are no real differences between men and women in language learning ability" and for this reason propose the following possible interpretations of their results: "gender bias in the testing instruments; a skew in the sample of men and women; and a difference in learning opportunities in-country." In order to investigate the third possibility, the researchers refer to a Ford Foundation-sponsored study of the ethnography of language learning in the study-abroad context.

References

Abrams, Kathy
    1989   Gender discrimination and the transformation of workplace norms. *Vanderbilt Law Review* 1183–1203.

Bacon, Susan
    1992   The relationship between gender, comprehension, processing strategies, and cognitive and affective response in foreign language listening. *Modern Language Journal* 76, 160–178.

Bacon, Susan and Michael Finnemann
    1992   Sex differences in self-reported beliefs about foreign-language learning and authentic oral and written input. *Language Learning* 42, 471–495.

Bem, Sandra
    1993   *The Lenses of Gender*. New Haven, CT: Yale University Press.
    1996   Dismantling gender polarization and compulsory heterosexuality: Should we turn the volume down or up. *Journal of Sex Research* 32, 329–334.

Bing, Janet and Victoria Bergvall
1996   The question of questions: Beyond binary thinking. In Bergvall, Victoria, Janet Bing, and Alice Freed (eds.), *Rethinking Language and Gender Research: Theory and Practice*. London: Longman, 1–30.

Boyle, Joseph
1987   Sex differences in listening vocabulary. *Language Learning* 37, 273–284.

Brecht, Richard, Dan Davidson, and Ralph Ginsberg
1995   Predictors of foreign language gain during study abroad. In Freed, Barbara (ed.), *Second Language Acquisition in a Study Abroad Context*. Amsterdam: Benjamins, 37–66.

Burstall, Claire
1975   Factors affecting foreign language learning: A consideration of some recent research findings. *Language Teaching and Linguistic Abstracts* 8, 5–25.

Burton, Pauline
1994   Women and second language use: An introduction. In Burton, Pauline, Ketaki Kushari Dyson, and Shirley Ardener (eds.), *Bilingual Women: Anthropological Approaches to Second Language Use*. Oxford: Berg, 1–29.

Butler, Judith
1990   *Gender Trouble: Feminism and the Subversion of Identity*. London: Routledge.

Cameron, Deborah
1990a   Demythologizing sociolinguistics. In Joseph, John and Talbot Taylor (eds.), *Ideologies of Language*. London: Routledge, 79–93.
1990b   Why is language a feminist issue? In Cameron, Deborah (ed.), *The Feminist Critique of Language*. London: Routledge, 1–28.
1995   *Verbal Hygiene*. London: Routledge.
1996   The language-gender interface: Challenging co-optation. In Bergvall, Victoria, Janet Bing, and Alice Freed (eds.), *Rethinking Language and Gender Research: Theory and Practice*. London: Longman, 31–53.
1997   Theoretical debates in feminist linguistics: Questions of sex and gender. In Wodak, Ruth (ed.), *Gender and Discourse*. London: Sage, 21–36.

Code, Lorraine
1995   How do we know? Questions of method in feminist practice. In Burt, Sandra and Lorraine Code (eds.), *Changing Methods: Feminists Transforming Practice*. Peterborough, Ontario: Broadview Press, 13–43.

Crawford, Mary
    1995   *Talking Difference: On Gender and Language.* London: Sage.

Eckert, Penny and Sally McConnell-Ginet
    1992a   Think practically and look locally: Language and gender as community-based practice. *Annual Review of Anthropology* 21, 461–490.

    1992b   Communities of practice: Where language, gender and power all live. In Hall, Kira, Mary Bucholtz, and Birch Moonwomon (eds.), *Locating Power: Proceedings of the Second Berkeley Women and Language Conference.* Berkeley: University of California Press, 89–99.

    1999   New generalizations and explanations in language and gender research. *Language in Society* 28, 185–201.

Ehrlich, Susan
    1997   Gender as social practice: Implications for second language acquisition. *Studies in Second Language Acquisition* 19, 421–446.

    2001   *Representing Rape: Language and Sexual Consent.* London: Routledge.

Ehrman, Madeline and Rebecca Oxford
    1989   Effects of sex differences, career choice, and psychological type on adults' language learning strategies. *Modern Language Journal* 73, 1–13.

    1990   Adult language learning styles and strategies in an intensive training setting. *Modern Language Journal* 74, 311–327.

Eisenstein, Miriam
    1982   A study of social variation in adult second language acquisition. *Language Learning* 32, 367–392.

Ekstrand, Lars
    1980   Sex differences in second language learning? Empirical studies and a discussion of related findings. *International Review of Applied Psychology* 29, 205–259.

Ellis, Rod
    1994   *The Study of Second Language Acquisition.* Oxford: Oxford University Press.

Ellison v. Brady
    1991   924 F.2d 872, 878–81 (9th Cir.1991)

Farhady, Hossein
    1982   Measures of language proficiency from the learner's perspective. *TESOL Quarterly* 16, 43–59.

Freed, Alice
   1996   Language and gender research in an experimental setting. In Bergvall, Vic-
            toria, Janet Bing, and Alice Freed (eds.), *Rethinking Language and Gender
            Research: Theory and Practice*. London: Longman, 54–76.

Freed, Alice and Alice Greenwood
   1996   Women, men, and type of talk: What makes the difference? *Language in
            Society* 25, 1–26.

Freeman, Rebecca and Bonnie McElhinny
   1996   Language and gender. In McKay, Sandra and Nancy Hornberger (eds.), *So-
            ciolinguistics and Language Teaching*. Cambridge: Cambridge University
            Press, 218–280.

Gal, Susan
   1978   Peasant men can't get wives: Language change and sex roles in a bilingual
            community. *Language in Society* 7, 1–16.

Gardner, Robert and Wallace Lambert
   1972   *Attitudes and Motivation in Second Language Learning*. Rowley, MA:
            Newbury House.

Goldstein, Tara
   1995   "Nobody is talking bad": Creating community and claiming power on the
            production lines. In Hall, Kira and Mary Bucholtz (eds.), *Gender Articu-
            lated: Language and the Socially Constructed Self*. New York: Routledge,
            375–400.

Goodwin, Marjorie
   1990   *He-Said-She-Said: Talk as Social Organization among Black Children*.
            Bloomington, IN: Indiana University Press.

Harvey, Penelope
   1994   The presence and absence of speech in the communication of gender. In
            Burton, Pauline, Ketaki Kushari Dyson, and Shirley Ardener (eds.), *Bilin-
            gual Women: Anthropological Approaches to Second Language Use*. Ox-
            ford: Berg, 44–64.

Hill, Jane
   1987   Women's speech in modern Mexicano. In Philips, Susan, Susan Steele, and
            Christine Tanz (eds.), *Language, Gender & Sex in Comparative Perspec-
            tive*. Cambridge: Cambridge University Press, 121–160.

Hyde, Janet and Marcia Linn
   1988   Gender differences in verbal ability: A meta-analysis. *Psychological Bulletin* 104, 53–69.

Kitzinger, Celia and Hannah Frith
   1999   Just say no? The use of conversation analysis in developing a feminist perspective on sexual refusal. *Discourse & Society* 10, 293–316.

Kitzinger, Celia and Alison Thomas
   1995   Sexual harassment: A discursive approach. In Wilkinson, Sue and Celia Kitzinger (eds.), *Feminism and Discourse: Psychological Perspectives.* London: Sage, 32–48.

Kline, Rebecca
   1993   *The social practice of literacy in a program of study abroad.* Ph.D. dissertation, Pennsylvania State University, State College.

Kramsch, Claire and Linda von Hoene
   1995   The dialogic emergence of difference: Feminist explorations in foreign language learning and teaching. In Stanton, Domna and Abigail Stewart (eds.), *Feminisms in the Academy.* Ann Arbor, MI: University of Michigan Press, 330–357.

Larsen-Freeman, Diane and Michael Long
   1991   *An Introduction to Second Language Acquisition Research.* London: Longman.

Maccoby, Eleanor and Carol Jacklin
   1974   *The Psychology of Sex Differences.* Stanford, CA: Stanford University Press.

Macaulay, Ronald
   1978   The myth of female superiority in language. *Journal of Child Language* 5, 353–363.

Maltz, Daniel and Ruth Borker
   1982   A cultural approach to male-female miscommunication. In Gumperz, John (ed.), *Language and Social Identity.* Cambridge: Cambridge University Press, 196–216.

Marecek, Jean
   1995   Psychology and feminism: Can this relationship be saved? In Stanton, Domna and Abigail Stewart (eds.), *Feminisms in the Academy.* Ann Arbor, MI: University of Michigan Press, 101–132.

Medicine, Bea
　1987　The role of American Indian women in cultural continuity and transition. In Penfield, Joyce (ed.), *Women and Language in Transition*. Albany, NY: State University of New York Press, 159–166.

Ochs, Elinor
　1992　Indexing Gender. In Duranti, Alessandro and Charles Goodwin (eds.), *Rethinking Context: Language as an Interactive Phenomenon*. Cambridge: Cambridge University Press, 335–338.

O'Malley, J. Michael and Anna Chamot
　1990　*Learning Strategies in Second Language Acquisition*. Cambridge: Cambridge University Press.

Oxford, Rebecca
　1993　Gender differences in styles and strategies for language learning: What do they mean? Should we pay attention? In Alatis, James (ed.), *Strategic Interaction and Language Acquisition: Theory, Practice, and Research*. Washington, DC: Georgetown University Press, 541–557.
　1994　La différence continue ... Gender differences in second/foreign language learning styles and strategies. In Sunderland, Jane (ed.), *Exploring Gender: Questions and Implications for English Language Education*. London: Prentice Hall, 140–147.

Oxford, Rebecca and Martha Nyikos
　1989　Variables affecting choice of language learning strategies by university students. *Modern Language Journal* 73, 219–300.

Oxford, Rebecca, Martha Nyikos and Madeline Ehrman
　1988　Vive la différence? Reflections on sex differences in use of language learning strategies. *Foreign Language Annals* 21, 321–329.

Polanyi, Livia
　1995　Language learning and living abroad: Stories from the field. In Freed, Barbara (ed.), *Second Language Acquisition in a Study Abroad Context*. Amsterdam: Benjamins, 271–291.

Rampton, Ben
　1991　Second language learners in a stratified multilingual setting. *Applied Linguistics* 12, 229–248.

Schiffrin, Deborah
　1996　Narrative as self-portrait: Sociolinguistic constructions of identity. *Language in Society* 25, 167–203.

Schumann, John
   1976   Second language acquisition: The pidginization hypothesis. *Language Learning*, 26, 391–408.

Siegal, Meryl
   1994   Second-language learning, identity and resistance: White women studying Japanese in Japan. In Bucholtz, Mary, A.C. Liang, Laurel Sutton, and Caitlin Hines (eds.), *Cultural Performances: Proceedings of the Third Berkeley Women and Language Conference. April 8–10, 1994*. Berkeley, CA: University of California, Berkeley Women and Language Group, 642–650.
   1996   The role of learner subjectivity in second language sociolinguistic competency: Western women learning Japanese. *Applied Linguistics* 17, 356–382.

Spolsky, Bernard
   1989   *Conditions for Second Language Learning*. Oxford: Oxford University Press.

Steinem, Gloria
   1983   *Outrageous Acts and Everday Rebellions*. New York: Holt, Rinehart and Winston.

Talburt, Susan and Melissa Stewart
   1999   What's the subject of study abroad?: Race, gender, and "Living Culture." *The Modern Language Journal* 83, 163–175.

Thomas, Alison and Celia Kitzinger
   1997   Sexual harassment: Reviewing the field. In Thomas, Alison and Celia Kitzinger (eds.), *Sexual Harassment: Contemporary Feminist Perspectives*. Buckingham, England: Open University Press, 1–18.

Thorne, Barrie
   1990   Children and gender: Constructions of difference. In: Rhode, Deborah (ed.), *Theoretical Perspectives on Sexual Difference*. New Haven, CT: Yale University Press, 100–113.

Wenden, Anita
   1991   *Learner Strategies for Learner Autonomy*. Englewood Cliffs, NJ: Prentice Hall.

Wenden, Anita and Joan Rubin
   1987   *Learner Strategies for Language Learning*. Englewood Cliffs, NJ: Prentice Hall.

West, Candace and Don Zimmerman
  1987   Doing gender. *Gender and Society* 1, 25–51.

Zentella, Ana Celia
  1987   Language and female identity in the Puerto Rican community. In Penfield, Joyce (ed.), *Women and Language in Transition*. Albany, NY: State University of New York Press, 167–179.

2. Negotiation and performance of gender in multilingual contexts

"How am I to become a woman in an American vein?": Transformations of gender performance in second language learning

Aneta Pavlenko

1. Introduction

Recently, I have argued elsewhere that successful second language (L2) learn-ing by adult immigrants involves, above all, agency, and, as a consequence, 'discursive assimilation', (re)positioning and self-translation (Pavlenko 1998; Pavlenko and Lantolf 2000). 'Self-translation', in this view, refers to the rein-terpretation of one's subjectivities in order to position oneself in new commu-nities of practice and to 'mean' in the new environment since "the person can only be a meaningful entity, both to himself or herself and to others, by being 'read' in terms of the discourses available in that society" (Burr 1995: 142). In this paper, I address one aspect of this discursive (re)construction of iden-tity – transformations of gender performance – situating it within a language socialization perspective that views second language learning as an essentially social process, whereby the relationship between the learner and the learning context is dynamic and constantly changing (Peirce 1995).

Since gender identity is a social and cultural construct, societal conceptions of normative masculinities and femininities may differ cross-culturally and thus lead to modifications of previous models according to the new circum-stances. Cultural changes in immigrants' and refugees' individual and commu-nity understandings of gender roles are well documented in the literature on immigrant women (Buijs 1993; Gabaccia 1994; Gordon 1995; Hegde 1998; Lieblich 1993) and refugee communities (Camino and Krulfeld 1994; Cole, Espin, and Rothblum 1992; Ledgerwood 1990). Krulfeld (1994) suggests that immigrants' gender concepts, roles, and behaviors are most likely to change in the areas of greatest articulation within the dominant society (for immigrants in the United States, for instance, this change may entail a reconceptualization of the role of gender in education and employment). The modification will also be mediated by individuals' race, ethnicity, class, and sexuality, as well as by gender ideologies in the communities in question. The changes in gender roles in the process of cultural adaptation may lead to tensions and difficulties in relations between men and women in the minority community, between spouses, between parents and children, and to individual concerns and anxieties with regard to professional and social status (Benson 1994; Gordon 1995; Krulfeld 1994; Ledgerwood 1990; Lieblich 1993).

The study of gender as an important constitutive aspect of immigrant and refugee experience is a relatively new field: it came to light only in the last decade under the influence of feminist and postmodernist reconceptualizations of history and sociology. So far, changes in individual and community views of gender roles have been explored with regard to available subject positions, intimate relationships, parent-child relationships, and employment (Buijs 1993; Camino and Krulfeld 1994; Cole, Espin, and Rothblum 1992; Gabaccia 1994; Gordon 1995; Hegde 1998; Ledgerwood 1990; Lieblich 1993). While acknowledging the importance of language mastery for assimilation in a new society, none of the studies so far have considered language learning as a separate area of concern. On the other hand, existing literature on second language acquisition, bilingualism, and gender (Burton, Dyson, and Ardener 1994; Ehrlich 1997) does focus on language learning and use as mediated by gender, but has not yet considered what possible transformations may occur in discourses of L2 users as they attempt to occupy new gendered subject positions. Thus, while acknowledging other important aspects of gender transformations, a discussion of which can be found in the literature on immigrant experience, my study focuses on changes in the discursive performance of gender in the process of second language socialization.

2.   Theoretical framework

The present work is informed by feminist poststructuralist perspectives, which emphasize the constitutive role of language, suggesting that it is the speech communities that produce gendered styles, while individuals make accommodations to those styles in the process of producing themselves as gendered subjects (Cameron 1996). As a result,

> who one is is always an open question with a shifting answer depending upon the positions made available within one's own and others' discursive practices and within those practices, the stories through which we make sense of our own and others' lives. (Davies and Harré 1990: 46)

From this viewpoint, it comes as no surprise that a transition to a different culture, a different society, may involve a change in how one views and performs gender. This is not to say that gender performance within a particular society is predetermined, but to point out that the range of subjectivities validated within each community, subculture, or culture is ultimately limited – even though constantly negotiated and reconstituted. The assumption of a limited range of available subjectivities is of crucial importance here, as a theory of multiple, fragmented, and fluid identities that does not distinguish between a range of discourses and subjectivities available within and between cultures, is not particularly helpful and informative. Assuming that such a range exists – and that it may not coincide between the two communities in question – allows us to explain why transitions between cultures may result in changes of ideologies, discursive practices, and meanings allocated to various categories, in particular, the category of gender. Border-crossers may find themselves in a situation where their previous subjectivities cannot be coherently and/or legitimately produced and understood and, thus, appear discontinued, while the subjects resist or produce new social identities through repeated performances of various acts that constitute a particular type of identity (Butler 1990; Cameron 1996; Pavlenko 1998). This dilemma is illustrated in a well-known memoir by Eva Hoffman (1989), *Lost in Translation: A Life in a New Language*, where the Polish-born protagonist is informed by her fellow classmates at Rice University: "This is a society in which you are who you think you are. Nobody gives you your identity here, you have to reinvent yourself every day" (p. 160). She then proceeds to ask:

> ... I can't figure out how this is done. You just say what you are and everyone believes you? That seems like a confidence trick to me, and not one I think I can pull off. Still, somehow, invent myself I must. But how do I choose from identity options available all around me? (Hoffman 1989: 160)

Alice Kaplan (1993), the author of another memoir, *French Lessons*, suggests that it is the possibility of inventing and adopting a different identity that may prompt people to move away from the culture that doesn't "name them" (p. 209). It is critical, however, to underscore that one's subjectivities are not entirely a product of one's own free choice and agency: they are co-constructed with others who can accept or reject them and impose alternative identities instead. Often, depending on the power balance, it is others who define who we are, putting us in a position where we have to either accept or resist and negotiate these definitions. In particular, language behavior that does not conform to the community norms is frequently seen as marked. This attribution of new meanings to one's speech acts and behaviors is illustrated in stories told by a well-known linguist, Anna Wierzbicka (1997), who came to Australia from Poland as an adult only to find out that her ways of performing femininity, being a mother or a daughter, may not carry the same value and elicit the same response in her new environment:

> ... when I tried to soothe my children in the first weeks of their lives with anxious Polish invocations of '*Córeńko! Córeńko!*' (lit. 'little daughter! little daughter!') my husband pointed out how quaint it sounds from the point of view of a native speaker of English to solemnly address a new-born baby as 'little daughter.' (Wierzbicka 1997:117)

> ... when I was talking on the phone, from Australia, to my mother in Poland (15,000 km away), with my voice loud and excited, carrying much further than is customary in an Anglo conversation, my husband would signal to me: 'Don't shout!' (Wierzbicka 1997: 119)

Individuals engaged in non-standard speech acts may oftentimes be seen as outsiders, which is, ironically, what happens to Hoffman (1989) who goes back to Poland twenty years after her family left the country. Meeting with her childhood friends, she runs into a series of misunderstandings as life stories are not always easily interpretable across cultures and dynamics of conversation may be entirely different. Her interaction patterns give her away: "Leave her alone, she's American," says one of her friends to another, irritated by Eva's urge to look for solutions, a speech act which has no appeal in Eastern European contexts (Hoffman 1989: 256).

Based on a theoretical framework which understands identities as dynamic, fluid, multiple, and socially constructed, in what follows I will demonstrate that linguistic and cultural transitions of immigrants and expatriates represent a meaningful and fertile site for exploring and problematizing the relationship between language, gender, and identity. To look at ways in which second language learners negotiate and transform gender performances in discourse, I will examine a corpus of first person narratives by L2 learners, which includes, but is not limited to, cross-cultural memoirs, a genre that recently came to attention in the field of second language acquisition (SLA) as a legitimate source of data, complementary to more traditional empirical paradigms (Kramsch and Lam 1999; McGroarty 1998; Pavlenko 1998, 2001, in press a; Pavlenko and Lantolf 2000; Schumann 1997; Young 1999).

Three terms will be used interchangeably to refer to the individuals discussed in the present study: 'L2 learners', 'L2 users' and '(adult) bilinguals'.

The first term, traditionally used in the field of SLA, underscores the fact that all the individuals in question have learned their second language later than the first. The second term emphasizes that all of them are legitimate and regular users of their second language. Finally, the term 'bilinguals' is used in agreement with Grosjean's (1998) functional definition of bilinguals as individuals who use both languages on a regular basis, regardless of whether they are equally fluent in both.

3.   Research design and methodology

The corpus of 30 L2 learning stories examined in the present study consists of two types of first person narratives: (1) 25 cross-cultural autobiographies which focus on second language learning and use, and (2) 5 oral narratives about second language learning. Three criteria guided the selection of narratives in the present study. First of all, I have limited the corpus to stories which discuss both second language learning and use and the relationship between language and gender. Second, to acknowledge social, linguistic, and cultural constraints on life-storytelling (see Linde 1993), I limited the corpus to stories written or told in English in the US (with the exception of two narratives I have elicited in Russian and two essays by Wierzbicka 1985, 1997, who resides in Australia). Third, all memoirs in the corpus were published between 1973 and 2000, as 1973 is considered to be the turning point for modern women's autobiography, coinciding with the strengthening of the feminist movement, which prompted women to create new spaces for themselves and to tell stories previously considered untellable (Heilbrun 1988).

The first set of narratives in the corpus consists of 12 book-length cross-cultural autobiographies (Alvarez 1998; Davidson 1993; Dorfman 1998; Hoffman 1989; Kaplan 1993; Kingston 1975; Lvovich 1997; Mar 1999; Mori 1997; Ogulnick 1998; Rodriguez 1982; Watson 1995) and 12 autobiographic essays (Baranczak 1990; Brintrup 2000; Chambers 2000; Hirsch 1994; Kim 2000; Lee 2000; Mori 2000; Reyn 2000; Rosario 2000; Saine 2000; Wierzbicka 1985, 1997). In addition, I will refer to a biography of a Polish-American writer Jerzy Kosinski, based on multiple interviews with the writer (Sloan 1996).

To offset the written nature of the first set of narratives, I supplement it with the second set of five oral life-story interviews, four of which I conducted myself. The first two second language learning narratives, elicited in English, are part of a larger corpus of L2 learning narratives I collected in the Summer of 1998 at Cornell University. None of the informants in the larger study were asked about gender issues, and the two participants, Christina and Dominik, were the only ones who raised these issues spontaneously. Christina is a Polish-English bilingual, who learned English as a teenager and came to the US in her twenties. Several years later, she became a literature scholar with an Ivy League Ph.D., feeling much more comfortable in English than in her native Polish. Dominik is a Hungarian-Slovak-English trilingual, who learned English upon arrival in the US three years prior to the interview; unlike Christina, he is planning to return to his native Slovak Republic after completing graduate study in the US. The other two interviews were originally conducted for another study in Russian with two Russian-English bilingual women, Marina and Natasha, in the Fall of 1999 at Cornell University. Both women studied some English in school in Russia, but mainly learned it in their twenties, upon arrival in the US, where they reside now. Natasha works in a research facility and Marina is in the process of completing her doctoral degree in psychology. The code-switching that occurred when the two women raised gender issues in their Russian narratives is extremely interesting for the purposes of this study. The fifth interview comes from a study conducted with a peasant Laotian woman, Pha, by Gordon (1995). Pha arrived in the US as a refugee and started learning English as an adult. Her interview was chosen in order to represent a voice of a working-class individual, whose socioeconomic circumstances differ from those of the other informants.

Based on the type of language socialization experienced by the narrators, the two sets of narratives can be subdivided into three categories: immigrant, ethnic, and expatriate language memoirs. Immigrant autobiographies include stories of informants who came to their new country and learned their second language – in which they now work and live – as teenagers and adults (Christina, Marina, Natasha, Pha; Alvarez, Baranczak, Brintrup, Dorfman, Hirsch, Hoffman, Kim, Kosinski, Lvovich, Mori, Reyn, Saine, Wierzbicka). Ethnic lifewriting is represented by the work of Chambers, Kingston, Lee, Mar, Rodriguez, and Rosario, who came to the US as children and/or grew up in ethnic neighborhoods and discuss a different language learning path – a transition from a minority to a majority language. It is important to note here that regardless of whether a particular person was born in the US or not, hyphenated identity terms, such as Japanese-American or Russian-American, will be used in the discussion to acknowledge the participants' own current identifications. Finally, to provide a contrast to the theme of 'Americanization', I included the interview with Dominik, who is getting ready to go back to his native country, and narratives of temporary expatriates who live in the US but had made linguistic journeys into French (Kaplan, Watson) and Japanese (Davidson, Ogulnick).

Three questions will guide my analysis of the corpus in the present study: (1) what can personal narratives tell us about possible stages in the process of the negotiation of gender identities in second language socialization; (2) what are the key sites of transformations of gender performance; (3) what linguistic changes take place in the transformation process. In order to carry out the data analysis, I first identified three types of references in the corpus: (1) references to the relationship between language and gender; (2) explicit attempts at repositioning, involving statements such as "I see myself as X" or "I no longer consider myself to be Y"; (3) implicit alignments with particular story participants or with the members of the audience. The length of references varied from one sentence to one thematically bound episode. These references were then coded and analyzed for information about particularly salient sites of transformation of gender identity, and the links between language and gender. The main analytical concept used to analyze the data in the present study was *positioning*, which, following Davies and Harré (1990), is viewed as the process by which individuals are situated as observably and subjectively coherent participants in the story lines. The narrative nature of the data allows me to illuminate the practice of reflective or self-positioning whereby storytellers signal, either explicitly or implicitly, that they occupy a particular subject position. The process of self-positioning is seen as closely linked to ways in which dominant ideologies of language and gender position the narrators and to ways in which the narrators internalize or resist these positionings. Two aspects of positioning will be emphasized in the study: the multiplicity of subject positions occupied by an individual at any given moment, and their temporality, whereby identity work is seen as an ongoing process. Only qualitative results of the analysis will be presented below, as quantitative information about the number of references to particular issues would be meaningless in this type of narrative inquiry, which sees any experience shared by two or more individuals as no longer fully idiosyncratic.

Three limitations of the present study need to be acknowledged before we proceed any further. To begin with, recognizing that different speech communities have different life-storytelling conventions (see Linde 1993), I chose to focus on stories told or written in English in the US. This choice limits my discussion to discursive performances of gender in American English, and leaves the question of how gendered subjectivities may be constructed in narratives in other languages to further investigation. Another important limitation is the fact that, with the exception of a few expatriate narratives, the L2 learners and users in the study are discussing their socialization into a society viewed as dominant where power relations between the majority and minority language are unequal. It is quite possible that the stories told in other cultures and in other languages may paint a very different picture of language socialization and transformations of gender performance. Finally, most of the narratives in question are written or told by relatively successful middle-class individuals who had successfully acquired English. While the narratives of Americans who had attempted to learn another language allow us some glimpses into the nature of 'failure' in L2 learning, it is a failure experienced by speakers of a powerful language. Only further study could illuminate the experiences of immigrants who did not achieve a similar success in L2 learning and/or positioning themselves in their second language.

Despite these limitations, which I hope will be overcome in future research, I am positive that examination of first person L2 learning narratives offers a productive way to expand the study of SLA. In the present chapter, these narratives will allow me to examine how gender subjectivities, shaped by ideologies of language and gender, may be questioned, challenged, negotiated, and restructured in the process of second language socialization.

4.   Transformations of gender in second language learning: data analysis and discussion

4.1. Language learning stories as a gendered genre

The analysis of the narratives in the corpus suggests, first of all, that language learning stories are in themselves gendered performances (for a detailed discussion of language memoirs as a gendered genre, see Pavlenko 2001). It is not accidental that 24 narratives in the corpus come from women and only 6 from men (Baranczak, Dorfman, Kosinski, Rodriguez, Watson; plus an interview with Dominik). Despite a careful search and a policy of including all memoirs which had a discussion of language and gender issues in at least one chapter (for books) or section (for essays), I was unable to locate any more relevant male language memoirs than the ones in the corpus. Similarly, except for Dominik, none of the male L2 learners I have interviewed about their learning invoked gender issues in their stories. In view of the theoretical framework assumed in the present chapter and volume, the 'unequal gendering' of language learning stories is easy to explain: gender is a category that is more visible for its less privileged members, just as we would expect the category of race to be more widely discussed by non-white writers. It also appears that the literary performance of contemporary American femininity – but not masculinity – is predicated on an explicit questioning of ideologies of gender and selfhood (Pavlenko 2001). In other words, "to be a woman in an American vein" may entail, among other things, questioning the meaning of being a woman.

The 'gendered' nature of L2 learning stories which portray the relationship between language and gender explains why my subsequent discussion appears to privilege women: they are the ones that talk about the issue explicitly and in-depth. Whenever possible, however, I will also attempt to comment on the negotiation of masculinities in L2 socialization, since the scarcity of discussions of the role of gender in L2 learning by male learners does not in any way suggest that gender as a system of social relations does not play a role in their learning experiences. Rather, as pointed out above, this silence indicates that at present the role of gender – unlike that of race, class, or culture – is obscured by the privileged ways in which male learners are often positioned (Polanyi 1995; for a discussion of a male L2 learner's trajectory, see Teutsch-Dwyer's chapter).

In what follows I will examine what L2 learning stories can tell us about transformations of gender in second language socialization. I will start my discussion by looking at ways in which dominant ideologies of language and gender are questioned in the L2 learners' narratives and proceed to look at the strategies of assimilation and resistance adopted by the narrators. Then I will single out four key sites, where, according to the narratives in the corpus, the traditional gender expectations are most often questioned, negotiated, and contested: intimate relationships, parent-child relationships, friendships, and work places. I will also discuss a number of ways in which linguistic devices contribute to changes in gender performance: from changes in pitch and voice quality (see also Ohara's chapter), to modifications of the lexicon, speech acts, and discursive repertoires. I will conclude by summarizing the results of the study and discussing its implications for further research on language and identity, and L2 learning and gender.

4.2. Questioning gender ideologies

Smith (1987) points out that every woman who writes autobiography ends up interrogating the prevailing ideology of gender, if only implicitly. This suggestion is fully borne out by the autobiographies in question where women – and only rarely men – are preoccupied with gender issues, in particular with social and cultural constraints on the construction of femininities which become particularly visible in transition. Due to the unique positioning of their authors, who often see themselves 'between two worlds', cross-cultural life stories question gender in unparalleled ways. It is not simply ideologies of gender that are questioned in the narratives, but ideologies of 'gender and X': gender and race, gender and ethnicity, gender and class, gender and culture, and, most notably for the present study, gender and language. The bilingualism and bicultu-ralism of the authors also allows them to examine things through multiple lenses, thus, deessentializing femininity, splintering the force of both their native and North American cultural authority, and reinventing and reimagining themselves in the process.

The depiction of gender inequality which dominated their primary language socialization is at the heart of a number of memoirs written by Asian-American and Latina women (Kim 2000; Kingston 1975; Lee 2000; Mar 1999; Mori 1997, 2000; Rosario 2000). The two Chinese-American authors, Maxine Hong Kingston (1975) and Elaine Mar (1999), separated by a quarter of a century, nevertheless share a memory of ways in which their language denied them their subjectivity. Mar (1999) recalls how her mother justified signing her school re-port cards with the father's name: "You always sign the man's name. It's the only one with meaning" (p. 160). Similarly, the Chinese-American protagonist in Kingston's (1975) memoir learns that "there is a Chinese word for the fe-male *I* – which is 'slave'" (p. 56). Not only the subjectivity may be denied to women in particular communities, they may also be pressured into submission and silence. "I hated having to limit my comments on politics in conversation with men," recalls Nelly Rosario (2000: 162), a Dominican-American. "I con-tinue to feel unsafe in Japan because of the way women are embarrassed or pressured into silence," admits a Japanese-American Kyoko Mori (1997: 243). For some women, such primary socialization, accompanied by ways in which the majority society continuously ignores Asian-Americans and Latinos, re-sults in a "subconscious, lingering sense that I, as a female, am not good enough" (Lee 2000:137). Many, like Alvarez (1998), Kingston (1975), Mori (1997), or Rosario (2000), link this internalized sense of oppression to the lan-guage of their childhood, to particular forms of politeness they were forced to use, to turns they were never allowed to take in conversations:

> I've been told that in Spanish my voice takes on a softer, pleasant, sometimes subservient timbre. The language does represent for me love and constraint, passion, warmth, and at times self-oppression. Self-oppression from obligatory Sunday mass, from parents with many rules for children growing up in New York, from a country where children and women are told too often to shut up. (Rosario 2000: 163)

It would be highly misleading, however, to say that it is particular languages, or especially first languages, that are blamed and criticized in the narratives in the corpus. Rather, the authors take on the ideologies they perceive as oppressive and the links between language, gender, and identity created by these ideologies. In doing so, they create new hybrid identities and new master narratives that were previously untellable in either language, in either community. Thus, a Panamanian-American, Veronica Chambers (2000), deconstructs the links between language, gender, and race, conventionalized in her racially mixed New York City neighborhood and proclaims herself to be a Latinegra, fluent in both English and Spanish:

> When I spoke only English, I was the daughter, the little girl. As I began to learn Spanish, I became something more – an *hermanita*, a sister-friend, a Panamanian homegirl who could hang with the rest of them. ... When Puerto-Rican girls talked about me in front of my face, looking at my dark skin and assuming that I couldn't understand, I would playfully throw out, "*Oye, sabes que yo entiendo?*" Being *Latinegra* – black and Latin, has become a sort of a hidden weapon, something that you can't see at first glance. I know that many people look at my dark skin and don't expect me to be fluent in anything but homegirl. (Chambers 2000: 24)

Similarly, Mori (2000), born into an upper-middle class Japanese family, problematizes the common portrayal of 'foreignness' as a "combination of ethnicity and poverty" (Mar 1999: 158), so often imposed on the newcomers. Viewing the conventionalized portrayal of immigrant women as 'othering' she refuses to tell the stories that people are waiting to hear:

> The stories ... of a brave but disadvantaged immigrant woman trying to understand an unfamiliar language, missing the customs and the foods of the homeland, overcoming one "culture shock" after another – have nothing to do with me. I resent being expected to tell such stories because I have none to tell and also because, even when they are the true stories for many first-generation immigrant women, there is something self-congratulatory or condescending in most listeners' attitudes. (Mori 2000: 139)

Moreover, it is not only immigrants, many of whom have no choice but to engage with the dominant culture, that recognize the role of gender as a powerful category shaping one's language learning and use. Similar critical questioning takes place in the narratives of temporary expatriates. "I have gone through most of my life with very little conscious awareness of how gender was affecting what and how I was learning," writes American scholar Karen Ogulnick:

> After first being immersed in Japanese language and culture for 2 years in 1987, I experienced changes in the ways I felt, acted, and perceived myself as a woman. ... My desire to be accepted and recognized as a speaker of Japanese overpowered

any subconscious resistance I may have had to complying with what I perceived as submissive female behavior. (Ogulnick 1998: 135–6)

Interestingly, social pressure makes Ogulnick conform despite her apprehensions about traditional gender roles, prescribed for Japanese women, and soon she finds herself speaking *onna rashiku* 'like a woman'. This experience makes her reconsider not only ways in which ideologies of gender work in Japan but also ways in which they had shaped her identity in America:

> ... my vantage point, not only as a white, English-speaking American but also a *woman*, in between cultures, sharpened my insight into how everyday language behaviors create and sustain larger social inequities. ... My diary gave me a tool to look within myself, to try to understand more deeply how I had been socialized to be a woman in my white, American, Jewish, working-class subculture and how I was learning to speak "like a woman" in Japan. (Ogulnick 1998: 136)

Another temporary visitor, Dominik, complains about incompatible gender ideologies of America and Slovakia and the resulting feeling that he is denied certain means of self-expression and, as a result, has to suppress a part of his identity. What is interesting about his comments is that Dominik questions neither his own beliefs, nor those in his L1 community, but rather the discourses of gender and sexual harassment of the country in which he temporarily resides:

> before I came here, lot of Americans warned me that ... that American culture, that these 'sexual harassment' rules, and I am, I am the type of person who jokes most of the time about sex, I mean, that's part of like ... culture ... back home, and I, I, I just feel that here, because I, I have to repress my natural personality, my natural thinking about sex ... I mean, I mean, I like to joke about it, and ... I just feel about two years, I just lost ... part of myself, or kind of like, sense for humor, as I was used to ... I just don't express myself in the same way, as, as, as I am used to ... (Interview with the author, Summer 1998)

Finally, I would like to point out that examination of gender ideologies is not restricted to narratives of middle-class educated women fluent in English and familiar with feminist discourses. Gordon's (1995) study shows that similar questioning takes place in the mind of Pha, a peasant Laotian woman who came to the US with her husband and children, nine years prior to the interview. While Pha had little if any exposure to feminism in educational contexts, her everyday interactions in Philadelphia prompted her to reappraise women's home-centered and silent role in Lao culture. In an interview with the researcher, Pha portrays this role not as women's choice but as a means by which men control women in Laos: "I am your husband. I go anywhere. I do everything. You cannot control me" (Gordon 1995: 55).

Thus, it appears that despite vast differences in the subjects' experiences and learning trajectories, many women in the study share the need to reconsider gender expectations they had lived – or continue to live – by. I suggest that this critical examination of ideologies of gender may constitute the first step in the process of transformation of gender performance.

4.3. Making choices: assimilation versus resistance

Facing new femininities and masculinities, often tied to new ways of self-expression, L2 learners may opt either for assimilation or resistance to new subjectivities. The desire to assimilate to the new community may be prompted by negative attitudes to gender ideologies and discursive practices of one's native speech community, where the language 'doesn't name' the individual or labels her wrongly, while the culture devalues her and limits her options of self-expression. Such is the choice consciously made by many L2 users in the corpus, some of whom explicitly say that they perceive English as liberating (see also McMahill's chapter). "We could go places in English we never could in Spanish," states Alvarez (1998: 64) on her own behalf and that of her sisters. Similarly, Rosario (2000: 163) sees her English as "much more liberating" than Spanish which she links to the silencing of women and children. Other narrators link their choice to identity options available in the new community. Christina, a Polish-English bilingual informant, starts talking about her attitudes toward Poland, and, suddenly, turns to gender, indicating that her disassociation from Poland may be 'gender-based':

> I have no natural desire to go back, no natural desire at all ... uhm ... to be Polish and to live in Poland, no connection to the land ... I have connections to my family but they are of a completely different nature, they seem to be unconnected to ... to the country ... uhm ... the sense of what a woman is supposed to do with her life ... and even though my mother is pretty independent and has an intellectual job, still, I have a sense that I wouldn't be ... uhm ... gender-free. Even here I am not really gender-free, to any extent, I am probably much less independent than most American women ... uhm ... but still ... I am ... more in control, I suppose, of what I do with my life than I would in Poland ... uhm ... I really would be an old maid in Poland by now, whereas here my choice to ... uhm ... choice, it's again a ... a problematic word ... but the fact that I am, I don't know, not married or don't have a family ... uhm ... at my age is not a problem ... (Interview with the author, Summer 1998)

Similarly, Mori (1997, 2000), who fled Japan at the age of twenty, describes her relocation to America as an escape from the restrictions of Japanese women's language and from the roles prescribed for women:

> There was no future in Japan for a woman from my upper-middle class milieu who wanted to be a writer more than she wanted to be a nice suburban home-maker. (Mori 2000: 139)

These feelings are also echoed in Gordon's (1995) interview with Pha, who states: "I like America, I love America because womans [sic] have freedom" (p. 63). Notably, the perception of the new culture as allowing for more gender freedom is not limited to inhabitants of countries which some may label 'patri-archal.' A similar attitude is also expressed by a former German citizen Ute Margaret Saine (2000):

> Perhaps not surprisingly, many of my German girlfriends from this and later schools emigrated, like myself, to Italy, England, Brazil, France, and, of course, the United States. In order to escape repression, particularly of gender. (Saine 2000: 172)

It is quite possible, however, that the perception of being gender-free while living in another country and speaking another language may be shaped by the fact that many new arrivals are joining their new community at a later age, having escaped childhood – and at times even school – gender socialization practices. Memoirs of Americans learning other languages clearly demonstrate that America is not a 'gender-free' heaven either (Ogulnick 1998; Watson 1995). As discussed previously, Ogulnick (1998) in particular acknowledges that her exposure to gendered discursive practices of Japanese makes her reflect back upon gendered discursive practices of English, which are similarly disempowering:

> In my reimmersion into Japanese culture ... the experience was more like looking into a mirror ... one that revealed, even where there were differences, much about the condition of being a woman in my own culture. This time by being there, and being aware of how I was learning Japanese, I was also learning the many subtle and not-so-subtle ways I had been taught to speak "like a woman" in my native language and culture. (Ogulnick 1998: 10)

> Flashbacks to childhood experiences brought me back to times when I was controlled, punished, and sexually suppressed. Although I perceived gender-specific codes of appearance to be more prominent in Japan, thinking back to my own cultural socialization process, I recall the gender-polarizing ways I was taught

how to speak, act, and look like a girl. I can still hear echoes of men's voices commenting on my clothes, hair, body – each one in conflict over how I should look – more modest, sexier, thinner, fatter, older, younger. Each one had an image around which I tried to mold myself. The two societies and languages may have been different, but the message that I received, implicitly and explicitly, was basically the same: that women's bodies, language, and thoughts are controlled by men. (Ogulnick 1998: 33)

Whatever the reason may be, whether it is an escape from childhood language socialization or the links perceived between American English and feminist discourses, many L2 users in the corpus appear to have chosen – or at least accepted – English as the language that gives them enough freedom to be the kind of women they would like to be. In other contexts, however, the links perceived between language and gender may prompt L2 learners, most often expatriates, to resist new subjectivities and discursive performances, often at a price of not being seen as fully fluent and proficient. This half-assimilation, half-resistance is portrayed by Ogulnick (1998) who at times feels hurt and excluded from conversation by her Japanese friends:

I may have also resented that I wasn't getting a certain attention or recognition I seemed to feel I deserved for not acting "like an American." In other words, here I was, the low woman in the hierarchy, this American woman not being appreciated for not wanting to be treated as an American woman. The irony of this is that I wanted to assimilate but didn't want to give up a certain privilege – the attention and status of being American. (Ogulnick 1998: 133)

A much stronger form of resistance is depicted in Richard Watson's (1995) memoir about his unsuccessful attempt to learn French. The author, an American philosopher and an expert on Descartes, could easily read and translate from French. At the age of fifty-five he decided to go ahead and learn spoken French in order to converse with his French colleagues. Unfortunately, his multiple attempts to master the language fail, due in part to his ambivalent feelings toward spoken French fueled by his childhood notions of idealized masculinity, incompatible with being French or sounding French:

I have a distinct dislike for the sound of spoken French. Many Americans do. Why? Because it's weak. For American men at least, French sounds syrupy and effeminate. (Watson 1995: 52)

... it was clear that it embarrassed me to speak French. I knew exactly why that was. I didn't want to sound like Charles Boyer in the movies of my childhood. We hooted and groaned when he breathed down the neck of some woman on the screen. And there was the suggestion that he might do things to them offscreen that no real man would ever be caught dead doing. A great suspicion came over me: Real Men Don't Speak French. (Watson 1995: 12)

While the discussion above portrays choices made by individuals as agents, it is necessary to underscore that the nature of agency, and thus the nature of assimilation and resistance, is always co-constructed. No matter how much an individual would like to assimilate to a particular community, she won't be able to if the community rejects or marginalizes 'outsiders'. Similarly, it would be misleading to suggest that individuals, particularly women who come from societies perceived as patriarchal, always attempt to occupy gender subjectivities of their new culture. It is equally possible that, as convincingly demonstrated in Blackledge's chapter, they may be engaged in attempts to maintain their gender identities, which are inextricably linked to ethnicity, culture, and religion.

4.4. Undergoing gender socialization

What happens to individuals who, despite all odds, decide to embark on a long journey of appropriation of new discourses, subjectivities, and ideologies? While the comparison of the old and the new may render familiar femininities unsatisfactory, learning to perform new femininities may be a confusing experience as well, as exemplified in a poignant excerpt from Hoffman (1989):

> The question of femininity is becoming vexing to me as well. How am I to become a woman in an American vein, how am I to fit the contours of my Texan's soul? The allegory of gender is different here, and it unfolds around different typologies and different themes. I can't become a "Pani" of any sort: not like the authoritative Pani Orlovska, or the vampy, practical Pani Dombarska, or the flirty, romantic woman writer I once met. None of these modes of femininity makes sense here, none of them would find corresponding counterparts in the men I know. (Hoffman 1989: 189)

For many women the absence of accepted landmarks for negotiating the paths to femininity, itself a contested cultural space, leads to recognition of mobility, plasticity, and mimicry involved in becoming a woman (Bartkowski 1995). In her discussion of Hoffman's book a Romanian-English bilingual, Marianne Hirsch (1994), suggests that even for teenagers and younger women the process may be very complex as "every transition into female adulthood is a process of acculturation to an alien realm" (1994: 74). Thus, her own and Hoffman's process of unlearning and learning, of resisting and assimilating was a double one which must have been doubly difficult to negotiate. It must have left us doubly displaced and dispossessed, doubly at risk, perhaps doubly resistant to assimilation. If most girls leave their "home" as they move into adolescence, Hoffman and I left two homes – our girlhood and our Europe. (Hirsch 1994: 75)

One does not simply learn a new set of grammar rules and apply them to new vocabulary; new discourses come with new ideologies and practices of embodiment. Does one flirt in this new space? And if yes, then how? What does dating mean? How does one become a parent if one's own models of parent-child relationship are no longer valid? Although these questions are disquieting to everyone who makes a transition into adulthood, the bewilderment is much more severe when linguistic and cultural transition is added to the normal sensitivities concerning intimacy and personal boundaries. Some narratives in the corpus suggest that transformation of gender often starts with changes in linguistic identities and corresponding changes in discursive interactions. Anna Wierzbicka (1985), who came from Poland to Australia as an adult, recalls:

When I came to Australia to live, one of my most keenly felt experiences was the loss of my (linguistic) identity. For my English-speaking acquaintances I was neither <u>Ania</u> nor <u>pani Ania</u> and not even <u>pani Anna</u>. I was <u>Anna</u> and this did not correspond in its socio-semantic value to any of the forms used in Polish. One thing which was good about this new name was that it could be used in self-identification. In Polish I have always found it difficult to speak to friends and acquaintances on the telephone because my name in Polish does not have any form which would be appropriate for self-presentation: <u>Anna</u> is so formal and so official that it can only be used with the surname, which is entirely inappropriate when speaking to friends or relatives; <u>Ania</u>, on the other hand, is childishly self-indulgent. ... the switch from the Polish <u>Ania</u> to the English <u>Anna</u> is more than a linguistic change: it is also a switch in the style of interpersonal interaction. (Wierzbicka 1985: 189)

Mar (1999) similarly outlines her transition path, listing various names she had been given and adopted at different stages and underscoring the multiplicity of her identities:

For the purposes of this book, my name is "Man Yee." On my birth certificate and passport, it's listed as "Man Yi." On my school and tax records, it's "Manyee." When filling out official documents, I always have to pause and double check before signing, to make sure I write the appropriate name. Otherwise, I would sign as "M. Elaine Mar" automatically. Without hesitation. It's an indication of who I've become – the self expressed in English, preceded by the vestige of a name that cannot be written, ending with the mystery of one that will never leave me. (Mar 1999: xii)

How is the transition path navigated and where do transformations take place? Usually, the transformation is achieved through participation in various discursive and social practices, most often, schooling. School plays an important role in several stories about the invention of acceptable hybrid identities, such as Chinese-American (Kingston 1975; Mar 1999) or Korean-American (Kim 2000; Lee 2000). The young women are portrayed in these stories in the process of trying out a range of linguistic devices, from a change in pitch to appropriation of new speech acts and discourses of femininity:

> Normal Chinese women's voices are strong and bossy. We American-Chinese girls had to whisper to make ourselves American-feminine. Apparently we whispered even more softly than the Americans. Once a year the teachers referred my sister and me to speech therapy, but our voices would straighten out, unpredictably normal, for therapists. Some of us gave up ... Most of us eventually found some voice, however faltering. We invented an American-feminine speaking personality ... (Kingston 1975: 200)

> Obviously, dieting wasn't going to make me taller or rounder, but I knew that by invoking that one word, the mantra of American womanhood, I was going to be accepted by my girlfriends in a way I'd never been before. (Mar 1999: 218)

For other learners, the process of socialization takes place later on in life, in college or at work, where a Chilean woman may become a Hispanic academic (Brintrup 2000) and a Japanese woman an American writer (Mori 1997, 2000). For Hirsch, who for many years chose to inhabit the margins, transformation is precipitated by participation in the feminist movement:

> The late sixties offer many opportunities for group identity, but even as I protest the Vietnam War and become involved in curriculum restructuring, I do so from the margins. The women's movement changes all that. I join a consciousness raising group in 1970 and experience a feeling of group allegiance for the very first time in my life ... During adolescence, friendship provided a form of displacement and resistance: to cultural assimilation as well as femininity. It was a place on the border between cultures, between girlhood and womanhood. Like those early friendships, feminism itself became a space of relation and relocation, a place from which I could think and speak and write, a home on the border. (Hirsch 1994: 85–88)

In addition to educational practices and participation in various communities of practice, four other spaces are singled out in L2 learning narratives as the key sites of the negotiation of gender performance: intimate relationships, friendships, parent-child relationships, and work places. Below I will discuss each one in turn, looking at what types of negotiation and transformation may take place in each space.

4.5. Negotiating gender: intimate relationships and friendships

Intimate relationships and friendships surface time and again as one of the most difficult areas for negotiation and an authentic performance of gender. To begin with, as illustrated in the interviews with Pha, in some minority communities women may be readier than men to depart from traditional gender roles and to embrace new ones:

> And Laotian families in here, in the North Philly, South Philly they get divorce a lot. ... Because the woman want to get divorce from the man, if man disagree, the woman don't care. ... I get the boyfriend and go out from you. I leave you at home. (Gordon 1995: 59–60)

New gender roles, however, may not be that easy to perform. "For a long time, it was difficult to speak these most intimate phrases, hard to make English – that language of will and abstraction – shape itself into the tonalities of love," confesses Hoffman:

> In Polish, the words for "boy" and "girl" embodied within them the wind and crackle of boyishness, the breeze and grace of girlhood: the words summoned that evanescent movement and melody and musk that are the interior inflections of gender itself. In English, "man" and "woman" were empty signs; terms of endearment came out as formal and foursquare as other words. ... How could I say "darling," or "sweetheart," when the words had no fleshly fullness, when they were as dry as sticks? (Hoffman 1989: 245)

The meaning of the social practice of American dating appears particularly mysterious to newcomers and has to be learned and negotiated, as seen in the excerpt from Hoffman:

> Dating is an unknown ritual to me, unknown among my Cracow peers, who, aside from lacking certain of its requisite accessories – cars, private rooms, a bit of money – ran around in boy-girl packs and didn't have a ceremonial set of rules

for how to act toward the other sex. A date, by contrast, seems to be an occasion whose semiotics are highly standardized and in which every step has a highly determinate meaning and therefore has to be carefully calibrated. (Hoffman 1989: 149)

Even Helie Lee (2000), who for the most part grew up in the States, feels that her American boyfriends continue to shy away from the vestiges of her Korean upbringing: "They felt crowded when I began each sentence with 'us' and 'ours' instead of 'yours' and 'mine'" (p. 133). Moreover, it is not only a performance of gender that may constitute a problem in a new culture, but also a reading of others' performances. Cathy Davidson (1993) points out that gendered speech acts of another culture may be impossible to read through the lenses of the first one:

More than once I've been baffled by Japanese male attentiveness, uncertain whether I'm on the receiving end of politeness or a proposition. In America I would sense a come-on immediately, but in Japan there are rituals of compliment and deferral – almost like flirtation – that I've seen men engage in among themselves. I've seen it with women, too, a jockeying among politeness levels and status codes that require a more intimate knowledge of Japan than I possess. (Davidson 1993: 90)

Difficulties in interaction with prospective partners are not limited to female bilinguals. Dominik finds it hard to talk to American women, be it friends or prospective dates, because in his native culture performance of masculinity is predicated on telling sex-related jokes:

... I always have in the back of my mind ... that you, you are not supposed to joke about sex so much, I mean, I, I still, with people who I feel really confident ... I tell some jokes, but it's much less, than I would probably do, while ... back home it's still like issue of confidence, but, but you would probably tell sexually-related jokes, or like kind of like hints ... to women you don't know so much, you know them but you, you are not so ... confident with them, while here ... it could be never a case, with me at least. (Interview with the author, Summer 1998)

When one's performance of masculinity is based on particular speech acts, such as risqué Eastern European jokes, flowery Georgian toasts, or bawdy Spanish compliments known as *piropos*, one may experience an acute discomfort in transition or cause discomfort to others. Julia Alvarez (1998) recalls how walking around the city with her father sometimes embarrassed her:

My father would stop on a New York City street when a young woman swung by and sing this song [a compliment to a woman with a lot of swing in her walk – A.P.] out loud to the great embarrassment of his daughters. We were sure that one day when we weren't around to make him look like the respectable father of four girls, he would be arrested. (Alvarez 1998: 41)

Baranczak (1990) tells a story of a well-known Polish writer, Antoni Slonimski, who after 12 years in London decided to return to Poland in 1951, at the height of totalitarianism. When asked why he had chosen to do so, he replied that he did not really feel lonely, materially deprived, or socially degraded: he was simply unable to tell jokes. The wittiest man in Poland, famous for his hilarious feuilletons, he could not stand not being funny, and opted for life under the oppressive communist regime. At approximately the same time another Pole, Jerzy Kosinski, left Poland for America. In his description of Kosinski's learning of English in America, Sloan indicates that his problem was the inability to perform another gendered speech act, flirting:

> Another translation problem also preoccupied Kosinski at that time. Love, supposedly, possesses a universal language, but Kosinski did not find it so. In Poland, his silver tongue had never failed him when it came to seduction, but America presented an altogether new sort of challenge. Not yet eloquent in English, or in the different vocabulary of seduction in America, he found himself at a loss. (Sloan 1996: 120)

One of the earlier episodes of life in America, later incorporated by Kosinski into a novel, involved him and an American woman sitting on a sofa, which in Poland is called a 'Castro convertible':

> ... he found himself unable to summon the words to request that she stand up so that he could turn the sofa into a bed. Every way he thought of putting it struck him as crude and unsatisfactory. He was trapped in every schoolboy's dilemma, finding a way to put the question that would not alarm the woman and push her away. Thus the plight of Warsaw's master seducer. Like the schoolboy rejected, he could only meditate on the inscrutability of language – the fact, for example, that the word for "Castro convertible" in Polish is *Amerykanka* – literally, "American woman." (Sloan 1996: 120–121)

With time, however, as seen in Hoffman's memoir, intimate words can acquire meaning in the second language and the politics of heterosexual interaction can be internalized:

But now the language has entered my body, has incorporated itself in the softest tissue of my being. "Darling," I say to my lover, "my dear," and the words are filled and brimming with the motions of my desire; they curve themselves within my mouth to the complex music of tenderness. (Hoffman 1989: 245)

Later, I'll come to recognize words like "responsibility" and "hurt" as a telltale buzz emitted by the men of my generation to signal that they don't really want to get involved. Once I do, my own freedom will be lost, and I'll begin to engage in those contorted maneuvers by which the women in the same generation try to conceal their desires so as not to scare the men off. (Hoffman 1989: 188)

In addition, not only intimate relations but also interactions with friends and casual acquaintances may be a difficult terrain to navigate in a second language. When asked about domains which she finds most complicated for fluent functioning, Christina pointed out that being the exotic 'other' may work quite well in an intimate relationship but less so in a casual one:

The most difficult ones?... the social scene, and, in fact, maybe not so much, not so much, uhm ... intimate relationships, like my relationship with Jim, but ... uhm, <u>really,</u> the party scene, the social scene, the kind of <u>casual,</u> friendly relationships, because in the intimate ones it becomes some kind of an exotic thing that you can play up on, whereas... in a kind of acquaintance sense... it's ... difficult to kind of hide behind... (Interview with the author, Summer 1998)

Ogulnick (1998) emphasizes that her interactions with Japanese friends are also colored by gender. She feels that she profited more from speaking Japanese to her female than to her male friends, and that the mere presence of males influenced the interactions:

Unlike the rigid boundaries I experienced with Keio, which made me feel blocked off and distanced from him emotionally, Akemi's personal stories, vivid details, imagery, and concreteness, helped to draw me in. ... Also in contrast to what I experienced as Keio's rigid and unyielding style, I experienced Akemi as nurturing and generous, which helped make learning Japanese with her much more pleasurable for me. (Ogulnick 1998: 60–62)

In sum, we can see that gender is negotiated in intimate relationships and friendships in a number of ways. To begin with, as seen in Alvarez's (1998) memoir and Dominik's story, in order not to be misinterpreted, L2 users may have to abandon some speech acts they see as central to their performance of gender. Like Hoffman (1989) or Kosinski (Sloan 1996), they may also have to internalize new expressions and speech acts, critical for full participation in gendered discursive practices of their new community. On the other hand, as we have seen from Christina's comment, a certain exotic 'otherness' may enhance one's sexual appeal to prospective partners in another culture (see also Piller's chapter). Finally, as seen in Davidson's (1993) and Hoffman's (1989) comments, L2 users also have to learn to interpret particular terms and speech acts in ways that conform to the norms of the L2 culture.

4.6. Negotiating gender: parent-child relationships

Parent-child relationships constitute another important domain where change is often inflicted as well as initiated. Two types of negotiation are illuminated in the L2 learning narratives in the corpus: renegotiation of the relationship with one's parents (Alvarez 1998; Chambers 2000; Dorfman 1998; Hoffman 1989; Kaplan 1993; Kim 2000; Kingston 1975; Lee 2000; Mar 1999; Mori 1997; Reyn 2000; Rodriguez 1982) and of that with one's children (Brintrup 2000; Lvovich 1997; Wierzbicka 1985, 1997). In both, cultural transition may have negative effects, such as the decline and loss of parental agency, status, and authority resulting from a marginal position occupied by parents in a new community (see also Blackledge's chapter).

In her analysis of Rodriguez's (1982) memoir which depicts a transition from a working-class Mexican background to middle-class America, Browdy de Hernandez (1997) suggests that Rodriguez rejected the model of selfhood offered by his father in favor of a model based on the "Great White father" of postcolonial society. Embarrassed by his father's inability to speak clear English, he distances himself further and further away from his father and from other Mexican males, described as "*los pobres* – the poor, the pitiful, the powerless ones" (Rodriguez 1982: 113). This language shift, prompted by the rejection of a particular ethnic, cultural, and social gendered identity, symbolizes emotional and cultural separation between Richard Rodriguez, a middle-class American man in the making, and his Mexican-American parents:

... as we children learned more and more English, we shared fewer and fewer words with our parents. (Rodriguez 1982: 23)

Kingston's (1975) and Mar's (1999) memoirs portray a similar refusal of a Chinese mother's version of femininity, that of a poor Chinese immigrant, usually performed through such speech acts as bargaining:

> At department stores I angered my mother when I could not bargain without shame, poor people's shame. She stood in back of me and prodded and pinched, forcing me to translate her bargaining, word for word. (Kingston 1975: 96)

> [Mother] described how she'd been walking by the Salvation Army store when she noticed a pile of furniture in its parking lot. ... I knew she meant the donation dropoff spot outside the store. It was clearly marked with big red letters on a white sign. If she could read English, she would know this too. I wanted to tell her, but I couldn't find the words. She sounded so excited. The truth would only make her unhappy. ... Wordlessly, I helped carry the coffee table home. (Mar 1999: 197)

In both cases, the rift between mothers and daughters is propagated by the mothers' lack of English skills as well as a general lack of understanding of the majority culture. The loss of authority, prompted by the cultural transition and the parents' poor performance in the majority language, is widely discussed in the literature on immigrant women (see, for example, Lieblich 1993). Clearly, many parents are conscious of the link between their loss of status and lack of mastery of the second language: the same Mar (1999) recalls her mother screaming "Go learn English so you don't end up stupid like your mother!" (p. 106). Another reason for the distancing between parents and children is the parents' difficulty in carrying out the familiar discursive practices of parenting in the new environment, as discourses of parenting may be very different across cultures and so are the understandings of schooling (see also Blackledge's chapter). Kim (2000) recalls that her parents knew or understood very little of what went on in her American school. Mar (1999) is equally unable to engage her mother in a meaningful conversation about her school experiences:

> I couldn't explain these [school] difficulties to Mother. Our language didn't leave room for such a conversation. The Chinese don't ask their children, *How was school today?* They say, *What did you learn?* and *Do you understand your lessons?* (Mar 1999: 69)

Hoffman (1989) describes her parents' despair, when they realized the impossibility of transferring Polish practices onto North American soil:

> They don't try to exercise much influence over me anymore. "In Poland, I would have known how to bring you up, I would have known what to do," my mother says wistfully, but here, she has lost her sureness, her authority. She doesn't know how hard to scold Alinka [Eva's sister] when she comes home at late hours; she can only worry over her daughter's vague evening activities. (Hoffman 1989: 145)

The same distance, from the parent's perspective, is portrayed in Gordon's (1995) interviews with Pha, who feels that she has lost control over her older son and is afraid that the same may be happening with the younger one:

> In Laos, the childrens is very honor for parents, for their parents. They talk parents, good and politely. And they do everything for parents. But in here, the children never help parents. ... Now, I stay confusing about children. ... The children in here, when they go to school and come back home, they get, they stay in their room, they don't want to talk with parents. Every children, every parents say like that. ... They don't want to talk, and they don't want to talk Lao, too. They only want to talk together in English in their room. (Gordon 1995: 64–65)

The linguistic and cultural rift between parents and children may cross ethnic, national, cultural, and class boundaries, and Natasha Lvovich (1997), quite assimilated into the American middle class, admits with disarming honesty:

> Watching my daughter growing up *American*, whatever that term means, is somewhat disturbing, painful, and confusing. (Lvovich 1997: 101)

The fact that the usual generation gap between parents and children is doubled and tripled when there is also a language and culture gap is a constant theme in the cross-cultural memoirs in the corpus (Kim 2000; Kingston 1975; Mar 1999; Lee 2000; Reyn 2000). Many authors attribute the loss of connection between parents and children to the children's desire to construct new identities in the new, more prestigious, language available to them:

> With my siblings I speak English. Spanish used to be a way of tattletaling. "Alex, *no digas malas palabras*." With our friends, too, English is the language of choice. Spanish used to be for us too right-off-the-boat, not hip enough. Spanish meant trousers and pointy shoes instead of Lees and fat-laced Pumas. (Rosario 2000: 164)

> ... by the time my Spanish-speaking parents were finally able to do battle for the Latino soul of their son, they discovered that they had lost me to the charisma of America, that what had begun in that hospital as a childish linguistic tantrum had, in the foster home, hardened into something more culturally permanent and drastic: the question of language had become ensnared in the question of nationality, and therefore of identity. (Dorfman 1998: 47)

> [our secret language] excluded our parents but not our neighbors; it defied my mother but not passersby at the supermarket. It was a code for power, moving us closer to the majority culture, further marginalizing our parents and memories of our past. (Mar 1999: 161)

As a result of this language shift, at times, instead of being socialized, it is the children who take on the roles of socializers and help their parents to assimilate in the new country, thus reversing the expected power relations:

> My parents were all too happy to let the transformation take place – it would allow me to slip painlessly and naturally into this new culture. Suddenly, my parents turned to me to construe this new world for them. I reveled in my power, child turned patient teacher. (Reyn 2000: 149)

> I had a dreadful power over my mother, one that grew with each word in my American vocabulary. As I gained fluency in English, I took on greater responsibility for my family, and parent and child roles became murky. Mother spoke and read virtually no English. She needed my help to buy groceries, interpret the news, and complete all manner of forms. (Mar 1999: 159)

> Assimilation came most immediately to my son, who was five years old. My husband and I placed him in charge of answering all calls in English. ... He was the tongue of the house, the role model of gestures and new ways of thinking. We looked to him as our permanent teacher. He brought in information about a variety of things. He taught us what to eat, how to buy it, when to eat it. He told us which people were our neighbors and educated us on the informality of dressing, the importance of sport, and the mentality of his teachers. (Brintrup 2000: 14)

Recognizing the linguistic advantage they have over their parents, some children may use language shift as a means of freeing themselves from the gender roles prescribed by the native culture of their parents:

> As rebellious adolescents, we soon figured out that conducting our filial business in English gave us an edge over our strict, Spanish-speaking parents. We could spin circles around my mother's *absolutamente no* by pointing out the flaws in her arguments, in English. My father was a pushover for pithy quotes from Shakespeare, and a recitation of "The quality of mercy is not strained" could usually get me what I wanted. ... Our growing distance from Spanish was a way in which we were setting ourselves free from that old world where, as girls, we didn't have much to say about what we could do with our lives. (Alvarez 1998: 63)

The discussion above clearly shows that a parent-child relationship, crucial to the process of language socialization, may itself undergo a transformation in a cross-cultural transition. In particular, the parents' attempts to engage in discursive practices of 'mothering' and 'fathering' may fail, as their own practices may not be easily transferrable to the new surroundings, not easily performed in the new language, and not listened to by children undergoing rapid assimilation to a new culture. In turn, children may perceive language shift as a way to 'set themselves free' of normative gender identities imposed on them by their first language community.

4.7. Negotiating gender: workplace interactions

The workplace is another important site where gender is performed and negotiated discursively, and where negotiation may make a difference in one's status. Mori (1997) presents her code-switching into English as a strategy that allows her to successfully perform an identity of a professional American female in conversation with her bilingual Japanese colleagues:

> Talking seems especially futile when I have to address a man in Japanese. Every word I say forces me to be elaborately polite, indirect, submissive, and unassertive. There is no way I can sound intelligent, clearheaded, or decisive. But if I did not speak a "proper" feminine language, I would sound stupid in another way – like someone who is uneducated, insensitive, and rude, and therefore cannot be taken seriously. I never speak Japanese with the Japanese man who teaches physics at the college where I teach English. We are colleagues, meant to be equals. The language I use should not automatically define me as second best. (Mori 1997: 12)

In a reverse situation, Davidson (1993), an American scholar in Japan, finds that simply being a Western female boosts her status and even puts her in a different gender category, neither male nor female, but that reserved for *gaijin* 'foreigners':

> In professional contexts, more than one Japanese woman remarked that I was often spoken of and to with forms of respect reserved for men in Japan. These women were broad-minded enough to be more bemused by this than resentful. When I pushed the issue, they also admitted that, if I was respected, it might be because in some sense I didn't really count. I was from another world, beyond the pale of professional competition, outside the battle of the sexes Japanese-style. It was as if my foreignness put me in some different gender category, on one level proximate and titillating, on another androgynous and remote. (Davidson 1993: 88)

> the word *foreign* complicated *female* in ways that I still don't fully understand. Perhaps because in 1980 most visiting foreign professors in Japan were men, the rules for how to treat a woman in my professional capacity just didn't exist.The Japanese professors I met were all friendly, but it was obvious that my male col-

leagues, in particular, didn't quite know what to do with me. Should they invite me out with them for the normal after-work drinking as they would a visiting male teacher, or would this be an insult to me (or, worse, to my husband)? Should they exclude me from such socializing, as Japanese women professors were routinely excluded, or would I consider that to be insulting, not to mention hopelessly sexist? (Davidson 1993: 87–88)

Ogulnick (1998) is similarly concerned about the role of her various subjectivities in her unsuccessful language sessions with a Japanese male colleague Keio:

> The categories Keio and I had available to us in our languages seemed to make it almost impossible for us to ever really speak the same language. Keio's maleness and the role he assumed as *sensei* when teaching me Japanese were dominant images for me; likewise my language, cultural identity, position at the university, and the color of my skin must have represented powerful symbols to Keio. (Ogulnick 1998: 49)

The quote above illustrates particularly well the co-constructed nature of language learner subjectivities: not only are the individuals in transition trying to read the mysterious signs of the new culture, but they are also read – and at times misread – by the culture.

A different issue with regard to performance of a workplace identity is brought up by Christina, a feminist and a literary scholar. During a recent trip to Poland, her native country, she found that differences in American and Polish ideologies of gender and related lack of vocabulary in Polish rendered it impossible for her to perform her professional identity of a feminist scholar:

> ...I suddenly worried that maybe my research is not complex enough or complex to satisfy me ... uhm ... because it seemed so mundane when translated into Polish ... but then again all the terminology that I was trying to translate didn't exist in Polish, I mean, even, even to talk about gender was impossible ... uhm ... not to mention certain theoretical issues in literature, that I was interested in, so it was not just difficult, it was also very anxiety-producing, because it was like confronting an impossibility to think about certain things in Polish... (Interview with the author, Summer 1998)

Thus, it appears that a gendered professional identity is also negotiated in a number of ways, through the lexicon, speech acts, even the choice of the language itself. This negotiation may be particularly acute in contexts where a specific culture does not accommodate female professionals or where authority is doubly difficult to perform for female non-native speakers. The difficulty is further compounded for scholars like Christina whose performance of professional identity is predicated on particular discourses, which may not exist in their countries of origin.

4.8. Becoming a woman in an American vein

Despite all the negotiation difficulties, many L2 users may successfully appropriate gender discourses of their new culture and find ways of positioning themselves authoritatively as its legitimate and authentic members. Thus, Rodriguez writes his autobiography "as a middle-class American man. Assimilated" (1982: 3). Similarly, Hoffman states at the end of her memoir:

> ... When I think of myself in cultural categories – which I do perhaps too often – I know that I'm a recognizable example of a species: a professional New York woman, and a member of a postwar international new class; somebody who feels at ease in the world, and is getting on with her career relatively well, and who is as fey and brave and capable and unsettled as many of the women here – one of a new breed, born of the jet age and the counterculture, and middle-class ambitions, and American grit. I fit, and my surroundings fit me. (Hoffman 1989: 170)

Hoffman explains her own understanding of becoming a woman in an American vein as it can be comprehended only through juxtaposition of two cultural perspectives on gender, Polish and American:

> I've acquired the assurance, which seems second nature to me but is relatively new for a person of my gender, that I can land in any city and within hours figure out how to get around it, use the metro, and find a good neighborhood restaurant and a decent midpriced hotel. Of course, it has helped in nurturing this confidence that I live in an imperial center whose currency is the international standard and whose language the Esperanto of the modern world. In all of this, I've developed a certain kind of worldly knowledge, and a public self to go with it. That self is the most American thing about me; after all, I acquired it here. (Hoffman 1989: 251)

For many learners, this 'becoming' also involves thinking of themselves in terms of new gender categories. Thus, Ogulnick was warned by her well-wishing Japanese friends that at twenty-five an unmarried woman turns into a piece of 'old Christmas cake':

> Satoko and I seemed to find ourselves in a more marginalized social space. Whereas single men in Japan are referred to in a more positive light, as *bacheraa* [bachelor], Japanese expressions for single women portray them as "old" and "unwanted": "old Christmas cake" [*furui kurisumasu keiki*], "unsold merchandise" [*urenokori*], and "spinster" [*orudo misu*]. (Ogulnick 1998: 90–91)

Soon, she finds herself internalizing these definitions and on an outing with a female friend sees herself through a Japanese lens:

> ...even just being out on a Sunday afternoon, standing apart from all the (seemingly) heterosexual couples around us made us feel the sting of the stigma many single women feel when they are referred to as *sabiishi* [lonely] and not *ichinin-mae* [complete human beings]... (Ogulnick 1998: 96–97)

At the same time, it is clear that while some learners, oftentimes Caucasian like Hoffman, manage to co-construct a new gendered identity in their new culture, other women may be positioned differently as their racial and ethnic identities do not neatly fit within the gender stereotypes created by the dominant ideologies and reproduced by the media which continue to ignore the racial, cultural, and linguistic diversity of contemporary America (see, for example, Lippi-Green 1997). Not surprisingly, this subtle 'othering' may be internalized by the L2 users who are not reflected in their new culture. "Over the years, I came to believe that being Chinese in itself constituted ugliness and asexuality," admits Mar (1999: 220). "To this day, after three decades of living in America, I feel like a stranger in what I now consider my own country" (1998: 44), poignantly states dark-skinned Julia Alvarez who internalized the blue-eyed and blond-haired images of American femininity. And, at the same time, she says

> The truth is that I couldn't even imagine myself as someone other than the person I had become in English, a woman who writes books in the language of Emily Dickinson and Walt Whitman, and also of the rude shopper in the grocery store and of the boys throwing stones in the schoolyard, their language, which is now my language. (Alvarez 1998: 72)

It is this positioning, this reinvention and reimagining of gender identities that is the most important feature of the narratives in the corpus. They do not simply tell us stories of 'fitting in'; instead, they rewrite what it means to be an American woman or an American man.

4.9. Losing gender in translation

While many bi- and multilinguals around the world manage to perform their gender identities successfully in their multiple languages, in some cases successful assimilation may entail a perceived loss of a gendered identity, or at least of a normative gendered identity, in the culture of origin. Thus, Rodriguez blames his socialization into English for becoming effeminate from the point of view of Mexican culture, for losing certain qualities that a real macho Mexican inevitably possesses, and in particular for becoming unusually talkative and proud of his way with words:

> I knew that I had violated the ideal of the *macho* by becoming such a dedicated student of language and literature. (Rodriguez 1982: 128)

The literal loss of a gendered voice, following the process of self-translation, is commented upon by Mori:

> In Japanese, I don't have a voice for speaking my mind. When a Japanese flight attendant walks down the aisle in her traditional kimono, repeating the endlessly apologetic announcements in the high, squeaky voice a nice woman is expected to use in public, my heart sinks because hers is the voice I am supposed to mimic. All my childhood friends answer their telephones in this same voice, as do the young women store clerks welcoming people and thanking them for their business or TV anchor women reading the news. It doesn't matter who we are or what we are saying. A woman's voice is always the same: a childish squeak piped from the throat. (Mori 1997: 16)

In sum, it appears that as a result of second language socialization in adulthood, one's performance of gender in the first language may no longer be seen as authentic. Even more serious problems are experienced by childhood bilinguals who escaped socialization into the gendered discursive practices of the first language and culture and, consequently, have trouble communicating. Alvarez, for instance, blames her limited Spanish vocabulary and discursive repertoires for the inability to express herself in her relationship with a Spanish-speaking boy:

> In the dark, periodically broken by the lights of passing cars, Mangú began to talk about our future. I didn't know what to say to him. Or actually, in English, I could have said half a dozen ambivalent, soothing things. But not having a complicated vocabulary in Spanish, I didn't know the fancy, smooth-talking ways of delaying and deterring. Like a child, I could just blurt out what I was thinking:

"Somos diferente, Mangú." We are so different. The comment came out sounding inane. (Alvarez 1998: 70)

In other contexts, it is the speakers' first language speech communities that lack particular discourses critical for gender performances by these individuals. This is the case with Christina, and also with two Russian women, whose life stories I elicited in Russian for a study of gender construction in Russian discourse (Pavlenko in press b). Thirty-one year old Natasha arrived in the US five years previously and learned English upon her arrival. Marina, who is now 25 and in the process of receiving her doctoral degree, came to the US and learned English at the age of 17. While the life trajectories and even second language socialization paths of these two women are quite different (Natasha studied English in ESL classes and then went to work as a researcher, while Marina went to an American high school and then college and graduate school), they became friends because they had something in common that separated them from many other members of the Russian community in their city – their feminist attitudes. While for most of the 90-minute life-story interview the two women speak Russian, in the part that deals with the reasons they chose their feminist identities both engage in code-switching:

Mne eto raskrylo glaza na pravdu ... na pravdu ... to, chto zhenshchiny sotni i sotni let byli ... oppressed ... mne ... ia seichas eto iasno vizhu ...
'It [feminism] opened my eyes to the truth ... the truth ... that women for hundreds and hundreds of years were *oppressed* ... for me ... now I see it clearly ...' (Marina, from the interview with the author, Fall 1999)

S etim kak-to smiriaiutsia, s etim kak-to zhivut ... vot eta vot oppression ...
'One puts up with this, one lives with this ... with this *oppression* ...' (Natasha, from the interview with the author, Fall 1999)

Zhenshchina ot property otsa stanovitsia property muzha ...
'A woman from being a *property* of her father passes on to being a *property* of her husband' (Marina, from the interview with the author, Fall 1999)

It is interesting to note that both words, *ugnetenie*/oppression and *sobstvennost'*/property, exist in Russian and are well-known to otherwise very fluent Natasha and Marina. In a further discussion with the researcher, the explanation offered by the two women for their use of the English translation equivalents was that in Russian discourse the two words are strongly linked to Marxist discourses about private and public property and oppression of working classes in capitalist countries. The notion of *ugnetenie zhenshchin*/oppression of women would amuse many monolingual Russian speakers, as feminist discourses are not widely known in post-Soviet countries (Pavlenko in press b). Finally, not only particular terms but even the life stories themselves, gendered and constructed in a particular place in time, may not be easily translatable into one's native language, as witnessed by the 'returning natives'. Hoffman describes one such 'loss in translation' which occurred in an encounter with one of her childhood friends upon her return to Poland:

> As we try to tell each other of our lives, I can see that she can't make out the sense of my story: that I am divorced, that I live on my own in a New York apartment, that I travel all over the place, that I have ambitions to write. (Hoffman 1989: 48)

These various quotes illustrate what can be in linguistic terms described as attrition of discursive competence in one's first language, or the mismatch between discourses of gender of the first and second culture. Alternatively, this phenomenon can be seen as the loss of one's ability to perform a gendered identity in one's first language or as resistance to such performance, prompted by the inability to perform one's current gendered subjectivity and to be understood on one's own terms. The mismatch in gender performances brings to the foreground the socially, culturally, and discursively constructed nature of gender: a transition to new gender ideologies, discourses, and social relations may not only entail performance of new gender subjectivities but also the loss of the previous ones, perceived as a loss of a normative femininity or masculinity.

5.   Conclusion

So, what have we learned about transformations of gender as a system of social relations – and of gender performances – in second language socialization? To begin with, it appears that 'transformations of gender', experienced by individual L2 learners and users in cross-cultural transitions, entail a wide range of inter-related phenomena, including changes in dominant ideologies of gender, normative gender roles, social and economic gender relations, and verbal and non-verbal gender performances. Examination of the first person narratives of these individuals allows us to identify some of the stages of transformation of the discursive performance of gender, the key sites where the negotiation takes place, and linguistic means involved in the process of transformation.

To begin with, my analysis of the narratives in the corpus demonstrates that different individuals may go through different stages in the negotiation of gender identities. At the same time, most women appear to share the need to question and ponder upon gendered subjectivities provided for them by their first and second cultures. It is through this comparison that some make a choice to assimilate to the second culture, prompted by the desire to adopt a particular identity, or even to be 'gender-free', while others choose to resist if possible. Those who decide to – or are forced to – assimilate may have to undergo a painful process of naming and renaming, which may invalidate some of their previous subjectivities and position them in undesirable ways, whereby an American 'single woman' may become an 'old Christmas cake' in Japan (Ogulnick 1998). This undesirable positioning or lack of validation by the majority culture may, in turn, be resisted by the L2 users. Many, as we have seen, choose writing as a unique public space, imbued with sufficient authority, where they do not only redefine themselves in terms of discourses available in the dominant society but also attempt to assign new meanings to the terms 'American man' and 'American woman' and, in doing so, to redefine the discourses that position individuals.

Examination of the L2 learning stories also allowed me to answer my second research question and identify the key sites where negotiation and transformation of gender subjectivities may take place. These sites include – but clearly are not limited to – educational establishments, such as schools and colleges, particular communities of practice, such as consciousness raising groups, friendships, intimate and parent-child relationships, and workplaces.

My third research question inquired about ways in which discursive performances of gender may change in cross-cultural transitions. The study identified a number of areas of linguistic indexing of gender involved in the process of discursive assimilation. First of all, as we have seen, even decisions to assimilate to or to resist assimilation to a particular community may be influenced by ways in which gender is indexed linguistically in that community. The means of indexing or performing gender which appear to influence decisions include – but are not limited to – pitch and overall voice quality (Mori 1997; Watson 1995), forms of politeness (Alvarez 1998; Ogulnick 1998), gendered rules of turn-taking in conversation (Mori 1997; Rosario 2000), speech acts such as bargaining or joking (Alvarez 1998; Baranczak 1990; Kingston 1975; Mar 1999; Dominik), and, most importantly, identity options afforded by particular speech communities (Christina; Kingston 1975; Mar 1999; Ogulnick 1998; Saine 2000). A similarly wide range of discursive practices is involved in the process of transformation and language choice. Some L2 users may consciously or unconsciously attempt to adjust their pitch and voice quality in order to come across as more feminine or more masculine in their L2 community (Kingston 1975; Mori, 1997; see also Ohara's chapter), while others simply sound different in the two languages (Rosario 2000; see also McMahill's chapter). Some L2 users may also modify their lexicon, discarding the terms which are not comprehensible or validated in their new community, and incorporating new terms, in particular identity terms, terms of endearment, and terms related to feminist discourses (Hoffman 1989; Ogulnick 1998; Wierzbicka 1985, 1997; Christina; see also McMahill's chapter on ways in which female Japanese learners use English subject pronouns). The appropriation of the new terms may, in turn, lead to code-switching, which was identified in the study as a strategy that allowed bilingual women Marina and Natasha to perform the gender identity of their choice in the L1. Not only the lexicon but also speech acts may be subject to modification. Some individuals (e.g., Dominik) may feel the need to abandon particular speech acts, such as ribald jokes or *piropos*, which in certain cultures are used to perform masculinities but in others may be perceived as instances of sexual harassment. Another area where change may be visible is turn-taking whereby adopting their gender subjectivities of choice some women may feel more entitled to voicing their opinions and participating as equal interlocutors (Alvarez 1998; Rosario 2000; see also McMahill's chapter). In addition, discursive assimilation is visible not only in performance but also in appropriation of new ways of interpreting particular terms, speech acts, and discursive practices, distinguishing, for instance, between flirting and politeness (Davidson 1993; Hoffman 1989). Not surprisingly, the study of narratives also targets narratives themselves, and particularly life story narratives, as language- and culture-specific, so that a change in speech communities may precipitate the need to retell one's gendered stories in different ways (Hoffman 1989). Finally, the analysis of L2 learning narratives demonstrates that not only do these narratives provide us with important insights into the nature of transformation of gender performances but that they also constitute gender performances, whereby American femininity – but not masculinity – is performed by focusing on gender as a theme (see also Pavlenko 2001).

Lastly, I have also argued in this paper that L2 learning stories, and in particular language learning memoirs, are unique and rich sources of information about the relationship between language and identity in second language learning and socialization. It is possible that only personal narratives can provide a glimpse into areas so private, personal, and intimate that they are rarely – if ever – breached in the study of SLA, and that are at the same time at the heart and soul of the second language socialization process. In the present study, the analysis of L2 learning narratives allowed us to see both where and how transformations of gender performance may take place in the process of second language socialization. It is up to future research, based both on personal insights and on third person observations, to examine, modify, and expand these suggestions.

In view of the approach taken here, some of the crucial questions in the future study of transformations of gender performance in second language learning become the following: What are the ideologies of gender in the learner's community of origin and how is the learner positioned in that community? What kinds of repositioning would a transition involve? How would the learner's gender, sexual, ethnic or cultural identity be read in terms of the second culture? What social practices is the learner permitted, enabled and/or encouraged to participate in? Which discourses, practices, and speech acts become the sites of struggle in the process of transition and internalization of new subjectivities? Only when these and many other questions are answered with regard to a wide range of learners from various linguistic, cultural, ethnic, racial, and socioeconomic backgrounds, will we be able to understand what it takes to become a woman – or a man – in an American – or any other – vein.

Acknowledgments

I am greatly indebted to Ewa Badowska, Claire Kramsch, Viorica Marian, and Tatyana Pyntikova for their invaluable advice, support, and inspiration at various stages of this project. I am equally grateful to my co-editors for their continuous assistance and encouragement throughout the writing process.

References

Alvarez, Julia
    1998   *Something to Declare*. Chapel Hill, NC: Algonquin Books of Chapel Hill.

Baranczak, Stanislaw
    1990   *Breathing Under Water and Other East European Essays*. Cambridge, MA: Harvard University Press.

Bartkowski, Frances
    1995   *Travelers, Immigrants, Inmates: Essays in Estrangemen*t. Minneapolis, MN: University of Minnesota Press.

Benson, Janet
    1994   Reinterpreting gender: Southeast Asian refugees and American society. In Camino, Linda and Ruth Krulfeld (eds.), *Reconstructing Lives, Recaptur-*

ing Meaning: Refugee Identity, Gender, and Culture Change. Basel: Gordon and Breach Publishers, 75–96.

Brintrup, Lilianet
  2000   Turbulent times. In Danquah, Meri Nana-Ama (ed.), *Becoming American: Personal Essays by First Generation Immigrant Women*. New York: Hyperion, 12–20.

Browdy de Hernandez, Jennifer
  1997   Postcolonial blues: Ambivalence and alienation in the autobiographies of Richard Rodriguez and V.S. Naipaul. *Auto/Biography Studies* 12, 2, 151–165.

Buijs, Gina (ed.)
  1993   *Migrant Women: Crossing Boundaries and Changing Identities*. Oxford/ Providence: Berg.

Burr, Vivien
  1995   *An Introduction to Social Constructionism*. London/New York: Routledge.

Burton, Pauline, Ketaki Kushari Dyson, and Shirley Ardener
  1994   *Bilingual Women: Anthropological Approaches to Second-Language Use*. Oxford/Providence: Berg.

Butler, Judith
  1990   *Gender Trouble: Feminism and the Subversion of Identity*. London: Routledge.

Cameron, Deborah
  1996   The language-gender interface: Challenging co-optation. In Bergvall, Victoria, Janet Bing and Alice Freed (eds.), *Rethinking Language and Gender Research: Theory and Practice*. London: Longman, 31–53.

Camino, Linda and Ruth Krulfeld (eds.)
  1994   *Reconstructing Lives, Recapturing Meaning: Refugee Identity, Gender, and Culture Change*. Basel: Gordon and Breach Publishers.

Chambers, Veronica
  2000   Secret Latina at large. In Danquah, Meri Nana-Ama (ed.), *Becoming American: Personal Essays by First Generation Immigrant Women*. New York: Hyperion, 21–28.

Cole, Ellen, Olivia Espin, and Esther Rothblum (eds.)
1992   *Refugee Women and their Mental Health: Shattered Societies, Shattered Lives.* New York: Harrington Park Press.

Davidson, Cathy
1993   *36 Views of Mount Fuji: On Finding Myself in Japan.* New York: Dutton.

Davies, Bronwyn and Rom Harré
1990   Positioning: The discursive production of selves. *Journal for the Theory of Social Behavior* 20, 43–63.

Dorfman, Ariel
1998   *Heading South, Looking North: A Bilingual Journey.* New York: Farrar, Straus, and Giroux.

Ehrlich, Susan
1997   Gender as social practice: Implications for second language acquisition. *Studies in Second Language Acquisition* 19, 421–446.

Gabaccia, Donna
1994   *From the Other Side: Women, Gender, and Immigrant Life in the U.S., 1820–1990.* Bloomington, IN: Indiana University Press.

Gordon, Daryl
1995   Shifting gender roles in the acculturation process. *University of Pennsylvania Working Papers in Educational Linguistics* 11, 1, 50–68.

Grosjean, François
1998   Studying bilinguals: Methodological and conceptual issues. *Bilingualism: Language and Cognition* 1, 131–149.

Hegde, Radha
1998   Swinging the trapeze: The negotiation of identity among Asian Indian immigrant women in the United States. In Tanno, Dolores and Alberto Gonzalez (eds.), *Communication and Identity Across Cultures.* Thousand Oaks: Sage, 34–55.

Heilbrun, Carolyn
1988   *Writing a Woman's Life.* New York: Ballantine Books.

Hirsch, Marianne
1994   Pictures of displaced girlhood. In Bammer, Angelica (ed.), *Displacements: Cultural Identities in Question.* Bloomington, IN: Indiana University Press, 71–89

Hoffman, Eva
  1989   *Lost in Translation: A Life in a New Language.* New York: Dutton.

Kaplan, Alice
  1993   *French Lessons: A Memoir.* Chicago/London: The University of Chicago
            Press.

Kim, Helen
  2000   Beyond boundaries. In Danquah, Meri Nana-Ama (ed.), *Becoming Ameri-*
            can: Personal Essays by First Generation Immigrant Women. New York:
            Hyperion, 113–125.

Kingston, Maxine Hong
  1975   *The Woman Warrior: Memoirs of a Girlhood Among Ghosts.* New York:
            Vintage Books.

Kramsch, Claire and Wan Shun Eva Lam
  1999   Textual identities: The importance of being non-native. In Braine, George
            (ed.), *Non-Native Educators in English Language Teaching.* Mahwah, NJ:
            Lawrence Erlbaum Associates, 57–72.

Krulfeld, Ruth
  1994   Buddhism, maintenance and change: Reinterpreting gender in a Lao refu-
            gee community. In Camino, Linda and Ruth Krulfeld (eds.), *Reconstruct-*
            ing Lives, Recapturing Meaning: Refugee Identity, Gender, and Culture
            Change. Basel: Gordon and Breach Publishers, 97–127.

Lee, Helie
  2000   Disassembling Helie. In Danquah, Meri Nana-Ama (ed.), *Becoming*
            American: Personal Essays by First Generation Immigrant Women. New
            York: Hyperion, 126–137.

Ledgerwood, Judy
  1990   *Changing Khmer Conceptions of Gender: Women, Stories, and the Social*
            Order. Ph.D. dissertation, Cornell University.

Lieblich, Amia
  1993   Looking at change: Natasha, 21: New immigrant from Russia to Israel. In
            Josselson, Ruthellen and Amia Lieblich (eds.), *The Narrative Study of*
            Lives. Vol. 1. Newbury Park: Sage, 92–129.

Linde, Charlotte
  1993   *Life Stories.* New York: Oxford University Press.

Lippi-Green, Rosina
1997   *English with an Accent: Language, Ideology, and Discrimination in the United States*. London: Routledge.

Lvovich, Natasha
1997   *The Multilingual Self: An Inquiry into Language Learning*. Mahwah, NJ: Lawrence Erlbaum Associates.

Mar, Elaine
1999   *Paper Daughter: A Memoir*. New York: Harper Collins Publishers.

McGroarty, Mary
1998   Constructive and constructivist challenges for applied linguistics. *Language Learning* 48, 4, 591–622.

Mori, Kyoko
1997   *Polite Lies: On Being a Woman Caught between Two Cultures*. New York: Henry Holt and Company.

2000   Becoming Midwestern. In Danquah, Meri Nana-Ama (ed.), *Becoming American: Personal Essays by First Generation Immigrant Women*. New York: Hyperion, 138–145.

Ogulnick, Karen
1998   *Onna Rashiku (Like A Woman): The Diary of a Language Learner in Japan*. Albany, NY: SUNY Press.

Pavlenko, Aneta
1998   Second language learning by adults: testimonies of bilingual writers. *Issues in Applied Linguistics* 9, 1, 3–19.

2001   Language learning memoirs as a gendered genre. *Applied Linguistics* 22, 2, 213–240.

in press a   "In the world of the tradition, I was unimagined": negotiation of identities in cross-cultural autobiographies. *The International Journal of Bilingualism*.

in press b   Socioeconomic conditions and discursive construction of women's identities in post-Soviet countries. In Kelemen, Mihaela and Monika Kostera (eds.), *Critical Eastern European Management: Current Issues and Research*. Harwood Academic.

Pavlenko, Aneta and James P. Lantolf
2000   Second language learning as participation and the (re)construction of selves. In Lantolf, James P. (ed.), *Sociocultural Theory and Second Language Learning*. New York: Oxford University Press, 155–177.

Peirce, Bonny Norton
   1995   Social identity, investment, and language learning. *TESOL Quarterly* 29, 1, 9–31.

Polanyi, Livia
   1995   Language learning and living abroad: Stories from the field. In Freed, Barbara (ed.), *Second Language Acquisition in a Study Abroad Context*. Amsterdam/Philadelphia: John Benjamins, 271–291.

Reyn, Irina
   2000   Recalling a child of October. In Danquah, Meri Nana-Ama (ed.), *Becoming American: Personal Essays by First Generation Immigrant Women*. New York: Hyperion, 146–155.

Rodriguez, Richard
   1982   *Hunger of Memory: The Education of Richard Rodriguez*. New York: Bantam.

Rosario, Nelly
   2000   On becoming. In Danquah, Meri Nana-Ama (ed.), *Becoming American: Personal Essays by First Generation Immigrant Women*. New York: Hyperion, 156–174.

Saine, Ute Margaret
   2000   Now is the time to try something – but have I got nine lives? In Danquah, Meri Nana-Ama (ed.), *Becoming American: Personal Essays by First Generation Immigrant Women*. New York: Hyperion, 165–175.

Schumann, John
   1997   The neurobiology of affect. *Language Learning*, a supplement.

Sloan, James
   1996   *Jerzy Kosinski: A Biography*. Plume Book.

Smith, Sidonie
   1987   *A Poetics of Women's Autobiography: Marginality and the Fictions of Self-Representation*. Bloomington, IN: Indiana University Press.

Watson, Richard
   1995   *The Philosopher's Demise: Learning French*. Columbia/London: University of Missouri Press.

174   *Aneta Pavlenko*

Wierzbicka, Anna
   1985   The double life of a bilingual. In Sussex, Roland and Jerzy Zubrzycki (eds.), *Polish People and Culture in Australia*. Canberra: Australian National University, 187–223.

   1997   The double life of a bilingual: A cross-cultural perspective. In Bond, Michael (ed.), *Working at the Interface of Cultures: Eighteen Lives in Social Science*. London: Routledge, 113–125.

Young, Richard
   1999   Sociolinguistic approaches to SLA. *Annual Review of Applied Linguistics* 19, 105–132.

(Re)constructing masculinity in a new linguistic reality

Marya Teutsch-Dwyer

1. Introduction

Some of the recent work on masculinity proposes that men's identities have become more problematic as a result of changes in society (Faludi 1999; Johnson and Meinhof 1997). Gender roles, within the poststructuralist view, have come to be regarded as socially constructed, fluid, and variable, with boundaries not as fixed as has been popularly believed (e.g., Bergvall, Bing, and Freed 1996). More importantly, masculinity is no longer viewed as the unproblematized norm against which female language is scrutinized and problematized (Johnson 1997).

Assuming that variability exists in masculine identities and that language plays divergent roles in the social construction of these identitites (Johnson 1997), how is masculinity fluid and unstable when confronted with new linguistic and new cultural realities? Are men subject to power relations similar to those that existed in the first language environment? What role does second language acquisition play in gender relations and masculine identities? Few of these questions have been addressed in the research literature so far (but see Pavlenko's chapter). Generally speaking, despite the new approach to research on gender and second language acquisition, male learners – as opposed to their female peers – have received relatively marginal attention so far. One wonders what are the reasons behind this obvious asymmetry. Is it the continuation among researchers of the tradition that men and masculinity are to be treated as the 'norm' against which women and femininity and female linguistic practices need to be scrutinized? Or is it, perhaps, the fact that the social pressures and social expectations 'disallow' men from divulging their inner failures and tribulations, including those associated with second language learning, thus making female informants more accessible and more informative? We may never find out.

In an attempt to bring some symmetry to research on gender and second language acquisition, this chapter focuses on one male's language development in a new linguistic and social reality. The research results are based on an ethnographic longitudinal case study of the naturalistic acquisition of English by a Polish man. I will argue that the gender role(s) that the learner chose to perform and the gender roles that he had been assigned due to fluctuating living circumstances may have had a significant influence on the acquisition process itself as well as on the outcomes of this process. The intricate relationship between this learner's self- and other-positioning in the structure of power relations and subsequent circle of language interlocutors have influenced his language practices. In particular, the study suggests that the social positioning of this male informant nurtured by his American girlfriend and other female linguistic 'caretakers' may have positively influenced the reconstruction of his masculinity in his new linguistic reality, and, at the same time, it may have slowed down the formal acquisition of the second language to a considerable degree. The next section of this chapter outlines the theoretical framework that influenced this study, with an emphasis on masculinity and second language learning and use. Then, I will present research questions and outline the methodological approach and techniques used in data collection. Next, I will illustrate and discuss the development of linguistic and non-linguistic markers of temporality the informant used in his personal narratives. Finally, the informant's initiation into language practices and the (re)construction of his masculine identity will be discussed and mapped onto his language development trajectory.

2. Masculinity, language use, and second language development

Unlike theories of second language acquisition, which had often assumed an idealized and abstract 'learner', more recent studies on gender and second language acquisition have investigated gender as a construct shaped by historical, cultural, social, and interactional factors (Goldstein 1995, 1997, and this volume; Peirce 1995). Within this new paradigm, second language learners are no longer viewed as unidimensional, ahistorical individuals whose language use and language acquisition are to a large degree influenced by a set of often clearly discernible characteristics (including sex), on the one hand, and a set of social variables in language learning, on the other (Peirce 1995; Woolard 1998).

When theorizing language and masculinity from a feminist perspective, rather than viewing "masculinity as an essentialist opposite to an equally essentialist femininity", Johnson (1997: 1–2) advocates a view which sees "masculinity and femininity as mutually dependent constructs in a dialectical relationship". More importantly, masculinities may vary not only within one individual, one group of individuals, but also across cultures. Thus, there is no one prototypical 'masculinity', but rather a range of masculine identities. Shaped by personal and societal values and subject to constant conditioning brought about by current life circumstances, the same individuals may articulate talk and gender differently under different social circumstances in order to situate themselves appropriately in a given social event (e.g., Goodwin 1999). Or they may also act according to culturally-defined norms of masculinity or femininity (Ehrlich 1997; Goldstein 1995; Hill 1987). In an experimental setting, Freed (1996) shows that the setting and communicative tasks the speakers engage in influence language practices to a much higher degree than the sex of the speakers. It has become known that conventional sex-role theory is not able to explain the use by both sexes of linguistic forms traditionally assigned to either men (de Klerk 1997) or women (Johnson and Finlay 1997).

Since gender, according to Cameron (1997: 60), is a "relational term, and the minimal requirement for 'being a man' is 'not being a woman', we may find that in many circumstances, men are under pressure to constitute themselves as masculine linguistically by avoiding forms of talk whose primary association is with women/femininity". The way in which masculine behavior is to measure up to a specific norm depends on the social expectations of the culture where this behavior is to be performed. Thus, conversationalists often construct stories about themselves and others, in order to perform certain kinds of gender identities (Cameron 1997). This practice is not invariant, however, and performing gender may involve different strategies in mixed and single-sex company, as also shown in this chapter, in private versus public settings, and in the various social positions one might occupy on a regular basis.

Recent studies have also shown that, when people do perform gender differently in different circumstances, they may behave in ways which would normally be attributed to the 'other' gender. Men, for example, contrary to commonly held beliefs, have been shown to indulge in practices of gossip similar in structure to those performed by women (Johnson and Finlay 1997). Also contrary to the myth, men – like women (Coates 1998 a, b) – consider small talk as a vehicle for affirming group solidarity. In her study of the different strategies women and men use when gossiping, Pilkington (1998) found that the aims of women's and men's gossip appeared to be similar in that they expressed solidarity and group membership. They differed only in the strategies adopted to achieve these aims. While the women tended to use positive :politeness strategies, the men used language in more aggressive ways. Similarly, Cameron's (1997) study found that the specific topics on which the talk among young males focused were conventionally and traditionally 'feminine' ones:

clothing and bodily appearance. The purpose of the gossip was, moreover, 'rapport talk' rather than 'report talk' which "serves one of the most common purposes of gossip, namely affirming the solidarity of an in-group by constructing absent others as an out-group, whose behaviour is minutely observed and found wanting" (Cameron 1997: 54).

It is common knowledge that successful second language acquisition involves opportunities to practice the target language. In the learning process, the learners' perceptions of their own identity are subject to change over time, as their social and cultural environments undergo changes. Following the idea that speakers' identities emerge from discourse, the language of the learner becomes an important tool for establishing one's social identity, one's self, in the changing reality within which second language speakers need to function. For example, in an extensive study on the gendered nature of narratives which include stories about language learning and gender, Pavlenko (1998 and this volume) demonstrates that cultural and social constraints of gender shape the ways in which both women and men learn and use second language. Both genders need to reinvent themselves to fit their new realities; however, the pressures may be much higher on some individuals than others. In another study on how second language settings may create restricted exposure to target language, Cumming and Gill (1991) show how the sociocultural factors and traditional family roles, in particular, had a significant influence on women's access to ESL classes and the target language and society at large. It was the husbands' role in the new community to take care of most family financial tasks, major purchases, and various institutional interactions, all carried out in the second language. By focusing on the women's access to ESL classes, the study revealed, indirectly, the gendered language practices that facilitated the males' access to the new cultural norms and contributed to their achievement of higher levels of language competence.

The current study argues for the importance of identity and language as the site of power and individual consciousness in the process of second language development. As poststructuralists would argue, rather than correlated with social variables such as gender, class, ethnicity, or age, identity, which Weis (1990: 1) defines as a "sense of self in relation to others", is "shaped moment to moment through the details of how participants interact with activities" (Goodwin 1999: 391). Following Peirce (1995), Weedon (1987), and Woolard (1998), I take the position that individual learner characteristics, including those of the male learner under investigation, are multiple, dynamic, and co-constructed. Learners create their own language and their own communicative strategies based on their perceptions of their positions as male or female in the social reality imposed on them in the new cultural, social, and linguistic environment. Those perceptions, Bourdieu (1999: 67) argues, may influence the speakers' linguistic practices, as "the value of the utterance depends on the relations of power that is concretely established between the speakers' linguistic competencies, understood both as their capacity for appropriation and appreciation". The definition of competence needs to include "an awareness of the right to speak" and "the power to impose reception" (Bourdieu 1977: 649). In other words, effective communication can be established in a situation which requires "that those who speak regard those who listen as worthy to listen, and that those who listen regard those who speak as worthy to speak" (Bourdieu 1977: 649). In a study of second language learning of immigrant women in Canada, Peirce (1995: 23) showed how women's identities changed over time: "... it was only over time that Eva's conception of herself as an immigrant – an 'illegitimate' speaker of English – changed to a conception of herself as a multicultural citizen with the power to impose reception". "As Eva continued to develop ... an identity as a multicultural citizen, she developed with it an awareness of her right to speak" (Peirce 1995: 25). Second language learning will, in turn, be seen here as socialization where language plays a significant symbolic role in how people constitute themselves (Weedon 1987) and others in terms of their attributes, activities, and participation in social practices (Eckert and McConnell-Ginet 1995). I believe, therefore, that the process of language acquisition is best viewed as a dynamic interaction between the social reality and the language learner. The present study focuses on this relationship.

3.   The study

My informant was recruited for the study at the time when I was on the Board of Trustees for the Polish Arts and Culture Foundation in San Francisco, California. Through this volunteer work I met a number of Polish visitors to the United States, many of whom shared a strong conviction that the only effective way to learn a second language was through natural exposure to that language. By "natural", my informants meant learning a language without and outside the rigidity of a structured language classroom setting. Many believed that highly desirable language acquisition results could be brought about only through "living" in a second language host society, through being exposed to the host culture, and by picking up the language on a daily basis. For this reason, I elected to observe longitudinally the morpho-syntactic development of English as a second language in a native speaker of Polish who would match my interlocutors' definitions of someone who would believe in naturalistic acquisition of a second language, i.e., by picking it up while living in the host country. From among several candidates I met through the Polish Arts and Culture Foundation, I chose Karol, who believed in "natural" acquisition of English, whose plans were to stay in the United States for at least a year-and-a-half, and who agreed to be my informant on a regular basis. Two questions were of primary importance in this study:

1.   How are the learning process and its outcomes influenced by a second language setting, its changing sociocultural factors, gendered language practices, and language experiences?
2.   What linguistic and non-linguistic markers does a naturalistic language learner use in the encoding of temporality, at different points in time?
      Specifically, the study looked at how the process of language acquisition correlated with (a) the male learner's access to the target language resources and (b) the learner's perception of his social positioning in the target language networks.

In what follows, I will describe in detail the setting and conditions of data collection and the importance of briefings and debriefings during every interview session.

3.1. The research setting

The study lasted 14 months. The recording sessions started one week after the informant arrived in the United States. It was agreed that the recording sessions, one hour each, for which he was paid in appreciation for his time, would take place every two weeks and that during that time he would use only English. Almost all the recording sessions took place in my house; only a few took place in his sister's house and later, once or twice, in his home.

Before and after each recording, the informant would update me, in Polish, on many of his cultural, linguistic, and personal experiences in the United States. These informal 'briefings' accomplished at least three things. First, over a period of 14 months I learned much about my informant's past and present life, future plans and dreams, opinions, and beliefs. He was an excellent and interesting storyteller who could weave his personal stories in fairly complex narrative structures, with many digressions, never losing track of the main story. While listening to his stories in his native tongue, I would take notes and jot down questions I would want to ask him during our interviews in English. To preserve a certain degree of uniformity in the data collection routine, the starting question would normally refer to the informant's daily activities between the current day and the previous interview. The questions that followed were based on the information gathered during the prerecording briefing sessions. In addition, every consecutive recording session was built around the ever-growing shared knowledge which served as a starting point for retelling of the 'new episodes' in the informant's most recent or distant past. To adhere to the natural discourse genre, however, the initiation of a topic or a change in topic introduced by the informant was not discouraged. Second, briefings as well as debriefings played an important part in verifying/validating the data. They provided the opportunity to check the correctness of my interpretation of the informant's linguistic output. Finally, the extra time spent before and after each interview contributed to the creation of a friendly and informal atmosphere. Rapport between the informant and myself was established and consistently supported. All these interview conditions resulted in obtaining language data that were as natural, or vernacular, as possible under the circumstances (see Labov 1972).

3.2. The informant

The informant, Karol, a male speaker of Polish, was thirty-eight years old at the time of the study. Prior to his stay in the US, he had never been exposed to English in any formal way, nor had he ever visited any of the English-speaking countries. In Poland, he received a university education and later worked as a high school physical education teacher and a soccer coach. He had a wife and two teenage daughters whom he had left behind. The main goal for his stay in the United States was to earn enough money to provide for his family in Poland. He had planned to return to his home country after three to five years. Karol projected a personality of someone who was friendly, helpful, and outgoing, with a highly positive attitude toward speakers of English. In addition, he loved to have fun, and he always showed willingness to use English in real communication – qualities that are often perceived to be desirable in good language learners (Naiman et al 1978 [1996]).

3.3. Data base

The results of this study are triangulated from the following types of data:

1. tape-recorded interviews of natural discourse collected bi-weekly from Karol;

2.   notes taken by the researcher during and after the tape-recorded inter-
       views;
3.   learner self-reports of strategies used in acquiring English, opinions on
       his newly-acquired target language abilities, stories about his language
       learning experiences, and accounts of many "adventures" encountered in
       his new culture; all these were reported in English and in Polish;
4.   informal interviews with the informant's American girlfriend;
5.   one audio-tape recording of a conversation between the informant and his
       girlfriend during dinner preparation time at their home; and
6.   one audio-tape recording of an informal conversation between the in-
       formant and his female co-workers during one of the customary lunch
       breaks at the informant's workplace. Data in situations (5) and (6) were
       collected without my presence, with the consent of all people involved.

4.   Language output: Temporality

The linguistic analysis of the learner's speech will focus on the grammaticalization process of temporality markers, which was shown to be a good index of
the formal acquisition of English as a second language. The ways in which time
and time relations are established can be determined by the context of utterances, the use of adverbials, the structure of a sentence, and the relationship between tense and aspect. These extralinguistic and linguistic elements in discourse make it possible for both the speaker and hearer to decipher the temporal meaning of the text and to assign a semantic representation to it. A
number of studies (Bardovi-Harlig 1999; Dietrich, Klein, and Noyau 1995;
Dittmar 1988; Giacalone Ramat 1992; Sato 1990; Teutsch-Dwyer 1995;
Teutsch-Dwyer and Fathman 1996; von Stutterheim 1984) have examined the
different ways in which temporal reference and temporal relations are expressed by second language learners of different ages, language backgrounds,
and in different learning contexts. As a general finding, temporality has been
shown to be expressed not only by more overt means, such as lexical and grammatical means, but also to a large degree by less overt discourse-pragmatic devices. As proficiency increases, so does the grammaticalization of the existing
lexical and discourse-pragmatic means (Meisel 1987; Sato 1990).

4.1. Analysis

The longitudinal micro-analysis of the language output focused on the ways in which temporal reference and temporal relations between events were encoded in personal narratives. Linguistic and discourse-pragmatic devices were analyzed and the relationship between the two types was observed over time. The fluctuations in the verbal behavior and the communicative strategies were then matched with the changes in the social context and the learner's self-perceptions of his position in the social and cultural reality within which he functioned during the study. The four most commonly found temporal relations were those of posteriority, anteriority, contaneity, and simultaneity.[1]

4.2. Means and devices used in marking time and temporal relations

The analysis of the learner's linguistic output, in particular the ways in which he encoded temporal reference and temporal relations in personal narratives revealed the use of three major devices: (1) discourse-pragmatic devices, (2) lexical means, and (3) morpho-syntactic structures.

I.   Among the discourse-pragmatic devices, four were found to be prevalent:

(1)   The Real Life Congruency (RLC) technique, a 'discourse organization principle' (Klein 1981) which makes use of a particular order of elements to deliver the desired message. In a temporal passage, events which occurred first appear first in an utterance, as in the following example:

> I was (at the)[2] gas station
> talk (with the) boss (of the) gas station
> and I start job[3]

(2)   'Anchoring', which is a device whereby a major event, or a series of events, is first located in time, by means of a deictic or calendric adverb, and then the story is recounted by means of tenseless verbs, e. g.:

> *Wednesday* I work (at the) gas station
> I go back home
> I sleep two hours.

(3)   'Conceptual transfer', which refers to a situation where a temporal re-
       lation may be expressed by non-temporal means, such as spatial refer-
       ence. Spatial reference, when associated with movement, or 'locomo-
       tion', may be used to express reference to time by identifying the point of
       origin, the Source, and/or the destination of the object, the Goal, which is
       understood to occur at a later point in time (Fillmore 1975), e. g.:

>   everybody Roma to New York
>   to San Francisco

(4)   'Conceptual transfer', where a temporal relation can be expressed by a
       repetition of the previous item in order to secure continuity, as in the
       example below. The item that is repeated refers to locality. The difference
       between this conceptual transfer and the conceptual transfer in (3) is that
       in (3) the narrative moves forward on a path *between* different localities,
       whereas in this example, the *same* locality is repeated to move events for-
       ward on a time axis, e. g.:

>   I work in *garden*
>   *garden* I plant flowers

II.   Lexical means constitute the most widely used linguistic means. They in-
       clude the following two forms:

(5)   adverbials:

>   *Last week* I go to school
>   and *then* I talk to my friends.

(6)   base verb forms:

>   Tuesday *work* in gas station
>   I *take* bus Market Street in office
>   *go* back home

III.   Morpho-syntactic means constitute the last category. They appear
       relatively infrequently in the learner's language output. They include two
       types:

(7) inflected non-target verb forms:

Last week we eat*ing* here.

(8) target-like past tense forms:

My friend *had* job

4.3. Language development over time

The longitudinal analysis of the data revealed a number of interesting tendencies, which may be attributed to the linguistic and social realities this learner was exposed to. To begin with, discourse-pragmatic means remained the most common device used to encode temporal relations at all the stages of Karol's second language development. The learner's heavy reliance on discourse-pragmatic means was strengthened by the initial successful communicative practices with his female co-workers. As the learner himself later stated he did not have to use "correct" English because his stories were well received and his jokes laughed at. Rather than focus on grammatical development, he continued to expand the gamut of discourse-pragmatic devices.

Aiding him in the communicative practices were lexical means (adverbials and base verb forms). Karol was quick to admit that vocabulary expansion was the key to communication. Indeed, the findings show that his lexicon underwent a steady expansion. The ratio of use of time adverbials to the number of utterances increased from 16% at the beginning stages to close to 45% towards the end of the first year. The lexical development is visible in the increased use of verbs as well. At the beginning of the study as many as 41% of the utterances did not have a verb in them, as opposed to only 8% in the final stage of the study. The data provides us with some evidence of the grammaticalization process; however, it is primarily evident in non-target like forms (e.g., we eat*ing*). Moreover, the use of the base verb forms remains very high (at 51% – 66%) throughout the 14-month period of the study. At the same time, as illustrated above, the use of different discourse-pragmatic devices continues to be favored in reporting past events. Table 1 shows the percentages of the past time events that were encoded by means of base verb forms, inflected non-target-like tense verb forms, and target-like past tense verb forms over a period of fourteen months. It also shows the percentage of utterances which lacked a verb altogether.

Table 1. Frequency of past-time events expressed by verbless utterances, base verb forms, inflected non-target-like verb forms, and target-like past tense forms, at six points in time over a period of fourteen months

	Time 1	Time 2	Time 3	Time 4	Time 5	Time 6
Verbless	41	25	18	9	12	8
Base VB	59	66	58	58	51	59
Non-Base	0	2	16	25	30	17
Past T VB	0	7	8	7	6	16

Interestingly, the use of adverbials dropped to 33% at the end of the study, co-inciding with Karol's and Karol's girlfriend's reports of the easiness of communication between them, due to the fact that Karol's girlfriend anticipated his intended utterances and filled in the words for him or came up with entire sentences to which Karol was merely expected to provide a positive or negative short answer.

5.   The social (re)construction of masculinity

5.1. The initiation into language practices

In this section I will discuss possible explanations for Karol's language developmental path and his language practices, which became rewarded at a fairly early stage, thereby slowing down the grammaticalization process. Unlike many female visitors who come to the United States as wives of university students, included in the category of 'sojourners' (e.g., Uchida 1998), single females, or married breadwinners who, for the lack of the host-country language skills, seek blue-collar jobs in Canada (Norton 1997; Peirce 1995), this male so-journer encountered very different welcoming routines into the host culture and host language practices. In sharp contrast to the predicaments the women in the studies above went through, including in some cases social harassment due to gender-based expectations on the part of either the home- or the host-country society, Karol's social and linguistic situation rendered, it would seem, a more favorable basis for language acquisition from the beginning of his stay in the United States. During the first month, he was hosted and taken care of by his bilingual sister, whom he hadn't seen for ten years, and by his monolingual American brother-in-law. The household, which also included a little daughter and her Spanish-English bilingual babysitter, provided a sheltered language learning environment. Since only Karol's sister spoke Polish, Karol either heard people in the house speak English to each other or he was addressed directly in English by the household members, especially by his brother-in-law. The latter often asked Karol questions about the current political and economic situation in Poland. Even though Karol's sister functioned as interpreter during these exchanges, Karol, as the male interlocutor, had the advantage of not only being the focus of these traditionally gendered exchanges but also of being the sought-after source of information, which he was prepared and eager to deliver. At least initially, his social position in the household validated by its male member and co-constructed by Karol's own agency appeared to place him in a favorable position in the social power relations. Karol reported that relatively soon he relied less and less on his sister's help, as he was increasingly more successful at understanding or guessing from the conversational context the content of his brother-in-law's follow-up questions and statements. His responses obviously still required his sister's assistance, however. This situation makes it clear that this man's initial speech practices, however entirely inadequate from the prescriptive point of view, set the tone for his future linguistic and social self- and other-positioning as male in the new linguistic environment.

5.2. Masculinity undermined through language practices

The linguistic 'routines' the two brothers-in-law engaged in with the assistance of the bilingual female during the informant's initiation stage came to an abrupt end when Karol's stay at his sister's house was terminated by his brother-in-law. Karol announced this change during one of the regularly scheduled informal interviews during the second month into the study, in the following way:

(9)   sister talk with her husband
        (who told her) that I no live at home
        I say, "good, no problem"
        I leave

Consequently, he moved to a workers' hotel downtown where he maintained a very close contact with four other Polish men, with whom he remained friends throughout the study.

Because Karol was not welcome to stay in his sister's house, his subsequent conversations with his brother-in-law were limited only to necessary occasions. Moreover, the reason for the infrequent contacts was, among others, caused by the growing distrust and initially covert animosity between the two men. At the onset of the third month of the study, he described his brother-in-law in an animated voice in somewhat pejorative terms:

(10)   brother-in-law is American
        he have this hobby
        money, family
        and no ... (other) persons in home

Like the males in Cameron's study (1997), Karol attempted to reconstruct his "hurt" masculinity by distancing himself from his brother-in-law who, he believed, lacked truly masculine qualities: he was too homey, too ostentatiously family-oriented, was too much involved in money making enterprises, and he did not like to entertain people at home.

The animosity became more obvious when Karol realized that *his* masculinity was severely undermined in the eyes of the one male he looked up to during the initiation stage and who initially gave him the impression of full acceptance of his linguistic trials. He expressed his disappointment in this way:

(11)   and he like speak business every time
        with me no possible (because)
        I no have money
        I no have business
        and I no speak English
        I no good partner for him (because)
        I no money no business
        no friends with lota money

Thus, Karol realized that his brother-in-law's standards of what constituted an appropriate male conversational partner were far from what he could offer at the time. Karol was not a man of means, nor did he have friends with money. He was not about to enter any business deals, and above all, he had insufficient English language skills. For face-saving reasons, however, he repeatedly criticized this overly materialistic approach to life.

Another important male in Karol's daily encounters was his boss in the factory he worked at on a full-time basis throughout the study. The contacts with his boss centered on the job tasks he had to perform. His boss would give him hands-on training from time to time, which consisted of explanations of how to operate a big cutting machine and how to hold the material to be cut. The verbal instructions were always accompanied by visual demonstrations. Thanks to the latter, Karol was able to compensate for his inadequate listening comprehension skills by relying on his own general knowledge and inferencing abilities to understand the instructions. He was, in fact, so good at 'following' the instructions that fairly soon his boss gave him – and again 'explained' – more complicated tasks to perform. On several occasions he was asked to work overtime, as he described in the following passage:

(12)　　last week is same as every week
　　　　I work every day and ten hours
　　　　because my factory get big order from United Airlines
　　　　and we working every day ten hours
　　　　and Saturday half day only four hours we work

What seems to be interesting, however, is that despite the fact that the informant's boss expressed his satisfaction with his job abilities, he did not extend this praise to his linguistic development. In fact, he indicated to Karol's girlfriend (who worked at the same factory) that were it not for his poor English language abilities, he could be promoted to a higher position, as Karol expressed below:

(13)　　My friend Danielle tell me that Michael talk
　　　　Karol good speak English
　　　　Karol get a job controller man

Thus, the second most important male in his life in the host country failed to acknowledge the great strides he felt he had made in his language development. The awareness of his linguistic inadequacy and the impossibility of advancing at work prompted this informant to think about learning English in a more systematic (structured) way; he even attempted to make some Polish-English tapes with his girlfriend. The plans were short-lived, however, and he continued the 'natural' acquisition of English, especially since his linguistic and non-linguistic attributes of male behavior were very welcome among his female circle of co-workers, as will be shown below.

5.3. The reconstruction of masculinity

The work place provided Karol with the opportunity to communicate socially with his co-workers during lunch and two coffee breaks. It did not take much time before he formed a social circle during those breaks, particularly with three female co-workers: a monolingual speaker of English and two bilingual speakers, one of Italian and one of Chinese origin. They would sit at a table (which he had built for that purpose) outside the building, have lunch or coffee, and "chat" in a friendly manner. Sometimes, he reported, he would just sit and listen to his friends' conversations; on other occasions, however, he would answer a lot of their questions about various aspects of life in Poland and his personal situation. Karol reported he would gladly tell them as much as he could. He soon realized, to his stated content, that he became a very popular "guy" with the three women and he felt free and encouraged to entertain them. Consequently, more and more often he volunteered to tell funny or "incredible" stories from his life. As part of his entertaining routine, he would tell jokes – which he was good at and which he had always enjoyed doing in his native language (for a discussion of jokes as a means of performing masculinity in Eastern Europe, see also Pavlenko's chapter). This new linguistic reality stood in sharp contrast to his social position vis-à-vis his brother-in-law and his boss, where his position of power was minimized and his English tolerated to the bare minimum. In the new situation, he regained the "power to speak" (Peirce 1995). His maleness among the female circle of friends was restored, and he felt his position was elevated to the position of an equal in conversations.

Karol reported that after a while he did not have to struggle to use "very correct English" among his circle of female friends because he knew they could by now understand what he had intended to say – that is, they got used to his language and his communicative strategies. His position strengthened, his masculinity restored, and his English abilities acknowledged and appreciated, Karol felt empowered and encouraged to expand the vocabulary element of his language system. He would periodically reiterate that even though he wanted to go back to Poland having reached his monetary goal, he also wanted to "make life easier for him here", in the United States. He would repeatedly announce that he wanted to get to know America better, and that he wanted to communicate with people. Language was the key to that, he stated. To this informant, the concepts of "language" and "language learning" were strongly associated with vocabulary and vocabulary acquisition since by now he had discovered that his grammatical constructions were positively reinforced by his listeners.

Not long after he had been employed, he started dating the American female member of his 'lunch' social circle. Soon the two moved into an apartment and shared it with two other Polish-speaking male friends of Karol's. During this time Karol's vocabulary was rapidly and visibly developing. Admittedly, Karol reported using a lot of Polish every day after work with the two friends and with his sister on a weekly basis. He also continued to be an avid reader of books and magazines in Polish. However, he continued to communicate only in English with the woman and at work with his co-workers. The two spent a lot of free time together, a large portion of which was in the kitchen since Karol loved to cook. For the most part, he reported that he lived a happy and contented life, as the excerpt below illustrates:

(14)   on Saturday maybe maybe we have small party and my friend
         I think we we dinner everybody
         and small drink
         my friends and American friend woman small dance
         drink long time
         finish maybe three o'clock at night this party
         and Sunday Sunday I maybe very tired and sleep

With time, Karol realized that his girlfriend modified her speech when she addressed him. According to him, she used primarily two techniques. First, she would slow down when speaking to him. Second, she would try to use the words that she remembered he had already acquired. On occasions when somebody else addressed him and he did not understand the message, she would 'translate' the message for him into the language that she knew was accessible to him. 'Translations' involved using synonyms known to Karol, using circumlocutions, and simplifying the structural content. Karol reported that with the passage of time, just as in the case of his co-workers, he stopped trying to 'speak correctly' to his girlfriend because he knew that she would understand him anyway. His girlfriend corroborated these statements by saying that she had always tried to anticipate what he intended to say and would either finish the sentence for him or would answer whatever question she guessed he might have intended to ask. She not only cared for him in the linguistic sense by using some form of "motherese" (Snow and Ferguson 1977) but also took care of his personal business which required phone calls or visits to banks, doctors, even the court. Being doted upon and living in somewhat sheltered social circumstances, it was not surprising that Karol, as he himself admitted, could not write a check or withdraw money until the end of the first year (compare the study by Cumming and Gill (1991) on women's restricted exposure to target language referred to above). Occasionally on weekends, his girlfriend would invite her American friends who often were second or third generation Poles or who were in some measure interested in Polish culture. Karol found them easier to converse with, as there was always some mutual interest to talk about. One of them, to Karol's surprise and admiration, could even speak some Polish.

(15)   John this John have mother is born here,
        and grandmother and grandfather born in Poland
        and he very good speak Polish
        he read Polish book
        Iota know of Polish history, geography

The learner in this study received much of what would be considered comprehensible input (Krashen 1981) during the initial period of his language acquisition although it was somewhat sheltered. A number of studies suggest a link between interactional modification and increased comprehension (Long 1985; Pica, Young, and Doughty 1987) and the importance of interaction and opportunities to communicate for second language acquisition (Loschky 1994; Schmidt and Frota 1986). However, despite the fact that this learner had ample opportunities to engage in interactional exchanges and was exposed to comprehensible input, the lack of feedback to his malformed utterances as well as the false supportiveness (Siegal 1996) which he received on a regular basis from his female interlocutors may have contributed to the stabilization (Preston 1989) of the linguistic forms he had acquired and proceeded to use in his daily output. The lack of negative feedback may have eventually led to fossilization (Preston 1989) of the formal elements of English in the early stages of language development. Thus, this chapter hypothesizes that the learner's substantial lack of the grammaticalization process during his language acquisition over a period of fourteen months is closely related to his perceptions of positive acceptance by the social female circles he was a member of and by the sheltered conditions he experienced in his private life.

6.   Conclusion

In this chapter, I have shown that a male learner's acquisitional path may be influenced by his image of masculinity and the fluctuating life situations encountered in the new cultural environment. The results suggest that this learner created his own language system and his own communicative strategies based on his perceptions of his position as a male in the social reality imposed on him in his new cultural and linguistic environment. It would appear that the masculinities transferred into a new cultural and linguistic environment do not necessarily disappear due to the lack of the required linguistic means. Rather, they undergo cosmetic transformations and manifest themselves through special linguistic and non-linguistic devices effective in maintaining the sought-after (as well as expected) status of a heterosexual male. The gender identity transposed into a new environment and the notions of how to act towards women, supported by the encouragement on the part of the feminine circles in the new reality, may facilitate communicative skills and enhance "the right to speak" and "the right to impose reception" (Bourdieu 1977; Peirce 1995) among females. The chapter raises the question of whether the social acceptance of male linguistic behavior among female circles leads to an optimal language development. As shown in the study, the role this male had been 'assigned' in his personal relationship with the American woman restricted the extent as well as the quality of interactions that would otherwise constitute the norm in the majority society (see Cumming and Gill 1991). His masculine identity and language investments (Peirce 1995) were rewarded at a fairly early stage of language development, thereby slowing down the formal acquisition of English.

The implications of the study call for a new conception of identity that entails "radically redefining the second language learner" (McKay and Wong 1996: 578). In full agreement with McKay and Wong, I strongly advocate the need for educators to see learners' identities more comprehensively and to "examine interconnections of discourse and power in the language learning setting" (1996: 578).

Notes

1. *A temporal relation of anteriority* expresses the idea that in an utterance we mark first those events that occurred first in time and later those that occurred later in time. In other words, the sequence of marking events in an utterance corresponds to the sequence in which these events occurred in real life.

   A temporal relation of posteriority is the mirror image of that of anteriority; in other words, instead of marking what happened first, we first mark what happened later and then what happened earlier in time.

   A temporal relation of contaneity expresses the idea that one event, or a series of events, is contained in another event, which occupies a larger time frame. Conversely, we can say that contaneity expresses the idea that one major event contains another event.

A temporal relation of simultaneity expresses the idea that two or more events appear alongside each other and occupy the same space on a time axis; more precisely, their time frames overlap at exactly the same points.

2.   Bracketed words are added to facilitate understanding of Karol's linguistic output.

3.   The informant's linguistic output has been transcribed following the principle of one proposition per line.

References

Bardovi-Harlig, Kathleen
    1999   From morpheme studies to temporal semantics: Tense – aspect research in SLA. *Studies in Second Language Acquisition* 21, 3, 341–382.

Bergvall, Victoria, Janet Bing, and Alice Freed (eds.)
    1996   *Rethinking Language and Gender Research: Theory and Practice.* London: Longman.

Bourdieu, Pierre
    1977   The economics of linguistic exchanges. *Social Science Information* 16, 645–668.

    1991 [1999] *Language and Symbolic Power.* Cambridge, MA: Harvard University Press.

Cameron, Deborah
    1997   Performing gender identity: Young men's talk and the construction of heterosexual masculinity. In Johnson, Sally and Ulrike Hanna Meinhof (eds.), *Language and Masculinity.* Oxford: Blackwell, 47–64.

Coates, Jennifer
    1998 a   Gossip revisited: Language in all-female groups. In Coates, Jennifer (ed.), *Language and Gender.* Oxford: Blackwell, 226–253.

    (ed.)1998 b *Language and Gender.* Oxford: Blackwell.

Cumming, Alister and Jane Gill
    1991   Motivation or accessibility? Factors permitting Indo-Canadian women to pursue ESL literacy instruction. In Burnaby, Barbara and Alister Cumming (eds.), *Socio-political aspects of ESL education in Canada.* Toronto, Canada: OISE Press, 241–252.

de Klerk, Vivian
1997   The role of expletives in the construction of masculinity. In Johnson, Sally
          and Ulrike Hanna Meinhof (eds.), *Language and Masculinity*. Oxford:
          Blackwell, 144–158.

Dietrich, Reiner, Wolfgang Klein, and Colette Noyau
1995   *The Acquisition of Temporality in a Second Language*. Amsterdam/Phila-
          delphia: John Benjamins.

Dittmar, Norbert
1988   Temporal means of expression in German as a second language. In Heinz,
          Vater and Veronika Ehrich (eds.), *Temporalsemantik*. Tübingen: Niemeyer,
          308–329.

Eckert, Penelope and Sally McConnell-Ginet
1995   Constructing meaning, constructing selves: Snapshots of language, gender,
          and class from Belten High. In Hall, Kira and Mary Bucholtz (eds.),
          Gender Articulated: Language and the Socially Constructed Self. New
          York: Routledge, 469–508.

Ehrlich, Susan
1997   Gender as social practice: Implications for second language acquisition.
          Studies in Second Language Acquisition 19, 421–446.

Faludi, Susan
1999   *Stiffed*. New York: Wiliam Morrow.

Fillmore, Charles
1975   *Santa Cruz Lectures on Deixis 1971*. Indiana University Linguistics Club.

Freed, Alice
1996   Language and gender research in an experimental setting. In Bergvall, Vic-
          toria, Janet Bing, and Alice Freed (eds.), *Rethinking Language and Gender
          Research: Theory and Practice*. London: Longman, 54–76.

Giacalone Ramat, Ana
1992   Grammaticalization process in the area of temporal and modal relations.
          Studies in Second Language Acquisition 14, 297–322.

Goldstein, Tara
1995   "Nobody is talking bad": Creating community and claiming power on the
          production lines. In Hall, Kira and Mary Bucholtz (eds.), *Gender Articu-
          lated: Language and the Socially Constructed Self*. New York: Routledge,
          375–400.

1997   *Two Languages at Work: Bilingual Life on the Production Floor.* New York: Mouton de Gruyter.

Goodwin, Marjorie Harness
1999   Constructing opposition within girls' games. In Bucholtz, Mary, A.C. Liang, and Laurel Sutton (eds.), *Reinventing Identities: The Gendered Self in Discourse.* Oxford: Oxford University Press, 388–409.

Hill, Jane
1987   Women's speech in modern Mexicano. In Phillips, Susan, Susan Steele, and Christine Tanz (eds.), *Language, Gender and Sex in Comparative Perspective.* Cambridge: Cambridge University Press, 121–160.

Johnson, Sally
1997   Theorizing language and masculinity: A feminist perspective. In Johnson, Sally and Ulrike Hanna Meinhof (eds.), *Language and Masculinity.* Oxford: Blackwell, 8–26.

Johnson, Sally and Frank Finlay
1997   Do men gossip? An analysis of football talk on television. In Johnson, Sally and Ulrike Hanna Meinhof (eds.), *Language and Masculinity.* Oxford: Blackwell, 130–143.

Johnson, Sally and Ulrike Hanna Meinhof (eds.)
1997   *Language and Masculinity.* Oxford: Blackwell.

Klein, Wolfgang
1981   Knowing a language and knowing how to communicate: A case study in foreign workers' communication. In Vermeer, A.R. (ed.), *Language Problems of Minority Groups.* Tilburg: Tilburg University Press, 75–95.

Krashen, Stephen
1981   *Second Language Acquisition and Second Language Learning.* Oxford: Pergamon Press.

Labov, William
1972   *Language in the Inner City: Studies of the Black English Vernacular.* Philadelphia: University of Pennsylvania Press.

Long, Michael
1985   Input and second language acquisition theory. In Gass, Susan and Carolyn Madden (eds.), *Input in Second Language Acquisition.* Rowley, MA: Newbury House, 377–393.

Loschky, Lester
   1994   Comprehensible input and second language acquisition: What is the relationship? *Studies in Second Language Acquisition* 16, 303–323.

McKay, Sandra and Sau-Ling Cynthia Wong
   1996   Multiple discourses, multiple identities: Investment and agency in second language learning among Chinese adolescent immigrant students. *Harvard Educational Review* 3, 577–608.

Meisel, Jürgen
   1987   Reference to past events and actions in the development of natural second language acquisition. In Pfaff, Carol (ed.), *First and Second Language Acquisition Processes*. Cambridge: Newbury House, 206–224.

Naiman, Neil, Maria Frohlich, H.H. Stern, and Angie Todesco
   1978 [1996] *The Good Language Learner*. Clevedon, UK: Multilingual Matters.

Norton, Bonny
   1997   Language, identity, and the ownership of English. *TESOL Quarterly* 31, 409–429.

Pavlenko, Aneta
   1998   Second language learning by adults: Testimonies of bilingual writers. *Issues in Applied Linguistics* 9, 1, 3–19.

Peirce, Bonny Norton
   1995   Social identity, investment, and language learning. *TESOL Quarterly* 29, 9–31.

Pica, Teresa, Richard Young, and Catherine Doughty
   1987   The impact of interaction on comprehension. *TESOL Quarterly* 21, 737–758.

Pilkington, Jane
   1998   'Don't try and make out that I'm nice!' The different strategies women and men use when gossiping. In Coates, Jennifer (ed.), *Language and Gender*. Oxford: Blackwell, 254–269.

Preston, Dennis
   1989   *Sociolinguistics and Second Language Acquisition*. Oxford: Blackwell.

Sato, Charlene
   1990   *The Syntax of Conversation in Interlanguage Development*. Tübingen: Gunter Narr.

Schmidt, Richard and Sylvia Frota
  1986   Developing basic conversational ability in a second language: A case study of an adult learner. In Day, Richard (ed.), *Talking to Learn: Conversation in Second Language Acquisition*. Rowley, MA: Newbury House, 237–326.

Siegal, Meryl
  1996   The role of learner subjectivity in second language sociolinguistic competency: Western women learning Japanese. *Applied Linguistics* 17, 3, 356–82.

Snow, Catherine and Charles Ferguson (eds.)
  1977   *Talking to Children*. Cambridge: Cambridge University Press.

Teutsch-Dwyer, Marya
  1995   *Means of Expressing Temporality in Untutored Adult Second Language Learner Variety*. Ph.D. Dissertation, Stanford University.

Teutsch-Dwyer, Marya and Ann Fathman
  1996   Marking time: A naturalistic and instructed second language acquisition. Paper presented at the TESOL Convention, Chicago, IL.

Uchida, Aki
  1998   Speaking English as a gendered praxis: Japanese women's intercultural experience. In Wertheim, Suzanne, Ashlee C. Bailey, and Monica Corston-Oliver (eds.), *Engendering Communication: Proceedings of the Fifth Berkeley Women and Language Conference, April 24–26, 1997*. Berkeley, CA: University of California, BWLG, 577–588.

von Stutterheim, Christiane
  1984   Temporality in learner varieties. *Linguistische Berichte* 82, 31–45.

Weedon, Chris
  1987   *Feminist Practice and Poststructuralist Theory*. Oxford: Blackwell.

Weis, Lois
  1990   *Working Class without Work: High School Students in a De-industrializing Economy*. New York: Routledge.

West, Cornel
  1992   A matter of life and death. *October* 61, 20–23.

Woolard, Kathryn
  1998   Language ideology as a field of inquiry. In Schieffelin, Bambi, Kathryn Woolard and Paul Kroskrity (eds.), *Language Ideologies: Practice and Theory*. Oxford: Oxford University Press, 1–28.

Linguistic intermarriage: Language choice and negotiation of identity[1]

Ingrid Piller

1. Introduction

As people's understanding of intimate relationships changes, spousal communication gains in importance. While in former times couples mainly came together to form an economic unit and to raise a family, today they tend to come together for "romantic" reasons, to share their free time and be friends. A "good spouse" is no longer just a good housekeeper, breadwinner, or sexual partner but a good communicator. According to Fitzpatrick (1990: 433), communication difficulties are a major cause of marital unhappiness and marital failure. With communication as a constitutive factor in the make-up of a modern romantic relationship, what does it mean for people to live in a relationship with a partner who has a different first language? How do they choose their language as a couple? What are the reasons behind those choices? Which identities do they construct for themselves in societies that continue to see monolingual and monocultural marriage (whether such a thing exists or not) as the norm? Do they celebrate a new bicultural consciousness or deplore their outsider status between two cultures? In this chapter I will attempt to answer these questions for a group of couples, in which one partner has English as a first language and the other German, and whose primary socialization was into two different national cultures. This chapter has the further aim to provide an overview of the sociolinguistic literature on linguistic intermarriage with a special focus on methods of data collection. The first part of this chapter can therefore be read as an introduction to data collection methods and approaches to the study of couple communication, particularly couple communication in a multilingual context. I will then go on to outline the theoretical framework for my own research project and the methodological choices I made based on that framework. Finally, I will discuss how the couples from English- and German-speaking backgrounds with whom I worked came to choose the language they use in the couple domain and how they find themselves positioned and re-positioned in their old and new linguistic and national communities.

2.   Methods in the study of linguistic intermarriage

For obvious reasons, private and intimate language is not readily available for observation and investigation (see also Deignan 1997: 24). Therefore, the methods employed in obtaining the data are of prime importance in studying private language contact. In many areas of linguistics, the fact that our results will be influenced by the methods used to obtain the data has become a matter of urgent concern (see, e.g., the section on "Methodological issues" in Gass and Neu 1996). In the following I will combine an overview of the literature on the linguistic practices of bilingual couples with a focus on the methods that were employed in these studies. As will become clear, the choice of data collection methods depends crucially upon the theoretical framework within which research is being conducted. Most research I will be reporting upon is concerned with the ways in which marriage outside one's linguistic group is related to language maintenance and shift. In other words, the typical research question asks whether minority partners in a bilingual relationship maintain their language (and pass it on to their children), or whether they shift to the majority language and do not pass it on to their children. Generally, it can be said that there is only a very small body of sociolinguistic research into language contact in the smallest social unit, the couple relationship (see also Varro and Boyd 1998: 23). There is, of course, a strong tradition of research into the language acquisition of the children of these couples. This focus on bilingual children and the simultaneous widespread disinterest in adults who have to learn to negotiate their lives with two languages reflects general assumptions that socialization and language learning in childhood are somehow more relevant than socialization and language learning in adulthood. In this chapter, I am solely concerned with adults from two different linguistic backgrounds who decide to share their lives as adults – a process which inevitably turns one partner, and often both, into second language learners and users.

2.1. Census data

Census data have mainly been used in the Canadian context to study the effects of Francophone exogamy, or "outmarriage", on language maintenance and shift. The context for this research is a widespread worry in the Francophone community and on the part of researchers that marriage of Francophone Canadians outside the Francophone community might be detrimental to the overall size and viability of the Francophone community. Thus, there is an overriding concern with counting Francophones, and sociolinguistic research with census data aims to show whether Francophones married to non-Francophones can still be counted as members of the Francophone community or whether they have to be "written off" as lost to another language community, most often to the Anglophone one. One particularly prolific author in demographic linguistics, or "demolinguistics", as this branch of linguistic inquiry is called, is Castonguay (e.g., 1979, 1982). The use of census data enables him to study extremely large samples: in one single table, Castonguay (1982: 266) presents information on the language practices of more than 400,000 bilingual couples. The drawback is that the information basis, i.e., the language practices investigated, is rather small: it relies exclusively on two census questions, the one on *mother tongue* (which was defined as "language first spoken and still understood"), and the one on *home language* ("what language do you most often speak at home now?"). He shows that a couple's linguistic environment will influence their language choices as "the frequency of the French option declines more rapidly than that of bilingual behavior as distance from Québec increases" (Castonguay 1982: 266). Castonguay (1979: 405) also shows that in most age groups the rate of shift towards English (from "mother tongue" to "home language") is higher than the rate of intermarriage. Thus, a certain number of Francophones will shift whatever their marital situation – despite the widely held belief that Francophone exogamy is a "danger" (Bernard 1994), a "Trojan horse" (Mougeon, Savard, and Carroll 1978) opening the doors to shift towards English. The limited number of linguistic questions asked in censuses (rarely more than two) is a major limitation of this form of data, as is their accessibility (many countries do not have censuses, or they may not contain language questions). However, work with census data such as the one by Castonguay can also help to disprove powerful "commonsense knowledge", e.g., that each exogamous Francophone is a numerical loss to the Francophone community in Canada. As Castonguay (1982: 267) points out: "A language shift as reported on the census questionnaire can quite possibly have occurred before, and not after, intermarriage: in such cases, the mixed marriage may well be viewed as an effect, rather than a cause of the language shift". However, census data cannot answer such causal questions. For these questions more fine-tuned data collection instruments are needed.

2.2. Questionnaires

Questionnaires can serve as a method of inquiry that is more context-sensitive and can be fine-tuned to specific research interests. One scholar using questionnaires in her study of the language practices of couples with a Dutch-speaking and an English-speaking partner in Australia is Pauwels (1985). She administered a language use questionnaire to 60 Dutch-born post-1945 migrants in Melbourne and elsewhere in Victoria. The sample consisted of three different groups: (G1) involving two Dutch-born partners, (G2) involving one Dutch and one Anglo-Australian partner, and (G3) involving one Dutch and one non-Anglo-Australian partner. The author was interested in the following four questions:

1) Is there a systematic difference in the language maintenance rate among the three groups?
2) Which domains (areas of language use) are greatly affected by the marriage situation and which domains are not?
3) Are there sex- and age-related differences?
4) Are there significant differences with regard to language shift in the second generation due to the marital situation of the parents? (Pauwels 1985: 4)

Pauwels' results show that Dutch is less well maintained in intermarried than in intramarried couples. Her most interesting finding in relation to bilingual couples is that no interviewee claimed to use one language exclusively with their spouse – all interviewees engaged in code-switching to a certain extent. However, details of these self-reported code-switching practices cannot be ascertained through a questionnaire. Such a research interest would require direct observation and recording of linguistic practices. Studies that use questionnaires as a means of data collection are – like studies using census data – typically not concerned with marital communication but with language maintenance or shift as a result of exogamy. Another example of such a study is Chiaro and Nocella (1999), who distributed 1,000 questionnaires to Italians living in the UK, 460 of which were returned and 452 incorporated into the sample as valid. It turned out that Italians married to an Anglo partner only transmitted Italian to their children if the mother was Italian. In other words, the authors found a major gender difference in linguistic practices resulting from exogamy.

Like censuses, questionnaires have the advantage that they can, comparatively easily, be administered to large-size samples. And, unlike census data, the questions can be tailored to a particular research interest. All the problems of what to ask, and how to interpret answers persist, though. Fasold (1984) compares self-reports on language usage to the weather forecast: sometimes they are right, sometimes they are wrong. All self-reports on language usage "are subject to variance in relation to factors such as prestige, ethnicity, political affiliation, etc." (Romaine 1994: 37). Only direct observation can help to gauge the relationship between self-reports and actual practice.

2.3. Interviews

Interviews have also been used in language maintenance studies of exogamous couples. Boyd (1998), for instance, taking her data from a larger interview project on "the development of immigrant languages in the Nordic region" (see also Latomaa 1998), investigates the maintenance of English in the children of US-Americans married to Danes, Finns, or Swedes. Like Chiaro and Nocella (1999), she finds that the children are more fluent in English (which is the minority language in this context) if the mother is the English speaker. Boyd (1998: 45–46) explains this pattern as a result of gendered family roles: a father who uses English "virtually all the time" with his child, will expose the child far less to English than a mother who uses English to the same degree.

Another illuminating interview-based study in the field is the one by Boix (1997). Although also interested in language maintenance, this author also takes into account the ideologies of the 59 Castilian-Catalan couples in his Barcelona-based study. Of particular interest is the fact that he does not link language maintenance or shift to gender as the studies discussed above (Boyd 1998; Chiaro and Nocella 1999) do, but sees class and network patterns as the decisive factors: "Catalanization" occurs in middle-class families with networks that value solidarity highly, while "Castilianization" occurs in working-class families.

A study that used interviews not to investigate language maintenance or shift but rather actual language use and linguistic attitudes is the one by Heller and Lévy (1992, 1994). Like Castonguay, they are concerned with Francophones married to Anglophones in Canada. Their research interest, however, differs significantly: rather than counting numbers on the macro-level they ask what it means on the individual, personal level to be socialized into one language community as a child, and move on to another one as an adult. The researchers interviewed 28 Francophone women married to Anglophone men in three Ontario cities about their lives: their schooling and that of their children, their work, family and social life, and their own, their spouses' and their children's use of French and English (Heller and Lévy 1994: 57). On the basis of the interviews the respondents were placed into three attitudinal groups, depending on the strength of their sense of Francophone identity. Then, the following factors were analyzed and put in relation to the attitudinal types: language choice in daily life, opinions about the usage of English and French, the notions of identity held by the interviewees, and the form of the interview discourse (i.e., code-switching, metaphorical expressions, or the characteristics of the French used). Most noteworthy, they found that marriage to an English-speaking partner does not inevitably lead to assimilation to English, and if it does "there is always a struggle, a least at some level, a concern, an ambivalent turning to what might be sacrificed by abandoning French, and often there is heartfelt pain" (Heller and Lévy 1992: 39). Ambivalence about the bilingual and bicultural marriage seems to be most common when the language groups to which the partners belong stand in an unequal power relationship. In such a situation, marriage partners will not only meet as individuals but also to a certain degree as representatives of their respective language groups. Another researcher who stresses the fact that unequal power relationships between linguistic and national groups will also play into the lives of the couples affiliated with both groups is Walters (1996). This researcher also found "ambivalence" to influence the access to the local language that Anglophone wives of Tunisian husbands enjoyed in Tunisia.

Interviews have enjoyed increasing popularity over the last decade since they yield data that allow for deeper insights into private language practices and how they relate to linguistic patterns at large than either census data or questionnaires. Often, they also allow access to actual practices in addition to the beliefs, assumptions, and ideologies that the interviewees hold about those practices. However, interviews are clearly research settings and it is difficult to know what couples do when they are not being researched, i.e., in the absence of a researcher (see the section on "Ethnography of communication" below for a further discussion of this point).

2.4. Experimental studies

Experimental research designs are most commonly employed by researchers working in the tradition of the social psychology of language (Auwärter 1988). Role-play, which is also frequently used in the study of cross-cultural communication (e.g., Clyne 1994: 17–19), can be regarded as a particular type of experimental setting, too. I am not aware of a research project that actually studied intermarried couples' communication experimentally but, potentially, one could, for instance, ask a bilingual couple to communicate for a certain time, possibly on a given topic, and tape them as they do so. In experimental studies of marital communication in monolingual contexts, couples are asked to engage in activities like the following: "to engage in pleasant conversation" (Fitzpatrick, Vance, and Wittemann 1984), to discuss a controversial issue

(Boucher 1995), "a neutral subject" (Spaine 1991), or "one current relational problem and one successfully resolved marital problem" (Weatherford 1985). In yet another study, of nonverbal communication in romantic dyads, couples were videotaped while playing the board game 'Trivial Pursuit' (Manusov 1990 a, b). In all these designs, participants are basically asked to role-play their own conversations (Baus 1992). This research design obviously has the advantage of yielding real communication between the partners, while most of the other possibilities involve a certain amount of self-reporting. However, it has the disadvantage of being artificial and making "subjects" feel very self-conscious. Ethnographers of communication, who will only accept observation of naturally occurring conversations as valid data, generally deny the validity of experimental approaches. Nevertheless, the presence of an observer is in many social situations also "unnatural" in a way (see discussion of the "observer's paradox" below), and in the case of the intimate dyad simply not feasible most of the time. However, despite its lack of ecological validity, experimental work can be a powerful tool because of its ability to tease out individual influences in language use (Crawford 1995).

2.5. Ethnography of communication

Ethnographers of communication see themselves as their major research "tool": by becoming participant-observers in a community they can observe the communicative practices of that community in a holistic perspective as they occur naturally. In other words, the central concern is to access communicative practices that are not being produced for research purposes (as interviews and experimental work are). The ethnographic approach has mainly been used with the bilingual couples of the Tucanoan peoples in the Vaupés region of Brazil and Colombia (Grimes 1985; Jackson 1983). The Tucanoans, who live in the North West Amazon Basin of Brazil and Colombia, are of interest to (linguistic) anthropologists because these groups have a strong taboo against endogamy, i.e., they have to choose a spouse from another group, and group membership is defined through the language one speaks. Thus, all the couples in the area are bilingual.

> Husband and wife each speaks his or her own language to the other. Each understands the language of his or her spouse, but does not speak it except in circumstances where it is necessary in order to communicate with other people who do not understand the primary language. A child becomes fluent in the language of both parents, yet considers his [sic!] father's language to be his own. (Grimes 1985: 391)

Thus, Tucanoan couples practice "dual-linguality", a communication pattern in which each partner actively uses her or his first language and receives the partner's first language back. They maintain this dual-lingual practice throughout their lives, and language maintenance of the indigenous languages is a lot better than in many other comparable indigenous communities around the globe (see Holmes 1992: 88).

Participant observation of marital communication in societies other than the Tucanoan is rare, particularly of bilingual marital communication. The simple reason for that is that the extent to which a researcher can be a participant-observer in an intimate dyad is fairly limited. The only research projects to use naturally occurring samples of couple talk as their data are, as far as I know, Fishman's (1978, 1980, 1983) work on the supportive nature of female contributions in monolingual-English conversations and the follow-up study by DeFrancisco (1989, 1991). Fishman and DeFrancisco asked monolingual white heterosexual married American couples to have all their home conversations tape-recorded for a certain period. Interestingly, the couples' willingness to let a tape-recorder "intrude" upon their private communications may be culture-specific as I tried to do the same for English- and German-speaking couples but could not find a single volunteer couple. A few couples who had intended to carry out these private recordings (e.g., of their dinner conversations) returned empty tapes to me claiming they had felt so constrained that they had, for the time being, given up dinner conversations altogether.

Both Fishman and DeFrancisco work within the dominance approach to female-male interaction (see Pavlenko and Piller's chapter, this volume), which assumes that a macrosocietal phenomenon such as the greater power of men as a group than women as a group will also show in microlinguistic interactions. This general assumption was borne out in the data of both: in Fishman's three couples and in DeFrancisco's seven couples, the women got to do the interactional "shitwork" (Fishman's term): if they wanted to have a conversation with their husbands, they had to start it, they had to introduce new topics, which were then frequently ignored by the men, they had to keep going despite their husbands' non-response, and they had to be supportive listeners to their husbands' comments. DeFrancisco additionally interviewed the partners in her study individually after their conversations had been taped and was able to show that her interpretations were also borne out by the participants' own perceptions.

Although participant observation is valued for its contextual validity, one has to be cautious about the naturalness of "natural" conversational data as the observer's paradox also applies in non-experimental settings (Wilson 1987). "Observer's paradox" is a term commonly used to refer to the impossible – and therefore "paradoxical" – task of the researcher to figure out what happens WITHOUT the presence of the researcher as observer (initially discussed by Labov 1972). As my experience with the couples who stopped having dinner conversations when they were to be "observed" by a tape-recorder shows, the observer's paradox is "an especially complex concern in research dealing with families and more particularly couples" (Walters 1996: 552–553). Because of taboos pertaining to the private and intimate nature of couple talk in many societies, naturally occurring couple talk that is not embedded in another situation, such as a party setting, is simply difficult to come by.

2.6. Fictional sources

One further possibility that recommends itself by the comparatively easy availability of the data is the study of bilingual couples in fiction. By fictional sources I do not only mean literary fiction, but also other forms of fictional representation such as movies or commercial advertising. Tannen (1986, 1990) and Leisi (1993), for instance, get most of their information on the language of (monolingual) couples from fictional sources. Of course, there is no way around the fact that fiction is not "real life" – but it offers something that is in a way even better than "real life": a model of reality.

> ... artificial dialog may represent an internalized model or schema for the production of conversation – a competence model that speakers have access to. If, then, we are interested in discovering the ideal model of conversational strategy, there is much to be gained by looking at artificial conversation first, to see what these general, unconsciously-adhered-to assumptions are; and later returning to natural conversation to see how they might actually be exemplified in literal use. (Tannen 1994: 139)

Fictional discourse does not represent reality but speakers may derive some of their communicative competence from it. Thus, it allows researchers access to linguistic ideologies, to ways in which people think they talk or ways in which they are thought to talk (by authors and their readers). This may be even more so as far as "love talk" is concerned, which is often said to contain a certain amount of re-enactment of literary models anyway (e.g., Leisi 1993: 74–109). In a study of the representation of bilingual couples in fiction (Piller 1998), I showed that, in a diverse fictional corpus including plays, novels, documentary films, and commercial advertisements from a range of sociolinguistic contexts, the lack of a common language is often represented as an advantage which leads to a mutual understanding that goes beyond language. "Understanding without words" becomes a sign of the deep connection between individuals that can result from love. Other authors represent a foreign language or an accent as a source of attraction that may be part of the reason why characters fall in love. Characters are sometimes drawn to another person because they are "exotic" and a non-native accent serves as a salient marker of the exotic in fiction. Characters may even fall out of love once the partner loses their foreign accent.

2.7. Introspection

In introspection, researchers rely on their intuitions as their "database". In general linguistics, introspection is one of the most frequently used "methods of data collection" and it is useful to answer questions about the grammaticality of morphological or syntactic structures. In sociolinguistics, however, the uses of introspection are much more limited. It may be used to generate hypotheses but not to verify them. In a very brief article that is based on introspection, Siguan (1980), for instance, suggests the following factors that might influence linguistic choice in cross-cultural couples: (1) They might choose the language of the monolingual area where they live. (2) They might choose the more prestigious language if they live in a diglossic area, i.e., an area where both a "high" and a "low" language are common in daily use.[2] (3) They might choose the non-native or less prestigious language for reasons of solidarity. (4) There might be a tendency for the language of the male partner to prevail. And, (5) there would be individual factors, i.e., choices that do not fall into the larger patterns previously identified.

Below, I will return to the complementary hypotheses (1) and (3), as well as (4). As English and German are not in a diglossic relationship in any of the contexts in which the couples I worked with live, hypothesis (2) is irrelevant. Generally, it is important to remember that introspection is not really a method of data collection, but rather a way to generate hypotheses.

2.8. Summary

To date, most of the research into the linguistic practices of couples from differing linguistic backgrounds has been concerned with language choice, maintenance or shift – issues which are amenable to data collection through self-reports rather than direct observation. This may be due to the fact that the couple domain is not easily observed by outsiders or also to the fact that language choice has been perceived to be the major linguistic issue faced by such couples. In these studies of their language choices, the language of the larger community was indeed shown to be the most decisive factor (Castonguay 1979, Pauwels 1985). Additionally, gender seems to have an influence on the transmission of the minority language to children (Boyd 1998; Chiaro and Nocella 1999). If the languages involved are small minority languages that are threatened by languages of wider communication (such as the Tucanoan languages in contact with Portuguese and Spanish), dual-linguality seems a useful strategy to maintain the minority language.

The comparatively fewer (and generally more recent) studies of the linguistic practices of bilingual couples that are less concerned with language maintenance and more with linguistic ideologies and the negotiation of identity (Boix 1997; Heller and Lévy 1992, 1994; Walters 1996), have shown that couples – supposedly one of the most private domains of language use – cannot escape the relationship their languages, cultures, and national communities at large find themselves in. In this way, the Francophone women married to Anglophone Canadians in Heller and Lévy's (1992, 1994) study have to come to terms with the ideology of treason that the larger society confronts them with; the Castilian-Catalan couples in Boix' (1997) study cannot escape the political and class ideologies of Barcelona society, and Anglophone wives in Tunisia (Walters 1996) may find that the neo-colonial and imperialist relations of their native countries with Tunisia and the Arab world constrain their (linguistic) choices in their marital and familial relationships. Furthermore, ideologies of the exotic "Other" may play an important role in initial sexual attraction and again constrain the choices of partners in a bilingual relationship in that the non-native partner may lose part of her/his attraction if they should speak too much like natives. This possibility is suggested by Piller's (1998) fictional data and also by some of the Anglophone wives interviewed by Walters (1996).

3.   Theoretical framework and research design

The discussion of methodological issues above has made it clear that each approach represents a certain trade-off, and a combination of as many methods as possible might yield the richest picture (see also Varro and Boyd 1998; Varro and Gebauer 1997). In my own research, I was aiming for the "rich" picture which goes beyond the questions of language maintenance and shift to address ways in which identities are constructed by these couples and co-constructed by the ideologies of the wider societies in which they live (see Introduction above). These aims derive from the theoretical framework within which my research is situated, and, therefore, I will in the following first introduce my framework and then go on to describe the methodological choices to which it led me.

In my research into the linguistic practices of bilingual (English- and German-speaking) and bicultural couples, I draw on postmodern conceptualizations of gender such as Butler's (1990), who regards gender as a performance which creates a (gendered) identity in the very performance. Such a view is social constructionist in that it sees gender as created in social interaction rather than resulting from the biology of sex. The postmodern view of gender eschews essentialist, dichotomous notions of masculinity and femininity, and regards them as socially constructed acts instead (e.g., Crawford 1995). If gender is not predetermined by sex, as this view claims, the performance of gender is a local construction that occurs in particular communities of practice (Eckert and McConnell-Ginet 1992; Holmes and Meyerhoff 1999), i.e., an act that differs within and across societies, cultures, and communities – in short, with the context. Gender becomes a heterogeneic act, which is not the only social category that is being performed in a given context. Rather, other aspects of personal identity such as professional status, nationality, ethnicity, or social class may also be part of the act. In this perspective, the meaning of being a woman or a man, and of studying their respective practices changes: "[It] is less about inhabiting some abstract and unitary category of 'women' or 'men' than it is about living one's other social identities (such as racial, ethnic, regional, subcultural) in a particular and gendered way" (Cameron 1997a: 33). Individuals do not only perform various aspects of their identity in a given context but they also participate in various communities of practice at a particular point in their lives and across the lifespan. The communities of practice they move into and out of may be the family, the workplace, a friendship group, an athletic team or a church group (Eckert and McConnell-Ginet 1995). For most people, the marital dyad or any other form of couple relationship – marital or non-marital, heterosexual or homosexual – is a major community of practice they are engaged in. Partners in a romantic relationship who come together from two different linguistic backgrounds are continuously performing a number of roles, in terms of gender, nationality, cultural background, or native speaker status (see Pavlenko and Piller's chapter for a fuller discussion). These performances are differently constrained in different languages because "... language is not a neutral medium that passes freely and easily into the private property of the speaker's intentions; it is populated, overpopulated – with the intentions of others" (Bakhtin 1981: 273–274). If partners in a romantic dyad come together from two different language backgrounds, at least one of them – and often both – is not living in their native country but find themselves positioned as "migrants". I speak of the "positioning as migrants" because – just like the conventional labels "man", "woman", "homosexual", "heterosexual", etc. – "migrant" is not a label for a social reality but for a reification of a conventional map of social reality. "These reifications structure perceptions and constrain (but do not completely determine) practice, and each is produced (often reproduced in much the same form) through the experience of those perceptions and constraints in day-to-day life" (Eckert and McConnell-Ginet 1995: 470). Another such reification that structures the perception and constrains the performance of one or both partners in a bilingual romantic relationship is that of "native" and "non-native speaker". Many linguists now agree that "the native speaker is dead" (Paikeday 1985), that s/he is "... an imaginary construct – a canonically literate monolingual middle-class member of a largely fictional national community whose citizens share a belief in a common history and a common destiny" (Kramsch 1997: 363). Nevertheless, native or non-native speaker status continues to be a powerful indicator of the identity people construct for themselves and have co-constructed for them by others.[3] For couples who come together in a community of practice from two different linguistic backgrounds, language choice may be an "act of identity" (Le Page and Tabouret-Keller 1985) whereby they proclaim their chosen identity to the world. Therefore, an investigation into the linguistic choices made by bilingual, cross-cultural couples may be a particularly fruitful site for an investigation into the linguistic construction of identity. One might argue that the preferred language choice of any person is the mother tongue. A person who uses her or his mother tongue can be conceived as being in a powerful position while the use of a second language always entails a certain amount of relinquishing of control. In one of his essays on English linguistic imperialism, Phillipson (1998: 106) writes: "Language rights will inevitably have to be limited further, but already in effect European politicians and bureaucrats often opt to function in a foreign language, or are pressured into doing so, rather than insisting on their language rights". The quote suggests that these politicians and bureaucrats would be better off expressing themselves in their mother tongue instead of another one. I am arguing that such a view is too simplistic. For many people their second language has become their preferred choice of expression as the examples in Coulmas (1997), and Pavlenko's and McMahill's chapters amply demonstrate.

As Cameron (1997b: 49) points out, our understanding of the relationship between language and gender has become "subtler and more complex" over the last few years due to the postmodern approach which suggests that "people are who they are because of (among other things) the way they talk". Researchers have moved away from a simple mapping of language onto gender and have started to investigate how a gendered identity is performed through language. Along with the other contributors to this volume, I am arguing that the prevalence of multilingual settings on this globe (Romaine 1995) calls for investigations that are even subtler: we need to study how gendered *identities* are being performed through *languages*.

This multiplex view of gender led me to search for a combination of as many methods as possible which would allow me to access the self-reports, attitudes, and ideologies of people engaging in bilingual couple relationships, as well as their actual practices. After my initial abortive attempt to recruit volunteers who would tape their "natural" dinner conversations (see above), I developed the following research design. I did not want to interview couples because an interview would turn "couple talk" into "couple-cum-researcher talk". At the same time, I wanted to access information typically elicited in semi-structured open-ended interviews. Therefore, I decided to ask couples to interview each other and record themselves as they did so. I developed a "discussion paper" on the basis of "models" emerging from a discourse analytic study of the representations of bilingual couples' communication practices in fiction (Piller 1998). The questions raised in the discussion paper also drew in part on the research results discussed above, particularly the work of Heller and Lévy (1992, 1994). The one-page discussion paper was developed in both English and German. This paper was given to German-English couples who volunteered to spend some time discussing the issues addressed in it, and tape themselves as they did so. The discussion paper served participating couples as a basis for the discussions which they were to self-record. Both the questionnaire and the discussion paper were prepared in English and German to give the couples the choice of their preferred language. Altogether, the discussion paper consists of 23 questions in four sections: language usage and skills (8 questions), language and culture (5 questions), language and identity (4 questions), perceived and self-reported attitudes towards bilingual and binational couples, and their children (6 questions).

The rationale for this design was twofold: on the one hand, it aimed to elicit self-reported information on the couple's language practices like in a semi-structured interview, and on the other hand, to yield samples of couple talk without the presence of a researcher. This design aims to combine aspects of an experimental design (a sample of couples engage in a comparable task) with more ethnographic approaches (semi-structured interviews over the recording of which the participants have full control). The design thus aims to ensure comparability as in experimental research while maintaining a natural setting without the presence of a researcher as in ethnographic research. All the participants were also asked to fill out a short questionnaire on demographic variables such as age, education, or occupation so that the results could be related to the analyses of the recorded conversations.

The sample of consultants was drawn on a voluntary, self-select basis from bilingual couples who could be reached through advertisements in bilingual interest publications, radio shows, or internet sites. Those couples who responded to the ad were sent a subject information statement together with the discussion paper and an audiotape. In this way, I collected conversations from 51 couples, 38 of whom lived in a German-speaking country (Germany, Austria), 10 in an English-speaking country (Britain, USA), and three in a third country (Belgium, Israel, the Netherlands).

4.   Language choice

Table 1 shows the community languages in relation to the self-reported couple language (which sometimes differs from the language that is actually being used in the taped conversation).

Table 1. Couple language and community language

Couple language	English	German	Mixed code	Total
Community language				
English	6	2	2	10
German	8	18	12	38
Other	2	1	–	3
Total	16	21	14	51

Of the 51 couples, 21 couples use German as their common language, 16 English, and 14 a mixed code (see Table 1). Those couples that report a mixed code use two different strategies: either they use a dual-lingual strategy in which each partner speaks her or his language all the time and receives the other language back, or both partners engage in code-switching. As was to be expected from previous research from a diversity of contexts (see the research report above), the community language is a powerful indicator of the language bilingual couples will use for marital communication (see Table 1). Six of the ten couples who live in an English-speaking country use English with each other (60%), and 18 of the 38 couples who live in a German-speaking country use German with each other (47%). However, it was also to be expected from these studies that the overwhelming majority of bilingual couples would opt for the community language as their common language – which is clearly not true for my sample. So which factors govern the choice of a common language according to the couples themselves? I will now look at two factors in some more detail: habit and compensation.

Many couples explain that they use the language they use, whether it is the majority language or the minority language, out of habit. It is the language they used when they first met that they stick to. Habit may account for the use of the majority language or the minority language. Deborah[4] (27 yrs old), an American woman who lives in Hamburg with her German husband, also adduces habit as the reason why they use English together in (1).

(1) Deborah:[5]   ... well, my husband and I erm decided to speak English together. and I guess mainly that has to do with the fact, that, when I first arrived here in Germany two years ago his English was considerably better than my German, and in order for us to communicate, even on a basic level, it was- it was necessary for us to speak English. and I think we've just kept that up, because it became a habit, and also I think it's sort of a ... a way for him to offer some sort of sacrifice to ME. because I had to give up, all my things, my culture, my language, my family, and my friends, to move to Germany. and he had everything here around him. and I guess the only thing he COULD offer me was his language. ... it- it's STRANGE for us when we speak German with each other. because we met in the States, he was teaching German at the university where I had studied. and I had already graduated but he was giving me private lessons. and that's how we became friends, and we just spoke English together THEN. and we have always spoken English together, and it just seems strange that- that once I came here, that we should then speak German.

Deborah finds it strange to use German, the language of wider communication in the country she lives in, with her husband because that is not what they did when they first met. The fact that couples find it difficult to change from the language of their first meeting to another one can probably be explained with the close relationship between language and identity. In a number of studies in the 1960s, Ervin(-Tripp) (1964, 1968) found that language choice is much more than the choice of the medium. Rather, content is affected, too. In a number of experiments, which have unfortunately not been replicated since, she demonstrated that in Thematic Apperception Tests (TAT) the content of picture descriptions changed with the language (English or French) a person used (Ervin 1964). When she asked Japanese-English bilingual women to do a sentence completion test, she got the same dramatic results: the sentence completion changed from one language to the other. Her most famous example is probably that of a woman completing the stimulus "When my wishes conflict with my family ..." with "It is a time of great unhappiness" in Japanese, and with "I do what I want" in English (Ervin-Tripp 1968: 203). More recently, Koven (1998), in an analysis of the narratives told by French-Portuguese bilinguals in their two languages, also showed that bilinguals perform the self differently in different languages.

If we say different things in different languages, it is quite obvious why cross-cultural couples stick to the language of their first meeting: they might lose the sense of knowing each other, the sense of connectedness and the rapport derived from knowing what the other will say in advance if they switched.

Habit also explains why the percentage of couples who use German in a German-speaking country is lower than the percentage of couples who use English in an English-speaking country (47% vs. 60%; see Table 1). English is much more likely to be the language of the first interactions – no matter where the couple will eventually settle down – as the proportion of speakers of German who have learned English as a second language is much higher than the proportion of English speakers who have learned German as a second language.

In (1), Deborah mentions a further factor that influenced her and her husband's choice of English as their common language. The use of English in Germany became a gift that was offered to compensate for the sacrifice Deborah had to make to live with her husband: migration. In cross-cultural relationships the partner in whose native country the couple live is privileged in society at large: legally, economically, and usually socially, too. In the linguistic construction of reality, power may also accrue to a person through being an undisputed expert manipulator of a code, a native speaker. Kouritzin (2000), an L1 speaker of Canadian English who lives with her L1 Japanese-speaking husband in Canada speaking Japanese in the family, describes how her husband has become the "ultimate linguistic authority in our home" (Kouritzin 2000: 321), an undisputed expert of Japanese whose pronouncements on language questions the family regularly seeks and unquestioningly accepts. Being a foreigner and having to use a non-native code places a person in a doubly weak position, while living in one's native community and using the native code places a person in a doubly strong position. The compromise to let one partner be the native, and the other the native speaker may well be conducive to a more egalitarian distribution of power in a relationship. Therefore, how does gender mediate these positions of native/non-native and native/non-native speaker?

Table 2. Language choice and gender

Female partner migrates and uses the community language with her partner	22
Female partner migrates and uses her native language with her partner	21
Male partner migrates and uses the community language with his partner	3
Male partner migrates and uses his native language with his partner	1
Total:	47[6]

Table 2 shows that, in my sample, about half of the female partners find themselves in a doubly weak position, i.e., they have given up their status as natives and their status as native speakers. However, only three male partners find themselves in such a weak position. Almost an equal number of couples have reached a compromise by "compensating" for migration with the use of the minority language. This includes a number of 'weaker' compromises, though, namely those that report the use of a mixed code.

Macro-sociological data on the residence of cross-national couples are notoriously unavailable (cf. Harding and Riley 1986: 23). However, there is no reason why my sample should be an unrepresentative one in terms of migration patterns. As the choice of residence for couples from Germany, the UK, and the USA is not complicated by glaring differences in the distribution of wealth, gender is the most likely explanatory variable for the migration/residence pattern observed (see Table 2). In most Western countries, husbands continue to earn more than their wives, and as migration is likely to involve downward occupational mobility, couples will figure that downward occupational mobility of the husband would hit the family as an economic unit harder than downward occupational mobility of the wife. As Breger (1998: 145) points out "the foreign spouse is at an economic disadvantage both in the employment market and in the marital relationship: economic asymmetry or downright dependence in the marriage relationship creates a potentially conflict-laden power imbalance".

5. Negotiating intercultural identities

In the previous section, I discussed the linguistic choices bilingual couples make and their reasons for these. In the following, I will describe how they view their cultural, national, and linguistic identities – identities acquired through birth and marriage. In (2), Christine (32 yrs old), a German woman who lives with Brendan (34 yrs old), her husband of 14 years, on a large British army base in Lower Saxony relates how she has been turned into an "English woman":

(2) Christine: I was always proud to be a German. and when I was abroad it's always nice to say, yes! I am German. I am different. but- erm and always look forward to coming back to England. but I think over the years, over fourteen years, living with the British communities erm I can't consider myself German anymore. now, having German colleagues at work. and I can see a big difference. I'm not one of them anymore. they actually call me Chris. the English woman. @@

Christine feels that her identity has changed because her communities of practice have changed. Although she continues to live in Germany, her context is "the British communities" now. Army bases are a striking example of the need "to look locally" and to refrain from sweeping categorizations. While they are "home away from home" for some, they may be "foreign territory in one's own country" for others. Christine is quite clear that it is not only her individual performance that has changed her feelings of identity but also the way she is being positioned by others. "Fellow Germans" no longer accept her as one of them but place her in the category of "the Other", and turn her into "the English woman". By engaging in a cross-cultural relationship her L1 community membership has become contested. One way of contesting her status as a German national is to deny her German first name and address her with an English version of it. Another way of "otherizing" her is to imply that something is wrong with her having a non-German-sounding surname by "giving her funny looks" as she describes in (3).

(3) Christine: if ... erm anybody sees my main- erm name tag, on- on my apron, you know, they give me a funny look cos it's a foreign name ... erm but in England I have no problems at all. and that's me being a German in England.

In sum, while all of the women in my sample relate that – because of their marriage – they are in many cases no longer perceived as natives of their original national communities, none of the men does. "Otherization" has a gendered pattern: while women are perceived as having passed from their original national identity to that of their spouse, men are not denied their status as natives in the same way. While the participation in new communities of practice will inevitably affect the performance of both, people seem to be more ready to perceive change in women than in men. I hypothesize that the reason for this difference in perception is due to outdated but maybe deep-rooted notions of ownership and marriage: if a woman marries a man from another country she becomes the "property" of another nation, and people expect this transformation to be tangible in one way or another. Anthropological literature on exogamy reports a virtually universal pattern whereby the outmarriage of women is much more strictly controlled by the group than that of men (Breger and Hill 1998: 14). If, however, a man marries a woman from another country, the "gain" is on the part of his nation, he is bringing in an "asset" so to speak. Naturally, people do not expect an owner to change with his property. Indeed, the direct incorporation of women into the nation as citizens is relatively recent. The Code Napoleon was the first modern statute to decree that the wife's nationality should follow her husband's – a regulation that was soon adopted by other European countries, too. That is "a woman's political relation to the nation was submerged as a social relation to a man through marriage. For women, citizenship in the nation was mediated by the marriage relationship within the family." (McClintock 1993: 65). For a long time this regulation resulted in the loss of citizenship for women, if they married a foreigner: until the 1970s, a British woman, for instance, would lose her citizenship if she married a foreigner and she would return to Britain a foreigner if she was widowed by him (Druce 1994). It goes without saying that there was no such regulation for men. Likewise, German law stripped German women who married non-German nationals of their citizenship until 1953, when the regulation was declared unconstitutional. The children resulting from a marriage between a German

man and non-German woman have always become German by descent, while the children of a German woman and a non-German man have only been allowed to acquire German citizenship by descent since 1973. There is a widespread belief that, with the advent of the Women's Rights Movement and secularization, restrictions on female exogamy have started to fall away over the past three decades, at least in post-industrial Western societies. This is certainly the case. However, the lowering of formal barriers does not mean that informal barriers have also given way:

> Just because there may no longer be any legal barriers to spouse choice does not mean to say that informal barriers are not effective, such as negative discourses on foreigners which may influence not only how the local community reacts to the marriage ..., but also may influence officials who have discretion in granting visas and entry permits ... (Breger and Hill 1998: 18)

Such informal barriers include not only discourses about foreigners, but also gender ideologies. In the sociolinguistic literature, women are often associated with more rigid boundary maintenance than men because they derive authority from who they are rather than from their accomplishments (Eckert 2000). Woolard (1997: 551), for instance, describes a similar pattern of "otherization" in friendship groups. She argues that in a Barcelona school, Catalan girls who hang out with Castilian girls are themselves perceived as Castilian, while this does not happen to Catalan boys who are friends with Castilian boys. No one doubts their "Catalanness".

So far, I have argued that L1 community membership in many cases becomes contested for women married to men from another national background. Of course, people do "really" change, too, not only in the perception of others. Time spent away from the country of origin results in language and culture "gaps" causing people to feel like strangers in both places (Varro and Boyd 1998: 12). Not only is L1 community membership a site of contestation and negotiation but also L2 community membership. The change from a native performance and the accompanying perception to a non-native one does not necessarily result in acquiring a new native persona. Those of my informants who mainly engage in non-native communities of practice not only report that they are denied the status of native by their original community but they also hardly ever acquire such a status in their communities of choice. Helga (29 yrs old), a German woman who lives in England with her Scottish husband describes her feelings of frustration at being identified as a non-native by strangers. It is not only her German accent that "gives her away" but also non-verbal forms of behavior as she describes in (4). In the utterance preceding the one in (4) she had related that a cashier had asked her where she came from although she had not uttered a single word in the store.

(4) Helga   *ich sage- ich sag so,*[7] "why?" I said. "I even didn't say a word."
                and she said: "yeah. but you parked your left-hand-drive car
                right in the front of the shop window." and I thought: "oh, my
                god!" I thought it was something special on me.
      Andrew   uhmhu.
      Helga   something tattooed on my fort head.[8] "you are German."

Helga describes her non-native identity as a kind of stigma, "something tattooed on my forehead" (see Piller 1999 for a further discussion of the non-native identity as stigma). The reduction to one's original national identity may be particularly painful because it does not have much psychological reality for my consultants. Most of them feel that they have acquired a new identity, which incorporates both national cultures (see (5) and (6)).

(5) Corinna   uhmhu. I find knowing or being able to speak another language
                an- an enrichment of- of my ability to express myself.

Like Corinna (28 yrs old), a German woman who lives in the US, all informants talk about their new identity in very positive terms. Incorporating a second language and culture into one's repertoire is described as "enrichment" just as in the old saying "A new language is a new life".

(6) Jordan   and I think, for me anyway, you gain another culture, as well as
                reading literature and- and other things of German culture
                which is an in- to- to- in some way made me feel partly Ger-
                man maybe, even though I'm an African-American of ethnic
                origin. I somehow feel now that I have, you know, th- some-
                what control the language. that's the way you get access to a
                culture and the people. I've adapted it. or adopted it, maybe
                that's a better word, as my own to some degree.

The statement of Corinna's husband Jordan (28 yrs old) (see (6)) further exemplifies the gap between performance and perception, between construction and co-construction that multilinguals experience in monolingual societies. While he has made German and German culture part of his performance, he acknowledges that "fellow Germans" will never perceive him as such because ethnic/racial considerations ("being German and African-American are mutually exclusive") will override other considerations.

While all informants have in one way or another experienced changes in the way they perform their cultural identities, the experience itself is gendered. As I mentioned above all informants celebrate their new identities but it is only women who also mention the costs of acquiring a new language and culture.

(7) Susan   but I mean, the things that we- we deal, almost on a daily basis with. always dealing with cultural differences. I mean there are so many things, that I always think, "oh, the Germans this, or, the Germans that." plus, we are dealing with the whole thing of, maybe, understanding, living in another country. the cultures being different. erm ... [oh, I=

Martin   [wha-

Susan   =wanted to say something, oh, now I forget what it was. the whole thing dealing with being far away from the family. it's a whole different- to me, when my family comes over, I mean, I think, we've learnt to be culturally erm sympathetic. dealing with other people. dealing with living in another country. trying- I think you become more ... [you know,=

Martin   [wha-

Susan   =OPEN to people, and the way they are. and differences, a lot more.

Martin   in what way does this- have this- does this have some influence on OUR relationship?

Susan   oh, don't you think it's a stress factor?

Martin   I don't [know?

Susan   [I think it's a STRESS FACTOR that you have to deal with.

Martin   I don't know. maybe- I don't-, maybe I haven't thought about it. so much. but I don't- /????/

In (7), Susan (31 yrs old) and Martin (34 yrs old) discuss their experiences of living with two languages and cultures. Martin, who, in contributions preceding and following this excerpt, mentions repeatedly that he is proud of having an American wife and that having a non-German partner has made his life much more interesting, finds it very hard to acknowledge that life with two cultures may also be "a stress factor". Other women in my sample are as adamant as Susan about the potential cost of a bilingual and bicultural relationship. I suggest that the evaluation of these new identities is gendered because of the migration pattern in my sample. Of the 47 couples whose self-reports I am discussing here, it was the female partner who migrated to her husband's native country in 43 cases, and the male partner who migrated to his wife's native country in only four cases (see Table 2). Having a second language, and particularly a prestigious one like English or German, in one's native country is an exceptional and coveted skill. Being a second-language speaker and migrant among natives is construed as a deficiency. One might argue that the label "migrant" is not really appropriate for the white, middle-class citizens of "First World" countries in my sample. Indeed, this class of migrants is more often referred to as "expatriates". However, even as such they are objectively weakened by their move from one country to another: they must obtain work permits, their education often does not fit the local system, their professional diplomas often do not get recognized. So, it happens that the "deficient" labels of "migrant" and "non-native speaker" cluster with the label "female" – making bilingualism and biculturalism a gendered experience. For women it is not only a boon.

6.   Conclusion

In this chapter I have looked at the gendered discourses of bilingual, German- and English-speaking, couples about linguistic and national identity, and discussed the methods which are commonly used to research linguistic intermarriage. I have argued that, in the study of linguistic intermarriage, both data collection methods and research questions have constrained each other. The difficulties in obtaining "natural" data from bilingual couples have led to a general favoring of census data and questionnaires, i.e., self-reported data. At the same time, the focus on language maintenance or shift also favored the collection of self-reported data. My research interest in actual language data of bilingual couples as well as their views of what it means to them to enter a bilingual community of practice as an adult, as well as objective difficulties in observing natural couple talk, resulted in my choice of an eclectic combination of data collection methods.

The question of linguistic identity was addressed through an analysis of the language choices these couples self-report. Through their language choices, the couples in my sample most often align themselves with the community they live in. However, they may also actively construct themselves as cross-cultural border-crossers by the use of a mixed code, or even as minority members, which happens when both minority and majority partner use the minority language. The reasons the couples themselves identify for their choices are 'habit' and 'compensation'. Both factors have wider implications for the study of multilingualism generally: we need to learn more about the ways in which content and identity constructions differ with language choice, i.e., how content and the presentation of identity differ from one language to the next in a multilingual's repertoire.

The question of national identity was addressed through an investigation of the reactions of old and new national communities to partners in a bilingual, bicultural relationship. Women are often denied the status of "natives" in both their national communities, the one they participate in by birth and the one they participate in by choice. Here, what needs to be investigated further is the question to what extent fluency, be it native fluency, near-native fluency, or second language fluency, is a matter of perception rather than performance. My data suggest that the distinction between native and non-native may be partly in the eye/ear of the beholder.

Notes

1. I am indebted to my co-editors for reading and commenting on a number of draft versions of this chapter. Their support through its longish gestation period is very much appreciated. Thanks also to Richard Watts and two anonymous reviewers for Mouton de Gruyter.

2. The use of Standard German and Swiss German in Switzerland, or local and classical Arabic in many Arab states are well-known examples of diglossic situations (Ferguson 1959).

3. Detailed discussions of native and non-native speaker identities can be found, e.g., in Braine (1999) or Singh (1998).

4. All the names are pseudonyms to protect the anonymity of my informants.

5. The following transcription conventions have been employed:

...	pause
-	truncation
,	clause final intonation ("more to come")
.	sentence final falling intonation
!	sentence final high-fall
?	sentence final rising intonation
[...]	parts of the utterance have been left out of the excerpt
/????/	inaudible utterance
CAPS	emphatic stress
Italics	German utterance; the translation is provided in an endnote

"..."   changing voice quality to mark reported speech
@   laughter
[beginning of overlap
=   one utterance latches on to another

6.   The three couples who live neither in an English- nor a German-speaking country have been excluded from this count, as has the only homosexual couple in my sample. While sexuality has not been a focus of my study, it is clear that the "heterosexual privilege" also accrues to bilingual, cross-cultural couples. For instance, the bureaucratic hassles that many of my informants mention in their conversations are even more severe for homosexual couples who cannot obtain a residence permit "by marriage". Significantly, all the homosexual couples I made contact with when I was recruiting consultants for this research were British and German nationals, who – as EU citizens – can take up residence in each other's country. "Simply" living as a couple must be fraught with many more hurdles for, e.g., American and German homosexual couples.

7.   German utterances are in italics. The German part of the excerpt translates as: "I say- I say like:"

8.   "fort head" is an error for "forehead."

References

Auwärter, Manfred
    1988   Das Experiment in der Soziolinguistik. In Ammon, Ulrich (ed.), *Sociolinguistics: An International Handbook of the Science of Language and Society*. Berlin: Mouton de Gruyter, 922–931.

Bakhtin, Mikhail
    1981   *The Dialogic Imagination*. [First published in 1929]. Ed. by Holquist, Michael. Trans. by Emerson, Caryl and Michael Holquist. Austin: University of Texas Press.

Baus, Raymond
    1992   An investigation of conciliation, control and intimacy in three couple types. *Dissertation Abstracts International* 53, 2, 346A.

Bernard, Roger
    1994   Les enjeux de l'exogamie. *Langue et Société 46, 38-39.*

Boix, Emili
    1997   Ideologías lingüísticas en familias lingüísticamente mixtas (catalán-castellano) en la región metropolitana de Barcelona. In Zimmermann, Klaus and Christine Bierbach (eds.), *Lenguaje y comunicación intercultural en el mundo hispánico*. Frankfurt: Vervuert, 169–190.

Boucher, Colette
1995   Développement et évaluation d'un nouveau systéme d'analyse des interactions verbales pour les couples. *Dissertation Abstracts International* 55, 8, 3634 B.

Boyd, Sally
1998   North Americans in the Nordic region: elite bilinguals. In Varro, Gabrielle and Sally Boyd (eds.), Americans in Europe – A Sociolinguistic Perspective: Probes in Northern and Western Europe. *International Journal of the Sociology of Language* 133, 31–50.

Braine, George (ed.)
1999   *Non-Native Educators in English Language Teaching*. Mahwah, NJ: Lawrence Erlbaum Associates.

Breger, Rosemary
1998   Love and the state: Women, mixed marriages and the law in Germany. In Breger, Rosemary and Rosanna Hill (eds.), *Cross-Cultural Marriage: Identity and Choice*. Oxford: Berg, 129–152.

Breger, Rosemary and Rosanna Hill
1998   Introducing mixed marriages. In Breger, Rosemary and Rosanna Hill (eds.) *Cross-Cultural Marriage: Identity and Choice*. Oxford: Berg, 1–32.

Butler, Judith
1990   *Gender Trouble: Feminism and the Subversion of Identity*. New York: Routledge.

Cameron, Deborah
1997 a   Theoretical debates in feminist linguistics: Questions of sex and gender. In Wodak, Ruth (ed.), *Gender and Discourse*. London: Sage, 21–36.
1997 b   Performing gender identity: Young men's talk and the construction of heterosexual masculinity. In Johnson, Sally and Ulrike Hanna Meinhof (eds.), *Language and Masculinity*. Oxford: Blackwell, 47–64.

Castonguay, Charles
1979   L'exogamie précoce et la prévision des taux de transfert linguistique. *Recherches Sociographiques*, 20, 3, 403–408.
1982   Intermarriage and language shift in Canada in 1971 and 1976. *The Canadian Journal of Sociology*, 7, 3, 263–277.

Chiaro, Delia and Giuseppe Nocella
1999   *Anglo-Italian bilingualism in the UK: A sociolinguistic perspective*. Paper presented at the 2nd International Symposium on Bilingualism, Newcastle-Upon-Tyne, UK.

Clyne, Michael
1994   *Inter-Cultural Communication at Work.* Cambridge: Cambridge University Press.

Coulmas, Florian
1997   A matter of choice. In Pütz, Martin (ed.), *Language Choices. Conditions, Constraints, and Consequences.* Amsterdam: John Benjamins, 31–44.

Crawford, Mary
1995   *Talking Difference: On Gender and Language.* London: Sage.

DeFrancisco, Victoria
1989   *Marital communication: A feminist qualitative analysis.* Unpublished PhD dissertation, University of Illinois, Champaign/Urbana.

1991   The sounds of silence: how men silence women in marital relations. *Discourse and Society* 2, 4, 413–424.

Deignan, Alice
1997   Metaphors of desire. In Harvey, Keith and Celia Shalom (eds.), *Language and Desire: Encoding Sex, Romance and Intimacy.* London: Routledge, 21–42.

Druce, Nel (ed.)
1994   The new politics of sex and the state. Special issue. *Feminist Review* 48.

Eckert, Penelope
2000   *Linguistic Variation as Social Practice: The Linguistic Construction of Identity in Belten High.* Oxford: Blackwell.

Eckert, Penelope and Sally McConnell-Ginet
1992   Think practically and look locally: Language and gender as community-based practice. *Annual Review of Anthropology* 21, 461–490.

1995   Constructing meaning, constructing selves: Snapshots of language, gender and class from Belten High. In Hall, Kira and Mary Bucholtz (eds.), *Gender Articulated: Language and the Socially Constructed Self.* New York: Routledge, 469–507.

Ervin, Susan
1964   Language and TAT content in bilinguals. *Journal of Abnormal and Social Psychology* 68, 5, 500–507.

Ervin-Tripp, Susan
1968   An analysis of the interaction of language, topic and listener. In Fishman, Joshua (ed.), *Readings in the Sociology of Language.* The Hague: Mouton, 192–211. [Repr. from: *American Anthropologist* 66 (1964), 86–102].

Fasold, Ralph
1984   *The Sociolinguistics of Society.* Oxford: Blackwell.

Ferguson, Charles
1959   Diglossia. *Word* 15, 325–40.

Fishman, Pamela
1978   What do couples talk about when they're alone? In Butturff, Douglas and Edmund L. Epstein (eds.), *Women's Language and Style.* Akron, Ohio: Land Books, 11–22.
1980   Conversational insecurity. In Giles, Howard, Peter Robinson and Philip M. Smith (eds.), *Language: Social Psychological Perspectives.* New York: Pergamon Press, 127–132.
1983   Interaction: The work women do. In Thorne, Barrie, Cheris Kramarae, and Nancy Henley (eds.), *Language, Gender and Society.* Cambridge: Newbury House, 89–101.

Fitzpatrick, Mary Anne
1990   Models of marital interaction. In Giles, Howard and Peter Robinson (eds.), *Handbook of Language and Social Psychology.* Chichester: John Wiley and Sons, 433–450.

Fitzpatrick, Mary Anne, L. Vance and H. Wittemann
1984   Interpersonal communication in the casual interaction of marital partners. *Journal of Language and Social Psychology* 3, 81–95.

Gass, Susan and Joyce Neu (eds.)
1996   *Speech Acts Across Cultures: Challenges to Communication in a Second Language.* Berlin: Mouton de Gruyter.

Grimes, Barbara
1985   Language attitudes: Identity, distinctiveness, survival in the Vaupes. *Journal of Multilingual and Multicultural Development* 6, 5, 389–401.

Harding, Edith and Philip Riley
1986   *The Bilingual Family: A Handbook for Parents.* Cambridge: Cambridge University Press.

Heller, Monica and Laurette Lévy
1992   Mixed marriages: Life on the linguistic frontier. *Multilingua* 11, 1, 11–43.
1994   Les contradictions des mariages linguistiquement mixtes: stratégies des femmes Franco-Ontariennes. *Langage et Société,* March issue, 53–88.

Holmes, Janet
1992   *An Introduction to Sociolinguistics.* London: Longman.

Holmes, Janet and Miriam Meyerhoff
1999   The Community of Practice: Theories and methodologies in language and gender research. *Language in Society* 28, 2, 173–183.

Jackson, Jean
1983   *The Fish People: Linguistic Exogamy and Tukanoan Identity in the Northwest Amazonia*. Cambridge: Cambridge University Press.

Kouritzin, Sandra
2000   A Mother's Tongue. *TESOL Quarterly* 34, 2, 311–324.

Koven, Michéle
1998   Two languages in the self/the self in two languages: French-Portuguese bilinguals' verbal enactments and experiences of self in narrative discourse. *Ethos* 26, 4, 410–455.

Kramsch, Claire
1997   The privilege of the nonnative speaker. *PMLA* 112, 3, 359–369.

Labov, William
1972   *Sociolinguistic Patterns*. Philadelphia: University of Philadelphia Press.

Latomaa, Sirkku
1998   English in contact with "the most difficult language in the world": the linguistic situation of Americans living in Finland. *International Journal of the Sociology of Language* 133, 51–71.

Leisi, Ernst
1993   *Paar und Sprache*. [1ˢᵗ edition 1978] Heidelberg: UTB.

LePage, Robert and Andrée Tabouret-Keller
1985   *Acts of Identity: Creole-Based Approaches to Language and Ethnicity*. Cambridge: Cambridge University Press.

Manusov, Valerie
1990a   The use of attribution principles for understanding non-verbal behavior: A test within romantic dyads. *Dissertation Abstracts International* 50, 7, 1849A.

1990b   An application of attribution principles to nonverbal behavior in romantic dyads. *Communication Monographs* 57, 104–118.

McClintock, Anne
1993   Family feuds: Gender, nationalism and the family. *Feminist Review* 44, 61–80.

Mougeon, Raymond, H. Savard and S. Carroll
    1978   Les mariages mixtes: le cheval de Troie de l'assimilation à Welland? *L'Express de Toronto* 3, 42.

Paikeday, Thomas
    1985   *The Native Speaker is Dead!* Toronto: Paikeday.

Pauwels, Anne
    1985   The effect of exogamy on language maintenance in the Dutch-speaking community in Australia. *ITL Review of Applied Linguistics* 66, 1–24.

Phillipson, Robert
    1998   Globalizing English: are linguistic human rights an alternative to linguistic imperialism? *Language Sciences* 20,1, 101–112.

Piller, Ingrid
    1998   Bilingual Love Talk in Fiction. In Parlog, Hortensia (ed.), *B.A.S. British and American Studies*. Timisoara: Hestia, 201–218.
    1999   'Something tattooed on my forehead:' gendered performances and perceptions of linguistic and national identity. In Pasero, Ursula and Friederike Braun (eds.), *Wahrnehmung und Herstellung von Geschlecht – Perceiving and Performing Gender*. Wiesbaden: Westdeutscher Verlag, 117–126.

Romaine, Suzanne
    1994   *Language in Society*. Oxford: Oxford University Press.
    1995   *Bilingualism*. Oxford: Blackwell.

Siguan, Miguel
    1980   Changement de langue dans le couple et dans la famille. In Nelde, Peter (ed.), *Sprachkontakt und Sprachkonflikt (Zeitschrift für Dialektologie und Linguistik, Beihefte* 32). Wiesbaden: Franz Steiner, 283–285.

Singh, Rajendra (ed.)
    1998   *The Native Speaker: Multilingual Perspectives*. New Delhi: Sage.

Spaine, Deborah
    1991   The nonverbal behaviors of intimate versus nonintimate married couples. *Dissertation Abstracts International* 51,12, 6120 B.

Tannen, Deborah
    1986   *That's Not What I Meant! How Conversational Style Makes or Breaks Relationships*. New York: Ballantine Books.
    1990   *You Just Don't Understand: Women and Men in Conversation*. New York: Ballantine Books.
    (ed.) 1994   *Gender and Discourse*. Oxford: Oxford University Press.

Varro, Gabrielle and Sally Boyd (eds.)
   1998   Americans in Europe – A Sociolinguistic Perspective: Probes in Northern
             and Western Europe. *International Journal of the Sociology of Language*
             133.

Varro, Gabrielle and Gunter Gebauer (eds.)
   1997   *Zwei Kulturen. Eine Familie. Paare aus verschiedenen Kulturen, am Beis-
             piel Frankreichs and Deutschlands.* Opladen: Leske und Budrich.

Walters, Keith
   1996   Gender, identity, and the political economy of language: Anglophone
             wives in Tunisia. *Language in Society* 25, 515–555.

Weatherford, Vicki
   1985   An exploratory study of perceived and observed confirmation/ disconfirm-
             ation communication behaviors in marital dyads. *Dissertation Abstracts
             International* 46, 6, 2082B–2083B.

Wilson, John
   1987   The sociolinguistic paradox: data as a methodological product. *Language
             and Communication* 7, 2, 161–177.

Woolard, Kathryn
   1997   Between friends: Gender, peer group structure, and bilingualism in urban
             Catalonia. *Language in Society* 26, 533–560.

Finding one's voice in Japanese: A study of the pitch levels of L2 users

Yumiko Ohara

1. Introduction

Recently, researchers focusing on the relationship between gender and language have begun to examine the issues and dilemmas faced by people who cross national and cultural boundaries as adults and (re)consider their own gendered identities in the face of the expectations and constraints of their target language and culture (Ogulnick 1998; Pavlenko, this volume; Peirce 1995; Piller, this volume; Price 1996; Siegal 1994, 1996). Unlike people who grow up within a culture, socialized to adopt certain linguistic practices appropriate to their gender in that society, second language (L2) users attempting to develop proficiency in the language and gain acceptance in the culture must often decide for themselves how willing they are to follow those practices used by native speakers (L1 users) to express gender in the target culture. Concerning Japanese, the language on which this paper centers, Siegal (1994, 1996) has noted the possibility that female learners resist using certain syntactic forms that are associated with a female speech register. Such a suggestion raises interesting questions about other aspects of language as well. For example, given that research on prosodic features of the Japanese language has demonstrated a strong correlation between high voice pitch levels and attributes associated with feminine identities, including being polite (Loveday 1986), cute, gentle, weak (Ohara 1993, 1997) and modest (Van Bezooijen 1995, 1996), we might speculate that some female learners of Japanese from cultures with different conceptions of gender would want to avoid projecting these images and hence resist employing a high pitched voice when speaking the target language.

In this chapter, in order to investigate some of the issues involved in L2 users' expression of gender in the Japanese language, I will examine the pitch levels of speakers of Japanese with different levels of proficiency and cultural competence. Using both phonetic analyses of laboratory recorded speech data and ethnographic interviews, I will attempt to describe how female learners of Japanese deal with the different cultural expectations and constraints related to the production of voice in Japanese society. I begin moving toward my analysis in the next section by briefly describing the results of some previous studies.

2. Pitch and gendered identities: Making the cultural connection

In previous research, I analyzed the voice pitch levels of Japanese L1 speakers who possessed high proficiency in English (Ohara 1992, 1997, 1999 a, b). Results showed that females produced a higher pitched voice when speaking in Japanese than in English while males did not alter their pitch level across languages. The results of my studies are in line with those obtained in a study by Loveday (1986), which drew comparisons between L1 speakers of Japanese and British English. To explain these results, I posited that cultural constraints were responsible for this difference, and not other factors generally claimed to be the cause of variation in pitch, such as anatomy (Laver and Trudgill 1979), physical and emotional states of a speaker (Baken 1987; Colton, Casper, and Hirano 1990), and the linguistic structures of the language being spoken (Yamazawa and Hollien 1992). These cultural constraints, I argued, center on expectations about femininity in Japanese society. One way Japanese females are expected to present a feminine image is through the use of a high pitched voice. Moreover, not only are female speakers expected to employ a high pitched voice, but it also seems to be the case that a female with a higher pitched voice has certain "advantages" within Japanese society. In a study in which female voices produced at various pitch levels were played for both Japanese female and male listeners, Ohara (1993, 1997) found that the higher the pitch of an utterance, the more likely the producer of the voice was perceived to be cute, soft, gentle, kind, polite, quiet, young, weak, and beautiful. On the other hand, it was observed that lower pitched voices were more likely to be perceived as belonging to females who were stubborn, selfish, strong, and straightforward. Furthermore, it was also discovered that a woman with a higher pitched voice was judged more likely to be able to marry someone desirable, while the lower the pitch the more a woman was perceived as being likely to remain single for life. There were virtually no gender-linked differences in these perceptions of pitch; both female and male participants perceived social meanings attached to different pitch levels in very similar ways. Also regarding perception, in a cross-cultural study of Dutch and Japanese, Van Bezooijen (1995) found that participants from both cultures consistently associated personal attributes, such as 'short', 'weak', 'dependent', and 'modest', with a higher pitch and the opposite attributes, namely, 'tall', 'strong', 'independent', and 'arrogant', with a lower pitch. The researcher also found that the association between the attribute 'short' and a high pitched voice is consistent with the idea of 'cuteness' in Japanese society. As Kinsella (1995) asserts, Japanese women often try to appear small, weak, and child-like in an attempt to display their 'cuteness'. In a later study, Van Bezooijen (1996) found, on the one hand, a correlation between a higher pitched voice and more feminine aspects of personality, such as dependence, modesty, lack of prestige, sensitivity, and explicit expression of emotions, and, on the other, a strong connection between a lower pitched voice and personality traits such as independence, arrogance, prestige, lack of sensitivity, and suppression of emotions. Based on these results, Van Bezooijen (1996: 765) contends that "this pitch would be chosen so as to approximate a particular vocal image reflecting desired personal attributes and social roles, of which gender identity forms an integral part". These studies further highlight the importance of voice pitch to gender roles and femininity. Together, the results of perception and production studies strongly suggest that female members of Japanese society are expected to sound polite (Loveday 1986), cute, soft, gentle, kind, quiet, young, beautiful (Ohara 1993, 1997), dependent, modest, sensitive, and emotional (Van Bezooijen 1995). At the same time, the females who do not conform to such expectations may suffer repercussions, and, in particular, be perceived as unlikely to find a husband (Ohara 1993, 1997). In mainstream Japanese society, where finding a husband is considered the ultimate goal toward which women are expected to strive (Edwards 1989), being thought of as 'non-marriageable' can be, and often is, a very serious problem.

In contrast to Japanese, speakers of English are not under the same kinds of cultural constraints regarding the pitch of their voice. As McConnell-Ginet (1978: 549) stated about American culture, "men lose by sounding woman-like, whereas women do not lose (perhaps they even gain in some contexts) by sounding manlike". Sachs, Lieberman, and Erickson (1973: 82) expressed a similar opinion when they wrote the following:

> Typically, in our culture having an 'effeminate' voice is a problem for a man. With the amount of overlap in physical structure that exists between men and women, perhaps some men learn, among other things, to lower their formants in order to sound more masculine. We expect that having a voice perceived as 'low pitched' is not a severe handicap for a woman, although an aggressive, 'masculine' speech style may be.

Furthermore, an experimental study of the perception of ideal voice types indicated that for a female voice in Mexican culture, medium pitch is preferred, while both medium and somewhat low pitched voices are preferred in American culture (Valentine and Saint Damian 1988). Thus, it is clear that the social meanings attached to voice pitch may vary across cultures. In Japanese society, certain social values are attached to a high pitched voice, which serve as an incentive for females to speak in a higher pitch. Yet, by way of contrast, such an incentive does not exist for speakers of different varieties of English.

This is not to say that females in English-speaking cultures are not under any kind of social pressure to express their femininity. They most surely are. Not only are there certain nonverbal ways, including makeup and ways of dressing, that women are expected to use to highlight their femininity, but linguists (Coates 1986, 1999; Holmes 1995; Mulac 1998; Tannen 1997, among others) have also suggested that there exist specific linguistic resources for expressing a female gender identity in the English language, including the use of a deeper, breathy voice to exude sexuality (Graddol and Swann 1989; Henton and Bladon 1985). In contrast, analyses of the Japanese data discussed above seem to suggest that in Japanese society the use of a high pitched voice is an important way of performing or 'doing' gender (e.g., West and Fenstermaker 1995; West and Zimmerman 1987). I use the word 'important' because, as just suggested, social pressures are such in Japanese culture that a woman opting not to employ a high pitch level risks hurting her chances of being thought of as a 'desirable' female.

Indeed, the fact that Japanese native speakers in previous research employed high voice pitch levels in Japanese and not in English serves as further evidence of the difference in social meanings of pitch across cultures. All of the Japanese participants in my previous research, both females and males, were university students at an American university, suggesting not only that their proficiency in English was sufficient to enter universities but also that they were familiar with American culture. Their voice pitch levels also point to a certain degree of awareness of the difference between the social meanings attached to voice pitch in the two cultures.

However, while the previous research has provided strong evidence that female native speakers of Japanese effectively deal with this cultural difference by using lower pitch levels when speaking English, one interesting question that remains is what happens in the opposite case. Do female L1 users of English who are either already proficient in or in the process of acquiring proficiency in Japanese employ a higher pitch when speaking in Japanese in order to satisfy cultural expectations? In an attempt to answer this question, I examine the voice pitch levels of two different groups of female L2 users of Japanese, those who are proficient in the language and those who have just begun studying it.

Although we might be tempted to assume that female learners of Japanese, in their attempts to acquire native-like proficiency, would want to emulate the speaking patterns of Japanese women, this may not necessarily be the case. Focusing on the linguistic behavior of female language learners in Japan, Siegal (1994, 1996) found that the learners "created their own language system based on their perception of Japanese women's language and demeanor" (1994: 648). She also highlighted the importance of identity construction for L2 learners: "second language learners do not merely model native speakers with a desire to emulate, but rather actively create a new interlanguage and an accompanying identity in the learning process" (Siegal 1996: 362). Based on such an observation, we might expect American females, not accustomed to the social expectation of using a high pitched voice, to actively consider, as a part of the process of acquiring proficiency in Japanese, what voice pitch means for their target culture identity. In order to determine how aware female L2 learners were of the social meanings attached to voice pitch in Japanese culture and how much their knowledge of these meanings affected their choice of voice pitch, I conducted a phonetic analysis of their performance on three different tasks and carried out ethnographic interviews with the participants. I offer more information about the data and procedures below.

3. Data and procedures

Three groups of female participants took part in the study: 1) beginning learners of Japanese whose first language is American English (L1-L5), 2) Japanese-English bilinguals, who have Japanese as their first language and American English as their second language (J1-J5), and 3) English-Japanese bilinguals, who have American English as their first language and Japanese as their second language (E1-E5). For the second and third groups, the term 'bilingual' is used interchangeably with 'L2 user' or 'L2 learner' to emphasize the fact that the participants possess a high level of proficiency in their second language. Judgments about the participants' proficiency were based on their educational level of attainment and experience in using the language. All of the Japanese-English bilinguals were officially enrolled in the University of Hawai'i at the time of the study; therefore, it was presumed that their English proficiency was relatively high. The English-Japanese bilinguals, also students at the University of Hawai'i, had all lived in Japan for at least one year; in addition, they had taken at least four years of Japanese at university level. The group of beginning learners was enrolled at the time of the study in the lowest level Japanese class offered at the University of Hawai'i; none of them had the experience of having lived in Japan.

In total, there were fifteen participants, five for each group. None of the participants had any history of speech or hearing disorders, nor did any of them exhibit symptoms of a cold or sore throat at the time of the recording. Their ages ranged between 22 and 33 for beginning learners, 25–33 for Japanese-English bilinguals, and 25–31 for English-Japanese bilinguals. Even though my focus in this study is primarily on the participants whose first language is American English, I have included the group of Japanese-English bilinguals for two reasons: 1) their performance will serve as a useful comparison to that of the other two groups, 2) the results will further confirm those of previous studies which have indicated a difference in the cultural expression of gendered identities. Since the Japanese native speakers were not monolingual speakers of Japanese but rather bilingual speakers of Japanese and English, they represented the most appropriate control group for other budding bilinguals (see, e.g., Cook 1999).

The participants were recorded in their performance on three tasks: 1) the reading of isolated sentences, 2) the performance of a scripted conversation with the researcher (the isolated sentences and conversations can be found in the appendix), and 3) the production of a telephone message to both a professor and a friend. All participants performed the tasks in both Japanese and English. The scripted conversations and the telephone message were designed to yield more natural speech samples than the reading of isolated sentences. This was particularly true of the telephone message task, because it required the participants to spontaneously create their own message, and was conceived to be the closest to natural speech. The participants were asked to leave a message in Japanese for a Japanese professor and a Japanese friend, and in English for an American professor and an American friend. In order to leave these four messages, the participants used the telephone in the lab to call a set telephone number, which in turn led them to an answering machine with a prerecorded message. Although the participants were not given prepared scripts to read for the message, they were not given complete freedom to make up their own messages either. The participants were directed to include the following in their message: 1) first, they were asked to identify themselves, 2) then state that they were looking for a particular book, 3) next explain that the library copy has been checked out, 4) then ask to borrow the professor's/friend's copy of the book, and 5) lastly, remark that they would call again later. Even though the participants were given directions, they still had to decide what kind of lexical items and grammatical constructions to employ when leaving the message. The order of languages in which the tasks were performed was randomized: some of the participants left the message in English first and then in Japanese, and others in reverse. Likewise, the order of the addressees, either professor or friend, was also alternated. The fundamental frequency of each participant's voice was measured and mean fundamental frequencies were obtained using the computer software Signalyze, Version 3.12.

After each participant completed the tasks, the ethnographic interview was conducted. As noted, the purpose of the interviews was to investigate how aware the participants were of their voice pitch levels when speaking in Japanese. In addition, the participants were asked to relate any interesting experiences they had when speaking Japanese, with particular emphasis placed on experiences that were related to their use of voice pitch. Since awareness and experience varied according to participant, the length and content of the interviews differed from one participant to the next. Those participants who were conscious of their voice pitch were prompted to explain their feelings in detail and were asked to express their beliefs about the relationship between voice pitch and identity. All of the interviews were conducted by the researcher and all were recorded with an audio-taperecorder.

4. Results

This section is divided into three subsections, which, respectively, present the results for beginning learners of Japanese, Japanese-English bilinguals, and English-Japanese bilinguals.

4.1. Beginning learners of Japanese

Table 1 shows the average mean fundamental frequency levels for the beginning level learners of Japanese on the three tasks: sentence reading, conversation, and telephone message.

Table 1. Beginning level learners of Japanese

| | Sentence | | Conversation | | Message | | | |
| | | | | | Professor | | Friend | |
	English	Japanese	English	Japanese	English	Japanese	English	Japanese
L1	199.22	188.25	186.32	188.98	170.81	173.22	184.18	174.23
L2	220.67	221.29	230.98	229.77	220.33	222.66	240.22	223.98
L3	250.98	251.99	267.00	270.00	252.00	253.77	283.00	255.21
L4	202.00	208.75	210.00	208.76	190.00	200.59	210.84	205.63
L5	254.00	256.00	270.00	265.00	271.22	272.88	289.23	270.76

In order to assess the statistical significance of the findings, the results were subjected to analysis of Paired-Samples t-Test (SPSS 6.1.1 Macintosh). The 2-tailed significance level was set at 95%. The difference in the language was not statistically significant for the sentence reading task (t = −0.71, df = 4, p = ns) nor for the conversation task (t = 0.34, df = 4, p = ns). Therefore, it can be assumed that beginning level learners were not using different pitch levels in English and in Japanese for these tasks. For the message task, the results were rather mixed. The difference in language was statistically significant in the message to friends (t = 3.99, df = 4, p = 0.002) but not in the message to professors (t = −2.28, df = 4, p = ns). In other words, in the message to professors the participants were not using different pitch levels in English and in Japanese, but in the message to friends they were. The difference in addressees was significant in English (t = 7.06, df = 4, p = 0.002) but not in Japanese (t = 1.18, df = 4, p = ns). This means that in English − but not in Japanese − the participants employed significantly different pitch levels in the message to a friend than in the message to a professor.

As is evident in Table 1, the beginning level learners of Japanese did not exhibit much difference in their fundamental frequency levels when speaking in Japanese and English. One interesting point concerning their pitch behavior can be witnessed in their performance on the telephone message task. The participants used a higher pitch in their messages to friends than they did to professors. This result is consistent with some studies which have suggested that for women a higher pitch level and variability in pitch can be used to indicate friendliness in mainstream American culture (Arnovitch 1976; Kramer 1977). It is also possible that in their message to a professor, the adoption of a lower pitched voice indicates an attempt to convey seriousness (e.g., Valentine and Saint Damian 1988).

4.2. Japanese-English bilinguals

As Table 2 demonstrates, the pitch behavior of the Japanese-English bilinguals widely diverges from that of the beginning language learners. The pitch levels observed in Table 2 further confirm the results of earlier studies which found that female participants employ higher pitch levels when speaking in Japanese than in English (Loveday 1986; Ohara 1992, 1997, 1999 a,b; Yamazawa and Hollien 1992). Although there is variation in the range of pitches used by these five participants, they all exhibit the following two patterns: 1) they use a higher pitch in Japanese regardless of the task being performed, and 2) they use the highest pitch in their messages to the professor.

Table 2. Japanese-English bilinguals

| | Sentence | | Conversation | | Message | | | |
| | | | | | Professor | | Friend | |
	English	Japanese	English	Japanese	English	Japanese	English	Japanese
J1	225.35	285.05	270.48	288.59	279.00	317.40	270.30	290.00
J2	235.56	263.30	270.56	288.59	262.87	299.44	232.40	278.78
J3	215.34	235.05	250.48	268.50	279.00	290.30	260.40	270.00
J4	215.32	275.00	270.22	289.74	270.92	297.42	250.22	270.34
J5	190.20	204.00	210.00	224.43	215.99	240.75	218.00	220.87

Concerning the statistical significance of this set of findings, the difference in language used was significant for the sentence reading task ($t = -3.75$, $df = 4$, $p = 0.020$) and for the conversation task ($t = -13.82$, $df = 4$, $p < 0.001$). At the same time, however, it should be pointed out that the difference across languages was greater for the conversation than the readings. For the message task, the results were rather mixed, just as they were in the case of the beginning learners of Japanese, but this time, in the exact opposite direction. There was no statistically significant difference across languages in the message to friends ($t = -2.10$, $df = 4$, $p = ns$). In other words, unlike the beginning language learners, Japanese-English bilinguals did not use different pitch levels in the message to a friend in English and in Japanese. Similarly, the difference in the addressees in the English message was not significant ($t = -2.29$, $df = 4$, $p = ns$). Thus, unlike the beginning language learners, the participants did not use different pitch levels in English when leaving a message for a professor and for a friend. However, the difference in the language had a significant effect on the message to professors ($t = -4.96$, $df = 4$, $p = 0.008$), i.e., pitch levels were significantly different in Japanese and in English. Also, the difference in the addressees was significant in Japanese ($t = 13.487$, $df = 4$, $p < 0.001$) which suggests that Japanese-English bilinguals used significantly different pitch levels in Japanese when speaking to a professor than when speaking to a friend.

4.3. English-Japanese bilinguals

While it has thus far been relatively easy to observe general patterns in the pitch levels used by beginner learners of Japanese and Japanese-English bilinguals,

Table 3 indicates that the situation is more complicated for the English-Japanese bilinguals.

Table 3. English-Japanese bilinguals

	Sentence		Conversation		Message			
					Professor		Friend	
	English	Japanese	English	Japanese	English	Japanese	English	Japanese
E1	178.76	182.30	195.78	200.23	195.94	200.61	210.55	220.25
E2	229.30	249.27	255.62	288.59	259.00	287.58	243.90	261.00
E3	234.73	262.63	240.34	268.09	235.12	284.43	244.28	284.66
E4	234.51	270.13	250.96	290.54	272.78	310.87	312.78	303.45
E5	236.80	238.10	246.37	240.95	217.90	216.41	227.53	223.14

As Table 3 demonstrates, the fundamental frequency levels used by the English-Japanese bilinguals in Japanese were rather mixed. Two participants, E1 and E5, show patterns that are closer to those of the beginning level learners and the other three participants, E2, E3, and E4, exhibit patterns that are similar to those of the Japanese-English bilinguals. Furthermore, in contrast to the beginning learners, this subgroup of English-Japanese bilinguals, E2, E3, and E4, was using an equally high pitched voice in the message to a professor and to a friend in Japanese while the beginning learners were using an equally low pitched voice in the same context.

In order to further emphasize the differences between those participants who generated results somewhat similar to the beginning level learners and those who resembled the Japanese L1 speakers, statistical analyses were conducted. Although the sample was rather small, the following results were obtained. For the first subgroup (E1 and E5), the difference in the language was not statistically significant for any of the tasks. This was true for the sentence reading ($t = -2.16$, $df = 1$, $p = ns$), for the conversation ($t = 0.1$, $df = 1$, $p = ns$), for the difference in language in messages to professors ($t = -0.51$, $df = 1$, $p = ns$), for the difference in language in messages to friends ($t = -0.38$, $df = 1$, $p = ns$), for the difference in addressees in the English message ($t = 4.96$, $df = 1$, $p = ns$), and for the difference in addressees in the Japanese message ($t = 2.04$, $df = 1$, $p = ns$). For the second subgroup (E2, E3, E4), the statistical results obtained resemble those of the Japanese-English bilinguals. For the sentence reading (t=–5.32, df=2, p=0.034) and for the conversation (t=–9.77, df=2, p=0.001), the difference in language was significant just as it was in the case of the Japanese-English bilinguals. For the message tasks, the difference in language was significant for the message to professors (t=–6.49, df=2, p=0.023) but not to friends (t=1.30, df=2, p=ns). Thus, these participants were employing different pitch levels in the message to the professor in Japanese and in English, exhibiting a pattern similar to that found in performance of the Japanese-English bilinguals. In the message to friends, the English-Japanese bilinguals were not using a different pitch, also resembling the Japanese-English bilinguals. The difference in addressees was not significant in English (t=0.65, df=2, p=ns). In other words, they were not using different pitch levels in the English messages to a professor and to a friend. This pattern was also exhibited by the Japanese-English bilinguals. However, one point which differentiates this subgroup from the Japanese-English bilinguals is found in the messages in Japanese to both a professor and a friend. While Japanese-English bilinguals vary pitch levels in their Japanese messages to professors and friends, the difference in the addressees was not significant in the performance of the English-Japanese bilinguals (t=–1.40, df=2, p=ns). In what follows, I will focus most of the discussion on these mixed findings, paying special attention to the results of the interviews conducted with the English-Japanese bilinguals. I will use the qualitative data to further substantiate my claim that the English-Japanese bilinguals in my sample can be divided into two subgroups: participants who exhibited pitch patterns similar to those of beginning learners, and participants who used voice pitch in ways similar to those of Japanese-English bilinguals.

5. The learners' views of voice pitch and Japanese 'women's language'

The fact that three of the English-Japanese bilinguals exhibited voice pitch patterns very similar to those of the Japanese-English bilinguals would, at a superficial level, seem to make a lot of sense. If one of the goals of learning and practicing a second/foreign language is to develop native-like proficiency, then we might want to praise participants E2, E3, and E4 for their native-like performance on the tasks. Especially when we consider the time that these three participants have devoted to their study of Japanese (over four years of university-level study and at least one year in Japan), it might give them a sense of satisfaction to know that at least in terms of their voice pitch levels, they seem to have acquired a proficiency comparable to that of L1 speakers. However, by the same reasoning, the performance of the other two English-Japanese bilinguals, E1 and E5, is troublesome. Are we to assume, based on their performance on the tasks, that their language ability is far from native-like? Likewise, noting the similarity between E1's and E5's performance and the beginning level learners in Japanese, are we to conclude that despite their years spent studying Japanese in the classroom and living in Japan, they have failed to acquire competence that exceeds that of students who are in their first year of study? And, going one step further, are we to think that the fact that E1 and E5 do not emulate this important aspect of identity of Japanese women will have a negative effect on their attempts to be accepted into the Japanese culture? Although Miller (1977, 1982), with his 'law of inverse returns', used anecdotal evidence to suggest that Japanese people have difficulty accepting L2 speakers who are fluent in the language, more recent research has indicated that L2 speakers themselves believe that the better they speak Japanese the more likely they are to be accepted by Japanese society (Ohta 1993). Furthermore, additional research focusing on the attitudes of the Japanese toward Japanese language learners has shown a positive orientation towards learners who do their best to learn 'correct' Japanese and assimilate into the culture (Haugh 1998).

Below, I will argue that the answer to the three questions just posed should be negative. Despite the divergences in the English-Japanese bilinguals' pitch levels, we should not assume that some of them have failed to attain high proficiency in the Japanese language or to find an identity that can gain them acceptance into Japanese society. What we should not forget is that, at the same time as they exist as learners of a foreign/second language working to achieve proficiency in Japanese, they also remain rational and interpretive social beings who base their decisions not only on a desire to emulate L1 speakers of Japanese. The results of the interviews revealed that all five English-Japanese bilinguals were very conscious of the kind of images that the pitch levels of their voice might be associated with. Indeed, it became apparent for these women that the voice pitch levels they employed correlated neatly with their attitude toward the kinds of images typically associated with Japanese women. In fact, this is precisely the point where the two English-Japanese bilinguals, E1 and E5, diverge greatly from the beginning level learners. The interviews confirmed that the reason that E1 and E5 did not vary their pitch across language was their own conscious and rational decision. This was not the case for the beginning level learners who in their interviews did not show any kind of awareness of the social meanings attached to voice pitch in the Japanese culture. They had not yet been exposed, either through their studies or through contact with the target culture, to the kind of stimuli that would lead them to obtain the information about the connection between voice pitch and female identity in Japanese society.

Similarly, the interviews made it clear that the three participants, E2, E3, and E4, who raised their voice pitch levels when speaking in Japanese, did so not necessarily because they were enamored with the idea of projecting themselves in such a way. Rather, it seems to have been a result of their attempt to fit into the culture. As one of those three participants, E2, remarked:

> It's not like I enjoy talking in a high pitched voice but it's like you kind of have to do that when speaking in Japanese especially when you are talking to professors and, you know, older people.

A short while later in the interview, she again expressed her awareness of the connection between a high pitched voice, femininity, and politeness with the comment:

> You know the intonation pattern is different, it's a lot higher [in Japanese] and sounds politer and softer, more feminine.

E2's assessment of the connection between femininity and politeness in Japanese culture is consistent with previous laboratory-based studies of pitch (Loveday 1986; Ohara 1993, 1997; Van Bezooijen 1995, 1996) as well as a recent study that examined naturally occurring speech of Japanese employees in businesses located in Hawai'i (Ohara 2000). The latter was a longitudinal case study of two female and two male employees, which found that the females employed a much higher pitched voice when speaking to customers than when speaking informally to acquaintances. Higher pitched voice was, in short, used by the female employees to express politeness.

The three participants in the present study also displayed a keen awareness that their employment of these high pitched voices was deeply tied to their attempts to adopt, or at least project, an identity that was very different from their identity in their native culture. For example, one of the participants, E3, stated the following:

> When my mother called me in Japan, she did not recognize my voice, not because I answered the phone in Japanese but because of the way I said *moshi moshi* ['hello' (high pitched)]. There were times my friends and relatives from back home called me and thought I was some other Japanese girl. I know I sound very different in Japanese.

Another one of these three participants discussed her use of voice pitch in terms of a 'search' for her Japanese identity. She remarked that often before she would go out with Japanese friends, she would practice in front of the mirror at home in order to make sure she was producing the right kind of identity in Japanese. As the next comments indicate, she describes part of this process as her attempts to "find her voice":

> I was always conscious of how my Japanese friends saw me. I didn't want to sound too aggressive or direct. I can remember practicing at home in front of the mirror so I could find the right voice and the right facial expressions and body language.

Thus, as these comments strongly suggest, not only were these three participants actively and consciously attempting to adopt or project a Japanese identity as a female, but they also viewed the pitch of their voice as an important way of expressing and conveying this identity.

In sharp contrast to these three participants, all of whom attempted to conform to the Japanese culture, the two participants who did not alter their voice pitch across languages, while still displaying awareness of the cultural significance of a high pitched voice, expressed a very different opinion about the necessity of adopting a Japanese identity. Specifically, both of these participants were quite critical of the images they observed Japanese females to be producing with a high pitched voice. For example, E1 remarked:

> I just don't want to sound like them. They sound too unnatural, fake, because their tone is too high. I just use my natural voice.

The other participant, E5, was even more critical in her assessment of the voice pitch behavior of some Japanese females she had observed:

> Sometimes it would really disgust me, seeing those Japanese girls, they were not even girls, some of them were in their late twenties, but they would use those real high voices to try to impress and make themselves look real cute for men. I decided that there was no way I wanted to do that.

Thus, as both of these remarks indicate, these two participants did not alter their voice pitch levels across the two languages as a result of a rational and conscious decision based on their own perceptions of the language habits of Japanese women and their greater social implications.

While the English-Japanese bilingual participants' responses may answer questions about their proficiency, certain questions about their identities in their second language and second culture still remain. If employment of a high pitched voice is expected of females in Japan, it would seem that a decision not to make use of such a practice could potentially hinder their efforts to assimilate and generally get along in the Japanese culture. Yet, at least according to the participants, this did not seem to be the case; neither of them reported any difficulties in being accepted by the Japanese people they interacted with. E1 made the following comments:

> I did not have Japanese men beating down my door, but I was able to make many very good Japanese friends. I was very comfortable just being me. I think my voice is about medium pitch for a female in the US, and I just used my own natural voice when I spoke in Japanese. In fact, I think they were happy to get to know the real me rather than some fake person with a high pitched voice.

Of course, what cannot be forgotten is that both E1 and E5 are, as white Americans, particularly visible, not only as L2 speakers of Japanese but also as *gaijin* 'foreigners'. Indeed, both of the participants expressed the belief that their foreign appearance made them exempt from some of the constraints that apply to Japanese women. For example, E5 noted that while she was staying with a Japanese family, her host mother was particularly critical of her own high-school-aged daughter's linguistic habits but at the same time stated explicitly that these criticisms did not apply to E5:

> My host mother was always correcting her and telling her she should not use certain words, and I think she even told her a couple of times to speak in a higher voice. But she never said anything about my voice, and she even told me once that I did not have to worry because I am *gaijin* and it was okay for me not to use feminine ways of speaking.

The other participant, E1, offered a similar view:

> I felt kind of bad for the Japanese women I know because I know the men kind of expect them to act real cute and dress fashionably and stuff. I was glad that I was a foreigner and didn't have to worry about that.

These comments reveal that E1 and E5 believed that they were accepted by the Japanese people they came into contact with. Moreover, they are also consistent with the general notion that foreigners in Japan are not expected to assimilate fully into Japanese culture (e.g., Miller 1977, 1982). This is not to argue for Miller's 'law of inverse returns' and to suggest that Japanese people react negatively to foreigners capable of speaking Japanese at a high level. All five of the English-Japanese bilinguals seemed pleased that they were able, using Japanese, to construct friendships with L1 users and be accepted by those around them. The three participants who did raise the pitch of their voice in an effort to follow Japanese speech patterns reported no difficulties in being accepted by their colleagues and neighbors while living in Japan. Still, the statements made by E1 and E5 do suggest that the standards for L2 users in terms of language use and language proficiency are different from those for L1 users. Although further study will be necessary to confirm the results of these interviews, it may be hypothesized that while many L1 speakers of Japanese are willing to accept foreigners with native-like proficiency, there is also tolerance for L2 speakers unable or not willing to conform to L1 speech patterns.

One interesting aspect about the comments of E1 and E5 is how they revealed that the participants had reflected quite critically on Japanese culture, particularly the attitudes toward and expectations about gender. For example, E5, the same participant who said that the high pitched voices disgusted her, later revealed a very sympathetic but still firmly critical belief about gender and gender roles in Japan:

> I feel bad for Japanese women because men treat them so poorly sometimes, and I can understand how it would be so difficult for them to break out of their traditional roles. But even so, I think by willingly taking on such a cute way of acting and using language they contribute very much to being treated that way. If I were a Japanese, one of the things I would try to do by my action and my language is to show men that I was not willing to just be an ordinary cute, young Japanese girl. I think that is why I decided that there was no way I was going to act like them and why I chose to just use my natural voice.

Even E3, who did, like the Japanese-English bilinguals, use a higher pitch in Japanese than in English, revealed there were some situations in which she was unwilling to conform to the behavior expected of Japanese females:

> I guess with my voice pitch and other things I tried to follow the Japanese way as much as possible, but there were some situations where I just couldn't do it. At some *enkai* ['parties'] when some of the older men employees would get drunk and try to act a little too friendly, I made sure I changed my mannerisms and actions so they would know I didn't like that kind of stuff. I watched how some of the other younger women handled it and they either just took it or tried to play it off in a cute way. I couldn't do that. I was not conscious of lowering the pitch of my voice, but I am sure I did that too. I would try to sound as assertive and forceful as possible. I am sure it further reinforced my identity as a foreigner, but there were some things like that I just couldn't take.

Thus, even though this participant indicated that she was trying to emulate Japanese behavior as much as possible, her attempts to adopt a Japanese identity were not just an absolute shift from one culture to another. As this last remark indicates, she demonstrated, as a thoughtful and rational social actor, a keen ability to monitor different situations in the target culture and to choose and modify her behaviors, including the pitch of her voice, according to those situations. In the words of Siegal (1996), "language learning and language use is not simply a case of one target language variety, but rather a complicated task of discerning power structures within a social order and power hierarchy. Individuals view themselves as choosing a code that matches their (desired) identity in a given situation" (p. 358). Indeed, the ambivalence felt by E3 about her competing foreign and Japanese identities and her need to change her mannerisms and her identity according to the situation appear not to be uncommon among foreign women in Japan. In a book based upon her personal experiences in Japan, Ogulnick (1998) made the following remarks:

> My experience replicates the strong internal sense I had when I first went to Japan, of wanting to find my place among a group of women, even if it meant having to change the way I looked, acted and spoke. Conversely, I became more resistant to speaking "like a woman" or, *kirei na nihongo* 'pretty Japanese', when I sensed that, by doing so, I was submitting to patriarchal control. (Ogulnick 1998: 105)

Even though the participants sometimes spoke in absolute terms about their own desires to project or avoid a feminine Japanese identity, this last comment by E3, as well as most of the other remarks made by the participants, indicate that the English-Japanese bilinguals were all aware of the kinds of identities they wanted to project and when they wanted to project them. They were also aware of the important role that voice pitch played in Japanese society, and chose the appropriate pitch levels based on the kinds of images and identities they wanted to project for themselves in different contexts.

6.   Conclusion

Using both phonetic analysis and ethnographic interviews, I have explored in this chapter, at a very general level, the relationship between pitch, culture, and gender identity. More specifically, using previous research that has demonstrated that a high pitched voice is a resource for projecting femininity in Japanese culture, I have attempted to discern how salient this aspect of the Japanese language was to female L2 learners as they went about both learning Japanese and constructing their own identities in relation to the target culture. I found that voice pitch meant nothing to beginning level learners who have never been to Japan. At the same time, English-Japanese bilinguals have given considerable thought to the link between pitch and identity. In fact, it became obvious that the female English-Japanese bilinguals' decisions about their voice pitch were deeply entrenched in their perceptions of gender and femininity in Japanese culture. Based on these results, this chapter has, I believe, three significant implications for the study of the relationship between language and gender.

First, it further confirms the points made in some of the previous studies about the need to consider prosodic aspects of language, such as voice pitch, in the study of the connection between language and culture in general, and language and gender in particular. Although previous research has tended to focus mostly on L1 speakers of Japanese, the fact that English-Japanese bilinguals also seemed well aware of the social meanings attached to voice pitch in Japanese further confirms that voice pitch is one of the key resources for performing a female gender identity in Japanese society. These findings, in turn, suggest that we should not forget the extent to which something as seemingly transparent as the pitch of one's voice may serve as a cultural tool for highlighting and emphasizing gender.

Second, this chapter also strongly indicates that the examination of the connection between language and gender should not just be limited to the investigation of L1 users. Study of the linguistic practices of monolingual L1 speakers has, undoubtedly, enhanced our knowledge of ways in which gendered identities are constructed and expressed in different cultures. At the same time, however, we need to recognize that it is these linguistic practices that must be embraced by learners of that language who attempt to interact with target language speakers. As this study demonstrated, L2 users may decide not to employ certain linguistic practices that are used by monolingual L1 speakers. It also appears that the L2 learners' attempts to construct gendered identities raise issues for them and force them to make decisions about the identities they want to project that may not necessarily be the same issues and decisions facing L1 speakers. Given the fact that the number of people studying foreign languages and crossing cultures is increasing at a rapid pace, further consideration of and research into these issues will, in the long run, provide people with knowledge that will help them cross cultures and construct 'new' identities.

Finally, in terms of language teaching, the findings of the present study suggest that, at least in the case of the Japanese language, there may be a need to inform language learners at beginning levels about the correlation between voice pitch and gender identities in Japanese culture. Although, as this chapter has demonstrated, choosing the pitch of their voice was an issue that was very salient to the English-Japanese bilinguals, it was quite clear from the interviews that it was not until they went to Japan that these women discovered the importance of a high pitched voice as an expression of femininity. Japanese language courses, in other words, did not prepare them for the decisions they were going to have to make concerning pitch behavior in Japanese and their construction of an identity in this foreign culture. Foreign language pedagogies often give special priority to the acquisition of linguistic structures, but this study indicates that learners might also benefit from more discussion of the target culture. In particular, discussion of social meanings attached to linguistic items and linguistic resources, such as voice pitch levels, would benefit learners preparing to enter the target culture (see Ohara, Saft, and Crookes in press for further discussion of the merits of engaging in discussions about the target culture with students). As a result of this discussion, learners will be able to engage in the kind of critical reflection about the culture that will allow them to make informed decisions about identities they want to construct for themselves.

Appendix

Sentences (taken from Ladefoged 1982; translated into Japanese by the researcher)

The girl gave the money to her father.
He wanted to go to Germany.
Is water a liquid?
Do you want some coffee?
Do you take cream in your coffee?
Where did you put paper?
Give me some apples, oranges, and peaches.
His name is Peter.
I think so.
How are you?

Onna no ko wa otoosan ni okane o ageta.
Kare wa doitsu e ikitakatta.
Mizu wa ekitai desu ka.
Koohii ikaga desu ka.
Koohii ni kuriimu ireru?

Shinbun o doko ni oita?
Ringo to orenji to momo o kudasai.
Kare no namae wa piitaa desu.
Soo omoimasu.
Ogenki desu ka.

Conversation script

A: Hi! How are you?
B: Oh, Hi! Where are you going?
A: I'm going to the library.
B: Oh, this is the book I borrowed from you last time. Thank you very much.
A: You're welcome.
B: It was a big help.
A: That's good.
B: Well, goodbye.
A: Bye.

A: Konnichiwa. Ogenki desu ka.
B: A, konnichiwa. Dochira e.
A: Toshokan made.
B: A, soo soo. Kore kono aida okari shita hon desu. Arigatoo gozaimashita.
A: Doo itashimashite.
B: Tasukarimashita.
A: Yokatta.
B: Jaa, sayoonara.
A: Sayoonara.

References

Arnovitch, Charles
    1976   The voice of personality: Stereotyped judgments and their relation to voice quality and sex of speaker. *The Journal of Social Psychology* 99, 207–220.

Baken, Ronald
    1987   *Clinical Measurement of Speech and Voice*. Massachusetts: Little, Brown, and Company.

Coates, Jennifer
    1986   *Women, Men and Language*. New York: Longman.

1999   Changing femininity: The talk of teenage girls. In Bucholtz, Mary, A.C. Liang, and Laurel Sutton (eds.), *Reinventing Identities: The Gendered Self in Discourse*. New York: Oxford University Press, 123–144.

Colton, Raymond, Janina Casper, and Minoru Hirano
1990   *Understanding Voice Problems: A Physiological Perspective for Diagnosis and Treatment*. Baltimore: Williams and Wilkins.

Cook, Vivian
1999   Going beyond the native speaker in language teaching. *TESOL Quarterly* 33, 2, 185–209.

Edwards, Walter
1989   *Modern Japan Through Its Weddings: Gender, Person and Society in Ritual Portrayal*. California: Stanford University Press.

Graddol, David and Joan Swann
1989   *Gendered Voices*. Cambridge, MA: Basil Blackwell.

Haugh, Michael
1998   Native-speakers' beliefs about Nihonjinron and Miller's "Law of inverse returns". *Journal of the Association of Teachers of Japanese* 32, 2, 27–58.

Henton, Caroline and Anthony Bladon
1985   Breathiness in normal female speech: Inefficiency versus desirability. *Language and Communication* 5, 221–227.

Holmes, Janet
1995   *Women, Men, and Politeness*. London: Longman.

Kinsella, Sharon
1995   Cuties in Japan. In Skov, Lise and Brian Moeran (eds.), *Women, Media and Consumption in Japan*. Honolulu: University of Hawai'i Press, 220–254.

Kramer, Cheris
1977   Perceptions of male and female speech. *Language and Speech* 20, 2, 151–161.

Ladefoged, Peter
1982   *Course in Phonetics*. Los Angeles: University of California Press.

Laver, John and Peter Trudgill
1979   Phonetic and linguistic markers in speech. In Scherer, Klaus and Howard Giles (eds.), *Social Markers in Speech*. Cambridge: Cambridge University Press, 1–31.

Loveday, Leo
    1986   *Explorations in Japanese Sociolinguistics*. Amsterdam/ Philadelphia: John Benjamins.

McConnell-Ginet, Sally
    1978   Intonation in a man's world. *Signs* 3, 541–559.

Miller, Roy
    1977   *The Japanese Language in Modern Japan: Some Sociolinguistic Observations*. Washington D.C.: American Enterprise Institute for Public Policy Research.
    1982   *Japan's Modern Myths*. New York: John Weatherhill.

Mulac, Anthony
    1998   The gender-linked language effect: Do language differences really make a difference? In Canary, Daniel, and Kathryn Dindia (eds.), *Sex Differences and Similarities in Communication*. Mahwah, NJ: Lawrence Erlbaum.

Ogulnick, Karen
    1998   *Onna Rashiku* [Like a Woman]: *The Diary of a Language Learner in Japan*. Albany, NY: State University of New York Press.

Ohara, Yumiko
    1992   Gender-dependent pitch levels in Japanese and English: A comparative study in Japanese and English. In Hall, Kira, Mary Bucholtz, and Birch Moonwomon (eds.), *Locating Power: Proceedings of the Second Berkeley Women and Language Conference*. Berkeley: Berkeley Women and Language Group, 467–477.

    1993   *Koe no takasa kara ukeru inshoo ni tsuite* [Images of voice pitch]. *Kotoba* [Words]14, 14–19.

    1997   *Shakaigengogaku no kanten kara mita nihonjin no koe no takasa* [Japanese pitch from a sociophonetic perspective]. In Ide, Sachiko (ed.), *Joseigo no sekai* [World of Women's Language]. Tokyo: Meiji Shoin, 42–58.

    1999 a   Performing gender through voice pitch: A cross-cultural analysis of Japanese and American English. In Pasero, Ursula and Friederike Braun (eds.), *Wahrnehmung und Herstellung von Geschlecht*. Opladen: Westdeutscher Verlag, 105–116.

    1999 b   Prosody and context: An analysis of conversation in a work place. Paper presented at the Twelfth World Congress of Applied Linguistics (AILA), Tokyo, Japan.

    2000   A critical discourse analysis: Ideology of language and gender in Japanese. Ph.D. dissertation. University of Hawai'i at Manoa.

Ohara, Yumiko, Scott Saft, and Graham Crookes
  in press Toward a feminist critical pedagogy in beginning Japanese as a foreign lan-
             guage class. *Journal of the Association of Teachers of Japanese.*

Ohta, Amy
  1993 The foreign language learner in Japanese society: Successful learners of
         Japanese respond to Miller's "Law of inverse returns". *Journal of the As-
         sociation of Teachers of Japanese* 27, 2, 205–228.

Peirce, Bonny Norton
  1995 Social identity, investment, and language learning. *TESOL Quarterly* 29, 1,
         9–31.

Price, Stephen
  1996 Comments on Bonny Norton Peirce's "Social identity, investment, and lan-
         guage learning". *TESOL Quarterly* 30, 331–337.

Sachs, Jacqueline, Philip Lieberman, and Donna Erickson
  1973 Anatomical and cultural determinants of male and female speech. In Shuy,
         Roger and Ralph Fasold (eds.), *Language: Current Trends and Prospects.*
         Washington D.C.: School of Language and Linguistics, Georgetown Uni-
         versity, 74–84.

Siegal, Meryl
  1994 Second-language learning, identity, and resistance: White women studying
         Japanese in Japan. In Bucholtz, Mary, A.C. Liang, Laurel Sutton, and Cait-
         lin Hines (eds.), *Cultural Performance: Proceedings of the Third Berkeley
         Women and Language Conference.* Berkeley, CA: Berkeley Women and
         Language Group, 642–650.

  1996 The role of learner subjectivity in second language sociolinguistic compe-
         tency: Western women learning Japanese. *Applied Linguistics* 17, 3,
         356–382.

Tannen, Deborah
  1997 Women and men talking: An interactional sociolinguistic approach. In
         Walsh, Mary Roth (ed.), *Women, Men, and Gender: Ongoing Debate.* New
         Haven, CT: Yale University Press, 82–90.

Valentine, Carol and Banisa Saint Damian
  1988 Gender and culture as determinants of the 'ideal voice'. *Semiotica* 71, 2/4,
         285–303.

Van Bezooijen, Renée
  1995 Sociocultural aspects of pitch differences between Japanese and Dutch
         women. *Language and Speech* 38, 3, 253–266.

1996   Pitch and gender related personality traits. In Warner, Natasha, Jocelyn Ahlers, Leela Bilmes, Monica Oliver, Susanne Wertheim and Melinda Chen (eds.), *Gender and Belief Systems: Proceedings of the Fourth Berkeley Women and Language Conference*. Berkeley, CA: Berkeley Women and Language Group, 755–765.

West, Candace, and Sarah Fenstermaker
1995   Doing difference. *Gender and Society* 9, 1, 8–37.

West, Candace and Don Zimmerman
1987   Doing gender. *Gender and Society* 1, 2, 122–151.

Yamazawa, Hideko and Harry Hollien
1992   Speaking fundamental frequency patterns of Japanese women. *Phonetica* 49, 128–140.

3. Gender in multilingual educational settings

Gender and public space in a bilingual school

Monica Heller

1. Introduction

Research on language and gender has addressed such issues as the ways in which linguistic ideologies are gendered, how the gendered division of labor is linked to the unequal distribution of linguistic resources in a community, or how gender ideologies are played out on the terrain of language (Cameron 1992; Hall and Bucholtz 1995; Holmes 1999; Johnson and Meinhof 1997; Wodak 1997). In this paper, I will examine some dimensions of all three, drawing on fieldwork conducted in a French-language minority school in Ontario (Canada).[1] Before turning to the data, I will further discuss the general questions outlined above, as well as describe the research from which the data emerge. I will particularly focus on the questions asked by the research, and the ways in which the study tried to address these questions.

The relationship between language and gender, or any other social category for that matter, is of course dialectic. We have ideas about what languages are, how they work, and what they are like, and about values we attach to them. We also have ideas about social categories like gender, which are tied to language ideologies in that the construction of social boundaries and social inequality is connected to the distribution of linguistic resources; the division of labor includes the communicative dimensions of that labor; and socialization into social categories is a communicative process.

Most work on gender in these processes has focused on monolingual settings. Existing work on gender and bilingualism examines ways in which the gendered division of labor helps explain gender differences in access to and appropriation of bilingual resources (Gal 1978; McDonald 1990) and ways in which ethnic, class, and gender categories and ideologies intersect (Pujolar 1997, 2000). Here I wish to explore some aspects of both, by foregrounding how the intersection of ethnic, class, and gender categorization processes influences gender differences in access to bilingual resources (both in terms of type and degree) and to the possibilities for defining their value and ideological content.

In the school which I discuss here, male students had greater access than females to the public space where definitions of what it means to be bilingual or multilingual (in French and English, but also in other languages, notably Somali) were legitimized. "Bilingual" is understood here both as an identity category (standing in opposition to identity constructs associated with one language, at least one main language) and as a set of practices. The reproduction of gender and class ideologies which relegated females, gays and lesbians, and working-class students to the margins of public spaces ensured the reproduction of heterosexual, middle-class male control over the definition of ideologies of ethnicity and language, which in turn became imbued with ideologies of heterosexual middle-class masculinity. This control, however, as I will show, is only partly hegemonic, in the sense that while others in the school must position themselves with respect to the dominant discourse, many also find ways to contest or escape it. Nonetheless, these gestures of contestation or escape are not always successful, and indeed can have quite negative consequences (for example, one mode of escape is dropping out of school, with all that entails for individual life chances). For a few, they permit the development of alternative ideologies and positions at the individual level, without fundamentally challenging the gendered nature of the public discourse at school.

My approach is informed by an attempt to understand the role of the school as an institution of social and cultural reproduction (Bourdieu and Passeron 1977), and in this case in particular, of the ways in which the school's role in the reproduction of the ethnolinguistic and quasi-nationalist ideologies of francophone Ontario is tied to its role in the reproduction of relations of power constructed through the social differences of class, race, ethnicity, and gender. I operationalize the notion of power by understanding it as the control over the production and distribution of both material and symbolic resources, as well as over the definition of their value and their meaning.

Here I focus on French-English bilingualism as a set of valued resources, access to which is, on the one hand, in part controlled by schools such as the one I describe here, and on the other, quite hotly contested in Canadian society, and the nature and value of which are also a matter of some debate. These particular resources, however, are tied in complex ways to the fact that schools construct what counts as display of knowledge. Among the forms of knowledge constructed and regulated by school we find knowledge of linguistic forms and practices of many kinds, whether institutionalized as subject matter ("first", "second", "foreign", "modern", "classical" languages, and so on) or constructed more loosely through monitoring and evaluation practices in everyday life at school. In this latter sense, schools define what counts as "legitimate language", and who counts as legitimate speakers and receivers of that language (Bourdieu 1982). That is, they define what is valued and recognized in the way language should be used, and which language varieties one should use. This applies to all language practices, whether monolingual or multilingual.

At the same time, it is clear that, although schools these days mainly adhere to a democratic and meritocratic ideology, in fact, linguistic resources are unevenly distributed in the community, and schools often reproduce this inequality. The unequal distribution of linguistic resources is, of course, intimately bound up with the principles of social organization of the community. Gender, class, race, ethnicity, religion, and other concepts are all available as bases of social categorization and social inequality, that is, as ways to struggle over access to resources, and ways to legitimize the regulation of that access along certain lines. The mutual embedding of ideologies of language and ideologies of social categories facilitates the reproduction of relations of power, since linguistic resources are tied to the distribution of other symbolic, as well as material, resources (Heller and Martin-Jones 2001).

These are processes and, frequently, struggles which take place largely on the terrain of symbolic power, through attempts at exercising or contesting symbolic domination (in Bourdieu's sense; see Bourdieu 1982). My concern therefore is to understand the naturalizing ideologies which legitimate positions of power, how they are constructed and contested, and with what consequences for whom.

The data for this research come from an ethnography of a single French-language minority high school in the Toronto area, which I conducted with the help of a number of research assistants between 1991 and 1995 (see Heller 1999). The project had a number of goals; here I follow the thread of gender, which is but one of the cross-cutting forms of social organization which informed life at this school. My research assistants and I attended classes and extra-curricular activities, hung out in a wide range of social spaces at school (the gym, the parking lot, the hallways, the cafeteria, the smoking area, etc.), conducted interviews with staff, school board personnel, students and parents, read relevant texts and on occasion organized focus-group-like discussions with existing friendship groups. Many of these events, activities, and discussions were audio- or video-taped. The data I draw on here come from field notes and video recordings of public events and other activities in the school, from interviews, and from a series of group discussions organized by one of my research assistants, Phyllis Dalley.

The study has some things in common with other high school ethnographies with a focus on language or ethnolinguistic identity, conducted in the United States or Britain (see Eckert 1989; Foley 1990; Rampton 1995). Notably, it shares a concern to understand social categories as constructed by examining language practices as forms of social action, and therefore to understand

people as social actors, and not simply reflections of social structure (see Bucholtz 1999; Heller 2001). It also shares a concern to understand how language
connects with processes of multiple social categorization, that is, with the role
of language in the intersection of class, gender, and ethnicity or race. And it
shows many of the same configurations of male middle-class white dominance,
and attempts at avoidance or contestation from other quarters. However, perhaps more than the others, this study foregrounds the role of the school as an institution of social and cultural reproduction, rather than simply as a site where
adolescents spend much of their social life, or as a straightforward site of social
selection, since here the school itself is symbolically charged as an ethnolinguistic institution in a multilingual (and officially French-English bilingual) society. In addition, it foregrounds ways in which language itself is a terrain of
struggle over symbolic domination.

I will begin this chapter by describing the fieldwork setting, and the ways in
which it is significant as a site of production and distribution of bilingual language resources, focusing on the school as an arena of production of a certain
ideology and practice of bilingualism. Schools like this one are the product of a
long history of struggle on the part of minority francophones to gain some
measure of power without having to assimilate. This struggle transformed
itself in the 1960s into a nationalist political movement, both in Québec and
elsewhere, which seeks to permit francophones to gain access to the modern,
international world through the construction of monolingual French-speaking
spaces which are meant as bases of power from which to open out to the rest of
the world. No one contests the value of bilingualism in French and English, it is
the road to it which has been (and in many ways still is) the focus of struggle. In
Québec, the monolingual spaces are envisaged mainly as the territory and State
of Québec, and include a broadly understood sense of public space. Outside
Québec, the emphasis is on institutions, of which school has historically been
the most important, since it is felt that socialization is a key to social change
and education a key to social mobility. Today, Franco-Ontarian schools are
considered important avenues of access to the valued linguistic resources of
both French and English, and to the credentialized institutionalization of the
value of those resources.

For these reasons, the prevailing discourse of the school (as of the political
movement which gave birth to it) contains a specific ideology of bilingualism,
one which envisions bilingualism as a kind of standard double monolingualism. What I mean by this is that the school values (and some students collaborate in valuing) bilingual repertoires which consist of the ability to speak both
standard English and standard French as if one were a monolingual speaker of
each. The school devalues mixed, code-switching practices. In addition, again

because of the nature of the nationalist movement, the school has an ambivalent relationship with vernacular Canadian French. On the one hand, the vernacular is the mark of national authenticity, and as such legitimates the concept of "people" or of "nation" which lies at the heart of nationalist struggle. The school exists "for" the Franco-Ontarian community, understood (albeit mainly implicitly) as a historically-rooted nation, of which language is the most important emblem. On the other hand, the purpose of political mobilization has been to escape unfavorable life conditions, and to enter a globalizing world in which local vernaculars have little purchase. The (ideologically charged) language values of the school are actively constructed in its significant public spaces.

I will then go on to describe the ways in which the dominant discourse on bilingualism at school is gendered in two ways: first, by relegating working-class students, girls, gays, and lesbians to the margins of public spaces, and second by using these spaces to reproduce gender ideologies which legitimize these students' marginalization. Even the contestatory discourse produced by African students tends to be male-dominated and resolutely heterosexual. Finally, I will take up two attempts to oppose these trends. One consisted of a small group of working-class girls who engaged in two separate challenges in the school's public space, one with respect to language, and one with respect to gender, neither of which was successful. The second consisted of another small group of middle-class, academically successful girls, whose contestation may have been successful in creating an alternative space for themselves, although it cannot be seen as having had much effect on the public space of the school. In all these instances, we can see the complex interweavings of language and gender, in ways which have an effect on the chances for individuals to influence the public discourse of the school, to define and gain access to the linguistic resources the school produces and regulates, as well as to influence the nature and development of institutional discourses on language and gender. In particular, these discourses contribute to the reproduction of the ideology of bilingualism as "double monolingualism" consisting of standardized "international" varieties, and to the ability of males to control the definition of language values and practices.

2.   A Franco-Ontarian school

The school I want to discuss here is a French-language high school in a community dominated by English. (I will call the school Champlain; this, and all other names in this text are fictive.) I do not have space here to discuss the social and historical basis of the school in detail, but it is important to point out that it is the product of French-Canadian struggles for collective rights, and must be understood in the context of a long history of nationalism (see Heller 1994, 1999). It is understood as an institution which exists to preserve the French language and culture in Ontario, an English-speaking province, and which aims at producing individual bilinguals by providing them with a French monolingual space within which to develop the French part of their bilingual repertoire. (The general idea is that you don't have to worry about learning English in Ontario; people say, *"L'anglais, ça s'attrape"* 'you catch English, like you catch a cold'.) It is also understood as an institution which prepares its students for entry into the modern world.

The result is that the school, as a Franco-Ontarian institution, is subject to tremendous pressure to construct within its walls a monolingual French-speaking space, despite the fact that the community in which it is situated is mainly English-speaking, despite the fact that almost all participants in the school setting (with the exception of relative newcomers) speak fluent English, and in consideration of the fact that everyone agrees that speaking both French and English is a good thing. A second result has to do with the nature of the French that is valued; here the objective of social, economic, and political advancement, and of entry into globalized marketplaces, places an emphasis on what is variously called *le français international* 'international French', or *un français de qualité* 'quality French'. Note that speaking high-quality French is associated with being able to function beyond local markets and networks. It is also associated with the ideology of monolingualism, in that one aspect of "good" French includes speaking a variety which bears no traces of contact with English. At the same time, the school is meant to fight for social advancement for Franco-Ontarians understood as a marginalized and under-educated group. The representatives of this group who actually attend the school speak, of course, a vernacular which often bears major traces of contact with English.

The school contains within its clientele speakers of the standard and speakers of the vernacular, speakers of monolingual and bilingual (contact) varieties of French, and students who have varying degrees and kinds of mastery of English and other languages. All these students bring to school not only different linguistic resources, but also different kinds of interest in collaborating with or resisting the school's attempts to construct its image as a producer of a certain kind of bilingual, as well as collaborating with or resisting the school's attempts to cope with the various obstacles in the path towards constructing that image.

3.   Producing a gendered vision of bilingualism

One group of students clearly collaborated with the school (although it cannot be said that this group faithfully produced the practices the school would like to see). This is the group of students who had a long experience of life in a minority setting, and who were in the "advanced level" stream which leads typically to university studies. These are students who valued the kind of bilingualism to which the school provides access, in part because the school was their major form of access to bilingualism, and in part because they felt strongly that acquiring a credential from such a school would provide a capital of distinction which would serve them well in competition for university entrance and for jobs. They also often believed that the language skills they acquire would serve them later on in the development of their careers. It is these students who produced much of the public discourse of the school, through the organization and presentation of school-wide events.

It was mainly the males who did this; in and of itself this fact tells us much about the gendered division of labor in forming the public discourse of the school. In addition, it is useful to examine the nature of the discourse. The central themes varied, generally focusing on upcoming school activities, and aiming at developing something the students understood as "school spirit". Some of these, as we shall see below, were overtly gendered. For example, the two major events to be dominated by females were the fashion show, an event primarily devoted to the reproduction of a specific romantic ideology of gender relations, and the multicultural lunch. However, no matter what the overt theme, there were frequently sub-texts with elements of both linguistic and gender ideology.

The sub-text regarding language focused consistently on the creation of an opposition between Toronto/Ontario and Québec identity, the first understood as primarily bilingual and "international", the second as local and monolingual French. It also often incorporated a devalorization of non-standard French. "*Québécois*" (the students' name for a vernacular form of Canadian French) was associated with urban or rural working class culture (and hence at the same time with a certain rugged masculinity, as is often the case in both bilingual and monolingual settings; see Pujolar 2000). The central gendered theme was a specific vision of romantic love, in which the male is the (articulate) pursuer and the female the (silent) object of desire. Together we can see how the public discourse of the school shapes an orientation towards bilingualism and "international French" which is shaped by and for males; even an alternative vision encapsulated in the category of "*Québécois*" is unavailable to females.

Beyond active roles in traditional activities, which generally entailed not using language, the only other public role readily available to girls was as support to the central activities of the male-dominated student council. Within that context, girls could aspire to some degree of power within the school, but in ways that tended to be associated with nurturing school spirit. Nonetheless, it needs to be pointed out that academic achievement was not part of the arena of school spirit and school public discourse. Thus girls at the same time could aspire to (and achieve) academic success, as well as some degree of social and political power as agents of school spirit, and collaborate in their own objectification as objects of sexual desire or romantic love, as well as in their political marginalization as supporters of, rather than primary producers of, public discourse.

In marginalized groups, alternative options were equally gendered. In particular, boys seemed to have many more options for making a life outside school than did girls. Girls tended to act more conservatively, less radically challenging the school and its vision and its rules; they also tended to feel keenly the tension between their own strong ties to language and culture (whether Somali, Creole, French, or anything else) and the competing values of the dominant views of bilingualism, or of English as the primary means of resisting the power and authority of the school. But here as well, there was little to challenge traditional gender roles.

The embedding of traditional gender roles into the public life of the school was clearly problematic for gay students, who tended to remain in the closet, and usually left the school rather quickly. It was also a problem for a small group of girls who shared the dominant group's views on bilingualism, for the most part, who shared their values regarding academic success, but who were unprepared to share in the gendered behavior that participation in those networks entailed. Calling themselves the "Nerds", they attempted to create an alternative space for themselves. This space entailed rejecting the prevailing view of romantic love, by rejecting the notion of romantic love as an important part of female identity. The "Nerds" accomplished this through the construction of a (possibly) fictive lesbian identity, by separating their romantic life from life at school, or by focusing on sexuality and female sexual pleasure (in opposition to feminine stereotypes of passivity and focus on love rather than sexuality).[2] While these strategies worked well for some of the Nerds, and less well for others, in either case, they did little to directly challenge the gendered nature of public discourse at Champlain. In what follows, we shall examine each of these positions more closely.

4.   Studs and Juliettes

It is early February, soon Valentine's Day. The student council has organized a dance, and has decided to raise money by holding a sale of roses. To advertise these events, the council has called a *réunion générale* (a kind of general assembly held in the auditorium, and run by the student council). As had become usual, the meeting takes the form of a series of skits, performed by student council members and their friends on the school stage.

The skit is based loosely on a format known from television contests. The student council president, Marcel, acts as master of ceremonies. He announces that the school will now pick the school "stud" (while he speaks in French, he uses the word "stud" from English). Four boys from the senior grades are called up to sit in a row on the stage. Marcel passes from one boy to the next, asking each a question. He asks the first two boys where they will take their girlfriends for Valentine's Day. To the third, Ali, he poses the following question: *"Quel est le rôle de la femme dans la société?"* ('What is the role of women in society?'). Ali is visibly uneasy, and fails to answer. Luc says that he will answer the question, and eventually Marcel gives him the microphone. Luc answers: *"De servir et plaire aux hommes"* ('To serve and please men'). The audience responds loudly, with many boys cheering, and some girls (notably the Nerds) booing and giving the "thumbs-down" sign of disapproval. Marcel returns to Ali, and asks him what would be the most eloquent thing he could say to his girlfriend on Valentine's Day. Ali still has a hard time finding an answer; several girls from the audience call out: "I love you," and *"Je t'aime."* Finally, Ali says, *"Je t'aime."* Marcel then asks the audience to express which answer they liked the most by applauding for each boy. The volume and duration of the noise produced by the audience is a measure of their support for each boy. The one who receives the loudest and longest applause is Luc. Marcel tells him he has won a gift certificate worth twenty dollars at a local chocolate store (presumably so that he can buy a gift for his girlfriend, not for himself).

The boys descend from the stage, and Marcel announces that it is now time to greet the school's "Juliettes" (interestingly, the label for the male contest focuses on sexual desirability, while the label for the female contest focuses on romance). A procession of boys in drag takes the places of the would-be studs in the row of chairs on the stage. Now the event takes a different format. Instead of asking the audience to judge the "girls", Marcel asks each "girl" what "she" would most like to receive from "her" boyfriend for Valentine's Day: a diamond, a car, chocolate, money. Each "Juliette" says no, none of these things. So, Marcel asks, what *would* they like? At this, the "Juliettes" stand up and turn around, holding a piece of paper to their *derriéres* 'behinds'. On each piece of paper is one letter; put together, they spell out R-O-S-E-S. With this, Marcel announces the rose sale, and encourages everyone (by which he presumably means the boys) to buy a rose for their girlfriends.

This Valentine's Day skit was probably the most extreme, but by no means the only, example of the gendered division of public discourse at Champlain. Not only does it reproduce traditional gender stereotypes, it so clearly takes the male perspective that females are not even allowed on the stage to play themselves. By the same token, here as in other skits produced by Champlain students, males in drag are seen frequently on stage and are considered funny, while the rare females seen in drag (two during the time we worked there) portray highly serious male characters.

During the time we were at Champlain, the student council was consistently dominated by males; only four or five females were even members over the course of those four years, and they usually took a back seat to the males in public displays such as the *réunions générales*. In fairness, at other times, girls have been student council presidents, and there have been female-dominated student councils, but because this was not the case in the four years we were at Champlain, we cannot make any claims regarding those facts. During the field-work period, girls did take the lead in organizing activities related to the school's 25th anniversary, and put together a slate for the student council elections (which was, however, defeated). It is thus not impossible for girls to take on a leadership role at Champlain, but what we observed pointed to the difficulty of doing so in any arena dominated (however temporarily) by boys.

While the student council was dominated by males, girls did play a supporting role. They were the ones most involved in fund-raising activities, for example, selling pastries and pizzas in the front hall. They also organized the graduation dance at the end of the year. Otherwise, their opportunities for taking the public stage were limited, and frequently involved displaying traditional images of female beauty. For example, one student council skit involved sending students a message about recycling. Four students interrogated a vernacular-speaking granny about what can and cannot go into the recycling bin. The last question was whether or not such old grannies should go in, too. The students all decided that the answer was yes; they seized the granny in question, threw her in the recycling bin (an oversized box), and drew out the school beauty, a tall blonde, who walked off smiling silently on the arm of the chair of the environment committee, as the audience was told that indeed, recycling could turn trash into a thing of beauty. Clearly, here, the vernacular is associated not only with decrepit old age, but in particular garrulous, female old age, while silence is associated with female desirability.

The annual fashion show was the most important single event contributing to the public construction of images of female beauty and their association with a particular, heterosexual vision of romantic love. The show was held each spring, with clothes donated by local merchants. The event was considered a prestigious one, and participating students rehearsed every day for months.

A small group of students (two girls, Nadine and Sylvie, and a boy, Patrick) were responsible for the organization of the show, under the supervision of a female teacher, and while female students vied to be accepted as part of the show (they were selected through auditions, and not everyone was accepted), male students had to be cajoled (although being approached could be seen as a sign of the girls' approval of them as romantic or sexual partners, and so few actually refused the invitation). However, boys controlled all technical activities for the school, and were not reluctant to turn those skills to the organization of the fashion show (as they did for all public events). Thus boys were responsible for the construction of the catwalk, and boys ran the sound system, the lighting and the videotaping.

While Patrick let Nadine and Sylvie take care of most of the daily, routine issues, his word was law when it came to discipline or conflict resolution. For example, during one practice session, Sylvie had an argument with one of the boys in the show, who refused to do what she wanted him to do, and who ended up by asking why he should listen to her. Patrick, who had been sitting nearby, then got up and said, "Because I have the last word". That ended the argument. During another practice, someone turned out the lights, and Sylvie asked that they be turned on. The lights stayed off, and Nadine asked that they be turned on. They remained off until Patrick got up and shouted, "Turn on the fucking lights!"

In keeping with the dominant mode of public discourse at the school, the fashion show was organized as a series of skits, or dramatic set pieces, each designed to tell a story built around thematically linked clothes (sports clothes, beach clothes, work clothes, evening clothes, and so on). However, in contrast to the *réunions générales,* the fashion show was entirely silent, accompanied only by music. The students never said a word.

In each skit, students were paired off in heterosexual couples; Nadine explicitly ruled out any possibility of portraying homosexual couples, however fictive, although some of the boys playfully took a modeling stroll down the side of the stage together while the organizers' attention was somewhere else. The stories told in each skit were all scenes of courtship. In one such scene, a row of boys wait, sitting around a night-club set. One by one, four girls emerge, check out the boys, and each picks one as her escort. Only Luc (the acknowledged "Stud" of the school) is left standing alone, although the spotlight is on him, and he doesn't look particularly sad. Then a fifth girl emerges, and the last boy is happily paired off. After taking a turn on the catwalk, each couple returns to a chair, the girl perched on her escort's knee. In unison, the boys feel the girls' legs, from ankle to knee. At this point, the girls pretend to slap the boys' faces, and they rise and walk off in a huff. Virtue is protected. The fashion show closes with a formal dress scene; at the end, each tuxedo-clad boy gives a red rose to his evening-gowned partner.

Interestingly, the fashion show became an avenue for access to mainstream prestige for students from marginalized groups; two Somali-speaking girls and one Somali-speaking boy in particular gained wide attention through participating in the fashion show, although no one outside their own circles had ever spoken to them before. It is possible that the fashion show provided an opportunity for integration because little or no language was involved, and what English there was could be relatively easily understood; up until that moment, the bilinguals' propensity for using English among themselves acted as a means of excluding Somali-speakers, who in turn used Somali amongst themselves, hence erecting a barrier with respect to others. It also provided a common meeting ground in the construction of a shared vision of popular culture and romantic love, although the Somali girls had some trouble with some of the sexier dimensions of the image aimed at. They were permitted certain compromises; for example, the girls were not asked to parade in bathing suits, but were allowed to wear shorts instead for the beach scene. At about the same time, the two girls, along with others in their group, were starting to read romance novels in English, and to watch music videos on television. Later on, along with a third girl, they performed a contemporary, and very hip, dance at the annual talent show. The fashion show was thus part of their induction into Toronto bilingual society; learning English, learning contemporary dance and music, and learning how to act like a Canadian girl were all part of the same package.

It is important to note that despite being bound to traditional gender roles, girls at Champlain were as oriented to academic success as boys were, and as likely to do well. Nonetheless, it was necessary for them to accept the public domination of boys, or at least, not challenge it openly. Thus not only do the girls accept supporting roles with respect to boys, and engage in public displays of ideal images of romantic love and beauty, they also accept boys' sexual domination. For example, a favorite wintertime activity of some of the boys was to pick a female victim, carry her outside, and throw her into the snow. The girls would struggle and cry out, but also laugh. No one would ever come to the rescue of a girl in this predicament. Being a "popular" girl meant walking a fine line between assuming responsibility and credit for academic success, collaborating with the linguistic norms of the school, and accepting a degree of sexual objectification. The sexual objectification entailed keeping themselves to a supporting role with respect to the most important public discourse of the school; it meant not taking a public stand with respect to language and identity, but rather "getting along" with everybody, while limiting one's actual activities in the public domain to (silently) supporting the activities of the boys, and hence letting them define the shape of the public floor and their vision of Champlain as a Franco-Ontarian school.

5. Ways in and ways out

Just as the mainstream discourse on bilingualism at Champlain is gendered, so are the reactions of students who are positioned outside the group that dominates that public discourse. These include notably African students, schooled in European-based institutions, and initially upon arrival in Toronto, knowing no English; Canadian-born, usually working-class, sometimes monolingual francophone speakers of the Canadian French vernacular; gays and lesbians; and a small group of girls who styled themselves the "Nerds". In this section we will discuss the first three groups; the "Nerds" will be discussed in the following section.

For African students, reactions to mainstream bilingualism were connected to their relative access to activities inside and outside the school. Both boys and girls actively resisted what they saw as too narrow a vision of *la francophonie*; it was hard for them to identify with the French Canadian orientation which lies at the heart of the school's legitimacy. In this, of course, they were joined by many bilingual students, who also valued some notion of "international French". African students also had difficulty accepting the use of English in school; it failed to correspond to their idea that school should be a monolingual space in which to maximize access to French, and it also felt like an exclusionary practice on the part of their peers. In protesting their exclusion, and in advocating a more inclusive (but no less francophone) vision, it was nonetheless the boys who spoke the loudest on the public stage, while the girls, for the most part, organized and discussed more privately (although one girl in particular took an important leadership role).

African students notably organized in order to produce public skits parallel to those organized by mainstream bilingual white students; they appropriated public space (I do not have space to explain here how they were able to do so; suffice it to say that they were able to take advantage of institutional interstices.) It is important to note that in their skits, one of the central themes concerned the threat Canadian culture posed to students' traditional notions of gender roles, and in particular regarding the role of women. In one skit, a man ordered his wife to bring him coffee. She responded by throwing down her broom and stalking out of the room, saying that he could no longer tell her what to do. However, a few minutes later, she returned, holding her head in her hands, and lamenting, *"Qu'est-ce qui m'arrive? Je suis en train de perdre mes valeurs!"* ('What is happening to me? I'm losing my values!'). Similarly, African students felt uncomfortable with official positions on sexual harassment, saying that it seemed very strange to them that in Canadian society a woman in trouble would have to call a public phone number, and apparently could not count on her community to help her out.

At school, Somali-speaking female students, especially the older ones, tended to dress in conservative, elegant styles. Some wore veils, and sometimes wore Somali dresses. Many wore Somali dresses on the occasion of the annual multicultural lunch, which was also the major occasion for them to play a public role in the school: they took primary responsibility for organizing the event, and supplied a large proportion of the food. They formed close-knit friendship groups, mainly with other Somali-speaking girls, with whom they took classes, and spent time in the library and the cafeteria. Most of the males, as well as some of the younger females (such as the two who participated in the fashion show), oriented themselves quite differently to school and community. While sharing the girls' sense of the importance of French and Somali, and of their own cultural perspectives, the males (and younger females) also quickly discovered the powerful message of resistance to white authority embodied in African-American hip-hop culture. This was possible in large part simply because they have more opportunities to interact with the community outside home and school, but also because that community tends to construct all blacks as members of the same Afro-American cultural category, no matter where they are from. This is both an obstacle to self-definition, and an opportunity to take up a discourse of resistance to white domination. It was eventually reflected in these students' dress, in their musical preferences, and in their interest in basketball, which they played every day in the school gymnasium. This discovery also, ironically, laid the basis for a bridge between them and white students, who saw hip-hop culture as cool. In addition, through hip-hop, Somali-speakers also learned English, thereby allowing them to communicate more easily with other students.

The oppositional stance of the Somali-speaking students seems to have served the interests of the boys better than it did the interests of the girls. It gave the boys a position of strength from which to argue for the inclusion of their concerns in the mainstream discourse of the school, as well as a place from which to begin to build the bridges which would ensure that they were not simply speaking into the wind. While the Somali-speaking girls gained the respect of many teachers, their practices tended to maintain their marginalization. In addition, the boys' access to English gave them bridges and opportunities to which the girls, especially the older ones, did not have access.

The oppositional stances of Canada-born vernacular French speakers also differed along gender lines. Neither boys nor girls tended to be very vocal about the legitimacy of their perspective for the school's peer group culture, and many, both male and female, simply absorbed themselves into the bilingual mainstream. However, more boys than girls seemed to have options both inside and outside school. A few such boys managed to colonize the audio-visual club, creating a niche for themselves in which they could explore a certain version of masculinity (oriented towards technical things) without having to adopt prevalent bilingual practices. Some boys from Québec maintained, and exercised, the option of going "home", at first for regular visits, and eventually permanently. Most of these refused to speak English at school, maintaining both their monolingualism and their attachment to the local variety of French with which they arrived in Toronto. For some working-class boys, especially those who had grown up in and around Toronto, there was the option of obtaining work of some kind, usually in an English-speaking environment. These were boys whose French was not valued at school, and who spoke English well because of having grown up in an anglophone environment. Those boys often simply stopped speaking French at school, and then eventually stopped coming to school altogether.

Girls, on the other hand, did not seem to have these options so readily available. Their social life focused on school-based friendship networks, or, occasionally, friendship networks involving outsiders. The monolinguals sometimes found a few friends with whom they formed fast, highly solidary friendships, but most learned English fairly quickly. Bilingual working class girls often spoke English at school, feeling very insecure about their French; sometimes they attempted to participate in class through mixed, code-switched, practices; and sometimes they found ways to get around expectations for oral French performances, like singing. In all these cases, their practices were not highly valued by the school. At the same time, these girls tended to feel very strong attachments to their French identity, and would speak French in situations where they felt they would not be judged. The tension between French and English was much keener for them than for the boys.

One small group of such girls attempted to resist the school's imposition of its linguistic norms, arguing for their right to "write like we speak", since that, they said, was how their mothers taught them to speak. Despite their protests, their texts still came back "with all those red circles". Their linguistic resistance was, however, more like guerilla-warfare than traditional warfare, conducted on the sly in private spaces, poorly armed, and with no reinforcements. Interestingly, the only time these girls took the floor in public concerned a gender issue, and it coincided with a school-board wide campaign against sexual harassment (which may indeed have provided them with an institutional opening for more open contestation). Some of them argued that they had been harassed by a teacher. They further felt that their attempts to bring this issue up in a legitimated public space (a kind of "town hall" meeting of the entire school) had been curtailed, and so they organized a counter-meeting in the smoking section behind the school. Students seemed quite divided as to the legitimacy of the claim. In any case, the school followed common policy by removing the teacher from the school and allowing the charges to go forward to a hearing scheduled for the summer, when the school would in any case be closed. Here again, the oppositional stances of this group seem to work to the greater advantage of boys than of girls. The boys had choices open to them, choices they made; the girls were torn between the desire to resist their marginalization and the desire to conform to certain ideals of the school. Their acts of resistance were also, in the end, unsuccessful.

The final group that is clearly marginalized by the gender discourse of the school is that made up of homosexual students. Not only is the prevailing image of social life at school resoundingly heterosexual, homosexuality is seen as deviant; either repulsive, or, paradoxically, cool, but in either case, definitely deviant. For many students, "faggot" is one of the worst insults a student could hurl against a boy. The climate makes it difficult to be open about one's sexual orientation, to say the least. Here is what one gay student has to say about his experience after his orientation did become known:

> I got bashed, I don't mean physically, but I had some real bad comments... and then it was totally the opposite side of being abused, it was like almost a cool thing to hang around with a gay guy... at the beginning I thought it was quite funny somehow, but then it hurt me... you (the other students) just had to say "I know someone who is gay" and it was a big deal... "You know Bernard?" "No." "Yeah, you know, the faggot, ah, that's Bernard."

Bernard was one of the very few students at Champlain to attempt to be open about being gay. As an explicit attempt to challenge prevailing views, he decided to bring a male date to the graduation dance. When he announced this intention, a classmate became seriously concerned, arguing that Bernard simply could not do that: "You can't, you're supposed to bring a girl!" For most homosexual students, there are only two viable options. One is to keep one's sexual orientation a secret, and the other is to leave Champlain for a school where the climate might be less hostile (this is what Bernard did before his first year at Champlain was out). Obviously, neither strategy effectively challenges the discursive marginalization, indeed stigmatization, of homosexuality.

From the perspective of the dominance of the school's vision of bilingualism, and of that of the bilingual students, only the stance of the Somali-speaking boys could be seen as potentially posing a challenge. Their discourse is in part made audible by the existence of an institutionalized public discussion about anti-racist education. The other groups either manage to survive, or find themselves pushed out of school; either way, their perspectives remain marginalized. With the exception of the failed attempt on the part of a small group of girls to use a prevalent public discourse on sexual harassment to open discussions on their marginalization, none of these groups challenges the prevailing discourses of the school. It is not their monolingualism or bilingualism that the school values, and it is not possible for them to contribute to the construction of gender ideologies. Instead, the gendered social positions of all students constrain the strategies available to them.

6.   The "Nerds"

In contrast, one group of girls did seriously resist the prevailing organization of gender at Champlain. This group of seven girls (Farah, Denise, Lisa, Chloé, Carmelle, Carole, and Debbie) formed out of the common experience of rejection by the mainstream crowd. Most of them came to Champlain relatively late; four of them were graduates of French immersion programs who passed Champlain's entrance exams (although one of them is actually from a francophone family), and the others moved to Toronto after having completed elementary school elsewhere. They all found it difficult to gain acceptance into the strongly solidary peer group they found upon their arrival, the bilingual students who had gone to elementary school together. Their access to the mainstream, popular group, was further compromised by two things: for many of them, a relative lack of security in their French, and for almost all of them, a lack of fit with the valued image of the female body. Several of them recall at length having been made fun of by the others, because they were considered fat, or had acne. Some are also members of visible minority groups, while the popular group is principally made up of whites. The following is from a discussion session organized by Phyllis, and which took place on a fairly regular basis once a week for several months in the winter and spring of 1994:

(1) Discussion group 1, March 1994

Carmelle: In grade 12 11 class, there's basically two types of people, well, three types. You have the Somalians, they speak Somalian
Chloé: which tends to exclude those who don't
Lisa: yeah
Carmelle: a lot of them don't definitely exclude you but if you don't have a lot of confidence, you're not going to stay around and not (upset a thing?). You have another group of people, most of them have been together since I don't know when, and they'd come from grade seven and eight into this school, and they're all friends and they're all working toward the same goal and they all have one idea in mind. Some of them want to get married right out of high school that their boyfriends will know their past history. Then you have us, we're all weird in some way or another, and if we weren't basically physically abused like Lisa was, then we were emotionally abused, isolated from that crowd for some reason or another

Most of these girls spent several years alone, or in small friendship groups on the margins of school life. They are conscious of their marginality, and it hurts, although they try to see the positive side of things. Carmelle notes that she can sit quietly in the corridor at lunchtime, and listen to the others talk: "Because they don't even notice me, I can just sit there and listen to them. That way, I can know what is going on in the school." Lisa says: "That is one advantage of being a reject, you know, people don't notice you're there and you hear a lot of things". In the same discussion as that from which the first example was extracted, the Nerds say:

(2) Discussion group 1, March 1994

Carole: there's something I want to mention here, most of us here were the losers to some extent, the ones that were picked on
Chloé: oh yeah!
Carole: and I think that really has given us a better insight
Debbie: I think all of us (xx simultaneous talk)
Carole: even human nature, like the way people really are
Carmelle: not necessarily a better insight, but a different insight than
Carole: no, it gives you a better insight
Carmelle: no, a different insight
Chloé: I think people who have everything served to them on a silver platter (are less?) sensitized to other people

In the end, whether their insight is "better" or "different", they certainly feel that they know things that others do not, and can take perspectives that the "popular" girls cannot take. Of course, they are still somewhat angry about the way they were (and in many ways still are) treated, and may be somewhat jealous of the "popular" girls' perfect bodies; they say that the popular girls' breasts are the right size, not too big or too small like theirs, and their hair stays in place. Debbie and Farah in particular are unsure of how they feel, sharing the experiences and perspectives, as well as many of the practices, of both the popular crowd and the "rejects". At the same time, all six argue that this lack of fit has made them more accepting of who they are, more honest, and better able to see beyond physical beauty.

Over time, individually and collectively, the Nerds began to resist the image of femininity that was at the source of their marginalization. They rejected the practices of the popular group. For example, Lisa commented after the Valentine's Day skit described above that the student council (which had organized the skit) was obliged to use boys in drag to play the part of the Juliettes because no woman in her right mind would take a rose over money or a car. They disdained the popular girls as being mindless and only interested in boys. They had nothing but contempt for what they saw as the popular girls' participation in their own sexual objectification. One of the Nerds wrote to Phyllis: "They're nearly in their 20s and the "popular" girls are still getting molested (and they still love it. "Tee hee, stop, no! Don't take off my bra! Not in the hallway, tee hee!)". They reject the fuss made about the graduation dance:

(3) Discussion group 2, April 1994

Farah:	... there's so many girls in our school that I mean for the prom okay our graduation is coming up in May, and these girls are flipping through the magazines, "oh I want this dress, I want this dress, this is what I'm going to wear, don't you think this looks good", that's about it, it's basically brainwashing
Phyllis:	but does that get supported in the school?
All:	oh God yes
Chloé:	look who are the ones that are on the student council, and all the ones that are in. what do you call it, *Bureau de xx*, it's all the cute little people ...
Lisa:	a perfect example of how different the thinking is in this school is like when you get into the people who would be considered I don't know I guess (descended?) from the popular crowd. I have been asked in the last two weeks a total of fifteen times, three or four

times by the same person, what my prom dress looks like. I have not asked one single person, not one, and it doesn't stop there, okay. They want to know what kind of panty hose you're wearing, what shade. Does it matter? Does it matter whether I wear grey or taupe? Oh gee, I wonder.

They had the following to say about gender relations among the popular group, during a discussion about the student council:

(4) Discussion group 3, April 1994

Phyllis: do you think it's a coincidence that it's all guys in there?
Carole: no not at all, those guys have hung out with each other
Debbie: I think the girls are intimidated by them actually
Carole: oh they're a bunch of weak-willed spineless jellyfish, they're tee
            hee hee hee

Their rejection of the popular group's image of femininity is accompanied by the development of alternative practices. One set of practices involves being loud and sexually aggressive, rather than quiet and sexually passive, for example, talking and singing loudly in the hallways, making jokes, and making verbal sexual advances at boys (who would ignore them, or slink off down hallways when they approached). They would loudly insist on a turn at talk in class, although their remarks were not always well-received. They also took to making high-volume remarks about sex in public; for example, the boyfriend of Denise, one of the Nerds, came to her English class. After he left, another student said, "Look at her, she's so satisfied. She saw Tom." Denise replied, "Oh yes! I just had an orgasm sitting here. Now I'm basking in my afterglow."

Other strategies were designed principally to carve out an alternative sexual identity, or positioning, for themselves. Some of the girls did this by presenting themselves to the outside world as lesbian, and hence unavailable for sexual advances on the part of males. They reported themselves as having engaged in lesbian practices loudly within earshot of others, and they went to the graduation dance alone or as each others' dates. The image of lesbianism also allows them to take an active sexual role; they each act out in turn making sexual advances on others in the group, some of them rather sadistic, in what is perhaps a parody of male objectification of women (for example, "I'm going to stick a vacuum hose to your clit and drag you across the carpet"). Part of the purpose of this public discourse is to shock the popular students. Even Debbie and Farah, who were friends with both the popular group and with the Nerds, had a hard time with this kind of talk. For example, Debbie overheard the remark about the vacuum hose, and said, "You guys! How can you talk about things like that? You're hurting me, look, I'm crossing my legs." For the Nerds, this is a source of pleasure. One says that she "enjoys corrupting unjaded minds." Another writes to Phyllis, "Have you ever wondered about your sexuality? I have and reached the conclusion that I am hopelessly straight as a board, although I do enjoy giving the opposite impression, part of my shock appeal I suppose."

At the same time, while the construction of an image of lesbianism was largely a strategy for resisting dominant images of femininity, it was accompanied by a critical stance on the part of the Nerds towards the homophobic climate of the school. One of them accompanied Bernard and his male date to the graduation dance. Another befriended a lesbian student, and accompanied her on gay pride marches even after she had left Champlain. One day, Carole told several classmates that she had kissed another girl in front of her boyfriend, and that he had enjoyed watching. She then turned to Debbie, and said, "No, no, don't worry, I'm not a lesbian." Denise said, "Right, right, why do guys always think it's a turn on to see two girls make out? It's like gays should be shot and lesbians should be videotaped." Debbie says that guys who kiss guys and girls who kiss girls are disgusting: "If I saw that, I would puke right on them." Carole replies, "Oh right, don't you do that with your boyfriend? Walk down the street holding hands?"

Another element of the Nerds' strategy for carving out a different position on female sexuality was to adopt a discourse of Satanism, and indeed, to occasionally claim to be Satan. When a boy attempted to make an advance towards Lisa she rejected him saying that she was Satan, and that since Satan was an asexual being, it would be impossible for her to respond to the boy's advances. Indeed, taking up that position cast the boy's advances in a distinctly unfavorable light: what was he doing coming on to the devil? To be Satan not only gave the girls grounds for refusing to participate in prevailing gender relations, but it gave them a position of strength from which to do so, a position which protected them from accusations of either being too virginal and pure, or else lesbian.

Two other members of the group protected themselves through religion. Carmelle adopted adherence to some aspects of Celtic religions, which she valued in particular for what she understood to be the central role of women in those religious beliefs and practices. Farah was Muslim, and despite some episodes of acting like a member of the "popular" group, also had a commitment to more traditional Muslim gender roles, which made her relatively unavailable to non-Muslim boys. The final girl in the group was a member of a fundamentalist Christian group. She was somewhat marginal to the Nerds in several ways, among them her occasional flirtations with looking "sexy" (that is, wearing clothes the "popular" girls would approve of). However, she became pregnant; in and of itself, this would not have caused a problem for her relationship with the "popular" students, except that she decided to keep the baby and put it up for adoption, rather than have an abortion. The rest of the Nerds rallied around her, and supported her in many ways. In addition, it was necessary for her to defend herself from disparaging remarks from classmates (such as the one who suggested that she alone was responsible for what had happened), thereby committing her further to a stance outside of, and critical of, prevailing views of sexual relations.

But perhaps the most important form of the Nerds' resistance to the prevailing models of success at Champlain took place on the terrain of academic achievement. Doing well at school was a value the Nerds shared with the popular students; to their great delight, they were able to achieve more in that domain than the popular students were able to achieve.

(5) Discussion group, March 1994

Chloé: you'll see this later, but we were talking about this yesterday, about how the stereotype of the schools are like the bad kids are the ones that wear like the leather and they hang out together and they respond when teachers say something stupid or they kind of speak really loudly at *réunions générales* and all that stuff, and the other people, the ones that are the intelligent ones and the popular ones are the ones that look really nice and preppy

Lisa: but oddly enough

Chloé: it's the opposite

Lisa: out of the six people who are here, three of us got honor roll certificates today, and the other three of us maybe missed the honor roll by like .5%

Carole: and most of us are fast-tracking too in some way or another

No victory was as sweet as the graduation ceremonies in which several of the Nerds received academic prizes; Lisa wrote to Phyllis: "I deeply enjoyed going up to the podium five times as I watched their faces."

The Nerds found a variety of creative and imaginative ways to turn their initial rejection by the "popular" students into a position of strength. Their solidarity as a group also gave them a basis from which to develop a critique of their marginalization, and to cope with it. In addition, while their perspective allowed them to remain immune from the objectifying practices of their peers, it is only in the arena of academic achievement that they were able to set and achieve their own goals. As with most of the "popular" girls at Champlain, they were left orienting themselves with respect to their identity without being able to contribute anything to the public debate on this matter. In their emotional lives, it is far from clear that they were able to invent anything more satisfying than what the prevailing discourse had to offer. They clearly occupied a position on the margins of life at Champlain, and the creativity and originality of their perspective and achievements went largely unnoticed in public discursive space. In addition, while they were able to gain access to French through their academic activities, they staked their ground in English, removing themselves (or having been removed) from the construction of bilingualism at Champlain.

7. Conclusion

It is in the end mainly the male students of Champlain who are able to use public forums to construct specific versions of ethnolinguistic identity: *Québécois* as tough, rugged, authentic francophones; bilinguals as hip, plugged-in to North American popular culture in music, dress, and sports; Africans as privileged keepers of the European standard and simultaneously anti-colonialist, anti-racist warriors, street-wise and cool. They have concomitant negative stereotypes of each other: the *Québécois* uncultured lumberjack, the bilingual sell-out to the Anglos, the African as both victimized and threatening. Language is key to all these images, as Canadian and European French, English and Somali all become emblematic of specific visions of the school and its identity.

Female students are left to position themselves with respect to these discourses. Some simply associate with them, cheering on the boys, helping them, or playing their traditional roles within male-defined activities. Occasionally, they can exploit the window of opportunity presented by women's traditional role as primary agent of socialization to take control of events and committees such as the fashion show, the graduation dance, the multicultural lunch, the 25th anniversary celebrations, or even the student council. Others, notably the Nerds, resist, but in doing so they only marginalize themselves further from school life. Similarly, gay and lesbian students must position themselves with respect to prevailing norms, and find it impossible to participate in the main debates of life at school.

The struggle over the identity of the school is built on a gendered division of discursive labor. Male students have many more opportunities than do female students to say what they have to say about French and about *la fran-*

cophonie without having to be primarily concerned with what that has to do with being a male. At the same time, the intense focus on ethnolinguistic and ethnocultural identity which dominates the school's discursive space serves to obscure the gendered nature of that space. It makes it possible to use that space to construct gender ideologies which ensure that females and homosexuals are kept silent (or even invisible), and hence unable to participate in public spaces, as well as to construct linguistic ideologies which are associated with certain visions of masculinity. Resistance can only take place out of public view, and hence necessarily has only local, and possibly temporary effects. Academic success is the only competing field, but it too is not central to the school's public spaces.

Gender and linguistic ideologies are clearly intertwined, sometimes in surprising ways, and in ways which clearly are also tied to race and class. Their local workings at Champlain are no doubt specific to that school at that time; nonetheless, we can see here how much attention we do need to pay to sociohistorical conditions, and, perhaps more importantly, to the often hidden underside of bilingualism.

Notes

1.   Fieldwork was conducted in 1991–1994, and funded by the Social Sciences and Humanities Research Council of Canada and the Ontario Ministry of Education and Training Transfer Grant to the Ontario Institute for Studies in Education. The material drawn on here was collected and analyzed with the collaboration of Phyllis Dalley. A version of this analysis appears as Chapter 5, "Girls and Boys" in Heller (1999).

2.   Bucholtz (1999) describes a somewhat similar group of female "nerds" in a California high school. In her data, however, the girls are clearer about rejecting constructions of sexuality and romance. Bucholtz also claims that the construction of a "nerd" identity (see also Eckert 1989) should not be seen as mainly oppositional, nor the result of marginalization. As I hope to show below, in the case of the nerds of Champlain, the process of identity construction did seem to flow from initial experiences of marginalization, and was claimed by the girls themselves as overtly oppositional.

References

Bourdieu, Pierre
    1982   *Ce que parler veut dire*. Paris: Fayard.

Bourdieu, Pierre and J.-C. Passeron
1977   *La Reproduction: Éléments pour une Théorie du Systéme d'Enseignement.*
           Paris: Minuit.

Bucholtz, Mary
1999   "Why be normal?": Language and identity practices in a community of
           nerd girls. *Language in Society* 28, 2, 203–224.

Cameron, Deborah
1992 (1985)*Feminism and Linguistic Theory.* London: Macmillan.

Eckert, Penelope
1989   *Jocks and Burnouts: Social Categories and Identities in High School.* New
           York: Teachers College Press.

Foley, Douglas
1990   *Learning Capitalist Culture: Deep in the Heart of Tejas.* Philadelphia: Uni-
           versity of Pennsylvania Press.

Gal, Susan
1978   "Peasant men can't get wives": Language change and sex roles in a bilin-
           gual community. *Language in Society* 7, 1, 1–16.

Hall, Kira and Mary Bucholtz (eds.)
1995   *Gender Articulated: Language and the Socially-Constructed Self.* London:
           Routledge.

Heller, Monica
1994   *Crosswords: Language, Education and Ethnicity in French Ontario.* Ber-
           lin/New York: Mouton de Gruyter.
1999   *Linguistic Minorities and Modernity: A Sociolinguistic Ethnography.* Lon-
           don: Longman.
2001   Undoing the macro/micro dichotomy: Ideology and categorization in a lin-
           guistic minority school. In Coupland, Nikolas, Srikant Sarangi, and Chris-
           topher Candlin (eds.), *Sociolinguistics and Social Theory.* London: Long-
           man, 212–234.

Heller, Monica and Marilyn Martin-Jones (eds.)
2001   *Voices of Authority: Education and Linguistic Difference.* Greenwich, CT:
           Ablex.

Holmes, Janet (ed.)
1999   Special issue: Communities of Practice in language and gender research.
           Language in Society 28, 2, 171–312.

Johnson, Sally and Ulrike Meinhof (eds.)
  1997   *Language and Masculinity.* Oxford: Blackwell.

McDonald, Maryon
  1990   *'We Are Not French!' Language, Culture, and Identity in Brittany.* London
            and New York: Routledge.

Pujolar, Joan
  1997   Masculinities in a multilingual setting. In Johnson, Sally and Ulrike Mein-
            hof (eds.), *Language and Masculinity.* Oxford: Blackwell, 86–106.

  2000   *Gender, Heteroglossia and Power: An Ethnography of Youth Culture in
            Barcelona.* Berlin/New York: Mouton de Gruyter.

Rampton, Ben
  1995   *Crossing: Language and Ethnicity among Adolescents.* London: Longman.

Wodak, Ruth (ed.)
  1997   *Gender and Discourse.* London: Sage.

Cross-cultural excursions: Foreign language study and feminist discourses of travel

Claire Kramsch and Linda von Hoene

Opposite the full-page black and white photograph of a smiling railroad porter wearing a cap with the service number "Dienstmann 82" and a leather strap across his shoulder lie the neatly aligned rows of grammatical paradigms with their English translations featuring coordinating conjunctions and prepositional phrases in the third chapter of a beginning German textbook.

> *Dieses Jahr bleiben wir zu Hause*   This year we'll stay at home.
> *Aber naechstes Jahr fahren wir*   But next year we are going
> *nach Deutschland.*   to Germany.
> (Lohnes and Strothmann 1970: 51)

1. Introduction

Transportation and language pedagogy might have changed since the 1970s, but for the American student, learning German still means traveling, both literally and figuratively, to a new country and to a new language. The quintessential confrontation with the Other brought about by travel has been reflected upon by feminist scholars, who see gender as a paradigm for other differences, such as race, class, ethnicity, and those experienced while learning a foreign language (Kramsch and von Hoene 1995; von Hoene 1999). What can feminist theory contribute to our understanding of language learning *as travel*? And what kind of travel does the study of a foreign language foster?

In this paper we explore the question of how students travel to other cultures and encounter cultural and linguistic difference when studying a foreign language. We take travel to mean both the real and the imagined excursions into unknown geographical places on the map and the pedagogic excursions into new linguistic, cognitive, and social territory, i.e., the process of language learning itself. We first discuss recent work in feminist theory, where the focus of interest is not limited to differences between men and women, but encompasses the way difference itself gets constructed dialogically – gender being one significant, but not the only, outcome of this construction of difference. We then compare the modes of travel explicitly or implicitly encouraged by current textbooks and pedagogical practices with those suggested by recent work in feminist theory. We end with a reflection on the possibilities and the challenges presented by a feminist orientation to foreign language pedagogy.

2. Feminist theory as a discourse of difference

The work of feminist scholars, both in cultural studies and in linguistics, can provide a useful framework in which to rethink language study as a process of travel.[1] When students encounter difference, i.e., that which they perceive to be foreign, they have the opportunity to call into question and revise themselves as subjects. We first consider the notion of difference in feminist theory.

As we have elaborated in a previous article (Kramsch and von Hoene 1995), the history of feminist theory has been characterized by a dialogical and productively contentious process of bringing forth differences that exist both between and within subjects. In response to bourgeois feminist theory of the 1970s that took as its implied object of inquiry white, middle class, heterosexual women, writings by women of color in the early 1980s (e.g., hooks 1984; Moraga and Anzaldúa 1981) began to challenge these imperialist and universalizing assumptions and to articulate the myriad differences, such as race, class, sexual orientation, age, etc., that exist among and within people. This process of vigilantly teasing out differences rather than erasing or homogenizing them has also led theorists such as hooks (1989) and Anzaldúa (1987) to speak of the individual subject as a site of differences, one who is multivoiced and constructed dialogically through the interplay of these differences. Feminist theorists harking from psychoanalysis have also played an important role both in interrogating the univocality of the subject and in viewing subjectivity not as static but rather as a process of ongoing displacement and revision through the encounter with difference (von Hoene 1995). Julia Kristeva's (1976) concept of the *sujet-en-procès* 'subject-in-process', applied by von Hoene (1995) to foreign language study, theorizes the subject as one who puts herself "on trial" and calls herself into question by exploring that which is unconscious, i.e., foreign or other to the self. By bringing forth previously unconscious aspects of itself, the subject encounters the other or "stranger" in herself (Kristeva 1991) and participates in a process of ongoing transformation. Building on theorists such as Lacan and Fanon, the work of psychoanalytic feminist theorists, such as Kaja Silverman (1988), has also enabled us to understand that the subject is constructed through identification with the voice and gaze of the other.

By exploring the material and psychic sites of difference that had previously been denigrated and excluded by masculinist and colonialist discourses, feminism has resignified that which has been considered the "other" and enabled those who have been marginalized to speak for themselves. It is from this social, geographical, and fantasmatic space of the margins[2] that feminist psychoanalytic critics and postcolonial theorists have challenged the imperialist dictate of erasing difference and assimilating to a socially valorized ideal.

3.   Going native: The colonialist desires of second language acquisition

When we begin to apply the feminist attentiveness to difference to the learning of a foreign language, we quickly encounter what at first sight appear to be irreconcilable aims. While feminist theory, on the one hand, is invested in the avoidance of assimilation, the goal of foreign language study, i.e., to acquire native speaker fluency, takes as its implied goal identification with the native speaker ideal and the erasure of anything that would make the learner deviate from the native speaker ideal, whether it be in the form of an accent or code-switching. One could argue that the very term " 'native' speaker" connotes the colonialist image of a stereotyped, monolithic, foreign other.

In a chapter on T.E. Lawrence in her book *Male Subjectivity at the Margins* (1992), feminist psychoanalytic critic Kaja Silverman discusses the cross-cultural construction of subjectivity, highlighting two sides of desire that characterize the subject in colonialism. On the one hand, following postcolonial theorist Franz Fanon, the colonized seek to identify with the colonizer in an attempt to consolidate a semblance of power. This is the desire to assimilate so as not to stand out as different or other. On the other hand, as Silverman points out, the colonizer also might desire to abdicate his subjectivity – as does Lawrence – by identifying with the colonized. Lawrence thus attempts to remake himself in the image of the colonized other by donning Arab garb and by working on behalf of Arab independence. From the perspective of second language learning, the native speaker functions as a desired site of mimesis or identification, and like Lawrence in drag, students often attempt to make themselves over and to pass as natives by donning the clothing of the other (von Hoene 1999). In spite of the relative subject position of the learner vis-à-vis the power inhabited by the culture of the native speaker ideal, the process of assimilation, though at times resisted by learners, remains the implied top-down, desired goal of current theories that most frequently drive the teaching of foreign languages (Kramsch 1998).

In contrast to feminist theory, second language acquisition has not called into question its investment in and reliance upon the continual reproduction of colonialist modes of travel. Indeed, as von Hoene (1999) has argued, communicative theories such as the Natural Approach (Terrell 1977) are predicated on a dream of assimilation and a return to origins. With its equation of first and second language acquisition, the theory of the Natural Approach suggests that we can simulate the learning environment of a child acquiring a first language. Based on this stated premise, the Natural Approach wishes to return the adult learner to a prelinguistic, pre-subject space where, according to psychoanalytic theory, the separation of subject and object is foreclosed. Stated slightly differently, the dream of the Natural Approach is to erase the difference upon which the development of subjectivity is predicated. We would like to explicitly stress that the distinction between the theoretical claims of the Natural Approach and the often more cognitively oriented methods and exercises used in the language textbook and classroom activities point, out of necessity, to the inherent futility and impossibility of acceding to this theoretical ideal.

The reality of the foreign language classroom may indeed be in stark contrast to this ideal advocated by the Natural Approach. Learners may be ambivalent about identifying with the native speaker ideal and may indeed resist assimilation. For example, if the other represented by the native speaker is seen as negative or "less than" students, that other will be perceived as an undesirable site of identification. This ambivalence to identifying with the other who is perceived as negative may characterize, for example, the colonizer's or rebellious native's point of view. This ambivalence, one could argue, is consistent with the position of postcolonial subjects (Blunt 1994), who may both conform and resist, thus providing a site of productive transgression in their refusal.

4. Beyond assimilation: Poststructuralist and postcolonialist modes of travel

This resistance to assimilation has also been theorized in poststructuralist and postcolonialist thought. In *The Empire of Signs* (Barthes 1970), a book he wrote after his travel to Japan and his encounter with the Japanese language, Roland Barthes writes: "Open a travel guidebook: you will usually find a small lexicon, but this lexicon will oddly enough list boring and useless things: the customs, the post office, the hotel, the hairdresser, the doctor, the prices. And yet, what does it mean to travel? To encounter. The only important lexicon is the lexicon of the encounter" (Barthes 1970: 23).

What Barthes means here by encounter is not the casual contact between tourist and native described in handbooks for intercultural communication, nor even the more dramatic *encuentro* or encounter of colonists and colonized in the New World (Pratt 1992). Encounter for him is confrontation with difference:

> The dream: to know a foreign (strange) language and yet not to understand it: to perceive in it a difference without this difference ever being coopted by the superficial sociality of language, communication or vulgarity; to know, through the positive mirroring of a new language *(refractées positivement dans une langue nouvelle),* the impossibilities of our own; to learn the systematics of the inconceivable; to undo our "reality" under the effect of other categories, other syntaxes; to discover the unimaginable positions of the enunciating subject, to displace its typology; in short, to descend into the depths of the untranslatable, to feel its shock without ever absorbing it. (Barthes 1970: 11)

In the quote above, the encounter with difference via travel to a foreign language does not lead to a colonialist consolidation of identity that erases difference but rather to a poststructuralist, deconstructive process, i.e., a questioning and destabilization of the illusory naturalness of one's native language through the "positive mirroring" of a new language. Indeed, one could argue that Barthes' reference to the notion of mirroring alludes to the process of the construction of identity through the other that Lacan (1977) posits as the mirror stage. What Barthes suggests is that, in the encounter with a new cultural mirror, students have the opportunity to call into question the fiction of autonomy by realizing that they are always constructed through the gaze, the voice, and the language of the other (Silverman 1988). As von Hoene (1995), using Kristeva's concept of the *sujet-en-procès* suggests, learning another language can contribute to the revision of subjectivity through this interaction with difference. In learning a foreign language, students "make themselves strangers to themselves" by consciously adopting and identifying with the foreign language and culture. Through this encounter with the other, learners have the opportunity to call into question or "put on trial" the assumptions and beliefs that they bring from their own language and culture. Students change in the process by broadening the spectrum of differences through which they are constituted as subjects.

One of the most common criticisms of some poststructuralist theories, in particular deconstruction, has been that it often lacks attentiveness to sociohistorical situatedness, emphasizing instead the destabilization of meaning through the play of linguistic signifiers (Kaplan 1996). The inadvertent outcome of such an approach to cross-cultural travel is an erasure of the very differences that are at the heart of recent postcolonial feminist theory which emphasizes a "politics of location" (Rich 1986).

If we add the theoretical insights of postcolonial feminist writers like María Lugones and Gloria Anzaldúa to the psychoanalytic insights of poststructuralist theory, we can elaborate a more complex and socially inflected mode of cross-cultural travel that would enable language educators to be aware of the social nature of difference. This approach, which, following Rosi Braidotti, one might call "critical nomadic consciousness" (1994: 12), entails seeing travel not only as "movement" from one location to another but also as constant reflection on the privilege and power – or lack thereof – of those traveling. Though we use the terms of postcolonial feminism, we are at the same time aware that the foreign language classroom and the educational institutions in which it is situated often constitute sites of privilege. Indeed, we recognize that the study of foreign language is, for the most part, a process of voluntary, temporary, and mostly "fantasmatic nomadism" (von Hoene, in preparation) where the social consequences of transgression and the display of difference are very low indeed.

Feminist postcolonial theory can nonetheless enable the foreign language classroom to be instrumental in the development of a new cross-cultural consciousness by encouraging students to become aware of the desires of colonialist modes of travel, i.e., identification with or rejection of the other, desires that are often embedded in and sanctioned by current foreign language teaching methods and materials. Feminist postcolonial theory can also enable students to accept the impossibility and, indeed, the undesirability of identifying seamlessly with the other and to understand the value of identities constructed through and characterized by multiple differences.

What do feminist postcolonial modes of travel entail? We would like to examine two concepts, one denoting the process of travel – María Lugones' notion of "world-traveling" – and the other, Gloria Anzaldúa's notion of the "new Mestiza" which refers to a new type of multivoiced consciousness or identity constructed by inhabiting multiple cultures.

In her 1990 essay, "Playfulness, 'World'-Traveling, and Loving Perception", the feminist María Lugones describes a mode of travel that works against colonialist approaches to difference that either valorize or denigrate the other. Instead, Lugones (1990: 402) is interested in a dialogical relationship to difference that would have us call into question ideological and stereotypical notions of the other and to see others as active, complex subjects in specific social contexts:

> Through travelling to other people's 'worlds' we discover that there are 'worlds'
> in which those who are the victims of arrogant perception are really subjects,

lively beings, resistors, constructors of vision even though in the mainstream construction they are animated only by the arrogant perceiver and are pliable, foldable, file-awayable, classifiable.

Lugones' notion of world-traveling asks that we become noncolonialist travelers who are willing to see the world through the eyes of the other rather than through what Mary Louise Pratt (1992) has referred to as "imperial eyes". Lugones suggests that we adopt a stance that enables us to see others as subjects and to see ourselves from the destabilizing perspective of the other. In so doing, she provides a socially embedded variation of Barthes' mirror and Kristeva's *sujet-en-procès*: "... by travelling to their 'world' we can understand what it is to be them and what it is to be ourselves in their eyes. Only when we have travelled to each other's 'worlds' are we fully subjects to each other" (Lugones 1990: 401).

The feminist theorist Caren Kaplan aptly describes Lugones' theory of 'world'-traveling as a "critical practice" that "articulates connections between women based on the material histories of their differences. Such a politics of location undermines any assertion of progressive, singular development and alerts us to the interpellation of the past in the present" (1994: 150). Kaplan's statement can be productively extended beyond relationships and interactions among women to include all individuals, as Lugones' theory of "'world'-traveling" and feminist theory in general are central to a rethinking of how we travel to a wide range of differences that include but also go beyond gender.

Finally, Lugones' notion of "'world'-traveling" is active, intentional, and predicated on a nonlinear, nonteleological mode of being in the world where one is open to uncertainty and surprise. As opposed to erecting rigid boundaries between self and other, Lugones' traveler is "open to self construction" through the engagement with difference: "Those of us who are 'world'-travelers have the distinct experiences of being different in different 'worlds' and ourselves in them ... The shift from being one person to being a different person is what I call 'travel'" (1990: 396).

If María Lugones' concept of world traveling outlines a process, Gloria Anzaldúa's "new Mestiza" describes a new type of consciousness created in the interstices of cultures, "a consciousness of the borders" constructed through the engagement with difference. Anzaldúa's "new Mestiza", like Lugones' "world-traveler", is characterized by a state of transition and a willingness to "flounder in uncharted waters" (Anzaldúa 1987: 79): "She is willing ... to make herself vulnerable to foreign ways of seeing and thinking. She surrenders all notions of safety, of the familiar. Deconstruct. Construct" (p. 82). The new

Mestiza has a tolerance for ambiguity and seeks "to break down subject/object duality" (p. 80). The consciousness that Anzaldúa is describing is one that is formed through the process of "cross-pollination", "an alien consciousness" constructed through a "cultural collision" between two completely different frames of reference. This hybrid consciousness that results from the collision of cultures is what Anzaldúa refers to as a third way, the Mestiza consciousness. The struggle to uphold a Mestiza consciousness, one that calls for seeking out and being transformed by difference rather than squelching or avoiding it, is for Anzaldúa a struggle that is eminently feminist.

Taken together, Lugones' concept of world traveling and Anzaldúa's notion of Mestiza can provide a theoretical foundation upon which to rethink foreign language study as cross-cultural travel. But how can these concepts be operationalized in linguistic terms? For this, we need to look briefly at feminist linguistic theory.

5.   Speakers as travelers

Feminist linguists (Cameron 1985, 1990; Lakoff 1975; Mills 1995; Poynton 1989; Threadgold 1997) view language as a dynamic communicative practice rather than as a static system of signs. While in their early work, feminist linguists were keen on demystifying sexist practices (Cameron 1985) and on characterizing the verbal behaviors of women and men (Lakoff 1975), later feminist writings (Cameron 1995, 1998; Threadgold 1997) have drawn on anthropological linguistics (e.g., Hanks 1996) and critical discourse analysis (e.g., Fairclough 1995) to characterize the use of language to perpetuate or subvert social relations and gender relations in particular. Rather than viewing language as consisting of noun declensions, adjective endings, and the subjunctive mood, they see it as the actualization of potential meanings produced and received by language users in multiple contexts of communication and against multiple ideological horizons (Hanks 1996: 126, 165). Such a definition of language is reminiscent of Halliday's theory of language as social semiotic and actualized potential (Halliday 1978). Indeed, feminist linguists use Halliday's functional grammar as a social semiotic vocabulary to describe the systematic ways in which meaning is co-constructed by grammar in dialogue with other fellow speakers or writers. As we shall see in the next section, the structuralist metalanguage of nouns, adjectives, and verbs used in foreign language classes does not lend itself to discussing the ways in which texts construct the difference or lack of difference in the cultural realities they refer to. By contrast, with its systemic nomenclature that describes phenomena of cohesion, information structure, agency, point of view, modality, transitivity, Hallidayan linguistics can show how texts construct, perpetuate, or subvert social reality as seen from the perspective of a particular speaker/writer at a particular time.

In her recent book, *Feminist Poetics,* feminist linguist Terry Threadgold (1997) uses Hallidayan linguistics to reconnect the study of grammatical forms and the lived experience of the speaking subject. In this perspective, language learning is not the neutral and linear internalization of an artificially established standard, but an awareness that "every individual [speaker's] multiple positionings and constructions must be seen as forms of identity and experience which frame and constitute the sexed, classed and raced human subject's life history, which give it both its narrative coherence and its discursive and narrative multiplicity" (Threadgold 1997: 7). Furthermore, by drawing on such poststructuralist thinkers as Voloshinov/Bakhtin, Barthes, Foucault, and on feminist writers such as Kristeva and de Lauretis, Threadgold aims not at replacing but, rather, at putting in question traditional pedagogies by describing exactly what they do, how they came about, and what alternative pedagogies exist, from the perspective of the socially and historically situated enunciating subject.

Threadgold calls such a pedagogy a *poiesis,* i.e., a cultural and semiotic process of remaking or retelling well-known stories by making visible the subjectivities and intertextualities they assume in their recipients. It is a *performance,* because each of these rewritings is done from a specific corporeal position, and this performance is itself a critical metalanguage that says explicitly what traditional pedagogy keeps unsaid. It comprises *histories,* "histories of the making of texts and of the subjects who make or are made themselves, in negotiation with textual processes" (Threadgold 1997: 3). By engaging readers in a revisionist process of traditional pedagogies, texts can make learners into *subjects-in-process* on the margins of traditional pedagogy (von Hoene 1995).

6. The discourse of travel in foreign language textbooks

We now look at the three textbooks most widely used today to teach college-level German in the US: *Deutsch Heute* (German Today), *Neue Horizonte* (New Horizons), and *Kontakte* (Contacts).[3] How do these textbooks write into their goals and objectives the process of traveling to another culture? From the first editions to the current ones, *Deutsch Heute* (Moeller and Liedloff 1979–1996) and *Neue Horizonte* (Dollenmayer and Hansen 1984–1999), emphasize a "four skills" approach to language learning. The avowed goal of familiarizing students with German-speaking culture adds a "fifth" skill – culture. This cumulative process of skill building constitutes a linear approach to language acquisition, implicitly invested in an appropriation of the language and culture of the other. Together with this skill building approach, the two textbooks list a cross-cultural perspective as one of their objectives. Starting with the first edition in 1984, *Neue Horizonte* claims to teach students to "view their own culture more critically" (p. v). In its latest editions (1996, 1999) *Neue Horizonte* slightly restates this goal as "to view your own culture through the prism of another" (pp. vii, xvii). *Deutsch Heute*, in its sixth and most recent edition (1996), adds to the incremental mastery of linguistic skills the following goal: "*Deutsch Heute* strives to help students experience the relationship between culture and language while becoming more aware of their own culture and language" (p. xi). In adding this more self-reflexive goal, one that implies a dialogical, mutually informing relationship of native (L1) and foreign (L2) language, native (C1) and foreign (C2) culture, both *Neue Horizonte* and *Deutsch Heute* seem to invite students to call into question both C1 and C2 and to see as culture what they may have taken for nature. But, by equating culture with standard national cultures and standard national languages, both texts allow the encounter with the foreign to remain on a similarly standardized, generic plane.

The situation seems at first glance to be somewhat different with *Kontakte* (Terrell et al. 1996), which takes as its basic methodological premise Terrell's Natural Approach (Terrell 1977). The goal of this approach, based on Krashen's theory of second language acquisition, is to promote the experiential acquisition of language rather than the intellectual process of learning, thus opening the way for an unconscious identification with the other, even if, as in the other two textbooks, this other is of a rather generic kind. It appears, however, that the purpose of having students experience the foreign language and culture is not to promote the explicit goal of calling into question one's own culture but to ensure the maintenance of a low affective filter and to promote a sense of enjoyment and engagement in the class (p. xvi). In other words, *Kontakte*'s "contact zone" (Pratt 1992) fosters individual pleasure but not personal engagement with the foreign other.

How is the process of cross-cultural travel pursued across activities and exercises? In the 1996 edition of *Deutsch Heute* we find some prereading exercises that consciously ask the student to make contrasts and to see differences between C1 and C2 and to realize the relativity of their own culture and language. For example, in chapter two, students are asked to consider how they would describe their college experiences to a friend in preparation for reading a letter from a German student about her experience in Berlin; in chapter three, students are asked to consider the differences in the meaning of the word "cold" for people in Germany, Toronto, and Florida. But follow-up activities and grammar exercises focus exclusively on information retrieval and substitution drills, and thus miss an opportunity for cross-cultural reflection.

We find the same missed opportunities in *Neue Horizonte* (1996, 1999). Despite its goal to help students see their own culture through the prism of another, in its chapter on travel, *Neue Horizonte* presents Wilhelm Müller's (1794–1827) poem *Wanderschaft* 'hiking' [*Das Wandern ist des Müllers Lust* 'Hiking is a miller's delight'] without exploring cross-cultural differences with regard to the word *wandern* 'hiking' or the relationship between gender, travel, and yearning for difference. The exercises and activities that accompany the poem remain at the level of retrievable content, thereby trivializing the affective impact the poem could have in evoking travels to unknown and exotic places.

With its *Kulturprojekte* or 'culture projects', *Kontakte* incorporates a significant number of activities that ask the American student to view his/her own culture by comparing it to German, Austrian, and Swiss cultures. But like the other two textbooks, *Kontakte* also defines "German" and "American" as univocal nationalities with little variation within the larger cultures themselves. For example, in chapter one an activity asks what "Americans" and "Germans" like to do in their free time, with no attempt at specifying which Americans or which Germans the book is referring to. Gender, social class, age, regional affiliation, and ethnic differences are not brought into the discussion. Similar to *Neue Horizonte*, poetry plays a central role in *Kontakte*'s travel chapter. Eichendorff's (1788–1857) poem, *Wem Gott will rechte Gunst erweisen* 'Those upon whom God wishes to bestow his favors' (1826) and Tucholsky's (1890–1935) *Vornehme Leute, 1200 Meter hoch* 'Posh people, 1200 meters high' (1960) are rife with possibilities for cross-cultural exploration. Though *Kontakte* does provide an opportunity for students to discuss the travel habits of *vornehme Leute* 'posh people', one misses a deeper discussion about the motivations for travel, what the *weite Welt* 'wide world' in the Eichendorff poem has meant historically for Germans and Americans, what *vornehm* 'posh' means in various cultures within Germany and within the U.S., and what the historical relationship has been between gender and travel privileges.

If one looks at the evolution of these textbooks over time, one notices changes in the explicit depiction of cross-cultural differences. In the earlier editions of *Deutsch Heute,* for example, dating from the 1970s, reading passages were used to deploy the narrative of Americans studying or working in Germany, while more recent editions depict Germans or young American professionals traveling as tourists within Germany during their vacation. Even though the earlier editions present protracted contacts with the foreign culture, these contacts do not any more than those of the tourists in the 1990s lead to a really diversified acquaintance with the foreign, as they are limited in range and do not promote critical thinking. The reading selections in the most recent editions of all three books reflect this shift away from cross-cultural difference. In earlier editions of *Deutsch Heute* (e.g., 1979), we are privy to the cross-cultural tensions experienced by a foreign student or the wife of an American businessman in Germany. We see Robert Lerner going shopping with Frau Braun and becoming quite bewildered about things that are different such as whole bean coffee and day-old bread. We experience right along with Frau Fischer her difficulties in understanding why the German women she has invited for coffee will not eat her brightly decorated cake.[4] And we encounter Jutta Gruber puzzled at the differences between American and German conceptions of privacy as expressed through open and closed doors.[5] Although these differences may seem at face value superficial, they point to deeper levels of social difference and potential areas of productive cross-cultural tension. In subsequent editions much of what originally appeared in the central reading passages has been relegated to the culture boxes that form the margins of the chapter. When differences are discussed, they are done with greater distance; the individual is not depicted in the throes of cross-cultural conflict.

But students in earlier days did not experience the shock of the foreign any more than they do today. Earlier readings drew the reader into the emotional cross-cultural conflicts experienced by the protagonists, but they were often read as quaint characters in a fictional narrative, not as incarnations of real-life native speakers. In current editions cultural differences are presented in a more objective, documentary-like style, but they are subordinated to a rhetoric of similarity that denies national specificities and focuses instead on individuals as members of the "global village". In theory – but certainly not in practice – the image of this global village would have us believe that international differences are shrinking. The perception of greater proximity and access to German culture that is implicitly supported in many of these reading passages makes what once may have been seen as a voyage to discover difference into an assumption of global assimilation (Billig 1995; Kramsch 1987).

Ironically, the illusion of greater similarity between Germans and Americans seems to be promoted exactly at that moment in time when greater ethnic variation within Germany is being represented in the textbooks. Although the focus on diversity within Germany must be viewed as a positive development, it also tends to function as a site of displacement for international, cross-cultural differences that become absorbed in the globalization rhetoric of breaking down borders.[6] The attempt to represent a broader spectrum of differences within C2 lays bare the difficulty that foreign language study has in integrating a discussion of difference. Differences are often presented rather superficially and more often than not with an astonishing degree of segregation from the rest of the text. In *Neue Horizonte* (1996, 1999), for example, the final two chapters are devoted to foreigners and women as if to imply that they are not part of the culture that has been described in the earlier chapters. Of the three textbooks that we analyzed, *Deutsch Heute* (1996) did the most to offer a broader and less stereotypical array of visual images of ethnic diversity in Germany and did so from the outset of the book. In this textbook, people of color are presented not only as laborers, as they are in some of the other textbooks, but also as professionals, as students, as vacationers, and as a family taking part in the first day of school traditions with their children. But while the multicultural trend in textbooks emphasizes diversity, it too fails to emphasize difference. A focus on diversity merely juxtaposes various manifestations of the other; a focus on difference explores how the self and other are dialogically constructed.

In sum, recent textbooks demonstrate in theory a willingness to feature cultural difference and to initiate a dialogue between self and other, but, in practice, difference is replaced by multicultural diversity. Cross-cultural reflection is short-circuited by a shift to totally unrelated topics or by substitution drills that cushion rather than elicit the shock of the unfamiliar that Barthes writes about.

7. Feminist perspectives on language pedagogy

If we combine Lugones' *world-traveling*, Anzaldúa's notion of *multivoiced consciousness*, and Threadgold's emphasis on *poiesis, performance,* and *histories,* it might be possible to identify some common strands of a feminist pedagogy for foreign languages.

In a feminist pedagogy, the unit of learning would not be the word or the sentence, but the text (however short) uttered or written by someone for someone at some place and time. Thus, for example, the utterance *"Dieses Jahr bleiben wir zu Hause"* would be grasped not as the illustration of the use of prepositions and the present tense but as a speech act, proffered by some German speaker to some other German speaker with some purpose in mind and some shared knowledge of the context – a knowledge that would be different were it said in English to an English speaker in an English-speaking environment, *"This year we'll stay at home"*. Current communicative approaches to language teaching make a point of using as much authentic language as possible, in genuine contexts of use. But, as we have seen, authenticity is more often than not generic, genuineness is standardized, even stereotyped, eventfulness is essentialized. By contrast, a feminist pedagogy would attempt to recapture the uniqueness of the particular verbal event behind the standardized genre.

A feminist pedagogy would not view a word as a part in a linguistic system, but as a link in a system of intertextual resources:

> A system of intertextual resources – multi-medial, understood to be differentiated according to the subject's location in the social and cultural space, limited or constrained by the habitus of daily life, by class, race and gender – is put in the place of the linguist's system of language. Texts are now understood to be constructed chunk by chunk, intertextually, not word by word, and there can thus be no link between text and context except through the intertextual resources of this discursively produced subjectivity. (Threadgold 1997: 3)

What Threadgold stresses here is the fact that, by contrast with linguists whose role it is to identify words and their combinations at the sentence level, living users of the language construct spoken and written texts. They select lexical collocations or prefabricated chunks of speech like *die weite Welt* 'the wide world', *eine Gunst erweisen* 'to bestow a favor', or *bleiben wir zu Hause!* 'let's stay at home!', and combine them with others in accordance with the demands of the situational context.[7]

These chunks or combinations of chunks resonate with prior texts of which they were a part, e.g., folksongs or travel brochures for *in die weite Welt,* medieval-sounding phrases and romantic poems for *rechte Gunst erweisen,* or spoken utterances of everyday occurrence like *bleiben wir zu Hause!* By recombining these intertextual resources, speakers and writers define themselves as subjects-in-process in a social, cultural, and historical space and construct their ongoing dialogue with other speakers and readers through the incorporation of prior texts and cultural references. And indeed, these resources are socially and historically contingent: "the text can never be extricated from the complexities of these contextual encounters with socially and historically produced readers" (Threadgold 1997: 33).

So, for example, German concepts like *Wandern* 'hiking', *vornehm* 'posh', *Ferien* 'holidays', *Urlaub* 'paid vacation', have meanings that go far beyond their dictionary definitions – they may index social class, generation, gender, national culture, historical specificity, ideology in particular texts and contexts. The presentation of travel in feminist pedagogy would be concerned with the relationship between the individual interactions portrayed in the texts and the wider discursive and social structure they reflect. The first famous line of Eichendorff's poem, *Wem Gott will rechte Gunst erweisen /den schickt er in die weite Welt* 'Those upon whom God wishes to bestow his favors, he sends out into the wide world,' would not merely serve to illustrate a particular instance of relative clause construction (*wem . . . den*), or to point to a rather antiquated use of the phrase *rechte Gunst erweisen,* but would explore, for example, the potential meanings conveyed by the impersonal syntactic phrase. Frequently used in proverbs and folk sayings, this grammatical construction serves to express truths that seem eternal, i.e., necessary, precisely because it has no definite subject, no definite addressee, and it seems to establish a natural causality between traveling and God's favor. This natural order of things is expressed by the historical present indicative. The very grammar of this phrase captures the religious beliefs of a historically situated common folk speech community that the poet Josef Freiherr von Eichendorff identifies with, even though he himself did not belong to the "common folk". In addition, the impersonal relative clause construction with seemingly universal validity captures the universalizing tendencies of a certain German romanticism, that sees God's gifts bestowed on anyone who is pure of heart and has a romantic yearning for nature and adventure.

In a feminist foreign language pedagogy, attention would be focused in pre- and post-reading exercises on the way texts structure our vision of our own and of the foreign culture, how they mediate our understanding of the linguistic and cultural diversity among Germans and Americans in regard to (or disregard of) class, age, gender, region. Classroom interactions and students' writings would be used more consciously to examine the way students' discourse portrays travel to another culture – as a way of identifying with, exoticizing, or rejecting the other (Kramsch 1998; von Hoene 1999).[8] In addition, some of the materials and projects that already exist in textbooks and that do foster a more reflective approach to language study could be expanded and made more complex: *Kontakte*'s cultural projects and other cross-cultural activities; *Deutsch Heute*'s prereading exercises; *Neue Horizonte*'s inclusion of poetry.

A feminist pedagogy does not consider texts as so many sentences to be parsed like maps to be read: they are themselves roads to be traveled, roles to be embodied, acted out, performed. In traditional pedagogy, which focuses on destinations, outcomes, and products, texts are viewed as containers of information to be retrieved through sophisticated reading *strategies*, for which students need *tools* and *techniques*. A feminist pedagogy, by contrast, puts the subject in the center. It appeals not only to the learner's mind and behaviors, but to a subject's emotions, body, and his or her social and political habitus. According to Threadgold,

> The business of theatrical embodiment and performance as realised in rehearsal, the labour and pain of making meanings with the body, have become for me a metaphor of the much slower and less visible processes by which genres, discourses and narratives are embodied or rewritten as history and habitus in the business of everyday life and in the processes we call education. (Threadgold 1997: 125)

In a feminist pedagogy, rereading, like rewriting, recasting, recoding, rephrasing, become important activities, not to discover new information or to "get it right", but to reach new levels of personal recognition and understanding. Rather than so many repetitions, such reoccurrences are to be seen as recyclings, rhymings, variations on a theme – the essence of creativity and improvisation (Kramsch 1994). They are, according to Threadgold, the key to the construction of identity: "[Feminist writings] recognize that 'identity' is discursively produced, and that it is *not one;* that it is a network of multiple positions, constructed in and through many chains of signification, always realised in texts, enacted and performed, read and written, heard and spoken, in verbal, visual, graphic, photographic, filmic, televisual and embodied forms" (Threadgold 1997: 5).

Through the encounter with a new "acoustic mirror" (Silverman 1988; von Hoene 1999) foreign language learners can become conscious of how they relate to the other and can partake in shifts in how they perceive their own identities as Anglo-, African-, or Asian-Americans, as women or as men, as New Yorkers or as Californians, as immigrants or as U.S.-born. German can hold up to them the mirror in which they encounter for the first time the foreign in themselves (Kramsch 1995, 2000).

8.   Some difficult questions

It has to be said, however, that a foreign language pedagogy inspired by a discourse of difference and a discourse centered on the enunciating subject presents some dilemmas. For, making difference rather than diversity the key experience in language learning is already going further than many language teachers and learners are ready to go in the cultivation of the unfamiliar. In addition, centering language pedagogy on the varied and variable subjectivity of the language learner rather than on the standardized "native speaker" goes against the grain of traditional practice. A pedagogy based on linguistic and cultural difference can lead to relativism if it is not anchored in a socially and politically inflected definition of difference that moves beyond diversity as variation to a definition that focuses on the mutually constitutive relationship of self and other. In the following we address some of these questions.

The first question has to do with the imperatives of a communicative approach to language teaching. The metalanguage of feminist pedagogy does make visible the embodied experience of language learning by students and teachers. It allows speakers and readers to state their subject positions and those of others, and in that sense it is a pedagogy of difference as social awareness. But if it is used only as experiential material for public metatalk in the classroom, it may in turn colonize the learner as fodder for pedagogic talk and put on public display what should be, after all, a moment of private insight. Because the main purpose of language classes is arguably to talk, and because what is not displayed in the public arena of the classroom and cannot be captured and displayed on the test generally does not count as having been learned, not enough attention has been paid to the value of silence and of private speech, private reading, and writing in second language acquisition (Cook 1995). It is difficult to even talk of silence and privacy when the point of language instruction is ostensibly to make the language as publicly present as possible. Favoring silence seems to go against the efforts made in the last thirty years to increase communication and the amount of student talk in language classrooms. A feminist pedagogy would need to call into question the privilege given to talk versus silence, to the public use of language versus private reflection.

The second question has to do with the problem of normativity in language teaching. Both the need for public display of knowledge and the obligation to measure student production against a standardized norm seem to work against the notion of a feminist pedagogy. Language teaching is predicated on the notion of a stable, standard language, codified in grammars and dictionaries, monitored by nation-states and academic institutions, and their gatekeeping mechanisms. As such, how can it ever be taught through a feminist pedagogy that stands for difference and multiplicity?

For example, in the current multicultural classrooms where foreign languages are taught in the United States, students bring to class a variety of more or less oral, more or less literate educational traditions. But, as Cameron remarks, "the most important bias of dictionaries [and grammars] is toward the written rather than the spoken word ... The vitality of home and street vernacular is simply ignored" (1985: 83). The current debates brought about by the sudden accessibility of large electronic corpora of authentic vernacular language use like the *Collins Cobuild English Grammar* (Sinclair 1990) are symptomatic of the difficulty educational institutions have in dealing with language variation in a global world that, while it thrives on diversity, contrives in fact to minimize difference (see, e.g., Francis and Sinclair 1994; Owen 1993). Recent suggestions have been made to use once again the rich resources of oral tradition, routine, ritual, and verbal play in language classes (Cook 2000; Kramsch 1993; Widdowson 1992). But it only makes more visible the clash between the institutional demands of a schooling tradition that promotes a narrow definition of literacy based on the written language and the educational possibilities of a feminist language pedagogy that would like to broaden the concept of literacy to include multiple forms of orality and literacy (Kern 2000).

Finally, we have to face the tension between the demands of a "socially inflected" pedagogy and a pedagogy that focuses on linguistic and cultural relativity. How can feminist language pedagogy both teach critical social awareness and be attuned to a late modern world in which educators are rediscovering the educational value of verbal play and textual pleasure? The debates currently going on in the pages of professional journals[9] between those who promote a critical pedagogy (e.g., Fairclough 1996) and those who advocate a humanistically oriented pedagogy (e.g., Widdowson 1998) are about educational responsibility. Both sides are committed to various degrees to reforming schooling and deschooling education. They both argue for the ethical responsibility of the language teacher, but they understand responsibility differently. They travel in different ways, at different paces, and according to different times.

Much like feminist theory, which has been invested in bringing forth and 'living fearlessly with and within difference(s)' (Trinh T. Minh-ha 1989), so too the goal of a feminist orientation to language pedagogy should be to enable an ongoing forum in which to bring differences to the fore, differences among researchers, teachers, and among and within the students themselves. Ultimately, Julia Kristeva's notion of a subject-in-process, one that puts itself on trial, must apply to all engaged in the difficult mediation from theory to methodology, from methodology to practice in the exercise of professional research, the design of course materials, and the conduct of classroom practice. Such a mediation is not compatible with the traditionally prescriptive nature of pedagogy, even if it is of a critical kind. In addition to calling into question the traditional pedagogy, a feminist orientation must entail increasing student and teacher awareness of the dialogic construction of difference. Such an awareness is predicated on the ongoing interrogation of all aspects of teaching and learning.

Notes

1. We are aware that many readers of this chapter will not be familiar with the language of feminist theory. We have tried to keep it accessible within the bounds of a theory that has had to craft a new language to express a new way of seeing familiar realities.

2. The word 'fantasmatic' is used here to underscore how external social realities impact the imagination and the psyche.

3. We have chosen German textbooks since this is the common language that both authors have taught, but a similar analysis could be done on other language teaching materials as well.

4. This anecdote is meant to give American students an example of the German preference for all that is natural, fresh, and unadulterated by artificial colorings.

5. This cultural anecdote contrasts the American custom of leaving office doors open as a sign of social friendliness, with the German habit of closing doors when someone is in a room, as a sign of respect for privacy. (For a further exploration of such differences, see Troyanovich 1972.)

6. We are aware that the greater diversity of German speakers represented in the pages of American textbooks might be more a politically correct response to the demands of the domestic market than a desire on the part of the publishers to confront foreign language learners with real difference. In classroom activities, when diversity is acknowledged and even encouraged through pair and group work, students' diverse utterances are measured against the standard form to be learned (Doughty and Williams 1998), the normative task to be accomplished (Crookes and Gass 1993), and the objective content to be acquired (Byrnes 1998). Diversity is honored, but difference, dissonance, and divergence remain unexplored.

7. Under the influence of corpus-based linguistics (Sinclair 1991; Stubbs 1996), recent research in second language acquisition has focused on the way learners acquire pre-fabricated patterns and formulaic phrases rather than individual words and grammatical structures (e.g., Hakuta 1974).

8. The metaphor of writing as travel has been used by composition scholars like Clark (1988) to shift the focus from the product to the process of writing and to make the notion of readers and writers less static and more transient, dynamic, as belonging to "communities of practice" (Lave and Wenger 1991).

9. To get a flavor of that debate, see Toolan (1997).

References

Anzaldúa, Gloria
  1987   *Borderlands/La Frontera. The New Mestiza.* San Francisco: Spinsters/ Aunt Lute.

Barthes, Roland
  [1970] 1982 *The Empire of Signs.* Transl. R. Howard. New York: Hill and Wang.

Billig, Michael
  1995   *Banal Nationalism.* London: Sage.

Blunt, Alison
  1994   *Travel, Gender, and Imperialism: Mary Kingsley and West Africa.* New York: Guilford.

Braidotti, Rosi
    1994   *Nomadic Subjects.* Minneapolis: University of Minnesota Press.

Byrnes, Heidi
    1998.   Constructing curricula in collegiate foreign language departments. In Heidi
            Byrnes (ed.), *Learning Foreign and Second Languages: Perspectives in
            Research and Scholarship.* New York: MLA, 262–296.

Cameron, Deborah
    1985   *Feminism and Linguistic Theory.* New York: St. Martin's Press.
    (ed.) 1990 *The Feminist Critique of Language: A Reader.* 1st ed. London: Routledge.
    1995   *Verbal Hygiene.* London: Routledge.
    (ed.) 1998 *The Feminist Critique of Language: A Reader.* 2nd ed. London: Routledge.

Clark, Gregory
    1988   Writing as travel. *College Composition and Communication* 49, 1, 9–23.

Cook, Guy
    1995   Literary Theory and Pedagogy: The Conflict of Group and Individual.
            Paper presented at the AAAL Annual Conference, March 26, Long Beach,
            California.
    2000   *Language Play, Language Learning.* Oxford: Oxford University Press.

Crookes, Graham and Susan Gass (eds.)
    1993   *Tasks and Language Learning: Integrating Theory and Practice.* Cleve-
            don: Multilingual Matters.

Dollenmayer, David, Thomas Hansen, and Renate Hiller
    1984   *Neue Horizonte.* Lexington, MA: D.C. Heath.

Dollenmayer, David and Thomas Hansen
    1988   *Neue Horizonte*, 2nd ed. Lexington, MA: D.C. Heath.
    1996   *Neue Horizonte,* 4th ed. Lexington, MA: D.C. Heath.
    1999   *Neue Horizonte,* 5th ed. Lexington, MA: D.C. Heath.

Doughty, Catherine and Jessica Williams
    1998   *Focus on Form in Classroom Second Language Acquisition.* Cambridge:
            Cambridge University Press.

Fairclough, Norman
    1995   *Critical Discourse Analysis: The Critical Study of Language.* London:
            Longman.

1996   A reply to Henry Widdowson's 'Discourse Analysis: a critical view'. *Language and Literature* 5, 1, 49–56.

Francis, Gill and John Sinclair
1994   'I bet he drinks Carling Black Label': A riposte to Owen on corpus grammar. *Applied Linguistics* 15, 2, 190–200.

Hakuta, Kenji
1974   Prefabricated patterns and the emergence of structure in second language acquisition. *Language Learning* 24, 287–297.

Halliday, Michael
1978   *Language as Social Semiotic*. London: Edward Arnold

Hanks, William
1996   *Language and Communicative Practices*. Boulder, CO: Westview Press.

hooks, bell
1984   *Feminist Theory: From Margin to Center*. Boston: South End.
1989   *Talking Back: Thinking Feminist, Thinking Black*. Boston: South End.

Kaplan, Caren
1994   Politics of location as transnational practice. In Interpal, Grewal and Caren Kaplan (eds.) *Scattered Hegemonies*. 137–152.
1996   *Questions of Travel*. Durham: Duke University Press.

Kern, Richard
2000   *Literacy and Language Teaching*. Oxford: Oxford University Press.

Kramsch, Claire
1987   Foreign language textbooks' construction of foreign reality. *Canadian Modern Language Review*, 95–119.
1993   *Context and Culture in Language Teaching*. Oxford: Oxford University Press.
1994   In another tongue. *Profession '94*, 11–14.
1995   The applied linguist and the foreign language teacher: Can they talk to each other? In Cook, Guy and Barbara Seidlhofer (eds.), *Principle and Practice in Applied Linguistics: Studies in Honour of H.G.Widdowson*. Oxford: Oxford University Press, 43–56.
1998   Culture and self in language learning. In Cherrington, R. and L. Davcheva (eds.), *Teaching towards intercultural competence*. Conference Proceedings. Sofia, Bulgaria: The British Council, 14–29.

2000   Social discursive constructions of Self in L2 Learning. In James Lantolf (ed.), *Sociocultural Theory and Second Language Learning*. Oxford: Oxford University Press, 133–153.

Kramsch, Claire and Linda von Hoene
1995   The dialogic emergence of difference: Feminist explorations in the teaching and learning of foreign languages. In Stanton, Domna and Abigail Stewart (eds.), *Feminisms in the Academy*. Ann Arbor: University of Michigan Press, 330–357.

Kristeva, Julia
1976   *Revolution in Poetic Language*. New York: Columbia.

1991   *Strangers to Ourselves*. New York: Columbia.

Lacan, Jacques
1977   The Mirror Stage as formative of the function of the I. *Ecrits*. New York: W.W. Norton, 1–7.

Lakoff, Robin
1975   *Language and Woman's Place*. New York: Harper and Row.

Lave, Jean and Etienne Wenger
1991   *Situated Learning: Legitimate Peripheral Participation*. Cambridge: Cambridge University Press.

Lohnes, Walter and F.W. Strothmann
1970   *German: A Structural Approach*. Shorter Edition. New York: W.W. Norton.

Lugones, María
1990   Playfulness, 'World'-Travelling, and Loving Perception. In Anzaldúa, Gloria (ed.) *Making Face, Making Soul*. San Francisco: Aunt Lute, 390–402.

Mills, Sara
1995   *Feminist Stylistics*. London: Routledge

Moeller, Jack and Helmut Liedloff
1979   *Deutsch Heute,* 2nd ed. Boston: Houghton Mifflin.

Moeller, Jack, Helmut Liedloff, Winnifred Adolph, Gisela Hoecherl-Alden, Constance Kirmse, and John Lalande
1996   *Deutsch Heute*. 6th ed. Boston: Houghton Mifflin.

Moraga, Cherrie and Gloria Anzaldúa
1981   *This Bridge Called My Back. Writings by Radical Women of Color.* Watertown, MA: Persephone.

Owen, Charles
1993   Corpus-based grammar and the Heineken effect: Lexico-grammatical description for language learners. *Applied Linguistics* 14, 2, 167–187.

Poynton, Cate
1989   *Language and Gender: Making the Difference.* Oxford: Oxford University Press.

Pratt, Mary Louise
1992   *Imperial Eyes.* New York: Routledge.

Rich, Adrienne
1986   *Blood, Bread, and Poetry: Selected Prose, 1979–1985.* New York: Norton.

Silverman, Kaja.
1988   *The Acoustic Mirror.* Bloomington, IN: Indiana University Press.
1992   *Male Subjectivity at the Margins.* New York: Routledge.

Sinclair, John (ed.)
1990   *Collins Cobuild English Grammar.* London: Collins.
1991   *Corpus, Concordance, Collocation.* Oxford: Oxford University Press.

Stubbs, Michael
1996   *Text and Corpus Analysis.* Oxford: Blackwell.

Terrell, Tracy
1977   A natural approach to second language acquisition and learning. *Modern Language Journal* 61, 7, 325–337.

Terrell, Tracy, Erwin Tschirner, Brigitte Nikolai, and Herbert Genzmer
1996   *Kontakte: A Communicative Approach.* 3rd ed. San Francisco: McGraw Hill.

Threadgold, Terry
1997   *Feminist Poetics. Poiesis, Performance, Histories.* London: Routledge.

Toolan, Michael
1997   What is critical discourse analysis and why are people saying such terrible things about it? *Language and Literature* 6, 2, 83–103.

Trinh, Minh-ha
    1989   *Woman, Native, Other: Writing Postcoloniality and Feminism.* Blooming-
            ton, IN: Indiana University Press.

Troyanovich, John
    1972   American meets German. Cultural shock in the classroom. *Die Unter-
            richtspraxis* 5, 67–69.

von Hoene, Linda
    1995   Subject-in-process: Revisioning TA development through psychoanalytic,
            feminist, and postcolonial theory. In Kramsch, Claire (ed.), *Redefining the
            Boundaries of Language Study.* Boston: Heinle and Heinle, 39–60.

    1999   Imagining otherwise: Rethinking departments of foreign languages as de-
            partments of cross-cultural difference. *ADFL Bulletin* 30, 2, 26–29.

    in preparation. *Fantasmatic Nomadism: Psychoanalysis and Second Language Ac-
            quisition.*

Widdowson, Henry
    1992   *Practical Stylistics.* Oxford: Oxford University Press.

    1998   The theory and practice of critical discourse analysis. *Applied Linguistics*
            19, 1, 136–151.

Self-expression, gender, and community: A Japanese feminist English class

Cheiron McMahill

1. Introduction

The social impact of women's solidarity, accomplished through the medium of 'women's talk' or discourse, is seldom acknowledged in discussions of Japanese gender roles and the family. A 12/30/97 *Daily Yomiuri* article, for example, proclaims "Japan's divorce rate rising as age-old taboos fall away". It notes that one in three marriages now ends in divorce, and that the majority of divorces are now initiated by women. Factors such as women's increasing economic independence and the lessening of social stigma are cited. What is missing is the discourse of women, mothers and daughters, colleagues and friends, that both reflects and actively creates a culture in which women are valued regardless of their status as wives or mothers.

Even less recognized is the bilingual nature of women's social change and discourse, as Japanese-speaking[1] women appropriate English as a lingua franca for taking part in international lobbying, conferences, and research, and foreign-born, English-speaking women seek to support themselves economically in Japan, improve their Japanese, and gain access to Japanese feminist movements by offering their services as instructors, editors, and translators. Large numbers of women English students and instructors thus come together not only formally in university English departments and conversation schools, but in conversation exchanges and grassroots feminist[2] English classes across Japan (McMahill 1997; McMahill and Reekie 1996).

Japan-born female learners and their foreign-born English instructors share a belief that English ability gives women an edge in their careers and helps them achieve greater economic independence in a sexist job market. Activist teachers and students alike hope Japan-born women will use English itself as a tool for resisting their marginalization as non-native English-speaking women of color in international discourse (Fairclough 1992; Peirce 1986, 1995). Both learners and instructors may gain access to or create alternative linguistic and gender communities and ideologies through English language and teaching that serve them in both instigating and coping with personal and societal change.[3] These motivations or investments in learning and teaching English are obviously complex and contradictory. Here, I will show how they manifest themselves in the reality and imagination of a feminist English class community (Peirce 1995).

This article is a case study of one such grassroots feminist English class called "Colors of English". It was started by and for adult Japanese and Japan-born Korean women learners in the Tokyo area. First, I explain the historical and theoretical context of this particular community of practice. Next, I describe the site, coordinators, facilitators, participants, and my research methods. Then, I use excerpts from the class discussion to analyze and discuss how the participants use English and various feminist ideologies, especially the work of the American writer bell hooks, to deconstruct and pose alternatives to gender ideologies in their own families. Finally, I summarize the main points made by this study about English and the linguistic and gender identities and choices of the participants and facilitators.

2.   The context: feminist pedagogy, Japanese women's speech, and English

In order to create alternative societal structures that do not exclude or oppress women, radical and cultural feminists in the women's liberation movement of the 1960s and 70s in both the US and Japan experimented with various egalitarian and consensual forms of organization and decision-making (Tanaka 1995 a). One such structure was the largely leaderless consciousness-raising group in which women collectively created new theory and knowledge through the critical analysis of experience and emotion (Weiler 1994). Some of the participants in the women's movement went on to teach in universities, spearheading the development of women's, gender, and queer studies as academic disciplines. They re-envisioned the ideal role of the teacher as midwife rather than absolute authority (Belenky et al. 1997), as a radical working within the system to oppose the hierarchical organization of the university and the hegemony of established canons by raising students' intellectual consciousness about gender constructions and the invisibility of female experience (Lather 1984; Taylor 1995). How to achieve these goals best in classroom practice varies greatly from classroom to classroom, but in general there is a focus on giving students discursive space or "voice" and encouraging students to critically examine their own life experiences and connect these to historical and social structures (Middleton 1987); in other words, to empower students by helping them to develop a strong sense of not merely individual but collective identity and responsibility (Taylor 1995). These feminist critical pedagogies engage deeply with such critical and radical pedagogical theories as those of Freire (1971, 1973, 1985) and Giroux (1981, 1991), and struggle to address the complex intertwining of gender, language, and power with race, class, and sexual orientation (Collins 1990; De Castell and Bryson 1997; hooks 1994; King 1991; Lather 1987; McKellar 1989). Recently TESOL practitioners have applied feminist pedagogies to the university ESL classroom in the US (Schenke 1996; Vandrick 1994, 1995). This movement is active in Japanese universities in women's studies, cultural studies, and English as a Foreign Language (EFL) as well (Fujimura-Fanselow 1991, 1995, 1996; Smith and Yamashiro 1998). However, in the absence of radical institutional change, these experiments in empowering students and reimagining the roles of teacher and student in individual classrooms are to various degrees constrained and contradicted by the unequal and hierarchical structure in the wider university (Ellsworth 1989; Morgan 1996).

What is striking about the situation in Japan, however, is that since at least the 1970s Japan-born women have been taking feminist pedagogy into their own hands by forming countless study and discussion groups. One outgrowth of this feminist education movement has been to form and run "grassroots feminist English classes" and hire native English-speaking feminist women as instructors. I personally first got involved with facilitating feminist English classes in 1982, and over the years have heard about dozens of small classes or study groups around the country. In a survey of the organizers and/or facilitators of six different feminist English classes (McMahill and Reekie 1996), I found that the classes are with a few exceptions created and run privately and not for profit, and are often related informally to a non-governmental organization (NGO). Participants are virtually all-female, possibly because men are not interested in taking part or not active in circles where they would hear about the classes, and in some (few) cases are officially excluded by the decision of the organizers and/or participants. Without exception, the classes combine linguistic goals (usually improving one's English) with feminist goals such as translating feminist books or presenting at international women's conferences.

The participants themselves manage the classes, decide which foreign women to hire or invite, and negotiate the class content with these foreign women. The foreign women may be "uninvited" or fired if the participants are unhappy with them. The position of foreign women can thus be understood more as cultural and linguistic resource than institutional authority. The fact that our languages and experiences are privileged as resources is of course due to the currency given English and Western culture on a global level. Nevertheless, many of us involved as facilitators or guest speakers express an interest in developing counter-hegemonic feminist and critical pedagogies and see our work as a chance to combine education and social activism. These classes thus offer a rare opportunity to observe second language classroom interaction between foreign and Japan-born women that is under the control of the learners, and, compared to other school settings, outside the immediate constraints of hierarchical and male-dominated classrooms and institutions.

As for the motivation of the participants, I found that many of them believe that fluency in another language, especially English, helps them compete in the job market and also participate more actively in international events and thus is seen as congruent with feminist goals for oneself and for other women. This is in spite of heated debates in Japanese society and in the feminist English classes themselves about the role of English in perpetuating the hegemony of Western culture (Matsumoto 1996; McMahill 1997; Nakamura 1997; Park 1997; Pennycook 1994, 1995; Phillipson 1992; Tsuda 1994). In addition, some Japanese-speaking women are also interested in English because of its popular association with the discourses of feminism, as evidenced in the preference for English loan-words such as *uman ribu* for 'women's liberation', *feminisuto* for 'feminist', *jendaa* for 'gender', and *gei* for 'gay', instead of native Japanese words using Chinese characters (Summerhawk, McMahill, and McDonald 1998). The reasons for the association between gender equality and English are complex. Equality of the sexes was first written into Japanese law with the post-war constitution in 1947 (Fujimura-Fanselow and Kameda 1995). However, the status and rights of women have fluctuated greatly throughout the history of the various regions now called Japan. My own home of Gunma is known as the land of *kaa kaa denka* 'households ruled by wives' because women's traditional work of raising silkworms, making paper, and growing konjak roots brought in an important source of income and raised their social status. Women have organized to demand greater legal and political rights and societal participation independent of the West since at least the Popular Rights and suffrage movements of the Meiji Period (Buckley 1997; Fujieda 1995; Kaneko 1995; Pharr 1977). The fact remains, though, that women's history is not a focus in Japanese school textbooks (Fujieda 1995; Fujimura-Fanselow 1995). This may explain why popular images persist in and out of Japan of feminism as a Western import and Japanese women as being subjugated until after World War II.

As Pavlenko (1998, and this volume) notes in her study of the autobiographical narratives of bilingual writers, the ability to understand a second language can give one access to alternative gender ideologies, and the struggle to express oneself in a second language can entail the reconstruction of all aspects of one's social identity, including gender. What sorts of ideologies might a Japanese-speaking woman acquiring English be attracted to? As Kubota (1999) points out, much of the theory and research comparing English and Japanese communication tends to assume and reinforce essentialist cultural dichotomies between the East and the West. Much as paradigms presuming innate gender differences may shape the findings of applied linguistics research, in the field of cross-cultural communication, a focus on differences results in a construction of English communication as more direct and specific than Japanese, as less context-dependent and allowing less ellipsis (Hiraga and Turner 1995; Matsubayashi 1995; Matsumoto 1995; Romaine 1994; Rose 1996; Shibatani 1990). Women may be attracted to this mystique of English directness and specificity as a way to resist or even escape linguistic gender roles that proscribe a lack of assertion for females (McMahill and Reekie 1996; Siegal 1994, 1996; Tsuruta 1996).

Other linguistic work on gender in Japanese also reinforces ideologies of the Japanese language itself as oppressive to women. Lexically-based sexism, such as the lack of acceptable alternatives for the word *shujin* or 'master' for 'husband', receives much attention (Abe 1995; Nakata 1996). Research on *jo-seigo* 'women's speech' posits that Japanese sociolinguistic rules require women to use a less assertive or more polite style than men (Abe 1995; Reynolds 1993), as well as higher voice pitch and different intonation patterns (Mori 1997; Ohara 1997, and this volume). Further, standard Japanese is widely chastised for an abundance of not only sex-preferential but sex-exclusive terms, such as the use of distinct first-person pronouns, terms of third party address, and sentence-final particles for men and women (Ide 1979; Kanemaru 1997; McGloin 1997; Reynolds 1998 a, b).

As with all research on language and gender, care must be taken not to stereotype Japanese women's speech. The Tokyo or "standard" variety of Japanese spoken by young to middle-aged middle- and upper-class college-educated professionals in the major cities has tended to be studied, often out of context, to the exclusion of other speech communities (Abe 1995; interview with Aoki in Buckley 1997; Reynolds 1998 a,b). Much of the early research on women's speech has been criticized for this and for its anecdotal nature; when actual data is analyzed, there is much variation in conformity to the type of speech described as exemplifying women's speech (see Ohara's chapter; Okamoto 1995). Nevertheless, the idea that there is a proper, feminine way of speaking in Japanese is a powerful ideology, and as Okamoto notes, the decision not to adopt this way of speaking may be culturally "marked" (Okamoto 1995: 314–315). The women taking part in the feminist English classes I have studied are in fact the very college-educated, middle-class Tokyo dwellers whose speech has been collected as examples of "women's speech". Thus speaking in a foreign language such as English, while obviously entailing a

struggle with another set of linguistic gender ideologies, may be seen as a gendered linguistic choice, which offers them a linguistic space for re-examining
more consciously the norms of gendered speech and identity in Japanese.[4]

More recently, and in the class under discussion in this article, Japan-born
feminists and students of women's studies have been drawn to the discourses of
black and Asian feminist writers and theorists. They see these discourses as
providing them with useful tools for constructing new identities as both women
and people of color, and in the case of Japan-born Koreans, as cultural and/or
linguistic minorities (Hotta 1997; Sugiyama 1996). Most importantly for this
study, many women find identity construction and community-building inextricably linked. In feminist English classes, friendships with their Japan-born
co-participants are at least as much of an attraction as the presence of a foreign-
born facilitator, and the discussion itself is part of the process of creating an alternative gender discourse community.

3.   Overview of this research

3.1. The site

The class termed "Colors of English" started in 1996 and is organized by a
women's counseling service and publishing house called Femix. It is held
weekly in a meeting room in a women's center in Tokyo. About 50 women
have attended it in total over the years; an average of 15 women register per
term. I co-facilitated this particular class for two and a half years, seeing students on the average of once a month. In this study I undertake an in-depth
analysis of a single specific class I facilitated on November 28, 1997. The class
is billed as a "feminist" English class. The first flier explained the class goals as
follows:

> Why English? Why does English have the power of an international language,
> and why do we have to learn it? For women who don't want to simply imitate
> white middle-class English, but who wish to use English as a means for expres-
> sing and liberating yourselves, as a common language for sharing your thoughts
> and encountering women of all races and ethnicities ... this Fall, Femix will
> launch a feminist English class aimed at your empowerment (author's trans-
> lation).

3.2. The coordinators

"Colors of English" is run by two coordinators. One, referred to in the transcripts as P6, is the director of Femix and handles the class logistics and publicity. She is Japanese and draws on English books and articles on feminist therapy, psychology, and education as resources both for her work as a counselor and as a publisher of the magazine *Kurashi to kyoiku o tsunagu We*.[5] She started the class because:

> I now has a strong feeling that learning English can be a great weapon for Japanese women to get assertiveness. As we Japanese are not encouraged to express ourselves, especially our feelings, we need a sort of training to be articulate and assertive, which I think are most vital issues for a Japanese feminism (from a written response to early drafts of this article).[6]

The other coordinator handles the recruitment of instructors and curriculum coordination of the class. A Japanese-English translator and student of women's studies and linguistics, she is a Japan-born Korean who has participated in feminist NGO activities on an international level. She is responsible for the multi-cultural vision of the class and the decision to ask English-speaking women of various ethnic backgrounds and nationalities to take turns facilitating the classes once a month, or as one-time guest speakers.

3.3. The facilitators

Conscious preference is thus given to women of color in order to challenge the widespread linking of English to "white" ethnicity (Norton 1997). Thus, past instructors have included women of African and Asian descent, in addition to European. At the time of this research, one regular instructor was Chinese-American, one Japanese, one a white Canadian, and one, myself, a white American. In terms of linguistic diversity, almost all of the regular facilitators have been native speakers of standard North American English.[7] These English-speaking women act as cultural and linguistic resources and discussion facilitators rather than as traditional instructors. That is, the participants and coordinators generate or suggest many of the class topics and activities, and rather than formally teaching English language skills, the facilitators assist participants in their self-expression or comprehension of materials as needed.

I was the facilitator of the particular class analyzed here. Participants know me as in my thirties, white, American, a full-time university instructor, mother, Japanese speaker, feminist, divorced, and partner of a Japanese man. I had met the curriculum coordinator in a feminist group about 15 years previously in Tokyo, and ran into her again at various events when I moved back to Japan in 1992. I was interested in helping with the Colors of English class because of my desire to apply feminist pedagogy to the teaching of EFL in my university classes; this class gave me an ideal environment in which to try out new ideas. I continued offering to help facilitate the class because of the wonderful women I met there and the sense of community I enjoyed. In these senses, my motivation was similar to the participants as it was both academic and personal.

As mentioned above, the facilitators usually decide the topics of their classes in consultation with the curriculum coordinator. A selective review of audio tapes of twenty-five class sessions indicates that the following main themes have been treated in the class: ethnic identities, female identities, feminism, life choices, discrimination in employment, struggles with learning English, English (linguistic) imperialism, self-expression through discussion and free writing, personal histories, personal philosophies, relaxation, and healing.

3.4. The participants

In the class analyzed here, there are seven participants (including the two co-ordinators), all in their thirties and forties. The English proficiency of the class as a whole is high-intermediate to advanced. All of the participants studied English for six to eight years during their formal schooling in Japan and have taken private English conversation lessons throughout their adult lives. Time in English-speaking countries is noted below, and it is clear that the participants are already bilingual and bicultural or trilingual/tricultural to various degrees. Here is a brief overview of how they identify themselves in questionnaire responses and in the class discussion:

Participant 1: Japanese, married, homemaker, mother; has lived in the US as an adult

Participant 2: Japan-born Korean, single, full-time worker, lives alone, grew up bilingual in Korean and Japanese, attended university in an English-speaking country

Participant 3: Japanese, single, full-time worker, lives alone; must converse with foreign colleagues in English at work

Participant 4: Japanese, single, full-time worker, lives with parents; frequently visits English-speaking countries

Participant 5: Japanese, single, free-lance worker, lives with parents; lived in England for four years as a child, recently spent eight months in the US

Participant 6: Class coordinator, Japanese, married, full-time worker, mother; lived in England as adult, frequently travels abroad and reads English publications for her work

Participant 7: Class coordinator, Japan-born Korean, single, full-time Japanese-English translator, lives with mother; grew up monolingual in Japanese, attended university in an English-speaking country

As for their motivations for taking the class, in their journal entries,[8] class participants stress their interest in becoming more linguistically assertive and intellectually independent. A typical entry by participant 5 reads:

> My weak point is to do self-expression, but this class'es teacher'es are very powerful so I can get a lot of energy. I think this class is very different with another English class. Another English class'es are only English but this class is not. We can learn a lot of things- Feminist pedagogy, other people's idea, to express ourselves and so on.

The participants also combine English with feminist study because of the chance to develop a strong self-identity and improve their English for professional reasons. As participant 4 stressed in a questionnaire response:

> One of the most important things about me is just being myself. I want others to know my true intentions. Because since I was little, I always make a distinction between what I say and actually think. I hope I can say what I think in this class... I've never thought to combine the topics and style of this class with English practice. It's a kind of experiment for me.

At the same time, she notes that she needs English communication for her work. Many women, such as participant 3, stress the attractiveness of the participants and classroom community:

> I would like to study other idea and culture. I also like English. Moreover I am interesting in American woman's movement... I like Friday evening very much. Before the class, I often felt lonely. I struggle against conflicts. For example,

male society, verbal violence, prejudice, discrimination. I meet many friends in this class. I forget my stress ... because we exchange opinions, I get wide knowledge (questionnaire response).

This community seems to have different discourse rules from other "public" spaces in participant 1's daily life:

I'm a housewife now. Some of housewives around me stay home all day and some work as part-time workers. I think these people, including me, can't say their opinions everywhere. In my case, I can say my opinion at home but I can't at PTA meeting or to my husband's friends. If I have my own ideas and it's a little different from "normal" people's idea, once I say, I'm regarded as a kind of "strange" "strong" people (journal entry).

Participant 1 came to resist such discourse rules through her experience of living in another culture:

When I moved to the US, I noticed that the problem was not only my speaking English ability but also what I had inside and the best way to express my opinion. To express myself, I had to know about myself, for example, my background, philosophy, interests, future, ability, etc. However, it is not easy to seek self-identity and self-expression in Japan because we are not raised in such a way. Unconsciously, we are taught that it is the best way to be "normal" people and as same as everyone (journal entry).

Part of becoming aware of themselves as individuals is learning about their differences with others and the diversity of identities within the class. As participant 5 reflected,

I really enjoyed the class [by an African-American facilitator] last time. And I came to be interested in Asian-American, African-American women's history. As I spent 4 years in England when I was a child and spent 8 months in US recently, I can understand what these non-white women have to go through (journal entry).

Learning about the experiences of Japan-born Koreans in the class is also an eye-opener for the other participants. Participant 2 wrote about her experiences being bullied as a child and her anger when she realized that, as a foreign national, she would never be allowed to become a public school teacher in Japan. Participant 1 responded:

Before this class, I didn't know about minority esp. women. e.g. Korean American Korean Japanese. Before I had few knowledge about them, and I didn't try to know about them. I realized their status in Japan was lower than I imagined at this class. I was shocked and now I try to say it among my Japanese friends (journal entry).

3.5. Research methods

It is typical in the feminist English classes I have studied to use a reading, poem, song, video, or newspaper article dealing with women's issues as a catalyst for a speaking activity of some kind (McMahill 1997; McMahill and Reekie 1996). I chose the following excerpt from a memoir by the Black American feminist writer whose pen name is "bell hooks".[9] Students were given the passage a week ahead of time and asked to prepare their opinions for a discussion on its theme of mother/daughter relationships.

> I am always fighting with mama. Everything has come between us. She no longer stands between me and all that would hurt me. She is hurting me. This is my dream of her – that she will stand between me and all that hurts me, that she will protect me at all cost. It is only a dream. In some way I understand that it has to do with marriage, that to be the wife to the husband she must be willing to sacrifice even her daughters for his good. For the mother it is not simple. She is always torn. She works hard to fulfill his needs, our needs. When they are not the same she must maneuver, manipulate, choose. She has chosen. She has decided in his favor. She is a religious woman. She has been told that a man should obey god, that a woman should obey man, that children should obey their fathers and mothers, particularly their mothers. I will not obey. (hooks 1996: 81)

I use separate audio and video recordings, transcribed and triangulated with written and spoken comments by class coordinators and participants as a basis for analyzing the classroom discourse of the subsequent discussion. I also draw on participants' journal entries from the first nine months of the class, and their responses to a questionnaire I gave them just prior to the class studied here.

Because of the lack of previous research, I have borrowed from various theoretical disciplines in order to describe and explain all-female discourse in a "feminist" EFL classroom. I used certain key concepts of the interactional sociolinguistic approach developed by Goffman (1981), Gumperz (1982), and Schiffrin (1994). Within this approach, discourse is viewed as an interaction within which identities and relationships are constantly being constructed, and whose meaning can only be interpreted using contextual cues. Contextual cues refer to the parameters or participation framework of the specific interaction, the institutional setting, and background factors such as culture and ideology.

In the case of the Colors of English class, I take such contextual cues to be the individual situations of the participants, the values and traditions of Japanese culture, and feminism – especially the ideologies and traditions of feminist consciousness-raising and feminist pedagogy as in the work of hooks (1994), Vandrick (1994, 1995), and Weiler (1994). In this particular context, then, I pay special attention to the ideological context in explaining the significance of the utterances of speakers and the interaction of the group.

In addition, the work on classroom discourse analysis by van Lier (1988) and Fairclough (1989, 1992) provides some basis for comparing the turn-taking structure and facilitator – participant roles in the Colors of English class to more formal classrooms as well as to unstructured conversation.[10]

4.   Analysis and discussion

4.1. Personal experience as a source of authority

As noted by Schiffrin (1996), the topic of mother/daughter relationships, with their tension and ambivalence, tends to elicit a wealth of personal stories or narratives from women focusing on different expectations and obligations between their own and their mothers' or daughters' generations, and this is indeed what ensued in the class. The first participant (P1) sets the stage for the discussion by aligning herself with the mother in the bell hooks passage. P1 questions the reading not by referring to established theories or authorities, but on the basis of her own personal experiences and feelings. This respect for lived rather than learned truths has been a guiding principle of feminist consciousness-raising as well as Black feminist thought (Collins 1990; Weiler 1994).

In the passage, we only hear the author's interpretation of her mother; the mother is accused with no opportunity to respond. P1, speaking as a mother herself, voices a desire to protect her daughters:

P1:   For me, after reading this book, I was a little shocked, because I remembered about me and my daughter, not like not the relationship between me and my mother, I remembered me and my daughter.
    And um ... then my daughter is hurt, I want to protect-protect her if something happened I wanted to protect her, but this sentence,
    (She's hurting me,)

If I'm hurting my daughter, I'm hurting them, I didn't know the fact, it's very miserable situation for me, so I wanted to ask *them* I'm hurting you? but I couldn't do it ...

She challenges the other participants to let their mothers know their true feelings by reframing the problem so that daughters bear at least part of the burden of responsibility for this breakdown in communication:

P1: Many- at many other family, mother wants to talk her children but children don't want,
so their reply is just "sou" or "betsu ni"-ah "betsu ni" is a common expression-"betsu ni"-
"betsu ni" means they don't want to say about anything-

I attempt here to bring her back to her personal experience with her own daughters rather than speaking about Japanese society in general:

F: You mentioned about not wanting to know about what your daughters think or being afraid to ask them?
P1: Even I ask them they don't say real thinking,
maybe they say "oh you're a great mother, oh I like you very much."
Ps: ((laughter))
P1: To keep our relationship good, it's a good way they know,
and I also say them, to them, "oh you're a good [child for me"=
Ps: [((laughter))
P1: =but it's a part real, it's real, but um..further- further talking, more talking, maybe now it's a little difficult thing ...

She says she is willing to listen, but no one gives her any honest answers. She is not going to be put off with *betsu ni* or 'it's nothing.'

4.2. Emotions as a source of knowledge

The next three participants respond to P1 also from their personal experiences as daughters, explaining how they are silenced or empowered to speak to their mothers and why. In doing so, they seem to illustrate the psychological struggle of a daughter for an authentic self without sacrificing a close and nurturing relationship with her mother (Westcott 1997). The second participant (P2) testifies that because she wants different things than her mother does, her mother feels she is betraying their shared gender and ethnic identities:

P2:   Well, I read this over and over because- because I-I felt sympathy to this
       author.
       And um, I think I'm always fighting with my mother because, I don't
       know the real reason but what I want what I want to do or what I want
       something is always totally different from my mother's, and always my
       mother says I'm- I'm doing it only only for   you=
Ps: Ah!
P2:   =that's very a
       kind of burden for me.

I try here to characterize her mother's behavior as sacrificing, although she
seems to prefer the word "torn" from the reading:

F: Like she's sacrificing herself for you?
P2:   Yeah, and what's more also I thought, I'm a Korean and she's a Korean
       woman, and in this sentence, "she always torn", she's always very torn, so
       I felt guilty being as a kind of "bad girl" to her.

Of course, bell hooks is writing from her experience not only as a female but as
a member of a minority group in American society. It is noteworthy here that
only P2, as a Japan-born Korean, calls attention to the importance of racial or
ethnic oppression in understanding the guilt toward the mother implicit in the
reading text; according to Hotta (1997), it is mainly Japan-born Korean and
Chinese minorities, such as Jung (1994) and Tai (1995), who have turned the
attention of Japanese feminists to the multi-layered nature of oppression and
identity. P2 is not just unburdening herself emotionally here, but is offering important clues to theorizing the complexities of her relationship with her mother;
in other words, feelings are not "just feelings" with no place in "rational" discussion (Weiler 1994).

     Moving on, one of P2's mother's official duties as a mother appears to be
protecting her through mediating between her and her father; speaking out was
dangerous because it risked her father's wrath:

P2:   And also I reminded me of the relationship between my mother and my
       father. She didn't want him get angry- got angry with children, and always
       said that, please calm down to me, not to my father, you should not say that
       word, before I- before saying, you should not say that word because /?/

As facilitator, I again attempt to summarize and clarify what she is trying to
say:

F: It was like her responsibility to keep you from making your father angry?
P2:   Yeah, so ...

The third participant (P3) juxtaposes with P2's experience her and her mother's struggle to come to terms with their differences in the face of their great intimacy and identification:

P3:   =I always talk about many things, I-we talk about many things the neighborhood or job or family.
       My mother is similar to me, ["sokkuri"=
Ps: [((laughter))
P3:   and my character and face and talk are the *same,* like *twin.*
Ps: ((Laughter))

At one point, their close identification became strained when she did not follow her mother's advice and it became clear that she would not make the same choices her mother had. They were able to come to terms with their differences, however, and repair their relationship. This was thanks to her mother's ability to not pressure her and her sister about marrying by recasting that decision as a personal rather than a family or community problem. Notice also that P3 thus introduces the topic of societal pressure to marry conveyed by the mother, which other participants then build upon:

P3:   Um ... I have uh I have elder sister, two women don't get married yet, but she uh my mother worry about anything, but she uh decide this problem is personal, ah, oh so my mother enjoy her life,
       and I'm single, it's MY responsibility, not parents' job.
       She maybe she wait,
       but now it's independent each other.

The next participant (P4) recounts her long-term strategy to try and improve her relationship with her mother. She intends to separate herself from her mother and her mother's marriage to her father even if her mother will not:

P4:   =I don't want to live with my parents anymore=
Ps: ((laughter))
P4:   =and because, my, I, I don't like my father,
       because very my father is typical Japanese father
Ps: ((laughter))

P4:   =and very, and he thinks about only of himself,
       and my mother always obeys my father,
       and so it's not very- it's not so problem in my family,
       but um the anytime anytime my mother obeys my father,
       and I'm I'm so um irritate,
       so in that time I helped my father,
       but my mind is-my mind don't want to do that,
       so and uh but um, nobody argued about that in my family,
       so and um, probably my mother is double standard,
       she understands uh um.. my father do something all himself,
       but uh she never says about that,
       and uh, um, I don't know so,
       before I wanted to um, rebuilt a family relationship
       but, now I *give up* yes=
Ps: ((laughter))

This giving up, though, is not a passive action; instead, she makes a remarkable declaration that she intends to create a new type of family that is not based on marriage:

P4:   =give up maybe, so probably I should to make my family so even *own self*, single is probably I can say a *family,* yes=

Although economically independent with a stable job, she has been a devoted daughter and has lived with her parents past the age of forty. In Japan, since the imposition on the masses of the *ie* or household system of the samurai class during the Meiji Restoration, adult children have tended to live with their parents until they marry, the eldest son remaining even after marriage (Aoki 1986). For daughters especially, to live alone away from the family's supervision still risks sullying their sexual reputations and lowering their chances of being selected as a 'good', i.e., malleable and sexually inexperienced, bride in the future. In addition, as parents grow older, it is a source of comfort to have a child living with them to help out. Finally, in anticipating their deaths, parents hope that their children and grandchildren will maintain the family tomb and continue to perform the proper Buddhist or Shinto rites (Lebra 1984). Although traditionally these were the eldest son's duties, with fewer children being born, they now fall upon daughters as well. Creating her own family as a single woman would therefore seem to open up both herself and her mother to societal criticism and feelings of shame, not to mention fears of losing the support of children in both the parents' and the daughter's eventual old age and death. As

Ide notes, choosing not to marry or have children can seem frightening and dangerous because Japanese-speaking women know that "there is little or no state support for the elderly, and they can expect to live at least the last decade of life as widows dependent on their children" (Buckley 1997: 47). In the coda of her narrative, however, P5 resolves this radical choice by glossing her action as a positive example for her mother. What seemed initially a rejection of her mother can thus be redefined as nurturing behavior, because her own self-acceptance and acting in accordance with her own desires may actually lead the way to a more authentic life for her mother also. I try to bring her back to what is happening right now with her parents:

F: Are you living with your parents now?
P4: ((Nods))   =so I hope my mother lives own her life.
Ps: Mmm.
F: "Own her life" means away from your father? Away from you?
P4: [Both.
Ps: [((laughter))
P4: Yeah so and um she thinks about uh par-fathers or me,
      she never thinks about own self,
      and uh,
      I think she should think about her self, own self,
      and uh to make friends more or something to find a hobby,
      and if she wants to divorce it's *okay* yes.
      yeah.

In white American middle-class culture, we value "talking things out" face to face with someone when we are having trouble with a relationship. My next question seems to imply that this is what she should do:

F: Have you ever talked to her about that?
P4: Mm hm, yes, I [recommend=
Ps: [((laughter))
P4:   =to her about divorce.
      She answered, "if I win the [lottery"=
Ps: [((laughter))
P4:   =she will ...

P4 had stated earlier that she is still in the child's position in her family. Here, however, she seems to be reversing roles by advising her mother on divorce; one can imagine that she would back up this advice with emotional and economic assistance to her mother. In fact, there has been a surge in Japan of young women choosing to remain single and older women initiating divorces (Tanaka 1995b; Yoshizumi 1995). P4's reports of her conversations with her mother seem to link these two phenomena together in a way statistics cannot.

4.3. Personal narrative as a form of self-disclosure

All of the participants so far have used autobiography, or personal narrative, to persuasively argue their positions on the class topic. Personal narrative may dominate in feminist discourse for many reasons: it asserts the authenticity of one's own lived experience against, in this case, the "common-sense" of patriarchal society (hooks 1994; Rosen 1988); it creates rapport and thus in this case fosters female solidarity (Tannen 1988); it is face-saving in the case of disagreement, as it offers an embedded account of why one's opinions may differ from another's, again maintaining social solidarity (Schiffrin 1994).

The next participant (P5) now uses personal narrative to dramatize a current conflict with her mother:

P5: Um actually in a few days, I had a very very very tough time, and so, when I think of that I start to cry, so please don't look at me.
Ps: ((laughter))
P5: And um it was I think it was on Wednesday,
I and mother was talking about nothing, just stupid things,
then I- I don't remember, but the topic was just slided- slided on marriage, and uh uh she she suddenly talked about her friend – um actually "biyooin- biyooin no sensei" -"ano"- she's her friend-she talked to her that-"she" means the woman- excuse me how you [say=
F: [the beautician?
P5:   =the beautician knows me very much too, and the beautician told my mother that uh um, that uh, "I can't believe about the parents and you because-" ((laughter)) [((starts crying)) ...

P5 is relating here a case of "reported criticism" in which her mother, rather than criticizing her directly, reports the neighborhood beautician's criticism of her as a mother because P5, who is over thirty, has not married and produced children. While there are many positive aspects to such close relationships among the people in local areas and the tendency to patronize neighborhood businesses, being watched closely and commented upon may strongly influence conformity to local gender roles. Lebra (1984) also reports many instances of neighborhood gossip in Japan in pressuring women to marry. Because in my first culture, ideologies concerning individual privacy would make it unusual for a neighbor to even know about, let alone pass judgment on my marital status, in a somewhat shocked tone I try to get her to spell out her neighbor's expectations for me:

F: [What are you supposed to be doing according to the beautician? What should you be doing?
P5:   Maybe marriage, and that's all, I think.

According to Tannen (1989:105), such reported criticism is very damaging: "... opinions expressed in one's absence seem to have an enhanced reality, the incontestable truth of the overheard", and P5's reaction seems to bear this out:

P5:   then I couldn't stop crying and I couldn't leave the house and I-I just left home,
      and I couldn't come I, back to home until 11 or 12 in the night ((laugh)),
      and yesterday in the night I was just- I couldn't stop crying still,
      and I-I don't know how to sleep,

Tannen (1989: 105) observes that Americans typically direct their anger and criticism in response to reported criticism toward the quoted source rather than the speaker who conveys it. However, P5 seems to realize that the reported criticism was a strategy her mother utilized to pressure her daughter to marry, as reference to the opinions of others is one of the most common ways to discipline children in Japan. She immediately confronted her mother:

P5:   So I just talked to my mother, "if I am married, is it satisfied to you, *only* if I am married," and she said "yes" because,
      'cause she- my- her emotion was very hot at that time-
      I know that she doesn't think so,
      but it's part of true she hopes that I get married before now from now or anytime,
      she worries about my situation very much.

P5, pressed to analyze her mother's expectations more closely, indicates that women's happiness and security is dependent not only on having children, but on having grandchildren. One of a daughter's obligations is therefore to supply her and her husband's parents with these grandchildren; likewise, one of a mother's obligations is to raise a daughter to do so. P5's failure to marry and reproduce therefore violates not only her obligations to her mother, i.e., makes her a bad daughter, but makes her mother look as though she has failed in her obligations as a mother, i.e., been a bad mother. This mechanism illustrates how the obligations and expectations of women's gender roles are maintained from generation to generation through women themselves, in spite of the pain and suffering these roles may bring.

P5:   and I thought she was on my side,
        but yeah but when I was over thirty years old the situation is- has been changing,
F: She's starting to think [maybe it's gone too [far?
P5:   [Yes.   [Yes um.

"I thought she was on my side" may indicate P5's sense of betrayal at her mother endorsing the patrilineal and patrilocal customs of Japan that require a daughter not only to marry but to leave behind her membership in her own family and join a husband's household. As Ueno points out:

> A daughter is still seen as someone who will eventually marry out of the household and leave. Japanese girls grow up aware that if there is a son, he will take priority over them. It is a life lived in the shadow of abandonment, if not in childhood, then at marriage, when she is sent out into another household (in Buckley 1997: 286).

I seem to imply that perhaps her mother hasn't changed her basic position, and doesn't in fact want to abandon her, but was just succumbing to societal pressure in a moment of weakness:

F: She's starting- she feels pressure too sometimes-
P5:   Yes, she feels pressure too because all of most of her friends has babies now, and she was talked by them their friends like=
F: Grandchildren!
P5:   = "grand-
        children are really cute or so sweet or you have to see your own grandchild" and I-I understand what she thinks,
        it's very difficult for me.

Here I am anticipating her next word, finishing her sentence for her, out of a sense of solidarity with her due to my personal experience with my Japanese in-laws, who dote on my children from both my first and current marriage.

They had solicited twenty arranged marriage interviews for my husband prior to our own (unarranged) marriage in the effort to get him to become a proper *shakaijin* or full-fledged member of society. In modern families, this means work, marriage, and fatherhood for a man and housekeeping, marriage, motherhood, and care of her in-laws for a woman (Sukumune et al. 1993).

In fact, women's ability to give birth and their role as mother have been held in high esteem since ancient times. Yamagata (1999) sees links between the metaphors of childbirth in Japanese mythology with the way people think about the Japanese islands themselves and women's sexuality in the modern era. In ancient myths, the Japanese archipelago itself is lovingly envisioned as a litter of children while pregnant women's tendency to seclude themselves and restrict their activities echo the sacred rites of the goddesses and priestesses. The problem from a Japanese feminist viewpoint is not to reject this deeply-rooted ideology of childhood and motherhood in Japan, sometimes referred to as *boseiai*,[11] or 'maternal love', but to criticize the prejudice, discrimination, and even violence it can lead to for the women and men who do not or cannot conform to it through marriage and biological reproduction (Kanazumi 1997). In fact, I and two participants in the class that night are married and have children, but conspicuously refrain from talking about male partners, marriage, and children as positive sources of identity not just in this class, but in all of the classes I took part in. In this case, our *not* talking about certain (socially approved) aspects of our identities represents active resistance to the dogma of compulsory heterosexuality, marriage, and motherhood.

To go back to P5, to share such a personal problem would be very rare in an English class in another setting. The fact that it occurs here indicates that this class has special rules and is a place where participants are expected to actively voice their real feelings and problems. It may, however, not be uncommon in a feminist classroom: in both classes I observed at a completely unrelated feminist English site, in which a Japanese woman was the facilitator, a similar instance of self-disclosure occurred at a similar point in the class (McMahill 1997).

P5 uses an array of rhetorical devices for narrating the conflict with her mother and enhancing the listeners' involvement. One is her frequent reference to herself. Another is repetition: e.g., "I had a *very very very* tough time". Another is the use of emphatic particles such as "very" and "just." Another is parallel structure, which she emphasizes even further through her stress of the word "couldn't": e.g., "I *couldn't* stop crying and I *couldn't* leave the house and I-I just left home, and I *couldn't* come I, back to home until 11 or 12 in the night (laugh), and yesterday in the night I was just- I *couldn't* stop crying ...". Another is the use of direct quotes, as in "grandchildren are really cute or so sweet or you have to see your own grandchild". Finally, her extensive details create a vivid image of the conflict, while her tears and laughter clue us in to its emotional tone (Chafe 1982; Tannen 1989).

The result is that a connection has now been forged between the reading and the situation of the participants. At this point we are culturally and linguistically recontextualizing the reading and the topic of mother/daughter conflict in earnest and beginning to use them as tools for consciousness-raising and problem-solving.

4.4. Moving from victim to survivor

At this point, there is also, significantly, a shift in the turn-taking structure. We had been moving around the circle in a formal and constrained structure in which the facilitator opened and closed each person's turn and selected the next speaker. The immediacy of P5's problem, however, redefines the constraints of the classroom discourse rules so that participants can engage in genuine discussion, i.e., self-select their turn and build freely on each other's remarks without the facilitator necessarily intervening (van Lier 1988).

P5's problem is also reframed in ideological rather than subjective terms. This can be seen in two ways: one is through a shifting of the reference terms of the conversation away from P5 and her mother to "a woman", "women", and so on. Another is through indirect criticism of P5's mother's behavior by applying the feminist concept of "internalized sexism," in this case how women themselves oppress other women:

P4:   But sometimes a woman give-give a like that pressure to woman, women, yeah. And colleagues uh who worked at the same office before so sometimes uh come-comes to office I work, so and they very show off their life, that "I have good babies and good life, or you still work same position" or like that-yeah, it's a big pressure.

Notice how women in general, rather than P5's mother in particular, are accused of oppressing other women. This ideological construction of marriage and childbearing as natural, beneficial, and proper for all women is then countered in the class by a critical view of the family as a patriarchal institution which replicates itself by the legal and economic control of women, their sexuality, and their offspring (Aoki 1986; Ueno 1994). I use my identity as foreigner to bring this into the discussion by eliciting information on Japanese culture from one of the coordinators:

P7:   It- often it's related to the woman's reproductive capability, it's also, after a certain age the woman is no longer on the marriage market.

F: But during that time people are like you know, "It's not your womb, it's society's womb! You have to use it to reproduce! "

P7:   I think when people talk about marriage it's not relation to man and woman, it's a family, so marriage is implies the woman supposed to have a baby, supposed to have a family, so the pressure is as far as the womb is capable of reproducing.

F: So marriage is a kind of code word, or a kind of symbol, an indirect way to say, "reproduce"?

P7:   Yes.

In feminist consciousness-raising, women also support each other in getting in touch with their repressed anger and refusing to view themselves as passive victims.[12] P2 does this indirectly on P5's behalf by testifying that the pressure to marry is unfair gender-linked suffering, moving the tone of the class emotionally from hurt to outrage:

P2:   In these days, men-men don't get such a pressure to get married compared to women 'cause they /?/-
      I wonder why women have to have suffer such pressure even now because I think a single life is ...
      One of my coworkers, she's in-she's in forties, and she married
      but she said that she had to marry, so she married, but she said if she- if she were in twenty or thirty in now, she said, "I don't marry 'cause I can live by myself" but at that time she couldn't.
      But I agree with her, but *why* I have to suffer this kind of pressure even now, I can't-I can't believe it!

In the bell hooks passage, the particular patriarchal values internalized by the mother are identified as those of Christian morality. P2 answers her question of "why" by situating her own mother's behavior (and by implication, P5's mother's behavior) within a Japanese value system of *seken*, or concern for how others in one's family or community view one's actions:

P2:   I always talk to my mother, I always talk to my mother,
      you know, um, I don't know how to say in English "seken"=

F: Public
      opinion, the eye
      of society?

She then describes how she tries to raise her mother's consciousness. By implication, P5 might try a similar strategy with her own mother:

P2:   = Yeah, she always say, "I cannot say anything about you in neighborhood," but, "it's not your *neighborhood*, your neighborhood exists inside you,"
I said always,
"*your* opinion not *neighbor's* opinion, *your* opinion, so *you* have to change."

Changing the world, then, begins with changing oneself; this feminist insistence on personal accountability effectively counters the "impossibility" of social change (Moss 1995) and the resignation implicit in statements such as *shikata ga nai* or 'it can't be helped'.

It is important to note that the participants explicitly pinpoint the class itself as a source of critical consciousness of societal gender roles, and acknowledge that this critical consciousness is not always welcomed by their families. In the discussion analyzed here, the code words used for feminist ideologies are *women's issues* and *women's studies*, as in this example where I and P7 joke about our own lives and the "bad" role models we may be in terms of Japanese societal values:

P5: when I started to learn about women's studies,
first time she didn't want me to go to such group because when I came back to home I just talked about the woman who got divorced or=
P7:   was
never married
P5: =struggling with=
F: or married three times
P5:   =struggling with babies or the relationship with man ...

However, as one source of social validation is lost, a new source is taking its place. Throughout the class discussed here, there was frequent back-channelling through laughter and minimal responses that marked the listeners' affiliation with the speakers and encouraged the speakers to build on their stories, similar to Bucholtz's (1996) findings regarding African American women's construction of social identities through political alliance. The two coordinators also play an important role in reassuring the participants that they are not alone. P6 does this based on her experience in her work as a professional counselor:

P6:   I've heard so many similar stories from my clients, and my friends ...

The other coordinator, P7, further redeems P5's personal pain by likening it to the experience of growing up female and aware in a patriarchal society, a sort of psychic price that every woman has to "pay" for freedom, and a process that she herself has survived and come out of stronger. She thus brings the class full circle to the bell hooks reading again:

P7:   and so just hearing you, P5, I just want to say one thing,
      bell hooks- she can *see* the things you just suffered,
      because you can see, it's like a screen, the movie,
      once you see the structure, you are not *in* it, you are like a audience ...
      see um- she-she talks about the pain a lot, because she is so smart she can
      see everything and she- she knows she's different from other kids,
      but and because of the pain that's a kind of *price* she has to *pay* for the
      freedom, so after the pain, she can get the freedom,
      so that's why her book is so- um- give you- why her book becomes im-
      portant is that, it's *painful,*
      but that's the process you have to go through in order to get- to reach free-
      dom, liberty ...

At this point, it was time to end the class, so there is no recorded response to this statement. However, it seems important to note here that the source of P7's deep insight into the pain of growing up "different" is clearly complex and involves not only her gender, but her Korean and working-class identities as well. As she has stated in response to a questionnaire, "To continue thinking about world issues from three different perspectives – race, gender, and class – is very important to me". She is deeply interested in issues of language, oppression, and liberation, and has gained much from black feminist theory such as hooks (1994) and Lorde (1984), as well as the struggle of Japanese-speaking scholars such as Sakai (1991) and Ohsawa (1997) to challenge the hegemony of Western discourse. As she writes, "[I am] using the oppressor's language myself-being a Korean living in Japan, I am using Japanese as my first language-" (Park 1997: 12) and "What is at issue is to articulate how the colonized can formulate counter-discourses by using the colonizer's language for resistance" (Park 1997: 15).

5. Conclusion

In this study, I contextualized and interpreted the discourse that occurred in an all-female foreign language classroom in which there is a commitment to a feminist pedagogic approach. An analysis of one class session revealed myself, the facilitator, and participants struggling to make sense of the pain and conflict of mother-daughter relationships. Emphasizing our common feminist beliefs and our gendered experiences as women created a social solidarity that cut across ethnic and linguistic differences. Examining our individual and cultural differences, on the other hand, moved us from the personal narrative of a black American writer with a Christian background to critically examining and re-negotiating the morality of Japanese social values such as *seken* or concern for the opinions of family members and neighbors as they impacted on a class participant's relation with her mother. Cross-cultural discussion facilitated a recognition of the social rather than the biological bases of gender ideologies. Recognition in turn implies the possibility of unlearning, resisting, and rewriting gendered scripts (Talbot 1998).

Subsequent to the class described here, the class coordinators also decided to translate the source of the passage we discussed, the book *Bone Black: Memories of Girlhood* (hooks 1996), into Japanese over the coming year as a class project. In addition, the class participants have supported each other through extensive socializing in Japanese outside of class, accompanying each other to feminist conferences, and in sharing and creating a wide range of original feminist theory, not only in the work by Hotta (1997) and Park (1997) cited here, but also in presentations at various conferences throughout Japan. This article itself is a direct outgrowth of my participation in the class, and while I am no longer facilitating the class, I continue to cooperate with the participants, directly and indirectly, in various feminist projects. Supporting each other's personal and emotional well-being, translating and interpreting between Japanese and English for publications and events, enhances our careers and our economic independence at the same time that we hope it promotes the advance of women's rights internationally. These personal and political goals dynamically fuel each other.

The "Colors of English" class, then, is an example of Japan-born women attempting to appropriate English as a weapon for self-empowerment as women in Japan and as women of color in the world. While heatedly debating the imperialistic nature of English as an international language, these participants are not paralyzed by the contradictions of acquiring such a language, and optimistically conclude that the master's tools can be used to dismantle the master's house. They deliberately try to hire non-white instructors in order to get the

English without the racism, for example, but prefer only those instructors who speak prestigious varieties of English.

At the same time, English may be attractive for some of them precisely because of dichotomous discourses contrasting it positively with Japanese. I followed up in a later class session by asking the participants if they felt they were a different person when speaking English, and if so, how. Everyone said that they have a different identity as an English speaker. Some of the participants said they express themselves less stereotypically and more honestly, directly, and assertively in English than in Japanese. One example they gave was the insertion of subject pronouns such as 'I' or 'you'. They said that having to specify personal pronouns in English constantly drew their attention to the distinctions between their own opinions and those of their interlocutors and helped them to clarify their thoughts. They are familiar with research such as Maynard (1993) claiming that aspects of Japanese discourse modality such as omitting personal pronouns, or referring to one's self in relation to the other, foster interdependence and mitigate interpersonal conflict. Like the Western women learning Japanese in Siegal (1994), some of the participants in this feminist English class feel they are under special pressure as women to conform to a wider cultural ideal of showing concern for others and avoiding conflict. Speaking English rather than Japanese in their feminist consciousness-raising class can thus be one additional way to signal rebellion against such cultural and linguistic-specific ideologies of femininity.

Acknowledgements

Many thanks to the members of the "Colors of English" class for their cooperation with the initial study that led to this article. Special thanks to Hwami Park, Kyoko Inamura, and Aneta Pavlenko for their assistance and encouragement.

Notes

1.   I use the terms 'Japanese-speaking' women and 'Japan-born' rather than 'Japanese' throughout this chapter to acknowledge the diverse nationalities and ethnic backgrounds of women studying English in Japan. Approximately one percent of the population does not hold Japanese citizenship, and the majority of these are second- or third-generation Koreans or Chinese who were born in Japan, but whose parents or grandparents were stripped of Japanese citizenship at the end of World War II. In addition, there are unknown numbers of those with non-Japanese

descent or multi-ethnic descent who do not show up in official statistics because they have or have taken Japanese nationality.

2. I use the term 'feminist' throughout this paper for consistency's sake, but not all the participants in these classes are comfortable with labeling themselves as feminists because they feel a feminist is someone with special knowledge or membership in a certain political activist group. The common identity and the foundation for class membership is being a biological female who is interested in feminism, women's studies, and women's issues (see McMahill 1997).

3. I would like to stress that I am not saying that English or Western feminisms are better resources for women than other languages or ideologies; this is simply the case I am studying here.

4. It should be noted that Japanese-speaking women have a wide variety of responses to the use of 'women's language', from rejecting it altogether to working within it, researching its history, and reclaiming its positive aspects (see interviews with Ide and Kora in Buckley 1997).

5. English translation: "We – joining education with our lives".

6. Throughout this chapter, the participants' spoken and written English has not been corrected.

7. The curriculum coordinator notes that this has been a matter of facilitator availability.

8. For the first three months of the class, participants were asked to keep weekly journals in English and copy and share them with each other.

9. This writer has chosen not to capitalize her name.

10. The transcription method used is adapted from various conventions in Appendix 2 of Schiffrin (1994), as follows:

F	facilitator (the author)
P1, P2, etc.	first participant, second participant
(P6 and P7 are also class coordinators)	
Ps	several or all participants vocalize simultaneously
.	falling intonation followed by a noticeable pause
?	rising intonation followed by a noticeable pause
,	continuing intonation
...	noticeable pause or break in rhythm
-	halting, abrupt cutoff
–	stammering quality
!	animated tone
/?/	inaudible utterance
[	start of overlapping speech
]	end of overlapping speech
==	contiguous utterances
(( ))	description of some vocalization such as laughter
italics	emphatic stress

CAPS   very emphatic stress
" "   Japanese word
( )   parenthetical information

11. See Sachiko Ide's discussion of *boseiai* on pp. 37–42 and Chizuko Ueno's discussion of mothering and the maternal function on pp. 278–282 of Buckley (1997).

12. A classic example of this is the line in the novel *Surfacing* by Margaret Atwood: "This above all, to refuse to be a victim" (quoted in Greene 1994: 23).

References

Abe, Hideko
    1995   From stereotype to context: The study of Japanese women's speech. *Feminist Studies* 21, 3, 647–671.

Aoki, Yayoi
    1986   *Feminizumu to Ekoroji*. [Feminism and Ecology]. Tokyo: Shinhyoron.

Belenky, Mary, Blythe Clinchy, Nancy Goldberger, and Jill Tarule
    1997   *Women's Ways of Knowing*. New York: BasicBooks.

Bucholtz, Mary
    1996   Black feminist theory and African American women's linguistic practice. In Bergvall, Virginia, Janet Bing, and Alice Freed (eds.), *Rethinking Language and Gender Research: Theory and Practice*. London and New York: Longman, 267–290.

Buckley, Sandra
    1997   *Broken Silence: Voices of Japanese Feminism*. Berkeley: University of California Press.

Chafe, Wallace
    1982   Integration and involvement in speaking, writing, and oral literature. In Tannen, Deborah (ed.), *Spoken and Written Language: Exploring Orality and Literacy*. Norwood, NJ: Ablex, 35–54.

Collins, Patricia
    1990   *Black Feminist Thought*. Boston: Unwin Hyman.

De Castell, Suzanne and Mary Bryson (eds.)
    1997   *Radical Interventions: Identity, Politics, and Difference/s in Educational Praxis*. Albany, NY: State University of New York Press.

Ellsworth, Elizabeth
    1989   Why doesn't this feel empowering? Working through the repressive myths of critical pedagogy. *Harvard Educational Review* 59, 3, 297–324.

Fairclough, Norman
    1989   *Language and Power.* London: Longman.
    1992   *Discourse and Social Change.* Cambridge: Polity.

Freire, Paulo
    1971   *Pedagogy of the Oppressed.* New York: Herder and Herder.
    1973   *Education for Critical Consciousness.* New York: Seabury Press.
    1985   *The Politics of Education.* Westport, CT: Bergin and Garvey.

Fujieda, Mioko
    1995   Japan's first phase of feminism. In Fujimura-Fanselow, Kumiko and Atsuko Kameda (eds.), *Japanese Women: New Perspectives on the Past, Present, and Future.* New York: The Feminist Press, 323–341.

Fujimura-Fanselow, Kumiko
    1991   Women's studies in language education. *JALT Journal XV,* 7, 3–10.
    1995   Women's studies: An overview. In Fujimura-Fanselow, Kumiko and Atsuko Kameda (eds.), *Japanese Women: New Perspectives on the Past, Present, and Future.* New York: The Feminist Press, 155–180.
    1996   Transforming teaching: Strategies for engaging female learners. In Casanave, Christine and Amy Yamashiro (eds.), *Gender Issues in Language Education.* Fujisawa, Japan: Keio University SFC University, 31–46.

Fujimura-Fanselow, Kumiko and Atsuko Kameda
    1995   Appendix: Significant dates in the recent history of Japanese women. In Fujimura-Fanselow, Kumiko and Atsuko Kameda (eds.), *Japanese Women: New Perspectives on the Past, Present, and Future.* New York: The Feminist Press, 407–414.

Giroux, Henry
    1981   *Ideology, Culture, and the Process of schooling.* London: Falmer Press.
    (ed.) 1991 *Postmodernism, Feminism, and Cultural Politics.* Albany, NY: State University of New York Press.

Goffman, Erving
    1981   *Forms of Talk.* Philadelphia: University of Pennsylvania Press.

Greene, Maxine
1994 The lived world. In Stone, Lynda (ed.), *The Education Feminism Reader.* London: Routledge, 17–25.

Gumperz, John (ed.)
1982 *Language and Social Identity.* Cambridge: Cambridge University Press.

Hiraga, Masako and Joan Turner
1995 What to say next? The problem of elaboration for Japanese students of English in academic contexts. *JACET Bulletin* 26, 13–30.

hooks, bell
1994 *Teaching to Transgress: Education as the Practice of Freedom.* New York: Routledge.

1996 *Bone Black: Memories of Girlhood.* New York: Henry Holt and Co.

Hotta, Midori
1997 Beyond our invisibility: Diverse feminisms and the quest of Japanese women for self-defined identity. *Review of Japanese Culture and Society 9,* 66–78.

Ide, Sachiko
1979 *Onna no Kotoba. Otoko no Kotoba.* [Women's speech. Men's speech]. Tokyo: Nihon Keizai Tsushinsha.

Jung, Yeong-hae
1994 Hirakareta kazoku ni mukatte: fukugoteki aidentiti to jiko keiken [Facing my opened family: Complex identity and self-experience]. *Joseigaku Nenpo* [Women's Studies Annual Report] 15, 8–18.

Kanazumi, Fumiko
1997 Problematizing reproductive technologies. In Buckley, Sandra (ed.), *Broken Silence: Voices of Japanese Feminism.* Berkeley: University of California Press, 81–101.

Kaneko, Sachiko
1995 The struggle for legal rights and reforms: A historical view. In Fujimura-Fanselow, Kumiko and Atsuko Kameda (eds.), *Japanese Women: New Feminist Perspectives on the Past, Present, and Future.* New York: The Feminist Press, 3–14.

Kanemaru, Fumi
   1997   Ninshodaimeishi-kosho [Investigating personal pronouns]. In Ide, Sachiko
           (ed.), *Joseigo no Sekai* [The World of Women's Language]. Tokyo: Meiji
           Shoin, 15–32.

King, Joyce
   1991   Dysconscious racism: Ideology, identity, and the miseducation of teachers.
           The Journal of Negro Education 60, 2, 133–146.

Kubota, Ryuko
   1999   Japanese culture as constructed by discourses: Implications for applied lin-
           guistics research and ELT. *TESOL Quarterly 33, 1,* 9–35.

Lather, Patti
   1984   Critical theory, curricular transformation and feminist mainstreaming.
           Journal of Education 166, 1, 49–62.

   1987   The absent presence: Patriarchy, capitalism, and the nature of teacher work.
           Teacher Education Quarterly 14, 2, 25–38.

Lebra, Takie
   1984   *Japanese Women: Constraint and Fulfillment.* Honolulu: University of Ha-
           waii Press.

Lorde, Audre
   1984   *Sister Outsider.* Trumansburg, NY: The Crossing Press.

Matsubayashi, Yoshiko
   1995   Contrastive discourse analysis of decision-making negotiations between
           native Japanese speakers and native British English speakers. *JACET Bul-
           letin* 26, 61–78.

Matsumoto, Kazuko
   1995   Fragmentation in conversational Japanese: A case study. *JALT Journal 17,*
           2, 238–254.

Matsumoto, Michihiro
   1996   Eigo teikokushugi o megutte shijo debeeto [A debate in writing on English
           imperialism]. *Jiji Eigo Kenkyuu* [Research on Current Affairs English] Oc-
           tober–December issues, 26–27 in each issue.

Maynard, Senko
   1993   *Discourse Modality: Subjectivity, Emotion and Voice in the Japanese Lan-
           guage.* Amsterdam and Philadelphia: John Benjamins

McGloin, Naomi
  1997   *Shujoshi* [Final particles]. In Ide, Sachiko (ed.), *Joseigo no Sekai* [The World of Women's Language]. Tokyo: Meiji Shoin, 33–41.

McKellar, Barbara
  1989   Only the fittest of the fittest will survive: Black women and education. In Acker, Sandra (ed.), *Teachers, Gender and Careers*. Washington, D.C.: Taylor and Francis, 69–85.

McMahill, Cheiron
  1997   Communities of resistance: A case study of two feminist English classes in Japan. *TESOL Quarterly* 31, 612–622.

McMahill, Cheiron and Kate Reekie
  1996   Forging Alliances: Grassroots Feminist Language Education in the Tokyo Area. In Casanave, Christine and Amy Yamashiro (eds.), *Gender Issues in Language Education*. Fujisawa, Japan: Keio University SFC University, 15–30.

Middleton, Sue
  1987   Schooling and radicalization: Life histories of New Zealand feminist teachers. *British Journal of Sociology of Education* 8, 2, 169–189.

Morgan, Kathryn
  1996   The perils and paradoxes of the bearded mothers. In Diller, Ann, Barbara Houston, Kathyn Pauly, and Maryann Ayim (eds.), *The Gender Question in Education: Theory, Pedagogy, and Politics*. Boulder, CO: Westview Press, 124–134.

Mori, Kyoko
  1997   *Polite Lies: On Being a Woman Caught Between Two Cultures*. New York: Henry Holt & Co.

Moss, Gemma
  1995   Rewriting reading. In Holland, Janet, Maud Blair, and Sue Sheldon (eds.), *Debates and Issues in Feminist Research and Pedagogy*. Avon: Multilingual Matters, 157–168.

Nakamura, Kei
  1997   *Eigo teikokushugi o megutte shijo debeeto* [A debate in writing on English imperialism]. *Jiji Eigo Kenkyuu* [Research on Current Affairs English] March issue, 26–27.

Nakata, Hiroko
    1996   Are our husbands *shujin*? In The English Discussion Society (ed.), *Japanese Women Now II*. Kyoto: Shoukadoh Booksellers, 10–12.

Norton, Bonny
    1997   Language, identity, and the ownership of English. *TESOL Quarterly* 31, 409–429.

Ohara, Yumiko
    1997   *Shakaionseigaku no kanten kara mita nihonjin no koe no kotei* [Japanese people's voice pitch from a socio-phonological perspective]. In Ide, Sachiko (ed.), *Joseigo no Sekai* [The World of Women's Language]. Tokyo: Meiji Shoin, 42–58.

Ohsawa, Masaki
    1997   *Gengoteki na junsuisei/Gengogakuteki na zasshusei* [Linguistic purity/ Linguistic diversity]. *Shiso* [Journal of Thought], November.

Okamoto, Shigeko
    1995   "Tasteless" Japanese: Less "feminine" speech among young Japanese women. In Hall, Kira and Mary Bucholtz (eds.), *Gender Articulated. Language and the Socially Constructed Self*. New York: Routledge, 297–325.

Park, Hwami
    1997   The global spread of English: The possibility of counter-discourses. Unpublished manuscript, Temple University Japan.

Pavlenko, Aneta
    1998   Second language learning by adults: Testimonies of bilingual writers. *Issues in Applied Linguistics* 9, 1, 3–19.

Peirce, Bronwyn
    1986   Toward a pedagogy of possibility in the teaching of English internationally: People's English in South Africa. *TESOL Quarterly* 23, 401–418.

Peirce, Bonny
    1995   Social identity, investment, and language learning. *TESOL Quarterly* 29, 9–31.

Pennycook, Alastair
    1994   *The Cultural Politics of English as an International Language*. New York: Longman.

1995   English in the world/The world in English. In Tollefson, James (ed.), *Power and Inequality in Language Education*. Cambridge: Cambridge University Press, 34–58.

Pharr, Susan
1977   Japan: Historical and contemporary perspectives. In Giele, Janet Z. and Audrey C. Smock (eds.), *Women: Roles and Status in Eight Countries*. New York: John Wiley & Sons, 219–255.

Phillipson, Robert
1992   *Linguistic Imperialism*. Oxford: Oxford University Press.

Reynolds, Katsue
1993   *Gengo to seisa no kenkyu- genzai to shorai* [Research on language and gender- current and future]. *Nihon Gogaku* [Japan Linguistics] May, 224–234.

1998 a   *Onna kotoba no sai kenkyuu to jiko henkaku.* [Reexamination of research on women's language and self-reform]. Presentation given at Ochanomizu Joshidai Jendaa Kenkyuu Sentaa [Ochanomizu University Gender Research Center], July 16, 1998.

1998 b   Female speakers of Japanese in transition. In Coates, Jennifer (ed.), *Language and Gender: A Reader*. Oxford: Blackwell, 299–308.

Romaine, Suzanne
1994   *Language in Society: An Introduction to Sociolinguistics*. Oxford: Oxford University Press.

Rose, Kenneth
1996   American English, Japanese, and directness: More than stereotypes. *JALT Journal*, 18, 1, 67–80.

Rosen, Harold
1988   The autobiographical impulse. In Tannen, Deborah (ed.), *Linguistics in Context: Connecting Observation and Understanding*. Norwood, NJ: Ablex, 69–88.

Sakai, Naoki
1991   *Voices of the Past: The Status of Language in Eighteenth-Century Japanese Discourse*. Ithaca: Cornell University Press.

Schenke, Arleen
1996   Not just a "social issue": Teaching feminist in ESL. *TESOL Quarterly* 30, 155–159.

Schiffrin, Deborah
    1994   *Approaches to discourse.* Oxford: Blackwell.
    1996   Narrative as self-portrait: Sociolinguistic constructions of identity. *Language in Society* 25, 167–203.

Shibatani, Masayoshi
    1990   *The languages of Japan.* Cambridge: Cambridge University Press.

Siegal, Meryl
    1994   Second-language learning, identity, and resistance: White women studying Japanese in Japan. In Bucholtz, Mary, Anita Liang, Laurel Sutton, and Caitlin Hines (eds.), *Cultural Performances: Proceedings of the Third Berkeley Women and Language Conference.* Berkeley, CA: Berkeley Women and Language Group, 642–650.
    1996   The role of learner subjectivity in second language sociolinguistic competency: Western women learning Japanese. *Applied Linguistics* 17, 356–382.

Smith, Sandra and Amy Yamashiro (eds.)
    1998   Gender issues in language teaching. Special issue of *The Language Teacher* 22, 5, 5.

Sugiyama, Naoko
    1996   *Issei* mothers' silence, *Nisei* daughters' stories: The short fiction of Hisaye Yamamoto. *Comparative Literature Studies* 33, 1, 1–14.

Sukumune, Seisoh, Toshiyuki Shiraishi, Yoshiko Shirakawa, and Junko Tanaka
    Matsumi
    1993   Japan. In Adler, Lenore (ed.,) *International Handbook on Gender Roles.* Westport, CT: Greenwood Press, 174–186.

Summerhawk, Barbara, Cheiron McMahill, and Darren McDonald (eds.)
    1998   Introduction. *Queer Japan: Personal Stories of Japanese Lesbians, Gays, Bisexuals, and Transsexuals.* Norwich, VT: New Victoria Press, 5–16.

Tai, Eika
    1995   *Esunikku aidentiti no kojin kanri: Zainichi Taiwanjin josei no jirei o moto ni* [Individual management of ethnic identity: The case of Taiwanese women] *Joseigaku Nenpo* [Women's Studies Annual Report] 16, 109–118.

Talbot, Mary
    1998   *Language and Gender: An Introduction.* Oxford: Polity Press.

Tanaka, Kazuko
  1995 a   The new feminist movement in Japan, 1970–1990. In Fujimura-Fanselow,
           Kumiko and Atsuko Kameda (eds.), *Japanese Women: New Feminist Per-*
           spectives on the Past, Present, and Future. New York: The Feminist Press,
           343–352.
  1995 b   Work, education, and the family. In Fujimura-Fanselow, Kumiko and At-
           suko Kameda (eds.), *Japanese Women: New Feminist Perspectives on the*
           Past, Present, and Future. New York: The Feminist Press, 295–308.

Tannen, Deborah
  1988   Hearing voices in conversation, fiction, and mixed genres. In Tannen, De-
           borah (ed.), *Linguistics in Context: Connecting Observation and Under-*
           standing. Norwood, NJ: Ablex, 89–133.
  1989   *Talking Voices: Repetition, Dialogue, and Imagery in Conversational Dis-*
           course. Cambridge: Cambridge University Press.

Taylor, Sandra
  1995   Feminist classroom practice and cultural politics: 'Girl number twenty'
           and ideology. In Holland, Janet, Maud Blair, and Sue Sheldon (eds.), *De-*
           bates and Issues in Feminist Research and Pedagogy. Avon: Multilingual
           Matters, 3–22.

Tsuda, Yukio
  1994   The diffusion of English: Its impact on culture and communication. *Keio*
           Communication Review 16, 49–61.

Tsuruta, Yoko
  1996   Blind to our own language use? Raising linguistic and sociolinguistic
           awareness of future JSL teachers. In Casanave, Christine and Amy Yamas-
           hiro (eds.), *Gender Issues in Language Education*. Fujisawa, Japan: Keio
           University SFC University, 114–125.

Ueno, Chizuko
  1994   *Kindai kazoku no seiritsu to shuen* [The Establishment and Role of the
           Modern Family]. Tokyo: Iwanami Shoten.

Vandrick, Stephanie
  1994   Feminist pedagogy and ESL. *College ESL* 42, 69–92.
  1995   Teaching and practicing feminism in the university ESL class. *TESOL*
           Journal 43, 4–6.

van Lier, Leo
  1988   *The Classroom and the Language Learner*. New York: Longman.

Weiler, Kathleen
    1994   Freire and a feminist pedagogy of difference. In McLaren, Peter and Colin
            Lankshear (eds.), *Politics of Liberation: Paths from Freire*. London: Rout-
            ledge, 12–39.

Westcott, Marcia
    1997   On the new psychology of women: A cautionary view. In Walsh, Mary (ed.)
            Women, Men and Gender: Ongoing Debates. New Haven: Yale University
            Press, 362–372.

Yamagata, Hiromi
    1999   *Female genitals in Japanese mythology: A reexamination of the goddess
            Amenouzume*. Unpublished manuscript.

Yoshizumi, Kyoko
    1995   Marriage and family: Past and present. In Fujimura-Fanselow, Kumiko and
            Atsuko Kameda (eds.), *Japanese Women: New Feminist Perspectives on
            the Past, Present, and Future*. New York: The Feminist Press, 183–197.

Name index

Subject index